ENTANGLED DOMAINS

Set in colonial Northern Nigeria, this book confronts a paradox: the state insisted on its separation from religion even as it governed its multireligious population through what remained of the precolonial caliphate. *Entangled Domains* grapples with this history to offer an account of secularism as a contested yet contingent mode of governing religion and religious difference. Drawing on detailed archival research, Rabiat Akande vividly illustrates constitutional struggles triggered by the colonial state's governance of religion and interrogates the legacy of that governance agenda in the postcolonial state. This book is a novel commentary on the dynamic interplay between law, faith, identity, and power in the context of the modern state's emergence from colonial processes.

RABIAT AKANDE is an Assistant Professor at Osgoode Hall Law School in Toronto.

CAMBRIDGE STUDIES IN LAW AND SOCIETY

Founded in 1997, Cambridge Studies in Law and Society is a hub for leading scholarship in socio-legal studies. Located at the intersection of law, the humanities, and the social sciences, it publishes empirically innovative and theoretically sophisticated work on law's manifestations in everyday life: from discourses to practices, and from institutions to cultures. The series editors have longstanding expertise in the interdisciplinary study of law, and welcome contributions that place legal phenomena in national, comparative, or international perspective. Series authors come from a range of disciplines, including anthropology, history, law, literature, political science, and sociology.

Series Editors

Mark Fathi Massoud, *University of California, Santa Cruz*

Jens Meierhenrich, *London School of Economics and Political Science*

Rachel E. Stern, *University of California, Berkeley*

A list of books in the series can be found at the back of this book.

ENTANGLED DOMAINS
Empire, Law, and Religion in Northern Nigeria

Rabiat Akande
Osgoode Hall Law School, York University

Shaftesbury Road, Cambridge CB2 8EA, United Kingdom

One Liberty Plaza, 20th Floor, New York, NY 10006, USA

477 Williamstown Road, Port Melbourne, VIC 3207, Australia

314–321, 3rd Floor, Plot 3, Splendor Forum, Jasola District Centre, New Delhi – 110025, India

103 Penang Road, #05–06/07, Visioncrest Commercial, Singapore 238467

Cambridge University Press is part of Cambridge University Press & Assessment, a department of the University of Cambridge.

We share the University's mission to contribute to society through the pursuit of education, learning and research at the highest international levels of excellence.

www.cambridge.org
Information on this title: www.cambridge.org/9781009055048

DOI: 10.1017/9781009052108

© Rabiat Akande 2023

This publication is in copyright. Subject to statutory exception and to the provisions of relevant collective licensing agreements, no reproduction of any part may take place without the written permission of Cambridge University Press & Assessment.

First published 2023
First paperback edition 2024

A catalogue record for this publication is available from the British Library

ISBN 978-1-316-51155-8 Hardback
ISBN 978-1-009-05504-8 Paperback

Cambridge University Press & Assessment has no responsibility for the persistence or accuracy of URLs for external or third-party internet websites referred to in this publication and does not guarantee that any content on such websites is, or will remain, accurate or appropriate.

For you, mum.

CONTENTS

Acknowledgments — *page* viii
Note on Terms — x

Introduction — 1

PART I GOVERNING FAITH

1 Jousting for Souls: Indirect Rule, Christian Missions, and the Governance of Religious Difference — 31

2 Governing Shariʻa — 70

PART II CONSTITUTING DIFFERENCE

3 The Construction of Minorities: Late Imperial Secularity and the Constitutional Politics of Decolonization — 107

4 The Making of the 1958 Penal Code — 144

5 Constituting Rights: Christian Religious Liberty in the Late Colonial State — 189

PART III IMAGINING THE PAST

6 The 1977 Constitutional Conference and Beyond — 229

Conclusion — 267

Bibliography — 274
Index — 301

ACKNOWLEDGMENTS

This book is eleven years in the making, and I am fortunate for the sustained support that has brought it into being.

I began this project as a dissertation under the supervision of David Kennedy, Duncan Kennedy, and John Comaroff. I am fortunate to have these incredible scholars as teachers, mentors, and friends. I owe this book to their deep commitment and unrivaled generosity.

For excellent research assistance, I am indebted to Ola Mobarak, Malka Younas, Cecil Yongo Abugu, Misthura Othubu, and Nada Abdel Maksoud.

Several librarians and archivists have been invaluable to the success of this research. They include those at the National Archives of Kaduna, Nigeria; Lambeth Palace Library; Church of England Record Center; Center for the Studies of World Christianity, University of Edinburgh; Special Collections, School of Oriental and African Studies, University of London; University of Birmingham Cadbury Research Library Special Collections; National Archives, UK; Harvard Law School Library; and Osgoode Hall Law School Library. In particular, I am obliged to mention Yemisi Dina, Elyse Hill, Aslihan Bhulut, Stephen Wiles, Fred Burchstead, and Nkemka Eke for their tremendous help in retrieving often elusive records.

At Cambridge University Press, I thank Studies in Law and Society editors Mark Fathi Massoud and Rachel Stern for nurturing this project since its early days. I also thank Matt Gallaway, Jadyn Fauconier-Herry, Laura Blake, Jackie Grant, Sunantha Ramamoorthy, and Perrin Lindelauf for working with me to see this work come into print.

Sections of Chapters 2 and 5 have appeared in the *Law and History Review* (May 2020) and the *Journal of Law and Religion* (July 2022), respectively. I thank both journals for permitting me to reproduce those works.

I thank Winnifred Sullivan, Mashood Baderin, Brandon Kendhammer, Noah Feldman, Mridu Rai, and Mary Lewis for their invaluable commentary on an early draft of the manuscript at a March 2020 workshop. I thank Bruce Jackan of the Harvard Academy for International and Area Studies for convening that manuscript workshop and keeping it on schedule (in a virtual format) even as the COVID-19 pandemic upended life as we all knew it.

The Harvard Academy for International and Area Studies allowed me to immerse myself in the research that bridged the dissertation-to-book process. I thank Chris Gratien, Sophia Balakian, Brinton Ahlin, Sahana Ghosh, Zachary Howlett, Egor Lazarev, Melani Cammett, Mary Lewis, Bruce Jackan, Kathleen Hoover, and many other colleagues for making life at the Harvard Academy collegial, convivial, and truly gratifying even at the height of the COVID-19 pandemic.

I owe a debt of gratitude to several wonderful colleagues and teachers for their incredible support. Too numerous to mention, these include Intisar Rabb, Ruth Okediji, Noah Feldman, Obi Okafor, Faisal Bhabha, Anver Emon, Mitra Sharafi, Philip Girard, Ben Berger, and Ousmane Kane, among others. Some of these academics are at Osgoode Hall Law School, where I am fortunate to have wonderful colleagues.

It would be a challenge to produce an exhaustive list of the many friends and family members whose support, wisdom, and affection lurk behind every word in this book. I thank Khadijat Akande-Taiwo, Rukayat Akande, Yetunde Tijani, Ayodele Tijani, Ann Shafer, Titi Givans, Sara Minkara, Halimatou Hima, Salwa Petersen, Nkatha Kabira, Nadia Barakat, Clare Putnam, Kimberly Wortmann, Damina Khaira, Haleemah Suleiman, Sijuade Hamed, Helen Ouellette, Michael Ouellete, and many others.

Most of all, I thank Tayo, Fadl, and Hajar for their constant and unquestioning love and for bearing the many absences that have made this book a reality.

NOTE ON TERMS

Several Arabic and Hausa words are used in this book. A modified letter left half ring is used to represent the Arabic letter ʿ*ayn* as in "Shariʿa." I have attempted to be consistent in the transliteration; however, there are diverse English transliterations of some of the words employed: for example, "Shariʿa" is sometimes transliterated as "Shari'a," "Shariah," or "Sharia." These variations are found in the book to the extent that sources cited or institutions referenced (such as courts) utilize these variations. Variations will also be observed in the use of Arabic words such as "qadi," which have Northern Nigerian renditions: "alkali," or "khadi." I adopt the standard modern Arabic transliteration except when citing sources or referencing institutions that utilize alternative spellings.

In acknowledgment of the pejorative connotations of the terms "native" and "pagan," I limit their use to citations of sources (including the book's *dramatis personae* and scholarly literature) and analysis of colonial legal categories.

I refer to local Northern Nigerian religious groups other than Muslims as Indigenous in this book. This is not to signal the isolation of these groups from external (religious) influence prior to the encounter with the British imperial and Christian missionary agenda. Moreover, given that Islam's presence in Northern Nigeria dates to the ninth century and debatably earlier (since Islam arrived on the continent in the early seventh century), I use the Indigenous marker for non-Muslim faith communities to distinguish them from Muslims in the colonial governance project rather than to mark the nonindigenous presence of Islam in the territory.

INTRODUCTION

States' assertion of separation from religion – commonly understood as the thrust of the constitutional idea of secularism – is ubiquitous in the modern world. At the same time, however, religion remains a force, keeping its hold on the private lives of individuals and tenaciously maintaining its presence in the politics of individual states and the international legal order. The tension arising from the tenacity of religion and the ineluctability of claims of separation has heightened the need to understand how the modern state regulates religion and religious difference through its enactment of secular governmentality, to unveil the ambivalence that mode of governance entails, to identify the forms of empowerment and disempowerment it fosters, and to scrutinize how subjects contest its consequences.

Colonial Northern Nigeria provides a particularly unique opportunity to consider these questions. The meeting of the distinctive precolonial caliphate with Orientalist ideals in the late nineteenth century produced one of the most distinctive sites for the colonial governance of religion and religious difference. Empire's ostensible deference to Islam, manifesting in indirect rule through Muslim elites, its peculiar application of "Islamic" law in the public sphere (via criminal law), and extensive restrictions on Christian missionaries purportedly entrenched the precolonial caliphate. Yet, the colonial state insisted on its secularity. In unraveling this puzzle at the heart of colonial governance, this work presents the story of a sustained constitutional entanglement of religion and politics and illuminates its consequences for colonial and postcolonial subjects.

INTRODUCTION

Empire was entangled with religion from the onset. The origin of empire on the West Coast of Africa in 1841 was the product of an alliance between the British state and anti-slave-trade evangelicals. With the "sword of the steel" furthering the "sword of the spirit," imperial outreach was closely allied with Protestant Christian missions especially the Church Missionary Society of the Church of England (CMS) in the nineteenth century.[1] That alliance, which featured empire-backed CMS jurisdiction over Africans, would change to hostility between the colonial government and missionaries when formal empire commenced in Northern Nigeria at the turn of the nineteenth century. In founding colonial governance on indirect rule through Islamic institutions, the British administration separated itself from the missionary enterprise, asserting that this policy was necessitated by its secular approach to governance.

Colonies were "laboratories of experimentation."[2] It was the British Empire's experience confronting a dizzying array of religious faiths in its colonies, beginning in India, that led to its development of secularism as a statecraft technique of managing religious difference. The British colonial state considered church-state separation crucial to governing India.[3] This separation from the church was prompted largely by the experience of the 1857 Indian Revolt, which was widely interpreted as a rebellion against the anglicizing mission.[4] Beyond the fact that early colonialism featured a measure of cooperation with Christian missions, the imperial venture also professed a civilizing goal underpinned by Christian ideas.[5] The civilizing mission was based on two convictions.

---

[1] Emmanuel Ayankanmi Ayandele, *The Missionary Impact on Modern Nigeria, 1842–1914: A Political and Social Analysis* (London: Longmans, 1966).

[2] John L. Comaroff, "Colonialism, Culture, and the Law: A Foreword," *Law & Social Inquiry* 26, no. 2 (2001): 305–314.

[3] Peter van der Veer, *Imperial Encounters: Religion and Modernity in India and Britain* (Princeton: Princeton University Press, 2001), 22; Gauri Viswanathan, *Outside the Fold: Conversion, Modernity, and Belief* (Princeton, NJ: Princeton University Press, 1998). See also Catherine S. Adcock, *The Limits of Tolerance: Indian Secularism and the Politics of Religious Freedom* (Oxon: Oxford University Press, 2013); Nandini Chatterjee, *The Making of Indian Secularism: Empire, Law and Christianity, 1830–1960* (New York: Palgrave Macmillan, 2011).

[4] See Ilyse R. Morgenstein Fuerst, *Indian Muslim Minorities and the 1857 Rebellion: Religion, Rebels and Jihad* (London: Bloomsbury Publishing, 2017).

[5] See Ian Copland, "Christianity as an Arm of Empire: The Ambiguous Case of India Under the Company, c. 1813–1858," *Historical Journal* 49, no. 4 (2006): 1025–1054. See also van der Veer, *Imperial Encounters*. Copland argues that there was a degree of cooperation between empire and missions, deviating from the account of previous

The first was that "others" were capable of racial and religious "uplift,"[6] and the second was that these others could become "English in tastes, in opinions, in morals and in intellect."[7] The rebellion against the civilizing project inspired the colonial state's distancing from missions and, simultaneously, its adoption of Indigenous institutions as the vehicle for colonial governance. To be sure, notions of governing the "native"[8] through their institutions predates the 1857 revolt; as early as 1772, Warren Hasting's Judicial Plan had designed such a scheme.[9] Nevertheless, it was the 1857 mutiny that would catalyze these earlier proposals, marking a turn to indirect rule.

Theorists and historians of colonialism point out that the policy of adopting native institutions developed alongside the construction of the "native" as a legal and political identity.[10] With Britain's abandonment of its civilizing mission, it turned to liberal imperialism, premised on difference and simultaneously having as its goal, the construction and governance of difference.[11] Religious difference was, therefore, central to the liberal turn. Indeed, the famous 1858 Proclamation by

---

historians. See, for instance, Brian Stanley, *The Bible and the Flag: Protestant Missions and the British Empire in the Nineteenth and Twentieth Centuries* (Townbridge: Apollos, 1990).

[6] Chris Youé, "Mamdani's History," *Canadian Journal of African Studies* 34, no. 2 (2000): 397–408, 401; David C. Potter, *India's Political Administrators: From ICS to IAS* (Oxford: Oxford University Press, 1996), 47; Horst Gründer, "Christian Missionary Activities in Africa in the Age of Imperialism and the Berlin Conference of 1884–1885," in *Bismarck, Europe, and Africa: The Berlin Africa Conference 1884–1885 and the Onset of Partition*, eds. Stig Förster, Wolfgang J. Mommsen, and Ronald Robinson (New York: Oxford University Press, 1988), 100. See further Mahmood Mamdani, *Define and Rule: Native as Political Identity* (Cambridge: Harvard University Press, 2012); Mahmood Mamdani, *Citizen and Subject: Contemporary Africa and the Legacy of Late Colonialism* (Princeton, NJ: Princeton University Press, 2018).

[7] Thomas Babington Macaulay, Minute Dated February 2, 1835, cited in *Selections of Educational Records, Part 1, 1781–1839*, ed. H. Sharp (Calcutta: Superintendent, Government Printing, 1920), 107–117.

[8] The terms "native" as well as one I use later – "pagan" – are now regarded, at best, with ambivalence. I adopt them in this study in the vernacular sense in which they were employed by official colonial discourse and the dramatis personae in this book.

[9] This scheme had been designed for the East India Company. See Julia Stephens, *Governing Islam: Law, Empire, and Secularism in Modern South Asia* (Cambridge: Cambridge University Press, 2018).

[10] Mamdani, *Define and Rule*, 9; Karuna Mantena, *Alibis of Empire: Henry Maine and the Ends of Liberal Imperialism* (Princeton, NJ: Princeton University Press, 2010).

[11] Mamdani, *Define and Rule*; Mantena, *Alibis of Empire*. See further Tamir Moustafa, *Constituting Religion: Islam, Liberal Rights, and the Malaysian State* (Cambridge: Cambridge University Press, 2018). Liberal imperialism was not without critics

the English Crown ushered in late colonialism by declaring religious autonomy for colonial subjects:

> We declare it our Royal will and pleasure that none be in anywise favored, none molested or disquieted, by reason of their religious faith or observances, but that all shall alike enjoy the equal and impartial protection of the law; and we do strictly charge and enjoin all those who may be in authority under us that they abstain from all interference with the religious belief or worship of any of our subjects on pain of our highest displeasure.[12]

If the Indian mutiny inspired the state's distance from missions, Peter van der Veer points out that it was missionaries who advocated for the disruption of the state's ties with Indigenous religions. In response to what they perceived as the state's patronage of native religions, missionaries called for a separation of the state from these religions. Yet, it is important to note that this project was never intended to be a principled call for the disestablishment of all religions. On the contrary, the preference of missions was to be allied with the state and, failing that, to be free of restrictions in evangelizing to natives.[13] Indeed, missionaries remained fully committed to the establishment of the Church in England. Since Indigenous religions and religious institutions would continue to play a central role in civil and political life regardless of the claim of separation, the stage was set for altercations over the place of matters spiritual in the state. Regardless of these ambiguities, the classical requirements of liberal secularism – the assertion of religious freedom and of separation – were formally complete.[14] Invoked not only directly but also obliquely through a variety of ideas including neutrality, tolerance, and impartiality, secularism's essence – avowing the state's separation from religion and religious liberty – had come to be embedded in colonial thought and policy.

---

within the ranks of the colonial administration in India. To take an example, James Fitzjames Stephen (law member of the viceroy's council from 1869–1872) argued that the British, being members of a superior conquering race, should not "shrink from the open, uncompromising assertion" of that right by conquest to govern Indians whom he saw as "ignorant to the last degree" and "steeped in idolatrous superstition."

[12] "Proclamation by the Queen in Council to the Princes, Chiefs and People of India Published by the Governor-General at Allahabad," (1858). IOR/L/PS/18/D154 British Library, UK.

[13] Van der Veer, *Imperial Encounters*, 151. See Chatterjee, *The Making of Indian Secularism*.

[14] See John Rawls, *Political Liberalism* (New York: Columbia University Press, 2015).

GOVERNING DIFFERENCE: COLONIALISM AND RELIGION IN NIGERIA

The colonial state's turn from its nineteenth-century alliance with Christian missions in Northern Nigeria emerged from this broader imperial context. Yet, Northern Nigeria was quick to attain notoriety in missionary circles. By 1910, seven years after the commencement of formal empire, the World Council of Missions would devote much attention to the territory at its inaugural meeting, declaring the British Protectorate as an unusually daunting place to be a Christian missionary.[15] British Northern Nigeria's infamy was rooted in the peculiar brand of indirect rule on which colonial governance was based, and the religious differentiation policy it engendered.

As in much of the British Empire after the Indian mutiny, colonial governance took the form of indirect rule in Northern Nigeria, co-opting Islamic institutions in that predominantly Muslim territory.[16] This was complemented by a policy of religion differentiation. The state apprehended religious difference through a "grid of intelligibility"[17] that hierarchized faiths. It classified the colonized population into Muslims and non-Muslims. The colonial ideal of a non-Muslim native was the "pagan." In the colonial imagination, this pagan was "uncivilized,"[18] "living under mob law or arbitrary will"[19] without discernible means of political or judicial administration. Hence, the state sought, where possible, to place adherents of diverse

---

[15] World Missionary Conference, *Report of the World Missionary Conference, 1910* (Edinburgh: Oliphaunt, Anderson, and Ferrier, 1910).

[16] According to the 1952 Census, Northern Nigeria had a population of 16,835,582 with 12,289,975 identifying as Muslims, 4,091,046 identifying as adherents of other Indigenous faiths, and 454,561 identifying as Christian. *Population Census of Nigeria, 1952–1953* (Lagos: The Census Superintendent, 1953). The 1963 Census, which was the last time religious affiliation formed an index in the census, placed the population at 29,763,276 with 21,342,866 Muslims, 2,880,112 Christians, and 5,540,302 adherents of Indigenous religions. *Population Census of Nigeria, 1963* (Lagos: The Census Superintendent, 1964).

[17] Saba Mahmood, *Religious Difference in a Secular Age: A Minority Report* (Princeton, NJ: Princeton University Press, 2015), 25.

[18] Frederick John Dealtry Lugard, *The Dual Mandate in British Tropical Africa* (Edinburgh: W. Blackwood, 1922), 78; Frederick John Dealtry Lugard, *Political Memoranda Revision of Instructions to Political Officers on Subjects Chiefly Political and Administrative 1913–1918* (London: Frank Cass, 1970).

[19] Lugard, *The Dual Mandate*, 78.

Indigenous religions under the administration of the newly colonized caliphate institutions.[20]

The state featured a tripartite residential organizational structure among natives. Type I areas had a predominantly Muslim population (emirates) and were administered by the state through emirs (Muslim chiefs).[21] Type II areas were those understood to have Muslims and other Indigenous faith populations and were administered through Muslim chiefs of a lower status than emirs. The third category, Type III areas, were referred to as "pagan" areas and administered through the "pagan" chiefs. Therefore, much of the territory was governed through Muslim rulers, an arrangement that extended the political authority of the caliphate political elites – the Masu Sarauta ("possessors of governance") – beyond the precolonial years. Likewise, local chiefs were far from equal; emirs were at the highest rung of the hierarchy and "pagan" chiefs at the bottom. This arrangement extended to the jurisdiction of law. While the state applied "Islamic" law (including Islamic criminal law) and Islamic systems of courts in Type I and II areas, "pagan" native law and courts operated, subject to several restrictions, in Type III areas.

This political and legal arrangement also formed the basis of the state's policy regarding Christian missionary proselytization. Missionaries were prohibited from proselytizing in Type I areas and much of Type II areas but were permitted in Type III areas, a policy for which local and global missionaries castigated the state. Indeed, these Christian missionaries and the local converts they secured through the curtailed

---

[20] I refer to religious groups other than Muslims as Indigenous in this book. This is not to signal the isolation of these groups from external (religious) influence prior to the encounter with the British imperial and Christian missionary agenda. Moreover, given that Islam's presence in Northern Nigeria dates to the ninth century and debatably earlier (since Islam arrived on the continent in the early seventh century), I use the Indigenous marker for non-Muslim faith communities to distinguish them from Muslims in the colonial governance project rather than to mark the nonindigenous presence of Islam in the territory. See Rabiat Akande, Wendell Marsch, and Ann McDougall, "The Making of the Islamic World: Islam at a Crossroads in West Africa," January 2021, in Ottoman History *Podcast* (podcast), January 2021, www.ottomanhistorypodcast.com/p/the-making-of-islamic-world.html.

[21] Emirs were the political heads of provinces in the precolonial caliphate all acting under the overall authority of the sultan/caliph with the seat of the Caliphate at Sokoto. The colonial government initially abolished the title of the caliph in 1903, designating the new chief of Sokoto an emir. Even when the title was eventually introduced, the jurisdiction of the sultan had been reduced to that of emirs save in ceremonial matters. See Peter K. Tibenderana, "The Irony of Indirect Rule in Sokoto Emirate, Nigeria, 1903–1944," *African Studies Review* 31, no. 1 (1988): 67–92.

proselytization efforts described British colonial rule as tantamount to "Muslim sub-imperialism."[22] The Northern Nigerian colonial policy had its immediate roots in the guarantee of noninterference that was extended to emirs at the commencement of formal empire in 1903. The guarantee, that the government would "not interfere with the Mohammedan religion," was hardly novel[23]; it had parallels across the empire, including in the Queen's 1858 declaration set out earlier. However, in Northern Nigeria, it was extended only to emirs and the Muslim population. The guarantee was also paired with a generally applicable religious freedom declaration: "all men are free to worship as they please," which also found precedent in the Queen's Proclamation.[24] In addition, the legal instrument that had ushered in formal colonialism on the African continent in general, the Berlin General Act of 1885, mandated European powers to protect "freedom of conscience" and guarantee "religious toleration" to all "natives, subjects and foreigners" in their respective colonial territories.[25] Defending itself against accusations of Muslim bias, the state would therefore insist that it was committed to "impartiality," "neutrality," and religious liberty.[26]

---

[22] This appellation was very common in missionary discourse. See, for instance, Church Missionary Society, Report of Sub-Committee of Group III of the Church Missionary Society on Difficulties with Nigerian Government, January 26, 1916. CMS/B/OMS/A3/CL/1916. University of Birmingham Cadbury Special Collections (hereafter Cadbury Collections).

[23] Issued by Frederick Lugard. See Neville Brooke, *Report of the Native Courts (Northern Provinces) Commission of Inquiry Laid on the Table of the House of Representatives as Sessional Paper no. 1 of 1952* (Lagos, Nigeria: Federal Government Printer, 1952), i. For a discussion of the distinction between formal and informal empire, see Dane Kennedy, *Britain and Empire, 1880–1945* (London: Routledge, 2014). See also Martin Lynn, "British Policy, Trade, and Informal Empire in the Mid-Nineteenth Century," in *The Oxford History of the British Empire: Volume 3: The Nineteenth Century*, ed. Andrew Porter (Oxon: Oxford University Press, 1999) 3, 101–121.

[24] Colonial Reports-Annual, No. 409, Northern Nigeria, 1902 (HM Stationery Office: 1903), 16.

[25] Article 6, Berlin General Act 1885. The Berlin General Act was signed at the Berlin Conference, a gathering where European colonial powers carved out their respective African territories and set out the broad contours of the legal design of their relationship as colonial powers in Africa.

[26] See Lugard, *Political Memoranda*, 594; Donald Cameron, *The Principles of Native Administration and Their Application* (Lagos, Nigeria: Government Printer, 1934), 13–14, 26. See Joseph H. Oldham to Gordon Beacham October 18, 1932, CBMS/IMC/271, School of Oriental and African Studies Special Collections (hereafter SOAS).

Indeed, colonial administrators would also insist that Muslim chiefs were "secular chiefs," through whom the state governed.[27] In doing so, the state was invoking the post-mutiny mantra of imperial secularism: the assertions of separation or distance from religious authority (while governing through it), and of the religious freedom of colonial subjects.

DEFINING, DEEPENING, AND HIERARCHIZING RELIGIOUS DIFFERENCE

Historians and scholars of Islamic law, alike, have tended to ignore the state's assertion of its secularity, insisting that it perpetuated the precolonial theocracy. Consider the opinions of John Anderson, professor of Islamic law at the School of Oriental and African Studies in London, and Joseph Schacht, Oxford academic and later Columbia University professor, two prominent twentieth-century Western scholars of Islamic law. In separate surveys commissioned by the Colonial Office, both reached a similar conclusion: that the state had elevated Islamic law and perpetuated the precolonial theocracy.[28] Anderson and Schacht have been hardly alone in this view. Even contemporary historians of colonial Northern Nigeria espouse this opinion. Take the example of Moses Ochonu's *Colonialism by Proxy*, a fascinating account of colonial rule in Northern Nigeria.[29] Ochonu argues that the colonial

---

[27] See G. J. Lethem, Memoranda: Political Propaganda in Nigeria, Colonial Office, September 29, 1927, K5521/4 PP MS 60/2/1-7, 5. See also George John Frederick Tomlinson and Gordon James Lethem, "History of Islamic Political Propaganda in Nigeria," Colonial Office, 1927. Jean Boyd Papers SOAS, London, PP MS 36; Lugard, *The Dual Mandate*; Lugard, *Political Memoranda*; Muhammad Sani Umar, "Hausa Traditional Political Culture, Islam, and Democracy: Historical Perspectives on Three Political Traditions," in *Democracy and Prebendalism in Nigeria: Critical Interpretations*, eds. Wale Adebanwi and Ebenezer Obadare (New York: Palgrave Macmillan, 2013), 177–200.

[28] James Norman Dalrymple Anderson, *Islamic Law in Africa* (Oxon: Routledge, 2013); Joseph Schacht, "Islam in Northern Nigeria," *Studia Islamica*, no. 8 (1957): 123–146.

[29] Moses Ochonu, *Colonialism by Proxy: Hausa Imperial Agents and Middle Belt Consciousness in Nigeria* (Bloomington, IN: Indiana University Press, 2014). See also Olufemi Vaughan, *Religion and the Making of Nigeria* (Durham, NC: Duke University Press, 2016); Adamu Mohammed Fika, *The Kano Civil War and British Over-rule, 1882–1940* (New York: Oxford University Press, 1978); Obaro Ikime, "Reconsidering Indirect Rule: The Nigerian Example," *Journal of the Historical Society of Nigeria* 4, no. 3 (1968): 421–438; Matthew Hassan Kukah, *Religion, Politics and Power in Northern Nigeria* (Ibadan, Nigeria: Spectrum Books, 1993). See, however, Auwalu H. Yadudu, "Colonialism and the Transformation of the Substance and

governance of Northern Nigeria through Muslim proxies was in pursuit of the goal of sameness: the creation of a homogenous Northern Nigeria modeled on the Muslim caliphate.[30] Although Ochonu stresses that the colonial idea of the caliphate was an "imaginary" and not based on actual precolonial Islam, he concludes, as Schacht and Anderson did, that the essence of colonial administration was the reification of Islamic institutions.

To be sure, Northern Nigeria featured one of the most extreme forms of indirect rule in the British Empire. Save in parts of the Aden Protectorate, only there did Islamic law apply not just as personal law, but also as criminal law. For this reason, as well as the state's restrictions on missionary proselytization, received accounts present this colony as a unique and extreme case of the valorization of Islamic law, typical of theocratic governance. Nevertheless, the state's claim to secularism was just as palpable, laying not merely in its invocation of the post-mutiny mantra of separation and religious liberty, but also in its deployment of the late-colonial technique of defining, deepening, and hierarchizing religious difference. Whereas the state formally invoked separation and religious freedom, in essence, everyday colonial governance entailed this threefold technique.[31] And, in spite of the tension between this technique of governance and the conventional elements of secularism declared by the state, I argue that the former is, like the latter, characteristic of secular governance.

Scholarship in other colonial contexts illuminate the defining effect of colonial secularism on religion. C. S. Adcock's work on colonial India, *The Limits of Tolerance*, draws attention to the central governing feature of secularism: it "defines and confines" religion.[32] Similarly, in *Constituting Religion*, a study of the Malaysian context, Tamir Moustafa argues that not only did colonial law "constitute" religion, the postcolonial liberal state also remains inextricably implicated in this project

---

Form of Islamic Law in the Northern States of Nigeria," *Journal of Law and Religion* 9, no. 1 (1991): 17–47; Abdulmumini A. Oba, "Islamic Law as Customary Law: The Changing Perspective in Nigeria," *International and Comparative Law Quarterly* 51, no. 4 (2002): 817–850; and Sarah Eltantawi, *Shari'ah on Trial: Northern Nigeria's Islamic Revolution* (Oakland: University of California Press, 2017).

[30] Ochonu, *Colonialism by Proxy*, 8–13.

[31] Although in tension with governance practice, these formal elements of secularism are nevertheless crucial for understanding secular governance. I return to this point below.

[32] Adcock, *The Limits of Tolerance*, 25.

of religion governance.[33] This project of constituting religion, in fact, produces religious difference. What results, as Saba Mahmood argues, is that the secular state becomes "not simply a neutral arbiter of religious differences," but in fact, it "produces and creates them."[34]

To render religions legible to colonial governance and its purposes, the state defined religion as well as religious difference. As noted earlier, the state classified religion into two: "Islam" and "Paganism." The "Pagan" hardly mapped onto the precolonial category of non-Muslims. Not only did this group encompass a broad range of Indigenous spiritual tendencies, but members of this class within the precolonial Islamic polity (the *Maguzawa*) had the status analogous to that of *majus* (Zoroastrians) in classical Islamic jurisprudence. As such they were entitled to jurisdictional privileges comparable to that of the *ahl al kitab* (People of the Book), which included judicial autonomy as well as a measure of political autonomy. The colonial classification of the *Maguzawa* as *kafiri* (pagan) altered this precolonial identity, and overturned the caliphal governance arrangement, stripping this group of its autonomy. In the process, colonial rule not only deepened Muslim versus non-Muslim difference, it also hierarchized it far beyond the precolonial years.[35]

Ostensibly allied with the state, Islamic institutions were nevertheless not untouched by the colonial processes of defining, deepening, and hierarchizing religious difference. The state defined Islam, constructing a vision of the religion that could coexist with colonial governance. This was effected through a two-part process: the remaking of Islamic law through an unprecedented expansion of the precolonial doctrine of *siyasa* (discretionary powers of political rulers), and the making of an ideal Muslim subject.

From granting political authorities limited juristic authority in precolonial times, siyasa came to be expanded so as to overshadow *fiqh* (Islamic jurisprudence). This process did not only alter the content of Islamic jurisprudence; already, important studies like Sarah Eltantawi's *Shari'ah on Trial* reveal the colonial transformation of Northern

---

[33] Moustafa, *Constituting Religion*, 158. See also Stephens, *Governing Islam*.

[34] Mahmood, *Religious Difference in a Secular Age*, 22.

[35] See Allan Christelow, "Persistence and Transformation in the Politics of Shari'a, Nigeria, 1947–2003: In Search of an Explanatory Framework," in *Muslim Family Law in Sub-Saharan Africa: Colonial Legacies and Post-colonial Challenges*, eds. Shamil Jeppie, Ebrahim Moosa, and Richard Roberts (Amsterdam: Amsterdam University Press, 2010), 252; Mukhtar Umar Bunza, *Christian Missions among Muslims: Sokoto Province, Nigeria 1935–1990* (Trenton, NJ: Africa World Press, 2007), 7–13.

Nigeria Islamic law.³⁶ What is crucial to note and missing from existing accounts is the recognition that the expansion of siyasa, emerging as it did from a premise of Shariʿa governance, fundamentally recast the relationship between Islamic law and the state.³⁷ The state, in essence, now appropriated the power to define Islamic law. One of the central arguments of this book, therefore, is that the transformation of Islamic law in Northern Nigeria can only be apprehended by exploring the state's claim to secularity without losing sight of its utilization of caliphate institutions for the colonial enterprise. In their focus on the latter, works such as Eltantawi's tend to overlook the former – the state's assertion of secularism. Departing from this approach, this book engages both of these features of colonial governance by foregrounding the question: Who exercised the power to decide "Islamic" law and how was its exercise justified? Crucially, although Islamic law was invoked by *alkalai* (judge-jurists), emirs, and colonial administrators in deciding cases, the essence of precolonial jurisprudence had already been transformed by the reconfiguration of the precolonial constitutional balance between emirs and alkalai. At the same time, however, because the state continued to invoke Islamic law as the basis of governance – even while simultaneously asserting an ever-expanding executive authority over its content – it was able to claim fidelity to Islamic law and institutions while transforming its workings.

This assertion of colonialism's reform of siyasa wades into a debate over the relationship between siyasa and fiqh in premodern Islamic polities. On the one hand is the view, exemplified by Wael Hallaq, that regards premodern siyasa as compliant with the Shariʿa. Since siyasa remained within its constitutional boundaries, in other words, it did not encroach into the domain of jurists – the arena of fiqh.³⁸ In contrast, a burgeoning body of work insists that Hallaq's is an idealized view of precolonial governance and argues that the fiqh-siyasa distinction had started to break down long before the advent of

---

³⁶ Eltantawi, *Shari'ah on Trial*; Yadudu, "Colonialism and the Transformation of the Substance and Form," 17–47; Oba, "Islamic Law as Customary Law," 817–850.

³⁷ A notable exception is Brandon Kendhammer, *Muslims Talking Politics: Framing Islam, Democracy, and Law in Northern Nigeria* (Chicago: University of Chicago Press, 2016).

³⁸ Wael Hallaq, *The Impossible State: Islam, Politics, and Modernity's Moral Predicament* (New York: Columbia University Press, 2014).

colonial modernity.[39] While this work does not assume a naive view of the precolonial relationship between political authorities and jurists in the caliphate, it would nevertheless be a stretch to dismiss the precolonial fiqh-siyasa distinction as a mere "idealized cosmology."[40] Whatever the pull exerted on the sultan/emir-siyasa versus alkalai-fiqh balance by the realities of governance, deviations from the constitutional delineation of the jurisdiction was understood, by both precolonial emirs and jurists, as an exception.[41] This constitutional structure, I argue, was rewrought by colonial governance.

The state's construct of Islam was not limited to its transformation of Islamic law. The co-option of caliphate institutions that led to the remaking of that law also created a distinction between Muslims affiliated with the Masu Sarauta (Muslim political elites)[42] and those resisting the Anglo-Masu Sarauta alliance. The state's making and remaking of religious difference was therefore not limited to the Muslim versus Pagan dichotomy. Indeed, the political distinction between the Masu Sarauta's allies and their detractors would manifest as a theological difference, with the state sanctioning Qadiriyya Sufism, the theological predilection of the Masu Sarauta. In the process, the ideal Muslim subject was defined. Other Muslim groups were considered "dissident."[43] Of these "bad" Muslims, Mahdists, those who believed that the end of the

---

[39] See, for example, Samy Ayoub, *Law, Empire, and the Sultan: Ottoman Imperial Authority and Late Hanafi Jurisprudence* (Oxford: Oxford University Press, 2019); Kristen Stilt, *Islamic Law in Action: Authority, Discretion, and Everyday Experiences in Mamluk Egypt* (Oxford: Oxford University Press, 2011); Guy Burak, *The Second Formation of Islamic Law* (New York: Cambridge University Press, 2015); Ahmed Fekry Ibrahim, *Pragmatism in Islamic Law: A Social and Intellectual History* (Syracuse, NY: Syracuse University Press, 2015).

[40] Ayesha Chaudhry, *Domestic Violence and the Islamic Tradition* (Oxford: Oxford University Press, 2013). See also Moustafa, *Constituting Religion*.

[41] Umar, "Hausa Traditional Political Culture, Islam, and Democracy"; Mervyn Hiskett, *The Sword of Truth: The Life and Times of the Shehu Usuman dan Fodio* (Oxford: Oxford University Press, 1973); Mervyn Hiskett, "Kitāb Al-Farq: A Work on the Habe Kingdoms Attributed to 'Uthmān Dan Fodio," *SOAS Bulletin* 23, no. 3 (1960): 558–579; B. G. Martin, "A Muslim Political Tract from Northern Nigeria: Muhammad Bello's *Usul al-Siyasa*," in *Aspects of West African Islam*, eds. Daniel F. McCall and Norman R. Bennett (Boston: African Studies Center, Boston University, 1971), 63–86; Ibraheem Sulaiman, *The Islamic State and the Challenge of History: Ideals, Policies and Operation of the Sokoto Caliphate* (London: Mansell, 1987).

[42] Literally meaning "possessors of governance."

[43] Henry Willink, ed., *Nigeria: Report of the Commission Appointed to Enquire into the Fears of Minorities and the Means of Allaying Them* (London: HM Stationery Office, 1958) (hereafter Willink Report) CO957/41.

world was imminent and that colonialism was a form of corruption that marked the end of the world, were the most repressed in the early colonial era. Members of the other predominant Sufi sect, the Tijaniyyah, came to be labeled as dissident not merely for their contrarian theological positions, but also for their intense political opposition when they formed the base for the Northern Elements Progressive Union party challenging the Masu Sarauta in the years leading to decolonization. As a result of these and other measures, the state assumed the prerogative to define Islam, and thus deepened religious difference and hierarchized faith practices – both within and outside of Islam.

Therefore, far from freezing precolonial Islamic institutions, colonial rule redefined both Islamic law as well as the ideal Muslim subject, and in so doing, invented an Islam amenable to the state. In essence, the colonial governance technique and the co-option of caliphate institutions on which it relied did not elevate any religion, not even Islam. Instead, as demonstrated above, it confined and regulated all religions.

SECULARISM'S ENTANGLEMENTS

The defining, deepening, and hierarchizing processes so integral to the state's governance of religion points to a central feature of secular governmentality sui generis: the de facto entanglement of religion and politics. This insight is not only in tension with the state's assertion of religion-separation, it is also at odds with the received wisdom on secularism. According to that wisdom, popularly encapsulated in John Rawls' *Political Liberalism*, the constitutional idea of secularism emerged as a response to conflict over opposing values.[44] In this account, it was the need to manage religious diversity that led to the displacement of religion from the public sphere, which consequently became "secular." As the constitutional structure that created this separation between the public, secular, and political sphere on the one hand and the private and religious sphere on the other, secularism became the answer to conflicts triggered by religious diversity.[45] Secularism was, however, not merely beneficial to the state in ridding it of religious conflict, it

---

[44] See Rawls, *Political Liberalism*.
[45] Ibid. See also John Rawls, *A Theory of Justice* (Cambridge: Harvard University Press, 1971); Bruce Ackerman, *Social Justice in the Liberal State* (New Haven: Yale University Press, 1980); and Donald Eugene Smith, *India as a Secular State* (Princeton, NJ: Princeton University Press, 2015). Within the liberal democratic tradition, the

was also favorable to religion since it freed it of state interference.[46] In the Rawlsian model, therefore, the separation of religion and politics is the core of secularism. It also yields the other element of secularism – the promise of religious freedom.

Led by Talal Asad's *Formations of the Secular*, a wave of critical scholarship challenges the separationist argument at the heart of the Rawlsian narratives, arguing instead that the entanglement of the secular and the religious is the defining feature of liberal secularism. This entanglement, it adds, is not merely rooted in the intellectual origins of the idea of secularism, it is also reflected in the actual constitutional organization of "secular" states. Asad's work finds the emergence of the categories of religion and the secular from specific historical, political, and legal processes in Western Europe and also asserts that it was these conditions of their emergence that framed them in opposition to each other.[47] This realization that the law both constitutes the secular and the religious as well as frames their mutual opposition is now a core tenet of critical scholarship on secularism.[48]

Since this constituting power of law culminates in varying constructions of the secular and the religious across space and time, it is hardly surprising that studies of the enactment of secularism in particular constitutional contexts have proven fashionable in the anti-Rawlsian

---

Rawlsian separation thesis has come under attack for being inaccurate in asserting that separation of religion from politics is necessary to liberal governance. See Alfred Stepan, "Religion, Democracy and the 'Twin Tolerations,'" *Journal of Democracy* 11, no. 4 (2000). For examples of these states, see Stepan, "The Twin Tolerations," 219–220. Charles Taylor critiques this as secular-religion binary narrative as the "subtraction theory." See Charles Taylor, *A Secular Age* (Cambridge, MA: Harvard University Press, 2007). In the view of this minority, "almost all of the countries with the best claim to this form of government lack the wall of 'separation' and many have state churches." Alfred Stepan, a prominent critic of the Rawlsian separation idea, argues that the leading empirical analytical models of democracy (citing Robert Dahl and Juan Linz) do not include strict separation. Stepan proposes, instead, the "twin toleration model," which is "the minimal boundaries of freedom of action that must somehow be crafted for political institutions vis a vis religious authority and for religious individuals and groups vis a vis political institutions," "Twin Tolerations," 213.

[46] Michael J. Sandel, "Religious Liberty: Freedom of Choice and Freedom of Conscience," in *Secularism and Its Critics*, ed. Rajeev Bhargava (New York: Oxford University Press, 1999), 600.

[47] Talal Asad, *Formations of the Secular: Christianity, Islam, Modernity* (Stanford: Stanford University Press, 2003).

[48] Asad, *Formations of the Secular*; Moustafa, *Constituting Religion*; Stephens, *Governing Islam*; Mahmood, *Religious Freedom in a Secular Age*; Winnifred Fallers Sullivan et al., eds., *Politics of Religious Freedom* (Chicago: University of Chicago Press, 2015).

theoretical tradition.⁴⁹ With the legacy of the relations of power inscribed by colonial governance, the postcolony has provided a fruitful ground for research. Contemporary debates over Hindutva in India's constitutional politics,⁵⁰ the place of Islam in Egypt and Malaysia,⁵¹ and – since post-coloniality plagues both the former colonizer and colonized – French laïcité and its equivalents across Europe regarding the headscarf and other religious symbols⁵² are only a few examples of the contestations that have captured scholarly attention.

Unveiling religious-secular entanglements in these contexts has revealed that secularism is far from neutral. Not a few anti-Rawlsian accounts have therefore arrived at the conclusion that secularism qua secularism is being deployed by states to entrench majoritarian beliefs and practices and marginalize religious minorities. Saba Mahmood writes of secularism "intensif[ying] … religious inequality," by its "valuation of certain aspects of religious life over others" with the consequence of the increasingly precarious position of religious minorities in the polity.⁵³ Homi Bhabha remarks: "India forces us to think, sometimes in tragic moments, of the function of religious thought within secularism … If you look around the world today, this is a very important issue; this particular kind of … religious orthodoxy erupting within secularism."⁵⁴ This critical tradition, therefore, unmasks secularism for its biases.

---

⁴⁹ Saba Mahmood argues that secularism "entails a form of national-political structuration organized around the problem of religious difference, a problem whose resolution takes strikingly similar forms across geographic contexts." See, however, Mahmood, *Religious Difference in a Secular Age*; Linell Cady and Elizabeth Hurd, *Comparative Secularism in a Global Age* (New York: Palgrave MacMillan, 2010).

⁵⁰ See, for instance, Manohar Joshi v. Nitin Bhaurao Patil All India Reports, 1996 SC 796 and the commentary it generated, including: Brenda Cossman and Ratna Kapur, "Secularism's Last Sigh: The Hindu Right, the Courts, and India's Struggle for Democracy," *Harvard International Law Journal* 38, no. 1 (1997): 113.

⁵¹ Hussein Agrama, *Questioning Secularism: Islam, Sovereignty, and the Rule of Law in Modern Egypt* (Chicago: University of Chicago Press, 2012); Moustafa, *Constituting Religion*.

⁵² See Lautsi and others v. Italy (Application No. 30814/06 IHRL 3688 ECHR, 2011); Dahlab v Switzerland (Application No. 42393/98, ECHR 2001-V); Sahin v. Turkey, (Application No. 44774/98), Council of Europe: European Court of Human Rights, November 10, 2005, available at www.refworld.org/cases,ECHR,48abd56ed.html, and commentaries such as Peter G. Danchin, "Islam in the Secular Nomos of the European Court of Human Rights," *Michigan Journal of International Law* 32, no. 4 (2011): 663.

⁵³ Mahmood, *Religious Difference in a Secular Age*, 15.

⁵⁴ Ibid. "Secularism as an Idea Will Change," *The Hindu*, December 17, 1995, XIX, in Brenda Cossman and Ratna Kapur, "Secularism's Last Sigh: The Hindu Right, the

The anti-Rawlsian approach is rightly marshaled to challenge the relations of domination that the modern secular state produces. Nevertheless, it leaves no room for acknowledging the ambivalence inherent in the idea of secularism through its dual imperative of separation and religious freedom. In asserting the separation of religion from the state, secularism calls on the state to curtail, restrict, or even expunge religion from itself. Tugging in the opposite direction, however, is the second classical element of secularism – the notion of religious liberty.

Legal theory is no stranger to the idea that conflicting internal imperatives are often embedded in legal concepts. Although that idea was first comprehensively articulated in the realm of the law of property,[55] it has come to shed light on the workings of legal concepts outside of that domain, including in the constitutional thought on secularism. Writing on secularism's dual imperative of separation and religious freedom, Marc Galanter points out that these imperatives are "a set of potentially incompatible principles which may conflict in concrete situations."[56] Although critical theorists are right to assert that the de facto entanglement of the state and religion and the reality of the politics of religious freedom undercut secularism's imperatives, these principles nevertheless remain crucial to understanding the working of secular governance. The imperatives, and in particular, the tension between them, are useful not just to state actors carrying out multiple and often inconsistent projects but also to subjects contesting the state. This book makes a case for paying close attention to the ambivalence of secular governmentality. Doing so not only reveals how participants in constitutional struggles navigate the inevitable entanglement of the "sacred" and the "secular" entailed in secular governmentality, it also illuminates the potentially unstable hierarchy of relations produced by secular governance.

Courts, and India's Struggle for Democracy," *Harvard International Law Journal* 38, no. 1 (1997): 113; Ran Hirschl, *Constitutional Theocracy* (Cambridge, MA: Harvard University Press, 2010). On the sacred underpinnings of modern secular law, see John L. Comaroff, "Reflections on the Rise of Legal Theology: Law and Religion in the Twenty-First Century," *Social Analysis* 53, no. 1 (2009): 193–216.

[55] Wesley Newcomb Hohfeld, "Some Fundamental Legal Conceptions as Applied in Judicial Reasoning," *The Yale Law Journal* 23, no. 1 (1913): 16.

[56] Marc Galanter, "Secularism, East and West," *Comparative Studies in Society and History* 7, no. 2 (1965): 133–159.

NAVIGATING STATE-RELIGION ENTANGLEMENTS

The colonial enterprise was neither monolithic nor static. Differing conceptions of colonial administrators influenced colonial policy on state-religion relations, all justifiable under the banner of imperial secularism. To Frederick John Dealtry Lugard, the first high commissioner of Northern Nigeria, and his devotees, who had an Orientalist fascination with precolonial Islamic caliphate institutions, the success of native administration was premised on noninterference with Islam.[57]

The Lugardian emphasis on the administrative needs of indirect rule prioritized the religious freedom of the Masu Sarauta, the constraint of Christian missions, and the autonomy of Indigenous religious groups. The Lugardian emphasis on Muslim religious freedom was, however, in tension with the consequences of the state's co-option of caliphal institutions for governance. Notably, the Lugardian years witnessed the freeing of emirs' siyasa from the constraints of the Shari'a, a move intended to introduce reforms at odds with precolonial jurisprudence. In its Lugardian manifestation, therefore, notions of state-religion separation legitimated not only regulating and restricting missions but also the state's regulation and transformation of Islamic law and institutions.

Direct and indirect rule, Mahmood Mamdani points out, are not mutually exclusive, but are rather "two faces of power."[58] The second dominant colonial position on state-religion relations, which came to be espoused by Governor Donald Cameron, took an anti-Lugardian turn.[59] Cameron and his enthusiasts – administrators who did not adulate precolonial Islamic institutions – argued that "neutrality" ought to be the highest principle rather than the Lugardian emphasis on religious liberty of the Masu Sarauta. In favoring a more direct variant of indirect rule, Cameron departed from the ultra-indirect rule trajectory of earlier colonial years and sought to de-emphasize the role of Islamic institutions, and thus elevated state-religion separation. The Cameron years, consequently, witnessed the gradual transfer of judicial siyasa powers from emirs to English judges and colonial administrators, with the consequent curtailment of fiqh. Cameron's particular form of state-religion separation was not free of ambivalence, however; the

---

[57] High commissioner of the Protectorate of Northern Nigeria, 1900 to 1906; and governor general of Nigeria from 1912 to 1914.

[58] Mahmood Mamdani, "Historicizing Power and Responses to Power: Indirect Rule and Its Reform," *Social Research* 66, no. 3 (1999): 859–886.

[59] Governor of Nigeria, 1931 to 1935.

transfer of siyasa to colonial administrators, intended to de-emphasize the place of Islam in governance, effectively heightened the state's entanglement with the religion since colonial officials now governed Islam as well as its relations with other faiths.

As the Lugardian preference for Muslim religious freedom receded, Cameron's policies gained traction, although always in tension. Cameron's approach was inspired by the view that the best African was Christian, and thus grew his commitment to easing restrictions on Christian missions and granting them religious liberty. Yet, the exigencies of native administration curtailed the implementation of Cameron's ideas. For one, the Cameron state, as in Lugardian times, continued to utilize caliphate institutions for the purpose of native administration, including over non-Muslims. Moreover, Lugardian policy continued to command loyalty in the rank and file of the colonial administration. Therefore, in the last three decades of empire (1931–1960), the coexistence – and tension – between Lugardian and Cameronian thought was unavoidable.

These dueling colonial policies on religion governance, all plausible under secular governance, set the stage for contestations over state-religion relations, struggles that most prominently featured Christian missionaries and the Masu Sarauta.

THE EARLY COLONIAL YEARS

From the inception of empire in the Lugardian years, Protestant missionaries campaigned against the state's co-option of Islamic institutions.[60] Seeking to reinstate their early nineteenth-century alliance with the colonial enterprise, they argued that "true empire building" was a joint effort of missionaries and colonial officials.[61] Thus, once it was clear that Lugard was intent on utilizing local institutions, missionaries campaigned for the abandonment of the caliphal Muslim Fulani elites preferred by colonial administrators, and sought colonial governance through intermediaries of Hausa ethnicity.[62] This move was rooted in

---

[60] Henry Farrant, Secretary of the Annual Meeting of Missions in Northern Nigeria to Joseph H. Oldham of the International Missionary Council, August 11, 1931, CBMS/270 SOAS.

[61] Herbert Tugwell to Lewis Nott, December 19, 1905, CMS G3/A3/010 in Ayandele, *The Missionary Impact*, 126.

[62] On the hyphenation of the Hausa-Fulani identity by the twentieth century, see John N. Paden, *Ahmadu Bello, Sardauna of Sokoto: Values and Leadership in Nigeria* (Zaria, Nigeria: HudaHuda, 1986), 595. See also Ochonu, *Colonialism by Proxy*.

the missionaries' unfounded conjecture that Hausas, unlike Fulanis, were merely nominal Muslims open to missionary proselytization and conversion to Christianity. When this campaign failed, missionaries called for a restriction of the co-opted caliphal native administration institutions (chiefs, courts, and laws) to apply to Muslims only.[63] Therefore, contrary to the Lugardian emphasis on religious freedom, missionaries insisted on state-religion separation. Insisting on the state's separation from the caliphal institutions was, however, far from a principled call for separation. Instead, what missionaries really contested was the "unchristian" separation resulting from their loss, to the Muslims, of their nineteenth-century power-alliance with empire.[64]

Once this missionary campaign failed and the colonial government began to impose extensive restrictions on missionary proselytization, the campaign shifted to demands for religious freedom, articulated in the classic Protestant formulation: "freedom of conscience."[65] The missionary call for religious freedom hardly cohered with the Lugardian emphasis on the religious liberty of the Masu Sarauta, the broader political elite class brought into power by the 1804 revolution that established the precolonial Islamic caliphate. Missionaries insisted that Lugard's guarantee, in order to be consistent with the "Western civilization" principle of "religious toleration," must be construed consistently with "freedom of conscience" and could not confer a special status on Islamic institutions.[66] This call for "freedom of conscience," in essence, advanced missionary calls for the state's separation from caliphal institutions.

For the Masu Sarauta, on the other hand, the overriding principle was the 1903 guarantee of noninterference in Islam. These elites took the guarantee as a commitment to the retention of precolonial caliphal institutions, and consequently subscribed to the Lugardian emphasis on religious freedom. In their view, this primacy of the religious freedom of

---

[63] CMS 1916 Report.

[64] Rabiat Akande, "Neutralizing Secularism: 'Religious Antiliberalism' and The Twentieth Century Global Ecumenical Project," *Journal of Law and Religion* 37, no. 2 (2022): 290. See World Missionary Conference, *Report of the World Missionary Conference Commission I: Carrying of the Gospel to All the Non-Christian World* (Edinburgh: World Missionary Conference, 1910).

[65] World Missionary Conference Edinburgh 1910 Commission VII Report; Church Missionary Society, *Report of Sub-Committee of Group III*.

[66] Church Missionary Society, *Report of Sub-Committee of Group III*. See, for instance, minutes of meeting of the Christian Council of Nigeria with Governor Graeme Thomson, October 21, 1927. CO583/181/5. National Archives United Kingdom (hereafter NA, UK).

INTRODUCTION

caliphal institutions overrode claims of religious toleration by Protestant missionaries. Muslim elites, however, were divided over what Lugardian thought ought to mean for the fate of the Shariʻa. If emirs were content with its expansion of their siyasa powers, the alkalai, whose fiqh domain had begun to be curtailed, preferred an understanding of the Lugardian guarantee that granted the administration of the Shariʻa autonomy or distance from colonial governance. Nevertheless, alkalai remained impuissant critics of the colonial arrangement, and emirs' championship of Lugardian religious freedom – as well as missionary advocacy for state-Islam separation – marked the Lugardian years.

THE CAMERON ERA

The adversaries would switch positions in the Cameron years. From the early 1930s, when Cameron's ideas on native administration came to dominate the central colonial administration, emirs and alkalai began to invoke the guarantee of noninterference to call for the separation of Islamic institutions from the state. The thinking that underlay this shift was most comprehensively articulated in a 1938 fatwa issued by Annur Tingary, Bashir El Rayah, and Mohammed Swar El Dahab, three sheikhs of the Kano Law school, in which they called on emirs and elites to boycott the colonial government.[67] Arguing that Islamic law was an inseverable whole and a necessary foundation for Islamic governance, the sheikhs urged emirs and alkalai to abstain from cooperating with a regime whose overt reform project was at clear odds with Islamic law. The fatwa, in essence, asserted that service to the colonial regime amounted to complicity in its reform project and urged aloofness. Although this call ultimately failed, the state would take the hint and the most radical of Islamic law's transformation – the 1957 replacement of Islamic jurisprudence with an English penal code – would be presented in the language of Islamic law and with the active participation of national and transnational Muslim jurists recruited by the state.

For Christian missionaries, the transnational element would be decisive in influencing their discourse. By the late transwar period, Christian missionaries began to make their claims in the language of the human right to religious freedom. This turn to rights was inspired by

---

[67] Memorandum by Annur Tingary, Bashir El Rayah, and Mohammed Swar El Dahab, "Extension of Jurisdiction of Native Courts." Kano Prof. File #2182, 41–43, National Archives, Kaduna (hereafter NA Nigeria).

the work of the international ecumenical movement. For that movement, the late interwar to immediate postwar period was one of intense deliberation over the fate of Christianity and its missionary enterprise in a world plagued by two major threats: secularism and "Islamic orthodoxy." Faced with these threats, the ecumenical movement concluded that Christianity was in crisis.[68] Furthermore, ecumenical discourse viewed secularism not as the separation of state and religion, but as the de-Christianization of state and society.[69] Indeed, ecumenical thought during this period espoused the view that secularism inevitably led to the adoption of "false gods" to fill the void left by true religion.[70] Given this understanding, Islamic orthodoxy was far from contrary to secularism; it was complementary to it.

As a territory that was understood by missionaries as featuring both extreme Islamic orthodoxy and an espousal of secularism, Northern Nigeria, perhaps more than any other territory, embodied the unholy alliance of these two threats. In the vision of the movement, the solution lay in international legal protection for the right to religious freedom. The product was Article 18 of the Universal Declaration of Human Rights, brought into existence in 1948 through the direct efforts of the World Council of Churches. Among others, Article 18 protected the freedom of conversion and proselytization.

For missionaries in Nigeria and their emerging class of nationalist converts, postwar advocacy would hinge on the campaign to constitutionalize Article 18. In their doomed opposition to the missionary rights proposal, emirs invoked the guarantee of noninterference, arguing that the missionaries' constitutional rights proposal violated Lugard's assurance of state-Islam separation.

In the end, the product of these fierce contestations was the Independence deal on state-religion relations. That constitution deal featured three elements. The first was the replacement of Islamic criminal law with an English penal code, along with the abolition of emirs' siyasa. Presented to Muslim subjects as a product of sound deliberation among Muslim jurists, the reform was, in fact, set in motion

---

[68] See Terence Renaud, "Human Rights as Radical Anthropology: Protestant Theology and Ecumenism in the Transwar Era," *The Historical Journal* 60, no. 2 (2017): 493–518.

[69] Rabiat Akande, "Neutralizing Secularism"; Udi Greenberg, "Protestants, Decolonization, and European Integration, 1885–1961, *The Journal of Modern History* 89, no. 2 (2017): 314–354.

[70] Greenberg, "Protestants, Decolonization, and European Integration," 328–329.

by Christian missionary advocacy that fortuitously coincided with Colonial Office wariness of Lugardian claims of Northern Nigerian Islamic exceptionalism. The second element was the recognition of the Protestant-dominated non-Muslim bloc as religious minorities, a move that paved the way for the third element that ultimately sealed the constitutional deal. That third element was the successful domestication of Article 18 of the Universal Declaration, the postwar international religious freedom provision crafted by global ecumenists to protect the missionary enterprise.

POSTCOLONIAL CONTESTATIONS

Within seventeen years of Independence, the colonial struggle over state-religion relations resurfaced during Nigeria's first postindependence constitutional convention in 1977. The issue that rekindled the debate was the proposal for the establishment of a Federal Sharia Court of Appeal with jurisdiction over Muslims in personal law matters. It was at the 1977 Constitutional Conference that the struggle would, for the first time, be framed explicitly on the national terrain in terms of a debate between the forces of "secularism" (opposed to the court) and "anti-secularism" (championing the court).

For the successors to the missionary coalition, Christian groups now represented by the Christian Association of Nigeria, the battle cry was "secularism," understood as the separation of religion (in this case, Islam) from the state. In a shift from its advocacy for religious freedom at Independence, this group held up secularism as trumping Shariʿa proponents' religious freedom claims. The Christian coalition's advocacy for religious freedom at Independence had shifted to a commitment to separation. For proponents of the Shariʿa court, predominantly Northern Muslim political and intellectual elites, the overriding claim principle was religious freedom. This was, of course, a radical turn from these elites' impassioned opposition to religious freedom at Independence.

Unsurprisingly, these parties differed on the meaning of these ideas just as they had disagreed over them during the colonial years. Although the Shariʿa cum anti-secularism camp stood in opposition to separation, it argued that the Nigerian state was, at any rate, not separate from all religion as the Christian secular camp claimed. In an argument reminiscent of the colonial-era missionary critique of secularism as "unchristian separation," Shariʿa proponents argued that the postcolonial state was merely separate from and hostile to Islam. Specifically, this group argued that Nigerian law's common law origins were inextricable from that law's Christian heritage. This was not a call to displace the Christian common law; rather, the group advocated that the Shari'a be granted equal privileges. Ditto the invocations of religious freedom by the Christian coalition. Not only did the Christian coalition shift from its Independence position to argue that religious freedom was secondary to state-religion separation, it also insisted that the Shari'a proposal was inconsistent with the idea of religious freedom. Specifically, the Christian coalition argued that the religious freedom of non-Muslims would, in fact, be infringed by the establishment of the court. This freedom of non-Muslims, the coalition argued, superseded the demands of the Shari'a camp.

To be sure, parties to the postcolonial contestations had morphed from the colonial configuration. Beyond the expected cross-regional (Northern-Southern Nigeria) alliances inspired by postindependence constitutional politics, the makeup of the parties had changed in the intervening decades. On the Christian pro-secularism side, European missions were now visibly absent, replaced by Indigenous churches led by Christian converts. Further, indigenization also broadened the ecumenical coalition to now include the Catholic Church, a group that had been visibly absent from colonial struggles. The Muslim anti-secularism camp came to reflect a coalition beyond the monolithic Masu Sarauta representation of the colonial years to now include a new politically engaged intellectual elite class, among others. Expectedly, these new alignments produced tensions within the projects of each camp even though the parties insisted that the struggles were continuous from the colonial debates.

The 1977 constitutional convention did not mark an end to the struggles over state-religion relations. Although the Constituent Assembly decided against the Shari'a proposal after pro-Shari'a delegates walked out on the proceedings in protest, the Shari'a demand and hence, state-religion struggles, never disappeared from constitutional discourse. Indeed, the Shari'a proponents made a comeback in 1999 with an even more contested maneuver: the reintroduction of Islamic criminal law in Northern Nigeria.

CONTINUING ENTANGLEMENTS

The story of the relationship between religion and politics in colonial Northern Nigeria was therefore one of sustained entanglement, and struggles over the terms of that entanglement continue to haunt the postcolony. Accordingly, this book does not end with decolonization. I trace these contestations into the postcolony not to mobilize the past in service of the present, but rather, to affirm that postcolonial struggles are, to borrow Gayatri Spivak's words, "part of the unfinished nature of the past."[71]

The historical chronicle reveals a complex relationship involving both continuities and discontinuities. Not only have the contestants realigned their positions from the posture they inhabited at Independence, the debate has also evolved from the past by adopting the frame of secularism qua secularism. The significant reframing of the postcolonial debate aside, parties invoke state-religion separation to contest religious freedom as they did in the colonial years. Unsurprisingly, the change in the relations of power in the postcolonial state has altered the fealty of the parties to these principles just as their arguments transformed from the Lugardian to the Cameron years.

Despite the evolving arguments that its ambivalence engenders, the governmental technique of secularism, midwifed by colonial modernity, has continued into the postcolonial state. While its constitution articulates the classical state-religion separation element of liberal secularism,[72] the postcolonial state, like the colonial one, continues to be entangled with religion. The current religion governance project, which manifests as defining and confining religion, has encompassed even projects originally intended as a resistance to colonialism and uses techniques reminiscent of colonial governance. Most notably, the postcolonial Shari'a agenda, intended to reinstate precolonial Islamic law, relies on secular governance techniques strikingly reminiscent of the colonial years, such as penal codes and colonial-type courts. Such governance projects, referred to by Brandon Kendhammer as "Shari'a statism,"[73] continue to deepen and hierarchize religious difference.

The story of the evolving arguments of postcolonial contestants therefore coheres with the ongoing narrative of the continuity of colonial

---

[71] Ebrahim Moosa, "Colonialism and Islamic Law," in *Islam and Modernity: Key Issues and Debates*, ed. Muhammad Khalid Masud (Edinburgh: Edinburgh University Press, 2009), 160. See Prathama Banerjee, "Re-Presenting Pasts: Santals in Nineteenth-Century Bengal," in *History and the Present*, eds. Partha Chatterjee and Anjan Ghosh (Delhi: Permanent Black, 2002), 242–273, 261; Gayatri Chakravorty Spivak, *A Critique of Postcolonial Reason* (Cambridge: Harvard University Press, 1999).

[72] 1979 Constitution: Section 10 (separation); and Section 35 (religious freedom). The 1999 Constitution: Section 10 (separation); and Section 38 (religious freedom).

[73] See Kendhammer, *Muslims Talking Politics*.

secular governmentality. But the former also serves as my critique of the latter as it occupies the imagination of postcolonial scholarship on secularism. Much of the critical accounts of secularism, cutting-edge as they are, pay inadequate attention to secularism's internal ambivalence and in particular, its consequent contradictory deployment. Apprehending this crucial feature and effect of secularism illuminates how subject-stakeholders deploy its conflicting imperatives to challenge the state and attempt to advance their agendas within it. This work argues, in sum, that critiquing secularism as a governmental technique interlinked with the rise of the modern state as a globalized form of political arrangement is compatible with recognizing that secularism, like all legal ideas, is not free of internal ambiguities and competing external deployments.

INHERITING AN IMAGINED PAST

History is a potent weapon in the hands of all sides in the postcolonial debate over secularism. Undoubtedly, the struggle over the terms and meaning of the entanglement between religious and political power in the colonial state continues to shape postcolonial constitutional debates. That colonial history has clearly come to be reimagined and reinvented by all parties differently.

Today, when the pro-secularism camp asserts that Nigeria is secular, it is invoking a particular interpretation of Nigeria's colonial past, in which secularism was absent from the colonial state and only acquired at Independence. In this understanding, the gift of secularism was the product of a long history of national and international missionary advocacy against the disempowerment of non-Muslims in a colonial state that had privileged Muslims and Islamic institutions. When this group asserts the state's secularism and resists attempts to reintroduce the Shari'a into public institutions, it is forestalling a reversion to what it recalls as colonial Muslim sub-imperialism and disempowerment of religious minorities.

Like the pro-secularism coalition, the Shari'a camp's stance is also an assertion about Nigeria's colonial past. Reacting against the assertions of the secularism camp that colonial rule meant Muslim sub-imperialism, the Shari'a camp avers that the colonial state subjugated Islam and deprived Muslims of religious freedom. For them, the Independence package, especially the elimination of Islamic criminal law, was the final step in this process of displacing Islamic law and institutions and subordinating Muslims. This group maintains that the Independence deal, like earlier colonial moves, violated the 1903 guarantee of noninterference. The postcolonial Shariʻa agenda is therefore a project to reverse this effect of the colonial experience whose indignities have allegedly survived Independence. By wielding claims of religious freedom to champion Shariʻa against claims of the state's secularism, this group is rejecting the Independence deal and, with it, the colonial project.

This framing of the postcolonial debate between secularism and anti-secularism is impervious to the colonial experience it invokes. The predecessors of the postcolonial Christian secularism camp, Christian missionaries, spent the colonial years feuding with a state that insisted on its secularity while co-opting Islam. They contested the colonial state's secularism, first, by advocating for state separation from Islam and later, in the postwar years, wielding religious freedom claims against the unchristian separation that marked imperial secularism. They not only conceived of religious freedom as being external to secularism, they also deplored the latter for robbing state and society of its "religious glamor."[74] That postcolonial secularism advocacy is spearheaded by the Christian Association of Nigeria today is, therefore, a striking reversal. The same discrepancy holds true for the pro-Shariʻa, anti-secular group, as well. Considering the co-option of Islamic institutions by the "secular" colonial state, Masu Sarauta invocation of secularism's imperatives to advance their agenda in the colonial years and that group's fierce opposition to the religious freedom project during Independence negotiations, the postcolonial oppositional framing of the Shariʻa project in opposition to statist secularism is astonishing.[75] The binarization of the "sacred" and

---

[74] Report of the Oxford 1937 Conference of the International Missionary Council's Life and Work Movement.

[75] For examples of a few of the several scholarly interventions that take the binarism of the debate at its face value, see Andrew Ubaka Iwobi, "Tiptoeing through a Constitutional Minefield: The Great Sharia Controversy in Nigeria," *Journal of African Law* 48, no. 2 (2004): 111–164. See also Austin Metumara Ahanotu, ed., *Religion, State, and Society in Contemporary Africa: Nigeria, Sudan, South Africa, Zaire, and Mozambique* (New York: Peter Lang, 1992); Toyin Falola, *Violence in Nigeria: The Crisis of Religious Politics and Secular Ideologies* (Rochester: University of Rochester Press, 2001); Matthew Hassan Kukah and Toyin Falola, *Religious Militancy and Self-Assertion: Islam and Politics in Nigeria* (Aldershot, UK: Avebury, 1996); Vincent O. Nmehielle, "Sharia Law in the Northern States of Nigeria: To Implement or Not to Implement, the Constitutionality is the Question," *Human Rights Quarterly* 26, no. 3 (2004): 730–759; Johannes Harnischfeger, *Democratization and Islamic Law: The Sharia Conflict in Nigeria* (Frankfurt: Campus Verlag, 2008); and Rotimi T. Suberu, "Religion and Institutions: Federalism and the Management of Conflicts over Sharia in Nigeria," *Journal of International Development* 21, no. 4 (2009): 547–560.

the "secular" in constitutional discourse belies the sustained entanglement of law, religion, and empire in the colonial years, and the enduring legacy of that entanglement in the postcolony.

The quest for equality has remained the unarticulated crux of postcolonial struggles, just as it underpinned colonial debates. Its assertion of the equality of subjects notwithstanding, colonial governance was founded on hierarchizing religions, allowing substantive inequality to prevail. Not only did the state create a hierarchy between an Anglo-Masu Sarauta version of Islam and its others, it also recalibrated relations among Muslims with different theological leanings by infusing them with political and legal significance. In constituting the postcolonial state, the elimination of Islamic public (criminal) law and constitutionalization of Protestant human rights sent a signal that ecumenical Protestants had not only won hearts at the Colonial Office, but more significantly, that they had also won the fierce battle for the soul of the postcolony. The casualty, of both the colonial processes and its Independence resolution, was equality.

Tragically, the colonial technique of defining, deepening, and hierarchizing religious difference already predetermined the form and futility of resistance mounted by subjects. For missionaries resisting the subordination of non-Muslims (specifically, Protestant Christians), emancipation called for contesting the "secular Islamic" state through a hardly neutral notion of religious freedom that intended to invert rather than dismantle the colonial hierarchy. For the "bad Muslims," those Muslim minorities whose subordination was hidden by the state's alliance with Islam, resistance via an internal critique of the colonized caliphal institutions was doomed to fail from its inception. And, for those Masu Sarauta opposed to the colonial reform of caliphal institutions, resistance meant invoking empire's guarantee of noninterference to challenge a religion governance project that was itself integral to late imperial secularism. Nostalgic about the precolonial past but now steeped in colonial privileges and mired in colonial statist consciousness, these elites were left to feebly resist the state's secular project while simultaneously affirming its premises.

This book proceeds in three parts. Part I unearths the emergence and workings of secularism as a colonial technique of governing religious difference. With a focus on the two most contentious religion governance questions faced by the colonial state – the mission question and the fate of Islamic law – the two chapters comprising Part I uncover the ways through which the state defined, deepened, and hierarchized religious difference. Over the course of three chapters, Part II lays out the three elements of the Independence Constitution deal: the emergence of religious minorities as a political identity, the abolition of Islamic public law, and the constitutionalization of the right to religious liberty. Part II asks: what was the consequence of the colonial legal design described in Part I and the struggles it set in motion for the constitutional law and politics of decolonization? Part III examines the legacy of the colonial governance of religion for postcolonial constitutionalism. Through the lens of the constitutional proceedings of the first postindependence constitutional conference in 1977 and with highlights from other constitutional moments since then, the chapter unveils how and why the postcolonial struggles have inherited the complex colonial experience as an essentialist debate between secularism and anti-secularism. The concluding chapter reflects on what the unfolding of the career of imperial secular governmentality – in its colonial and postcolonial form – reveals about the complex connections between law, faith, identity, and power.

This book tells the story of the entanglement of law, religion, and empire in Northern Nigeria and traces the contestations set in motion by that entanglement into the postcolonial state. The Northern Nigerian story is unique, but the clash between the tenacity of religion and the inescapability of secular modernity, however, is ubiquitous. The account that follows is therefore crucial not only to understanding the tragedy of Nigeria's constitutional deadlock, but also to apprehending global postcolonial struggles over religion and religious difference.

PART I

GOVERNING FAITH

CHAPTER ONE

JOUSTING FOR SOULS
Indirect Rule, Christian Missions, and the Governance of Religious Difference

Delivering the keynote at the bicentennial gathering of the Church of England's Society for the Propagation of the Gospel in Foreign Parts on June 19, 1900, Prime Minister of England and Marquess of Salisbury, Lord Robert Gascoyne-Cecil, warned of the dangers of the British government's alliance with Christian missions in overseas colonial territories.[1] Cecil traced the alliance to the tendency of missionaries to "appeal to the Consul and ... the Gunboat" when faced with challenges in the mission field.[2] The prime minister argued that the entanglement that results from the British Empire perpetuating the ends of missionaries benefitted neither missions nor the imperial cause. In particular, he stressed that the entanglement of missions with the imperial project hinders the missionary venture by "diminish[ing] the purely spiritual aspect and action" of "Christian teaching" and raising suspicion of its religious motives.[3] The entanglement was, in his opinion, also detrimental to the imperial project because it portrayed the British Empire as partial to missionary interests, and as consequently failing to live up to its declaration of being a "secular colonial government" in its dominions.[4] Since the prime minister was delivering his address while the Boxer Rebellion, which featured attacks on Christian missionaries, was ongoing, he was quick to cite the Chinese example. Pointing out that several of the casualties of the revolt were Christian, Cecil asked his missionary audience: "Do

---

[1] "Lord Salisbury and Foreign Missions," *The Times Weekly Edition*, June 20, 1900, 10b.
[2] Ibid. [3] Ibid. [4] Ibid.

you imagine that they are slaughtered simply because the Chinese dislike their religion?" The prime minister went on to respond in the negative: "It is because they and other nations have got the idea that missionary work is a mere instrument of the secular government in order to achieve the objects it has in view. That is a most dangerous and terrible snare."[5]

This exhortation by the prime minister of an empire on which "the sun never set" was not received with favor by a missionary enterprise whose declared goal was to proselytize to the world.[6] After all, the global missionary project was the culmination of evangelicalism's spiritual premise – that Christ died for the world – into a political project whereby "the world must be changed for Christ."[7] Muslim Africa had a special place in this missionary design. As a historian, Thomas Prasch aptly points out, "For the late-Victorian missionary enterprise, Islam represented the quintessential Other: the faith that was most resistant, most competitive. And for Victorians, [black] Africa was the obvious arena of contention, the blankest continent on the imperial map."[8] Perhaps no territory encapsulated the pull that Black Africa had for Christian missionaries more than Northern Nigeria. Indeed, the area that came to be known as the British Protectorate of Northern Nigeria at the beginning of the twentieth century was home to the famed nineteenth-century Sokoto Caliphate of *Bilad al Sudan* (Land of the Blacks). Emerging from the 1804 Sheikh Uthman Dan Fodio-led revolt, Sokoto was "the largest, most heavily populated, most complexly organized and wealthiest system in nineteenth century west Africa."[9] Less prominent than Sokoto

---

[5] Ibid.

[6] For reactions to Salisbury's speech in missionary circles, see for instance, the Editorial of the August 1, 1900 edition of the *Church Missionary Gleaner* stating that Salisbury's speech was "hard" on the missionaries, 12.

[7] Talal Asad, *Formations of the Secular: Christianity, Islam, Modernity* (Stanford: Stanford University Press, 2003), 62. See also Jean Comaroff and John L. Comaroff, *Of Revelation and Revolution: Christianity, Colonialism, and Consciousness in South Africa*, vol. 1 (Chicago: University of Chicago Press, 2008).

[8] Thomas Prasch, "Which God for Africa: The Islamic-Christian Missionary Debate in Late-Victorian England," *Victorian Studies* 33, no. 1 (1989): 51–73.

[9] Michael J. Watts, *Silent Violence: Food, Famine, and Peasantry in Northern Nigeria*, vol. 15 (Athens, GA: University of Georgia Press, 2013), 49. For classical accounts of the caliphate, see Murray Last, *The Sokoto Caliphate*, vol. 1 (London: Open Humanities Press, 1967); Mervyn Hiskett, *The Sword of Truth: The Life and Times of the Shehu Usuman dan Fodio* (Oxford: Oxford University Press, 1973).

but no less crucial in shaping the Muslim identity of the area was the Kanem Bornu Empire, portions of which merged with Sokoto to become the British Colonial Protectorate of Northern Nigeria while France and Germany incorporated the remainder of Kanem Bornu into neighboring colonial possessions in the Lake Chad Basin. Northern Nigeria was far from exclusively Muslim; beyond Sokoto and Kanem Bornu, the area featured a variety of tribes practicing diverse religions, populations described in precolonial parlance as the *Maguzawa*. Yet, the area's Muslim character was undoubtedly its greatest attraction to Christian missions, especially the influential Church of England-affiliated Church Missionary Society. Muslim Africa's centrality to the missionary imagination was also rooted in a sense of competition. As the inaugural 1910 international gathering of world missions declared: "the ubiquitous and rapid advance of Islam is the great challenge to urgency in the evangelization of Africa."[10] Spreading the gospel to Northern Nigeria was therefore of primacy to missions.

For all of Northern Nigeria's allure, the feverish zeal to evangelize encountered such intense restrictions from the colonial government that the protectorate was quick to attain notoriety as an outlier in the global mission field.[11] Those restrictions were so extensive that they were perhaps unparalleled outside of the Arabian Peninsula. Indeed, after over a century of missionary presence in West Africa, only 2.7 percent of the Northern Nigerian population identified as Christian.[12] Moreover, that modest success was almost exclusively recorded among the other Indigenous faith populations to whom the colonial state permitted proselytization, contrary to its aggressive shielding of Muslims from missionary influence.

Colonial restrictions on missionaries are traceable to the imperial anxieties that inspired Prime Minister Cecil's 1900 speech. Specifically, missionary proselytization threatened the credibility of the British Empire's assertion, which was so commonplace by the time

---

[10] World Missionary Conference, *Report of the World Missionary Conference Commission I: Carrying of the Gospel to All the Non-Christian World* (Edinburgh: World Missionary Conference, 1910), 207.
[11] H. G. Farrant, Memorandum on Missionary Work in Northern Nigeria, December 16, 1929. CBMS/IMC BOX 270.
[12] Nigeria, Federal Census Office, Population Census of the Northern Region of Nigeria, 1952-3 (Lagos: Census Superintendent 1953).

of Cecil's address, that it was separate from religion.[13] That assertion of separation encompassed two claims. The first was that the colonial enterprise was devoid of a civilizing or Christianizing goal, and the second was that the state would not interfere with Indigenous religions.[14] These two notions of separation, which found expression in the "guarantee of non-interference" issued upon Britain's violent subjugation of Northern Nigeria, gave way to another imperial assurance – that the state was devoted to the religious liberty of colonial subjects. The dual insistence on separation and religious freedom formed the basis of the secular governmentality that came to animate colonial rule.

Crucially, neither the insistence on separation nor the declaration of commitment to religious liberty was principled. As the state invoked the notion of empire's separation from religion to restrict missions, it emphasized religious liberty in its dealings with Indigenous religions by declaring the religious and cultural autonomy of colonized populations. The state invoked its commitment to the autonomy of Indigenous populations as the bedrock for its turn to governing through Indigenous institutions – indirect rule.[15] Although premised on empire's separation from Indigenous institutions, indirect rule required the co-option of Indigenous institutions for the colonial project, and consequently called for the interference it appeared to prohibit. To further muddy the waters, colonial administrators' proclivities informed their understanding of these assurances and, therefore, influenced on-the-ground policies. This meant that the workings of imperial secularism and ultimately, of its corollary, indirect rule, were

---

[13] See Peter van der Veer, *Imperial Encounters: Religion and Modernity in India and Britain* (Princeton: Princeton University Press, 2001), 22; Catherine S. Adcock, *The Limits of Tolerance: Indian Secularism and the Politics of Religious Freedom* (Oxford: Oxford University Press, 2013).

[14] van der Veer, *Imperial Encounters*.

[15] For accounts of indirect rule, see, for example, William Malcolm Hailey, *Native Administration and Political Development in British Tropical Africa* (Nendeln, Liechtenstein: Kraus Reprint, 1979); Charles L. Temple, *Native Races and Their Rulers* (Cape Town: Argus, 1918); Margery Freda Perham, *Native Administration in Nigeria* (New York: Oxford University Press, 1937); Jonathan Reynolds, "Good and Bad Muslims: Islam and Indirect Rule in Northern Nigeria," *International Journal of African Historical Studies* 34, no. 3 (2001): 601–618; Kalu Ezera, *Constitutional Development in Nigeria* (Cambridge: Cambridge University Press, 1960); and Mahmood Mamdani, *Citizen and Subject: Contemporary Africa and the Legacy of Late Colonialism* (Princeton, NJ: Princeton University Press, 1996).

hardly constant. Even in that incoherence, however, the story of (the earlier decades of) colonial rule was, without doubt, one of an asymmetrical pact with Muslim rulers, and a marginalization of Christian missions. Against the background of the unfolding of imperial secularism as a historically contingent technique of managing religion and religious difference in Northern Nigeria, this chapter presents the struggles that arose from the frustration of missionary efforts in a much-coveted area of colonial Muslim Africa.

THE ENCOUNTER OF IMPERIAL AMBITIONS WITH THE MISSIONARY PROJECT

Not a few volumes have attempted to capture the story of missionary disappointments in Northern Nigeria.[16] These works evince differing views on the motivations behind the colonial government's restrictions on those missions. Andrew Barnes, for example, pinpoints the

---

[16] See Shobana Shankar, *Who Shall Enter Paradise? Christian Origins in Muslim Northern Nigeria, ca. 1890–1975* (Athens, OH: Ohio University Press, 2014); Emmanuel Ayankanmi Ayandele, *The Missionary Impact on Modern Nigeria 1842–1914: A Political and Social Analysis* (London: Longmans, 1966). See also Mukhtar Umar Bunza, *Christian Missions among Muslims: Sokoto Province, Nigeria, 1935–1990* (Trenton, NJ: Africa World Press, 2007); Jan Harm Boer, *Missionary Messengers of Liberation in a Colonial Context: A Case Study of the Sudan United Mission* (Amsterdam: Rodopi, 1979); E. O. Ayandele, "The Missionary Factor in Northern Nigeria 1870–1918," in *The History of Christianity in West Africa*, ed. Ogbu Kalu (London: Longman, 1982), 133–158; Chinedu Nwafor Ubah, "Problems of Christian Missionaries in Muslim Emirates, 1900–1928," *Journal of African Studies* 3, no. 3 (1976), 351–371; Edmund Patrick Thurman Crampton, *Christianity in Northern Nigeria* (London: Burns and Oates, 1979); Andrew E. Barnes, *Making Headway: The Introduction of Western Civilization in Colonial Northern Nigeria* (Rochester: University of Rochester Press, 2009); Andrew E. Barnes, "The 'Great Prohibition': The Expansion of Christianity in Northern Nigeria," *History Compass* 8, no. 6 (2010): 440–454; Andrew E. Barnes, "The Colonial Legacy to Contemporary Culture in Northern Nigeria 1900–1960," in *Power and Nationalism in Modern Africa: Papers in Honor of Don Ohadike*, eds. Toyin Falola and Salah M. Hassan (Durham, NC: Carolina Academic Press, 2008), 257–262; Andrew E. Barnes, "Christianity and the Colonial State in Northern Nigeria: 1900–1960," in *Nigeria in the Twentieth Century*, ed. Toyin Falola (Durham, NC: Carolina Academic Press, 2002), 281–292; Andrew E. Barnes, "'Evangelization Where It Is Not Wanted': Colonial Administrators and Missionaries in Northern Nigeria during the First Third of the Twentieth Century," *Journal of Religion in Africa* 25, no. 4 (1995), 412–441; and Peter K. Tibenderana, "The Emirs and the Spread of Western Education in Northern Nigeria, 1910–1946," *Journal of African History* 24, no. 4 (1983): 517–534.

cultural tensions between colonial administrators and missionaries, particularly the clash between the vision of civilization espoused by colonial administrators, and the Christianizing project of missions.[17] Others, like C. N. Ubah, have argued that emirs (Muslim political authorities) were the primary source of opposition to missions.[18] Yet, others such as the classical authority on Nigerian missions, Emmanuel A. Ayandele, argue that the missionary restrictions were a product of an indirect rule design that sought to placate Muslim vessels of colonial rule by keeping out Christian proselytizers.[19] In spite of more recent attempts to focus on the few instances of missionary breakthrough,[20] what is undeniable is that disappointment was the general experience of missions. These histories are useful for what they reveal of the fate of the missionary enterprise. In isolating the missionary question, however, they fail to interrogate the missionary experience for what it reveals of the broader colonial imperative to govern religion and religious difference.

As told in this chapter, the story is indeed one in which missionaries were frustrated by colonial restrictions. More importantly, however, it is an account of a broader struggle in which leading actors – missionaries, colonial administrators, emirs, and other Indigenous elites – wielded ideas on the proper relationship between the state and religion in shifting and incongruent ways. This contestation was precipitated by an enduring governmental technique that entailed the state insisting on its separation from religion even while both the state and religion were irreclaimably entangled.

The state's entanglement with religion is hardly surprising; after all, studies have drawn attention to the entanglement of religion and politics that secular governmentality entails.[21] As Hussein Agrama points out, secularism is "a process of defining, managing, and intervening into religious life and sensibility."[22] The entanglement that inevitably results is itself a reflection of the state's governance of religion and religious difference. The state categorized the religion of the colonized population into two – Muslim

---

[17] Barnes, "Evangelization Where It Is Not Wanted".
[18] Ubah, "Problems of Christian Missionaries in Muslim Emirates".
[19] See Ayandele, *The Missionary Impact*.
[20] See Shankar, *Who Shall Enter Paradise?*
[21] See, for example, Asad, *Formations of the Secular*; and Saba Mahmood, *Religious Difference in a Secular Age: A Minority Report* (Princeton, NJ: Princeton University Press, 2015).
[22] Hussein Agrama, *Questioning Secularism: Islam, Sovereignty, and the Rule of Law in Modern Egypt* (Chicago: University of Chicago Press, 2012), 26.

and non-Muslim, designating the latter as "pagan." This bifurcated classification then formed the basis of an elaborate administrative arrangement that stipulated, among other things, where colonial populations could reside, the elites through whom they would be governed, what courts were competent to resolve their disputes, and most importantly for the purpose of this chapter, whether they could be subjected to Christian proselytization. The binary Muslim–non-Muslim classification glossed over complexities in precolonial identity formation. Political wrangling in precolonial Sokoto had widened cleavages among Muslims (such as among those belonging to rival Sufi orders) in a way that questioned the homogenizing lens with which the state viewed that population.[23] Further, precolonial political or juristic discourse did not affix the ethno-religiously diverse non-Muslim communities with the pejorative *kafiri* (pagan) status with which they came to be treated by the state. Not all of these Maguzawa groups were political subjects of Sokoto; even those subject to caliphate overlordship had been granted jurisdictional autonomy.[24] Maguzawa were levied *jizyah*, a tax symbolizing their acceptance of the sovereignty of the Islamic state, and a levy in lieu of the military obligation binding on Muslim (men) – but lower than the *zakat* payment binding on all eligible Muslims. Religious faith was therefore closely tied to citizenship and governance in precolonial Northern Nigeria. That preexisting arrangement was incongruent with the grid through which the state came to understand and govern religion and religious difference. That grid, which defined religion as Muslim versus pagan, deepened precolonial difference and created a hierarchy that placed the colonial construct of the ideal Muslim over the colonial formulation of the pagan. In seeking to produce a colonial subject that was neither Muslim nor "pagan," evangelization threatened these classifications and the regulatory ambitions that motivated them.

Far from an isolated phenomenon in the British rule of Northern Nigeria, therefore, the missionary question can only be apprehended by unraveling the broader institutional context of the colonial governance of religion and religious difference. Accordingly, the account that follows presents the struggles over the state's restrictions on Christian

---

[23] See, however, Chapter 2 for a discussion of the intra-Muslim differentiation that indirect rule entailed.

[24] Bunza, *Christian Missions among Muslims*, 7–13.

missions as an encounter between imperial bureaucrats, missionaries, the colonial remains of the caliphate aristocracy, and other Indigenous religious elites over the governance of religious difference. If that encounter culminated in the dismal failure of the Christian missionary project to evangelize Muslims, the defining, deepening, and hierarchizing of religious difference that emerged from its ashes was its lasting legacy.

SECULARISM, MISSIONIZING, AND LATE LIBERAL IMPERIALISM

Cecil's bicentennial address to the Church Missionary Society was hardly the inaugural declaration of the British Empire's policy of separation from missions. That colonial policy and the constitutional idea underpinning it – secularism – emerged in mid-nineteenth-century British India.[25] The gradual unfolding of the Indian story was nearly paralleled by happenings in the seat of empire, in England. If one is to understand secularism as the statecraft principle of managing religious difference by the dual assertion of state-religion separation and religious freedom,[26] then strains of that idea began to emerge in England in the early decades of the nineteenth century. An initial step was the gradual "enfranchisement" of Catholics and dissenters, a process set in motion by a series of legislations, including significantly, the Sacramental Test Act of 1828[27] and Roman Catholic Relief Act of 1829.[28] Enfranchisement meant conferring on these marginalized groups citizenship and equality – rights that Protestants had long enjoyed. Although those legislative reforms meant the recognition of religious diversity and a modicum of liberty, it hardly meant the displacement of the Church of England, which endured as the state church. Other vestiges of church establishment would remain in several areas. This included public education, which had for long included Protestant instruction, a Christian

---

[25] van der Veer, *Imperial Encounters*, 41; Partha Chatterjee, "Secularism and Toleration," *Economic and Political Weekly* 29, no. 28 (1994): 1768–1777.

[26] John Rawls, *Political Liberalism* (New York: Columbia University Press, 2015); Bruce Ackerman, *Social Justice in the Liberal State* (New Haven: Yale University Press, 1980).

[27] This act repealed the requirement that government officials take communion in the Church of England.

[28] The Relief Act removed many of the restrictions on Roman Catholics introduced by the Act of Uniformity, the Test Acts, and the Penal laws.

"privilege" that even later vanguards of separation like the future Prime Minister Cecil would insist could not be "interfere[d] with, diminish[ed] or frustrate[d]."[29]

These features lend credence to Peter van der Veer's assertion that the enfranchisement of marginalized faiths was not a product of an ideological commitment to the twin principles of secularism, but was instead intended to "shift ... political loyalty from religious identity to national [European] identity."[30] In van der Veer's account, the shift in political loyalty from religious identity to national identity in Europe enabled the creation of a European Christian identity. With this, "the opposition between Britain as a Protestant nation and France as a Catholic nation became less relevant than the opposition between a Christian, civilized nation and colonized peoples without civilized religions."[31] Hence, secularism, as enacted in the metropole, was not so much about the state's separation from religion by expunging it from the public sphere and confining it to the private, within which the state granted subjects religious freedom. Rather, van der Veer argues that secularism entailed religion "creating the public sphere," and by so doing, it "transformed and molded" this sphere "into a national form."[32] The story of the development of English secularism was, in sum, that of a historically contingent governance project rather than of a neutral and predetermined implementation of the ideas of religious liberty and separation.

Even as the politics of secularism transcended commitment to ideology, that governance idea came to have a tenacious hold over constitutional discourse. In fact, as England was gesturing toward enfranchising marginalized religious groups at home, its empire began to realize that a "separation of church and state" was crucial to governing the jewel of colonial possessions – India.[33] This idea gained traction due to the experience of the Indian Revolt, understood in the upper ranks of the colonial administration as a rebellion against the civilizing mission of

---

[29] See Robert Gascoyne-Cecil, "Some Home Questions," delivered on October 7, 1885, at Newport, in Henry William Lucy, ed. *Speeches of the Marquis of Salisbury: With a Sketch of His Life* (London: Routledge, 1885). Until a 1974 legislation, the lord chancellor was required to be a member of the Church of England. See Lord Chancellor (Tenure of Office and Discharge of Ecclesiastical Functions) Act 1974.

[30] van der Veer, *Imperial Encounters*, 22.   [31] Ibid.   [32] Ibid.

[33] Ibid. Chatterjee, "Secularism and Toleration."

the colonial enterprise.³⁴ Although the civilizing mission was hardly synonymous with a Christianizing mission, those two projects were not independent of each other, both in the influence that missions exercised in colonial circles and in the inextricability of the two projects in the estimation of colonized populations. In response, the state not only sought to move from the civilizing project following the Indian Revolt, it also began to insist on its separation from missions and on the religious liberty of colonial populations.³⁵ Indeed, the rebellion inspired the Queen's 1858 declaration of religious and cultural autonomy for colonial populations.³⁶ The Queen's declaration also gave way to the shift from direct rule to the adoption of "native" institutions as the indirect vehicle for colonial governance. These dual commitments, therefore, already entailed a tension: on the one hand, empire declared Indigenous religions as autonomous from colonial interference.³⁷ On the other hand, however, colonial rule through "native" institutions necessarily called for interfering with, or at least, "instructing" those institutions.³⁸ Hardly passive bystanders, missionaries and Indigenous colonial subjects began to deploy these notions of separation and religious liberty to advance their projects. In particular, influential evangelists began to mount pressure on the state to distance itself from native religions just as it had affirmed its distance from missions. Far from being unconditionally committed to the notion of separation, what missions prized above all was a return to their original alliance with the state, and failing that, an empire expressing only the barest minimum neutrality toward indigenous religions.³⁹ On the other hand, however, colonial subjects would invoke the Queen's proclamation of religious

---

³⁴ See Thomas R. Metcalf, *Aftermath of Revolt: India 1857–1970* (Princeton, NJ: Princeton University Press, 2015).

³⁵ For an account of the shift to liberal imperialism, see Hugh Archibald Wyndham, "The Native Problem in Africa by Raymond Leslie Buell," *Journal of the Royal Institute of International Affairs* 7, no. 5 (1928): 335–337.

³⁶ Proclamation by the Queen in Council to the Princes, Chiefs and People of India Published by the Governor-General at Allahabad," (1858). IOR/L/PS/18/D154 British Library, UK.

³⁷ van der Veer, *Imperial Encounters*, 27; Nandini Chatterjee, *The Making of Indian Secularism: Empire, Law and Christianity, 1830–1960* (New York: Palgrave Macmillan, 2011).

³⁸ Frederick John Dealtry Lugard, *Report by Sir F. D. Lugard on the Amalgamation of Northern and Southern Nigeria, and Administration, 1912–1919* (London: H. M. Stationery Office, 1920), 70.

³⁹ van der Veer, *Imperial Encounters*, 21; Chatterjee, *The Making of Indian Secularism*.

and cultural autonomy and indirect rule on the perception of any form of interference.

Consequently, not only did religion defy the separationist assertion by maintaining a tenacious hold on public life, but what religious freedom (or, in the language of the Queen's declaration, "religious autonomy") meant also continued to be hotly contested. Nevertheless, the classical elements of secularism espoused in liberal political theory – religious liberty and separation – were formally fulfilled.[40] In deploying these ideas to govern missions and Indigenous religions, the state's assertions of secularism became, in essence, what van der Veer describes as "the tropes of a state that tried to project itself as playing the role of a transcendent arbiter in a country divided along religious lines."[41] Secularism, therefore, became an imperial agenda of governing religious differences – rather than a coherent project free of contestations.

Governing Religious Difference: Colonial Indirect Rule in Northern Nigeria

The imperial agenda arrived in Northern Nigeria in 1903, the year the British Empire declared its dominion over the Sokoto Caliphate and its contiguous territories, molding these precolonial entities into the British Protectorate of Northern Nigeria.[42] The restrictions on missionary activity that followed this formal colonization amounted to a shift from the cooperation between imperial and missionary interests that preceded it. In fact, the mid-nineteenth-century origins of the British presence in West Africa lay in the British government's alliance with overseas missions. The 1841 African Colonization Expedition, which was comprised of British missionaries, scientists, traders, and military officials, ushered in that presence. Setting out the vision of the mission-empire cooperation that inspired the expedition, British evangelical Thomas Foxwell Buxton pronounced: "Let missionaries and schoolmasters ... go together ... confidence between man and man will be inspired; whilst civilization will advance as the natural effect and Christianity operate

---

[40] Rawls, *Political Liberalism*; Donald Eugene Smith, *India as a Secular State* (Princeton, NJ: Princeton University Press, 2015); Ackerman, *Social Justice in the Liberal State*.
[41] van der Veer, *Imperial Encounters*, 35.
[42] On the circulations of colonial law, see Renisa Mawani and Iza Hussin, "The Travels of Law: Indian Ocean Itineraries," *Law and History Review* 32, no. 4 (2014): 733–747.

as the proximate cause, of this happy change."[43] This cooperation was reflected in the relationship that existed between the West African Frontier Force and British consuls and missions from 1841 through the turn of the twentieth century. With the backing of the imperial army, mission houses enjoyed wide liberties in pursuance of their project, including the exercise of jurisdiction over Africans on the basis of conversion to Christianity.[44] Moreover, the Berlin Treaty entered into by European colonial powers to delineate their African holdings placed missionaries under "special protection."[45] Remarking on the utility of missionary cooperation with imperial interests, C. C. Newton, a Baptist, famously remarked: "War is often a means of opening a door for the gospel to enter a country. A sword of steel often goes beyond a sword of the spirit."[46] To be sure, the friendship between missions and the British Empire suffered some strains since missionary efforts did not always enjoy the approval of the British government. Notably, Joseph Chamberlain, secretary of state for the colonies, disapproved of the first Church Missionary Society voyage into the Northern Nigerian hinterland in 1897. Yet, that hardly annulled the empire-missionary alliance; in fact, when the Emir of Kano humiliated the Church Missionary Society (CMS) missionaries by ordering them out of his domain, the British government-controlled West African Frontier Force was swift to retaliate with a military expedition.[47]

Missionary friendship with the British Empire, however, soured once Britain asserted formal dominion over Northern Nigeria in the early years of the twentieth century. On March 15, 1903, Sokoto fell to the British army, giving way to the declaration of a protectorate. Northern Nigeria was not free of imperial influence before that time. Although the nineteenth-century mission-empire project was mostly present in the southern part of the territory that would become Nigeria, the northern region was not untouched. Christian missions were present among communities contiguous to the Benue River and Niger River that demarcated the region that would come to be known as colonial Northern Nigeria. Moreover, these missions steadily strove to extend their reach

---

[43] Thomas Fowell Buxton, *The African Slave Trade and Its Remedy* (London: Murray, 1840), 454.
[44] See Ayandele, *The Missionary Impact*, 23–26.   [45] Ibid.
[46] C. C. Newton to Tupper, April 12, 1892, in *Foreign Mission Journal*, vol. 23, July 1892, in Ayandele, *The Missionary Impact*, 67.
[47] Ayandele, *The Missionary Impact*.

to the Muslim hinterland as depicted by the CMS voyage referred to above. The missionary efforts and the backing they enjoyed from the British government – a government understood by Northern Muslim elites to be Christian – only heightened these elites' sense of a Christian onslaught. In the last decades of the nineteenth century, pamphlets commonly circulated in Northern Nigeria warning "of the attack on Islam by the West" and calling for solidarity with Muslims being subjugated by what was regarded as Christian colonialism.[48] Early administrators of the Northern Nigerian Protectorate would seek to unsettle these assumptions of the Christian missionary leanings of the British Empire.

On the installation of Muhammadu Attahiru II, the inaugural colonial-era sultan of Sokoto, on March 21, 1903, the head of the British imperial army, Colonel Frederick Lugard, issued a declaration that "government will in no way interfere with the Mohammedan religion. All men are free to worship God as they please."[49] Although worded ambiguously, Lugard's guarantee, which was issued not only to the new sultan but also to all emirs, became a key referent point in the tussle over, among other things, the restrictions on missionary activity that would mark the colonial years.

The Lugard-led administration asserted that the guarantee called for the state's separation from religion. Moreover, the government argued that the state-religion separation required by the guarantee called for restricting Christian missionary activity.[50] With regards to the colonized, however, the administration argued that the fulfillment of the guarantee called for governing through precolonial caliphate institutions. While this understanding of the guarantee drew on the separationist notion that the state ought to leave religious matters to Indigenous institutions, it also rested on the idea of religious liberty for colonized populations, which was emphasized since the Queen's 1858 declaration in the aftermath of the Indian Revolt. As we will see below, the understanding that Lugard's administration adopted, the sensibilities from which it sprung, and its consequences for everyday administrative choices were not constant

---

[48] Hugh Clapperton, *Journal of a Second Expedition into the Interior of Africa from the Bight of Benin to Soccatoo* (Philadelphia: Carey, Lea and Carey, 1829).

[49] Colonial Reports-Annual, no. 409, Northern Nigeria, 1902 (HM Stationery Office, 1903), 16.

[50] See Colonial Reports-Annual, no. 409, Northern Nigeria, 1902 (HM Stationery Office, 1903), 77. See also a 1917 Manuscript Memorandum authored by Lugard and cited in May 1948 Report prepared by A. A. Williams. CO 554/1534. National Archives, United Kingdom (hereafter NA, UK).

across the colonial years. Yet, the governance design that emerged from this rationalization – indirect rule – would persistently center religion and religious difference in administering the colonial population.[51]

Articulating the foundations of British indirect rule, Frederick Lugard declared of colonial Africa: "The British Empire ... has only one mission – for liberty and self-development on no standardized lines, so that all may feel that their interests and religion are safe under the British flag." This religious liberty, Lugard went on, called for autonomy: "leaving them [colonized populations] free to manage their own affairs through their own rulers, proportionately to their degree of advancement, under the guidance of the British staff, and subject to the laws and policy of the administration."[52] Indirect rule through native institutions was, therefore, intimately linked with notions of the state's proper constitutional relationship with religion.

This emphasis on religion is not to deny the place of Indigeneity in the colonial encounter and colonial governance. Like elsewhere in the British Empire, Northern Nigerian indirect rule was based on the construction of a racialized identity distinction: the native versus the non-native.[53] In the colonial taxonomy, the native was African and "Indigenous" to a society. This was in contradistinction with a native alien who, though African, was considered nonindigenous.[54] The colonial notion did not reflect historical identities and relations; the historian Yusuf Bala Usman shows it relied on invented theories of origin.[55]

---

[51] It is striking that the doctrine of *ridda*, which prohibited apostasy from Islam, and classically imposed criminal and civil penalties were largely absent from the colonial discourse. For a historicization of *ridda* and its analogy to the modern doctrine of treason, see Abdullahi Ahmed An-Na'im, "Introduction: Competing Claims to Religious Freedom and Communal Self-Determination in Africa, in Abdullahi Ahmed An-Na'im," in *Proselytization and Communal Self-Determination in Africa*, ed. Abdullahi Ahmed An-Na'im (Eugene: Wipf and Stock Publishers, 2009), 15–16.

[52] Frederick J. D. Lugard citing General Jan Smuts in *The Dual Mandate in British Tropical Africa* (Edinburgh: Blackwood, 1922), 94.

[53] Mahmood Mamdani, *Define and Rule: Native as Political Identity* (Cambridge: Harvard University Press, 2012), 106.

[54] There was also the category of the "native alien" who, although a native African, is not Indigenous to the community in which he is found at the time the law struggles to deal with him. As I discuss the struggles over jurisdiction of the native courts in subsequent chapters, I highlight how this category of native alien was hugely contested.

[55] Yusuf Bala Usman, *Beyond Fairy Tales: Selected Historical Writing of Yusuf Bala Usman* (Zaria, Nigeria: Abdullahi Smith Centre for Historical Research, 2006); Mamdani, *Define and Rule*. Mahmood Mamdani, *Citizen and Subject: Contemporary Africa and the Legacy of Late Colonialism* (Princeton, NJ: Princeton University Press, 2018).

In the colonial schema, the "native's" identity was opposed to that of the "non-native," who was technically non-African but typically Caucasian.[56] Not all "natives" were, however, the same. Persons Indigenous to Southern Nigeria were classified by the state as native but nonindigenous. These nonindigenous natives and native aliens – sub-Saharan Africans who were Indigenous to neither Northern nor Southern Nigeria – were mandated by the colonial government to take residence in *sabon guruwa* (strangers reservations), usually located on the outskirts of the city far from Indigenous natives.[57] This process of defining and classifying natives was, therefore, central to colonial indirect rule.[58]

For all the legal and social significance of the construction of Indigeneity and its racial undertones, however, religion had a greater impact on the ordering of the state and took precedence in defining colonial subjects. Even the native versus non-native distinction could be upended by religious classifications. For instance, while non-native Muslims, particularly Arabs, were permitted to reside among natives, native but nonindigenous Christians (Christian Southern Nigerians) and native alien Christians (Christian sub-Saharan Africans) could not. Indeed, colonial governance was based on defining, deepening, and hierarchizing religious difference. As noted earlier, the state glossed over complexities in precolonial identity formations to classify colonial populations as either Muslim or non-Muslim. That classification, in turn, determined residential formations, political administration, and ultimately, jurisdiction.

Northern Nigeria was zoned into three areas under the colonial religion differentiation scheme. First, there were emirates under the control of emirs. Tagged "Type I areas," these were predominantly Muslim and consisted of Sokoto, Kano, Borno, Bauchi, and Katsina provinces.[59] Second were the Type II areas with a mixed religious

[56] Note that this construct was not merely a racial construct. For instance, "negro citizens of the United States" were not regarded as natives.
[57] David Edley Allyn, "The Sabon Gari System in Northern Nigeria, 1911–1940," PhD diss., (University of California, Los Angeles, 1976); Europeans lived in government reservations.
[58] Mamdani, *Define and Rule*.
[59] Provinces did not map onto the borders of precolonial emirates with the result that the jurisdiction of provinces tended to feature multiple emirs exercising jurisdiction over discrete spheres. Further, the number of provinces were not constant across the colonial years because the colonial administration periodically re-delineated the territory; although the twelve listed here are those that existed for much of the colonial years, other unlisted provinces were created and phased out during that period.

population that was governed through chiefs who were Muslim but did not have the status of emirs. Although some mixed religious areas had come under the control of the precolonial caliphate after the 1804 revolution and had been governed through Muslim administrators, the state expanded this category. In the colonial years, the Type II (mixed religious) provinces were Adamawa, Niger, Plateau, Ilorin, Zaria, and Benue. The third category, "Type III," was comprised of areas that were almost exclusively non-Muslim in the precolonial period. Given the expansion of *Masu Sarauta* (Muslim caliphal political elites) influence, only Kabba fulfilled the colonial-state designation of a pagan area. This territorial classification determined the extent of formal autonomy granted to native chiefs: emirs had the widest scope of powers and autonomy, Muslim chiefs of Type II areas were next, and the Type III area chiefs were at the bottom of the hierarchy. The classification not only determined political administration but also dictated the jurisdiction of laws and courts. "Islamic" law and its system of courts had jurisdiction in Types I and II areas, while customary law and courts operated, subject to restrictions, in Type III areas.[60] The colonial attitude to missionary proselytization mapped onto the above classifications with the state prohibiting missionary proselytization in Type I areas and in predominantly Muslim segments of Type II areas, while generally permitting missionary activity in non-Muslim segments of Type II areas and in Kabba, the Type III area.[61]

It was common for administrators to invoke "order" as a justification for restricting missionary activity. Defending the colonial administration against accusations of "favor[ing]" Islam, Lugard emphasized that the colonial policy centered on "neutrality, tolerance and impartiality in all religious matters."[62] Nevertheless, Lugard pointed out that the general rule admitted a "good order" exception.[63] By arguing that missionary proselytization was at odds with the requirements of order, administrators contended, in essence, that the missionary demand to proselytize could not be grounded in a claim of religious liberty.

---

[60] See Chapter 3.
[61] See Colonial Reports-Annual, no. 409, Northern Nigeria, 1902 (HM Stationery Office, 1903), 77.
[62] Emphasis added. Frederick John Dealtry Lugard, *Political Memoranda, Revision of Instructions to Political Officers on Subjects Chiefly Political and Administrative 1913–1918* (London: Frank Cass, 1970), 594.
[63] Ibid.

The "order" limitation to missionary religious liberty was championed by colonial administrators rather than the colonized Muslim population. Although certain Muslim elites argued that missionary proselytization came with a risk of unrest, Lugard and subsequent colonial officials took the lead in invoking the order justification.[64] Following its initial subjugation of Sokoto and its neighboring states, the British Empire sought to avoid the use of force for day-to-day administration. The colonial government did not hesitate to deploy brutal force to cripple real and perceived threats to authority.[65] Yet, senior administrators tended to reserve force for colonial subjects unallied with the Indigenous officials through whom empire governed. Otherwise, the deployment of force was not only regarded as costly, but also as a threat to governance because it threatened revolt. In fact, Lugard and several officials worried that missionary proselytization in Muslim areas would provoke a violent backlash not by jurists or the Masu Sarauta, but by the general population. These officials were further concerned that the backlash would compel the state to deploy force in defense of Europeans contrary to the general inclination to avoid resort to force.[66] The officials often cited the Sudan Mahdist War (1881–1898) in support of this concern, although Sudan was hardly analogous to Northern Nigeria.[67]

Certain administrators even invoked "order" to discourage missionary activity among Indigenous religious groups by arguing that missionary influence invited disorder through undermining the legitimacy of the institutions of those communities. These officials pointed to Southern Nigeria to illustrate this point, arguing that missionary influence had

---

[64] For instance, in a letter to Edmund Morel, publisher of *West Africa Magazine*, the emir of Kano would write: "Know that as regards the preaching which we discussed here, my opinion is that it is better to stop it altogether, from the first – because, if our people are disturbed about their religion they will become suspicious and afraid. Hence the country will become unsettled. Neither you nor we desire the country to become unsettled for that would be harmful." Edmund Dene Morel, *Nigeria: Its People and Problems* (Oxfordshire: Taylor and Francis), 135.

[65] See Chapter 2 for prominent examples.

[66] Lugard, *Dual Mandate*, 359. See also Colonial Reports-Annual, no. 704, Northern Nigeria, 1902 (HM Stationery Office, 1912), 77.

[67] Although anti-colonial and anti-missionary, the Sudan Mahdist war was, in large part, a tussle among Muslims over competing visions of the state and society. Heather J. Sharkey, "Jihads and Crusades in Sudan from 1881 to the Present," in *Just Wars, Holy Wars, and Jihads: Christian, Jewish, and Muslim Encounters and Exchanges*, ed. Sohail H. Hashmi (Oxford: Oxford University Press, 2012), 263–282.

weakened the authority of colonial intermediaries, and ultimately, of the state.⁶⁸ As we will observe in the pages that follow, not all officials subscribed to this inclination to shield all colonial subjects from missionary activity. Curiously, however, invocations of "order" would become constant throughout the colonial years, wielded by diverse administrators to delimit what activity came under the scope of religious liberty and state-religion separation and what was exempt from it.

The appeal to "order" was hardly dispassionate. In a critique of postcolonial Egypt's governance of religious difference, Hussein Agrama points out that secular states affirm "equality, neutrality and impartiality," while simultaneously privileging "the sentiments and values of the majority" on the grounds that these are "integral to the cohesiveness of society."⁶⁹ Colonial administrators invoked "order" as an exception to imperial secularism's commitment to religious liberty and state-religion separation. Yet, the construction of "public order" was central to that technique of governing religion and religious difference. First, the notion of public order affirmed the state's assertion of separation: the public "secular" sphere, as opposed to the private "religious" sphere, was the space within which the state sought to impose order. Since this assertion of separation was already tenuous given the state's entanglement with the Masu Sarauta through whom it governed, it is hardly surprising that the colonial notion of public order sought to protect Masu Sarauta sensibilities by preventing proselytization in Muslim areas. In essence, far from being the "exception" that it was framed as, "order" was integral to the colonial construction of religious liberty and state-religion separation. The everyday effectuation of these imperatives was consequently bound up with the needs of colonial administration.

The ideas of religious liberty and state-religion separation did not only suffuse the discourse of colonial administrators, they were also invoked by missionaries to contest the state's restrictions. A 1915 memorandum issued by the Church Missionary Society General Committee III is demonstrative. Charged by the CMS with "justifying the claim for complete freedom of missionary work," the Committee made two claims. The first, which called for "Freedom of Conscience," sought

---

[68] Lugard to Alvarez, August 2, 1912, CMS Minute Book. University of Birmingham Cadbury Special Collections (hereafter Cadbury Collections).

[69] Hussein Agrama, "Secularism, Sovereignty, Indeterminacy: Is Egypt a Secular or a Religious State?" *Comparative Studies in Society and History* 52, no. 3 (2010): 495–523. See also Mahmood, *Religious Difference in a Secular Age*, 150.

an "official declaration" that "freedom of conscience is granted to all persons in Nigeria."[70] By seeking a universal declaration of religious liberty, missionary advocates sought to extend religious freedom privileges beyond the addressees of Lugard's guarantee. Importantly, the committee stressed that freedom of conscience includes not only the liberty to believe, but also the freedom to convert. Hence, obstacles to conversion were in contravention of religious liberty. This formulation, quite novel at the time, was aimed at guaranteeing the freedom of the proselytized to convert to the faith of the proselytizer.[71] The CMS Committee further argued that the realization of the ideal vision of religious freedom called for dissociating "civil obligations from their religious purpose."[72] In an administrative design that tied civil obligations to cultural/religious institutions, the CMS call to demarcate civil obligations from their religious purpose sought to erode the power of Indigenous institutions, particularly, the Masu Sarauta-operated remains of caliphal institutions. The CMS notion of a robust religious liberty regime, therefore, sought to free its target audience from all constraints to Christianization.

The second CMS proposal set out the missionary vision of the ideal relationship of the state with religion. As with the proposition of religious liberty, however, missionary demand for the colonial government's distance from religion was hardly disinterested. Rather than a blanket call for the colonial government's separation from religion, the CMS called for "Non-Introduction into Pagan Districts of Moslem Officials and Islamic forms of Administration."[73] This proposal sought to oust caliphal authority over non-Muslims in Type II areas. As noted earlier, Type II areas were governed through Muslim intermediaries, an arrangement that extended Masu Sarauta control over Indigenous religious communities beyond the precolonial arrangement. The CMS suggested that the arrangement was one that defied the state's avowed commitment to its separation from religion and autonomy of colonial populations since these Muslim intermediaries "possess[ed]

---

[70] Church Missionary Society, *Report of Sub-Committee of Group III of the Church Missionary Society on Difficulties with Nigerian Government*, January 26, 1916. CMS/B/OMS/A3/CL/1916. Cadbury Collections.

[71] For a genealogy of the right to convert, see Linde Lindkvist, *Shrines and Souls: The Reinvention of Religious Liberty and the Genesis of the Universal Declaration of Human Rights* (Lund, Sweden: Bokbox förlag, 2014).

[72] Church Missionary Society, *Report of Sub-Committee of Group III*.

[73] Ibid.

a quasi-religious status."[74] As such, governing through Muslim elites was tantamount to establishing Islam in non-Muslim areas. In a tacit acknowledgment of the limits of its influence, the CMS suggested an alternative to its demand to abolish Muslim intermediaries: that the state take "special care" to ensure that "Moslem officials should not abuse their position for the spread of the Moslem religion or the repression of Christianity."[75] Together with its idea of religious liberty, the CMS and other prominent missionary groups in the colony would deploy the idea of state-religion separation in furtherance of the proselytization project.

To be sure, missionary advocacy was not limited to calls for state-Islam separation or calls for religious liberty. Ideas of Christian morality were sometimes invoked by both national and international missionary actors. At the 1910 World Missionary Conference, for instance, ecumenical missionaries pointed out that the government's policy regarding missions in Nigeria was a "disgrace."[76] Robert Williams of the CMS declared that he, like "other Christian people" was "ashamed that it could be possible for a Christian Governor of a Christian State to say that a missionary could not enter any city in Northern Nigeria until the permission of the Mohammedan Emir had been obtained."[77] Indeed, beyond the missionary desire to evangelize to natives, they were gravely concerned with the "unchristian conduct" of certain administrators. Although they considered these administrators "brave ... genial, good natured," they thought them "utterly ungodly, all living loose lives, all having women brought to them wherever they are,"[78] as well as with being "excessively violent" toward the local population.[79] These missionaries contended that Lugardian hostility to missions sprung from their fear that they (the missionaries) would bear information of their immoral lifestyles to England. These moral recriminations were, however, rarely invoked in direct contestations with the colonial administration. Rather, the justifications invoked

---

[74] Ibid.   [75] Ibid.
[76] World Missionary Conference, *Report of Commission VII*, 151. For an in-depth discussion on the involvement of global missionary ecumenists in the Nigerian debate, see Chapter 5.
[77] World Missionary Conference, *Report of Commission VII*, 151.
[78] Walter Miller to Frederick Baylis Sept 5, 1902. CMS/B/OMS/A9 G3 O Cadbury Collections.
[79] Ibid. See further W. R. S. Miller, "The Nigerian Government and Missionary Work," undated. CBMS/ IMC 271 SOAS.

by missionaries often centered on some notion of religious freedom and/or state-religion separation. Whether missionary advocacy would emphasize separation or religious freedom would depend on colonial practice which was, in fact, a complex amalgam of sensibilities and strategies.

The Practice of Imperial Secularism
Colonial administrators were not always of like mind on the means or ends of colonial rule. There were two main positions on the ideal design of colonial rule, particularly with regard to the state's relationship with religion. As set out above, Frederick Lugard, the first high commissioner of Northern Nigeria, regarded the success of colonial administration as hinging on an indirect rule design built on noninterference. This idea, which was further developed by Lugard's adherents in the colonial administration – the Lugardians – emphasized the religious liberty of Muslims, elevated emirate institutions (which survived the caliphate's destruction) in the hierarchy of Indigenous institutions, and interpreted empire-religion separation as calling for missionary restrictions. The Lugardian design hardly granted Islam or emirate institutions unfettered autonomy; yet, these administrators regarded the formal supremacy of these institutions as grounds for restricting missions.[80] To Sir Donald Cameron, a later colonial governor, and those who subscribed to his view, native administration required a more direct variant of indirect rule. Calling for reduced powers for all Indigenous chiefs, including emirs, Cameron veered from Lugard's emphasis on Muslim religious liberty to insist on the state's neutrality. As understood by Cameron, state neutrality called for eliminating the privileged status of emirate institutions, including the shielding of Muslims from missionary influence. These two views on state-religion relations and colonial administration had different consequences for Christian missions. Further, they evinced different conceptions of what constituted missionary proselytization, with Lugard's being more expansive than Cameron's. Yet, neither the Lugard nor the latter Cameron phase featured constancy. It was the residents in each province, and ultimately, the district commissioners, who gave life to colonial policy. Many of these officials remained Lugardians even after Lugardians lost power in the central administration. Although attitudes are generalizable enough to permit an analysis of colonial

---

[80] On the transformation of precolonial caliphal institutions, see Chapter 2.

practice, individual differences among colonial administrators meant that uniformity was elusive. These variations did not only intensify the struggles, but they also provided important tools in jousting for the souls of colonial subjects.

LUGARD'S YEARS OF AUTHORITY

As the progenitor of Northern Nigeria indirect rule, Frederick Lugard[81] was considered the "High Priest" of that form of colonial governance. Missionaries conferred this appellation on him as a criticism of what they regarded as his undue adulation of native institutions. As Henry G. Farrant, missionary of the Sudan United Mission (SUM) and secretary of the Annual Meeting of Northern Nigerian Missions put it, officials like Lugard saw their primary role as "conservators" of native institution, thereby assuming the role of "Priests rather than administrators."[82] Lugard's fascination arose from an Orientalist interest in the exotic "other." Capturing this adulation for native institutions, Walter Richard Samuel Miller, a CMS missionary who had attained notoriety for his unrestrained criticism of the state's alliance with Muslim emirs complained: "There is more remaining of the old bourgeoisie spirit among the white people in Northern Nigeria than probably anywhere else in the colonies! A perfectly medieval conception of Kingship and chieftainship exists."[83] Lugard's fascination did not extend to Indigenous religious groups. Islam, in his view, was the highest standard of civilization attainable by Africans. Although Lugard considered Islam as being "incapable of the highest development," he argued that the religion's "limitations ... suit[ed] the limitations of the people."[84] In particular, Lugard stressed Islam's "civilizing effect" on "pagans" and in particular, the religion's promotion of "a higher standard of life

---

[81] First high commissioner of Northern Nigeria, and later the first governor general of Nigeria, Lugard was also the governor of both Northern and Southern Nigeria from 1912 to 1914 and the governor general of Nigeria from 1914 to 1919.

[82] The Brooke Commission on the Native Courts System in Northern Nigeria named Lugard the "High Priest of Indirect Rule." The missionaries had, however, named Lugardians "priests" of indirect rule long before then. See also Henry Willink, ed., *Nigeria: Report of the Commission Appointed to Enquire into the Fears of Minorities and the Means of Allaying Them* (London: HM Stationery Office, 1958), 58.

[83] Walter Miller to Rev. Hooper, May 1927. CBMS/IMC Box 271. School of Oriental and African Studies Special Collections, UK (hereafter SOAS).

[84] See Lugard, *Dual Mandate*, 78.

and decency, a better social organization and tribal cohesion and a well-defined code of justice."[85] Lugard, therefore, regarded Islam as ideal for Africa and Africans.

In comparison, Lugard considered Christianity unsuitable. He highlighted Christianity's "more abstruse tenets, its stricter code of morality, its exaltation of peace and humility, its recognition of brotherhood with the slave" as unappealing "to the temperament of the negro."[86] Lugard argued that these features of Christianity produced in converts an "attitude of intolerance" toward native ways.[87] In particular, Lugard worried about Christian missions "weakening the authority of the Moslem Religion," thereby threatening the sanctity of "real Africa."[88] Lugard nevertheless cultivated the friendship of missionaries of the CMS. After all, he had missionary roots himself – his mother had worked for the CMS in India, and his father, although not a missionary, had been a chaplain in the East Indian Company; Lugard himself had first gone to India in the service of the church. In Northern Nigeria, Lugard's missionary friends strongly urged him to accompany colonial rule through emirate institutions with a Christian civilizational project. Notably, Walter Miller, who had close ties to Lugard, set out such a proposal in a 1903 letter wherein Miller suggested replacing Islamic education with missionary education, exempting parents of pupils from taxation, and taxing polygamists, among other things.[89] In concluding the letter, Miller emphasized that "the great hope for this country is the spread of Christianity in it." In his reply, Lugard indicated his agreement with Miller's vision. Lugard, however, pointed out that the actualization of Miller's idea was hindered by a shortage of officials. Lugard wrote: "if we had unlimited money … and could flood the country with European officers, no doubt we could do much in a short time."[90] At the inception of colonial rule, the 320,000-square-mile protectorate with 8.7 million population had only 104 European colonial administrators.[91] The manpower shortage would continue into later colonial

---

[85] Ibid.   [86] Ibid.   [87] Ibid.   [88] Ibid.
[89] Walter Miller to Frederick Lugard, July 29, 1903, CMS G3/A9/01, in Ayandele, *The Missionary Impact*, 145.
[90] "Lugard's Memo on Dr. Miller's Paper," August 9, 1903, CMS G3/A9/01, in Ayandele, *The Missionary Impact*, 145.
[91] Colonial Reports-Annual, no. 346, Northern Nigeria, 1900–1901 (HM Stationery Office, 1902), 19; Colonial Reports-Annual, no. 437, Northern Nigeria, 1903, 20.

years even if it would be slightly ameliorated. As such, Lugard's attachment to caliphal institutions and the Masu Sarauta, the elite class through which they were governed, did not merely stem from an Orientalist fascination. It was also necessitated by administrative exigency.

Long before Lugard came to be labeled the "High Priest" of indirect rule for his zeal for emirate institutions and his restrictions on Christian missions, missionaries had begun to worry about the fate of the missionary enterprise under indirect rule. Prior to the commencement of formal colonial rule in 1903, Christian missionaries began advocating for empire to directly govern through a close cooperation with missionaries. Accustomed to their alliance with empire for much of the nineteenth century, missionaries dreaded the prospect of indirect rule through Muslim emirs. To force the hand of empire even before the conquest of Sokoto, the 1897 edition of the Anglican *Church Missionary Society Intelligencer* reported that the caliphal governance was to be "superseded by the direct exercise of British Authority."[92] Through these efforts, missions tried to forestall indirect rule.

When advocacy for direct administration failed, missionaries campaigned for the exclusion of caliphal elites from governance. Notably, missionaries suggested that the precolonial caliphate's Islamic identity was tied to the dominance of the Fulani ethnic group and argued that the Revolt of 1804 that had brought the caliphate into existence was a Fulani insurgency that displaced Hausa elites. Missionaries preferred Hausas not only because they regarded Muslims of that ethnicity as intellectually superior to Fulanis, but also because they considered Hausas to be "lax" in faith and open to conversion.[93] As early as 1891, missionaries allied with the Royal Nigeria Company to form the Hausa Association to not only study Hausa culture but also to advocate the overthrow of Fulanis and restoration of Hausas to power.[94] The ethnic dichotomy advanced by missionaries was tenuous, not least of all due to the hyphenation of Hausa-Fulani elite identity in the aftermath of the early nineteenth-century inception of the Sokoto Caliphate.[95] Nevertheless, missionaries insisted on the distinction, and when indirect rule

---

[92] *The Church Missionary Intelligencer* (1897), 355.
[93] "Unlike the Fulani, they [Hausas] seem to have no ferocious fanaticism and the tenets of Islam are followed in a very lax manner." *Sudan Leaflet*, no. 1, January 1890.
[94] See Ayandele, *The Missionary Impact*, 123.   [95] Ibid.

became inevitable, missionaries advocated that Hausas be appointed in place of Fulani emirs, stressing that "the Fulani is not, will not be and cannot ever be loyal to the British Government."[96] Although the demand to displace caliphal aristocrats was unsuccessful, it ushered in calls for separating the state from the Muslim faith.

Governor Lugard was adamant that the 1903 guarantee of noninterference conferred religious liberty on Muslims and excluded missionary proselytization. Lugard persuaded senior officials like Colonial Secretary Chamberlain to adopt this meaning by arguing that only such an interpretation could dispel emirs' suspicion that the British Empire retained its nineteenth-century alliance with missionaries. The concern that the Masu Sarauta operated from an assumption that missionaries were indistinguishable from the colonial government would weigh on Lugard heavily during his years as administrator just as that worry had featured prominently in Salisbury's bicentennial address to the CMS.

Lugard's concern was not misplaced. As noted earlier, Muslim elites perceived the colonial encounter as a religious encounter. In a 1902 letter written to Lugard while the British army was advancing upon Sokoto, Sultan Muhammadu Attahiru I declared: "Between us and you there are no dealings except as between Mussulumans and Unbelievers."[97] Discussing with a prominent journalist sympathetic to Lugard years later, the emir of Kano, Muhammad Abbas, argued that proselytization was more than an invitation to voluntarily convert since it exerted undue pressure on Muslims due to the "prestige all white men have."[98] Evincing a desire to protect Muslims from such coercion, Lugard stressed that "it would be a misuse of the power and authority of the Government" to request that the Masu Sarauta accept missions.[99] Lugard further argued that "if they [missions] were established by the order of the Government, the people have some cause to disbelieve the emphatic pledges I have given that their religion shall in no way

---

[96] Walter Miller to Frederick Lugard July 29, 1903. CMS/G3/A9/01, in Ayandele, *The Missionary Impact*, 145.

[97] See Henry Fleming Backwell, *The Occupation of Hausaland, 1900–1904, Being a Translation of Arabic Letters Found in the House of the Wazir of Sokoto Bohari in 1903* (London: Frank Cass, 1969), 13. In a poem composed by the Sultan, he declared: "Muslims do not consent to obey the Christians." See Bunza, *Christian Missions among Muslims*, 22.

[98] Quoted in Morel, *Nigeria, Its Peoples and Its Problems*, 133.

[99] CMS/A3/L5/1898. Frederick Lugard to Frederick Baylis in Crampton, *Christianity in Northern Nigeria*, 46.

be interfered with."[100] Given elites' understanding of the colonial encounter as a religious confrontation between Islam and Christianity, Lugard feared that a loss of faith in his 1903 guarantee could signal the end of empire's hold over the territory without resort to force.

Deploying the ideas of (Muslim) religious liberty, the imperative to separate the colonial government from the missionary project, and the demands of order, Lugard imposed extensive restrictions on missionary activity in areas that had a significant Muslim population. To proselytize in these (Type I and II) areas, missionaries had to apply to the colonial resident officer for a permit. Official guidelines required that these residents forward applications to emirs for consideration. In practice, however, residents denied applications without forwarding them to emirs, arguing that to do so would exert undue pressure on emirs and contravene the state's commitment to liberty.

Lugard, however, made an exception in the sphere of education wherein he permitted missionary activity other than those involving direct attempts to convert. In fact, Lugard's ostensible deference to the Masu Sarauta did not translate into an aversion to Western education. That attitude was informed by the need to generate manpower; Lugard approved of limited educational instruction in order to provide "satisfied clerks, capable officials and loyal Emirs."[101] Lugard was, therefore, not antithetical to missionary education for Muslims, although he remained averse to Christian religious instruction. This attitude is also demonstrated by Lugard's approach to the mission-Masu Sarauta dispute over the guardianship of former slaves following the abolition of domestic slavery.[102] The colonial government, under Lugard, asserted custody over the freed slaves and set up a Freed Slaves Home for that purpose. Lugard then expressed his willingness to employ a CMS employee as the matron of the home if that missionary would exclude religious education from the curriculum. The CMS could not, however, accept Lugard's condition without a special waiver from its Home Office in England. The CMS Home Office did not grant that waiver although it would later assume a tactical posture and grant a waiver for similar

---

[100] Lugard, *Political Memoranda*, 24.
[101] Sonia Graham, "A History of Education in Relation to the Development of the Protectorate of Northern Nigeria 1900–1919, with Special Reference to the Work of Hans Vischer," PhD diss., (University of London, 1955), 108.
[102] Domestic slavery was abolished in the early colonial years. See Slavery Proclamation of 1900 and Slavery Proclamation of 1907.

institutions in Zaria and Bida.[103] With the support of the British colonial secretary, Lord Elgin, Lugard issued grants to missions schools that did not provide religious instruction.[104] These restrictions on mission education did not apply to areas populated by adherents of Indigenous religions, although in those (Type III) areas, the provision of religious instruction precluded mission schools from government funding. With the restrictions on religious instruction, Lugard's embrace of missionary education was hardly conducive to proselytization.

If Lugard's years of authority were hardly idyllic for the missionary enterprise, Lugard's successors would come to espouse a notion of Masu Sarauta religious liberty and state-mission separation that would subject missions to extensive constraints that were unprecedented even in the light of Lugard's practice.

LUGARDIANS AND THE MISSIONARY ENCOUNTER

Lugard's ideas found many adherents in the colonial administration, the earliest and most ardent of which were Governor Percy Girouard and Lieutenant Governor Charles Temple.[105] These officials, the Lugardians, instituted a form of indirect rule that was so centered on the Masu Sarauta that Lugard's biographer, Margery Perham, named it "ultra indirect rule."[106] Acknowledging the deviation from Lugard's invention, Girouard informed Lugard that he had inherited a "direct" system of administration from him and had changed it to an "indirect" one.[107] Lugardians espoused a notion of religious liberty for the Muslim vessels of rule that prohibited any form of missionary activity. Although these ideas were sourced from Lugard's manuals for colonial administrators, *Political Memoranda* and *The Dual Mandate*, they were

---

[103] The CMS had established a mission station in Zaria in 1900 before the colonial policy restricting missions was firmed up.

[104] However, officials such as Winston Churchill, undersecretary of state for the colonies, dissented. Churchill warned that "it would never do to prejudice education in Nigeria by suspicion of Christian proselytizing." Minutes C.O 446/60 No.36412, 28 NA, UK.

[105] Other prominent Lugardians were colonial residents: Temple, Gower, Arnett, Burdon, Hewby, and Festing. Lugardian policy also gained admirers outside colonial ranks, especially among commercial interests. Of this group, Edmund Morel, publisher of *West Africa Magazine*, stood out.

[106] Margery Perham, "Preface to Lugard," in Lugard, *The Dual Mandate*, xl.

[107] "Girouard to Lugard April 28 1909," in Ayandele, *The Missionary Impact*, 146.

applied without the measured flexibility and limited camaraderie (with missions) that marked Lugard's tenure.[108] So intense were restrictions of the Lugardian years that Thomas Alvarez, secretary of the CMS in Northern Nigeria, commented in 1912 that there had come to exist "a definite policy – unprecedented in the last 60 years – to keep Christian missionaries out of a British protectorate."[109] In missionary estimation, the Lugardian years were the pinnacle of missionary repression.

Lugardians often justified their unrivalled restrictions on missions as a necessary consequence of the 1903 guarantee's requirement of Muslims' religious liberty and state separation from Christian missions. Far from a self-evident reading of the guarantee, however, that understanding was inspired by Lugardian hostility to Christian missions. Girouard, for instance, was of the view that the missionary project produced "half civilized" populations such as the Southern Nigerian Christian converts he and fellow Lugardians despised.[110] Temple, the most infamous Lugardian in missionary circles, regarded Christianization as a "mistaken philanthropy" that violated indirect rule's mission of "assist[ing] the native to develop that civilization which he can himself evolve."[111] Temple further argued that doing such would ultimately result in the "overthrow and abolition of native institutions by a misguided paternal government."[112] Another Lugardian and Giroaurd's successor, Hesketh Bell, pointed out to the Royal African Society in 1911: "We want ... no transmogrification of the dignified and courteous Moslem into a trouser burlesque with a veneer of European Civilization."[113] Already discernible in everyday colonial correspondence, the roots of this intense Lugardian hostility to missions were laid bare in an October 19, 1911 letter to the archbishop of Canterbury by Edmund Dene Morel, publisher of West Africa Magazine. Although Morel was not a colonial administrator, he had close ties with Lugardians and sympathized with their views. In the letter to the archbishop and Church of England principal,

---

[108] Lugard, *The Dual Mandate*, 78; Lugard, *Political Memoranda*.
[109] Thomas Alvarez to the Home Society undated 1912 (received on July 5). CMS/B/OMS/A9/G3 P.
[110] Ayandele, *The Missionary Impact*, 146.
[111] Temple, *Native Races and their Rulers*, 30.
[112] Ibid. See also Minutes by T. Davies, officer in the Prime Minister's Office advising the prime minister as to the suitable response to a letter written by Captain Jones dated October 28, 1931, to the prime minister querying the restrictions placed on missionaries, CO 583/181/5.
[113] Hesketh Bell, *Journal of African Society*, July 1911, 391.

Morel accused missionaries of seeking to "subvert the entire fabric of native society" by introducing ideas that undermined native institutions such as limitations on polygamy.[114] Christianity, Morel argued in another context, had a "denationalizing effect" by encouraging Indigenous peoples to change their culture. Morel described the Christian produced by this denationalization, as a "hybrid, ... neither one thing nor another."[115] In comparison, Morel argued that Islam "intensifies the spirit of nationality, ... imbuing his spirit with a robust faith in himself and in his race."[116] Morel further compared the devotion of the African Muslim with the laxity of the European Christian, declaring: "there is more evidence of spiritual influence out here, than in our great congested cities."[117] Morel, like Lugardians, therefore insisted that the devotion of the African was better addressed to the "God of Africa" than to the "God of Europe" being promoted by missions.[118]

So intent were Lugardians on frustrating the missionary project that it was under Lugardian authority that the *Sabon Gari* system was institutionalized in Northern Nigeria. Designed by Resident Charles Temple during the tenure of Governor Girouard, the Sabon Gari system kept missionaries and nonindigenous Africans out of Muslim areas. This residential segregation system was targeted at shielding Muslims from the influence of missionaries and Christianized Africans (especially Southern Nigerians), and it restricted nonindigenous Africans to the *Sabon Guruwa* and missionaries to government reservations.[119]

Lugardian aversion to missionary work among Muslims extended to missionary education.[120] The few mission schools established during Lugard's tenure were forced out of operation, and by 1916, the CMS school in

---

[114] E. D. Morel to the Archbishop of Canterbury October 19, 1911, and Archbishop Jones to Bishop Tugwell, January 20, 1912. Davidson 179 Lambeth Palace Library.

[115] Edmund Dene Morel, *Affairs of West Africa* (New York: Routledge, 2013), 230.

[116] Ibid., 229. [117] Ibid. [118] Ibid., 351.

[119] The law that would formally institutionalize this system of residential segregation – the Cantonments Proclamation – would come into existence after Giroaurd's tenure in 1914. See David Edley Allyn, "The Sabon Gari System in Northern Nigeria, 1911–1940," PhD diss., (University of California, Los Angeles, 1976). Southern Nigerians, many of whom had received missionary education and converted, moved to Northern Nigeria in droves to staff the lower cadre of the colonial administration in the early colonial years.

[120] A major exception was the custody of freed slaves. Girouard regarded missionary rehabilitation of freed slaves as a necessity and supported mission-operated Freed Slave Homes by issuing a grant for each ward aged fifteen years and below.

Zaria was the only mission school in a Muslim area.[121] As if to prevent the establishment of another, an Education Ordinance was enacted that year, prohibiting grants-in-aid to Muslim-area mission schools that did predate the Ordinance.[122] That prohibition was officially repealed in response to missionary advocacy[123]; in practice, however, Lugardians continued to keep missions out of Muslim areas. To fill the void left by the prohibition of mission education, Girouard established a Department of Education in 1910, ushering in the era of government-owned and operated schools.[124] Those schools relied on government grants; however, since colonial revenue depended on taxes, grants were minimal with the consequence that few schools were established in Types I and II areas. Even in the absence of missions, great care was taken to avoid Europeanizing pupils, and contrary to Lugard's vision of an education that would produce administrative staff, Lugardians sought to train colonial subjects in their own ways. Government education in Muslim areas, therefore, meant Islamic education in the Hausa language. Unlike the situation in Muslim areas, mission schools in Type III areas provided unrestricted education alongside Christian religious instructions. Indeed, by the time a latter colonial governor, Hugh Clifford, would assume office in August 1919, he would bemoan the fact that "after two decades of British occupation," Muslim Northern Nigeria had "not yet produced a single native ... sufficiently educated to enable him to fill the most minor clerical post in the office of any government department."[125] Those disparities were rooted in Lugardian insistence on shielding Muslims from missions.

Although Lugardian restrictions centered on predominantly Muslim areas, their anti-missionary attitude also manifested among Indigenous religious groups. As Girouard observed in 1908, "Personally, I should like to see the missions withdraw entirely from the Northern States, for the best missionary ... will be the high-minded, clean living British

[121] The other school – that in Bida – had closed in 1915.
[122] Section 13 of the Education Ordinance 1916.
[123] Amendment to Section 13(e) by July 1917 *Gazette*.
[124] In Kabba – operated by G. P. Bargery of the CMS Mission.
[125] Thomas Jesse Jones, *Education in Africa: A Study of West, South, and Equatorial Africa by the African Education Commission, under the Auspices of the Phelps-Stokes Fund and Foreign Mission Societies of North America and Europe* (New York: Phelps-Stokes Fund, 1922), 175. Two years after the Stokes report, 6.88 percent of the children of school age in Southern Nigeria were enrolled in school as compared to the 0.244 percent of children of a similar age in Northern Nigeria. Government of the Colony and Protectorate of Nigeria, Blue Book Colony, and Protectorate of Nigeria 1922 (Lagos: Government Printer, 1923).

Resident."[126] Two cases of restrictions among non-Muslim communities attained notoriety.

The first involved the imprisonment of the Chief of Tong, a village classified as a sub-unit of Garam town.[127] Under the instructions of the Chief of Garam, the Tong Chief was imprisoned for thirty days for permitting missionary activity in Tong contrary to the Garam Chief's express directives. Missionaries' pleas to the colonial district officer, Mr. Smith, to secure the Tong Chief's release were unsuccessful. Further, although Smith averred at the ensuing trial that "everyone had freedom of conscience," he did not comment on Tong's pretrial imprisonment or reprimand the Garam Chief.[128] Neither did Smith intervene in the Garam Chief's punishment of the Tong Chief following the court's release of the latter from detention. When the Tong Chief responded by attempting to petition the colonial government for a general religious freedom declaration and autonomy from Garam, the Garam Chief ordered the arrest and beating of Tong residents. Both the district officer and the colonial resident continued to maintain their silence, refusing to intervene even when Tong residents ultimately fled their village in fear of reprisal attacks.

Another case involved Tuwam, a village under the supervisory authority of Kabwir. As a punishment for the refusal of the Tuwam Headman and villagers to perform a "heathen rite in connection with tilling," the Kabwir Chief imposed a penalty – that the Headman offer "a sacrifice to the spirits" in expiation.[129] The Headman of Tuwam refused, citing his Christian faith. With the intervention of CMS missionaries, the Headman appealed to the resident, who referred the matter to Governor Hesketh Bell. After eight months of silence, Bell responded that he was "not prepared to interfere with native customs even though they appear to us to be unreasonable and superstitious as long as they are not repugnant to humanity."[130] Here, as in the Tong

---

[126] Ayandele, *The Missionary Impact*, 116, 147.
[127] See "Statement re: the Treatment of Tong, an ungwa [suburb] of Garam," July 1916. Report by Wedgwood addressed to G. J. Manley from Northern Nigeria CMS Mission. CMS/B/OMS/A9 G3 O, Cadbury Collections.
[128] Ibid.
[129] Revs. J. W. Lloyd and G. T. Fox to the CMS dated March 11, 1912. CMS/B/OMS/A9 G3 O, Cadbury Collections.
[130] Ibid. Because Tuwam involved a labor question, one might easily understand Bell's reaction, as colonial policy did not generally grant labor exemptions on the ground of religion even in Southern Nigeria. See Andrew E. Barnes, "Evangelization Where It Is Not Wanted," 412–441. Yet the Lugardians adopted a restrictive policy even with regards to non-labor questions.

case, Lugardians argued that interference constrained the religious liberty of natives and was at odds with indirect rule.

The constant refrain of missionaries in the Lugardian years, as in Lugard's era, was the proposal of a constitutional arrangement in which the state would be favorably disposed to the Christianization project. In response to the common situation presented in cases such as Tuwam, the CMS called for the dissociation of culture from religion.[131] That argument was premised on missionaries' resignation to indirect rule's reliance on Indigenous elites. Nevertheless, the CMS argued that elite authority ought to be rooted in culture rather than religion, stressing that enforcement of social laws and customs amounted to a violation of "religious toleration" when those obligations are associated with religion.[132] In sum, missionaries did not only call for religious liberty for the targets of their proselytization, but they also sought the colonial government's distance from competing faiths. Nevertheless, ambiguities inherent in those ideas of ordering state-religion relations made it plausible for Lugardians to deploy the same concepts to impose unparalleled restrictions on missions.

THE CAMERON YEARS

The upper echelons of the colonial administration saw a definite break from Lugardian policy with the inception of Donald Cameron's tenure in 1931. Cameron was not the first to depart from Lugardian indirect rule. Hugh Clifford (governor 1919–1925) first set out the ideas that would form the cornerstone of Cameron's governance ideology. However, Clifford's bid to sway the Colonial Office from Lugardian ideals was unsuccessful, and Lugardian thought commanded the support of senior officials of the British Empire until the inception of Cameron's tenure as governor.

Contrary to Lugardian distaste for the Christianized population that missionary proselytization had produced in Southern Nigeria, Cameron (and before him, Clifford) regarded Southern Nigeria as an ideal. Unlike

---

[131] See Church Missionary Society, *Report of Sub-Committee of Group III*. Examples of cases highlighted by missionaries include the demolition of a church in a Katareigi on the orders of the assistant resident (Thomas Alvarez to G. J. Manley Secretary of Home Society) and Bell's 1912 denial of applications for missionaries on the basis that conversion to Christianity would inspire rebellion against their Muslim overlords: Alvarez to G. J. Manley July 10, 1916. CMS/B/OMS/A9 G3 O.

[132] Church Missionary Society, *Report of Sub-Committee of Group III*.

Northern Nigeria, Southern Nigerian colonial administration was less reliant on Indigenous chiefs even in those areas where the colonial government formally ruled through these elites. That design, coupled with the nineteenth-century history of mission-empire alliance in Southern Nigeria, produced a colonial policy in which missionaries operated freely and recorded much success. Cameron also expressed great admiration for the colonial subjects that half a century of missionary activity had produced in Southern Nigeria and noted that "to be a good African and a good chief depended ... upon the man becoming a Christian."[133] Cameron was, therefore, no Lugardian adulator of emirs and Islamic institutions. Instead, Cameron regarded indirect rule as "a means and not an end"[134] and insisted that emirs (and other colonial intermediaries) were merely "instruments."[135] Moreover, Cameron opined that these instruments and the colonial subjects they administered were "primitive and ignorant,"[136] and argued that exposure to "western civilization" was necessary.[137] Cameron's outlook, therefore, favored missionary access not only to adherents of Indigenous religions, but also to Muslims.

Cameron put forth a notion of state-religion relations that advanced this project of Christianizing the native. To Cameron, Clifford, and those administrators who shared their ideals, the 1903 guarantee called for the state's neutrality with regards to religious matters. Cameron likened the Lugardian policy to the drawing of a "curtain" over Muslim Northern Nigeria, shielding it from the benefits of Western civilization, including Christianity.[138] Instead, Cameron advocated for a posture of neutrality that withdrew that curtain.[139] This connoted the government's complete separation from and noninterference with

---

[133] Handley Hooper to Walter Miller, June 9, 1931.CBMS/IMC/271 SOAS.
[134] Donald Cameron, Address to the Legislative Council, March 6, 1933, Supplement to the *Extraordinary Gazette*, March 6, 1933, Margery Perham Papers 688/ 1 4 Rhodes House Library Oxford cited in Casper Andersen and Andrew Cohen, *The Government and Administration of Africa, 1880–1939: Recruitment and Training* (London: Routledge, 2017), 244.
[135] Ibid., 245.   [136] Ibid., 241.   [137] Ibid., 247.
[138] Donald Cameron, *The Principles of Native Administration and Their Application* (Lagos, Nigeria: Government Printer, 1934), 12–13, 26. Henry Farrant to Joseph Oldham August 11, 1931 CBMS/IMC/270 SOAS. Joseph H. Oldham to C. Gordon Beacham October 18, 1932) CBMS /IMC/270 SOAS.
[139] Cameron, *The Principles of Native Administration*, 12–13, 26. See Precis of August 6, 1931 meeting of Governor Cameron with representatives of the CMS, the Sudan United Mission, and the Sudan Interior Mission. CBMS /IMC/270 SOAS. See further Joseph Oldham to Henry Farrant October 8, 1931 CBMS/IMC/270 SOAS.

native religions or missions. Since Cameron actively sought the making of a Christianized subject, that notion of neutrality was hardly dispassionate. Indeed, Cameron's approach earned him praise within missionary circles with the colonial governor being described not only as the "master of indirect administration and not its servant,"[140] but also as espousing a governance principle with "solid roots in Christian theology."[141] At a 1927 meeting sought by the secretary of the International Missionary Council, Joseph Houldsworth Oldham,[142] Graeme Thomson (a successor to Clifford) agreed to grant missions access to Muslim areas. Invoking the ideas of neutrality already declared by Clifford, Thomson declared that the government would not exert pressure on emirs to allow missionary work in their territories. At the same time, however, Thomson assured the missionaries that the government would neither "induce" emirs to refuse permission nor represent that the government was averse to emirs' approval of missionary activity.[143] Thomson further pointed out that the government intended to "educate the Emirs to an understanding and recognition of the principles of religious toleration which are characteristic of Western civilization."[144] The policy change, which was ultimately approved by the secretary of state for the colonies, was not announced to the Masu Sarauta and its knowledge was limited to colonial administrators and missionaries.

As it turned out, more than a change at the upper echelons of the administration was needed to facilitate missionary access. Several residents and district officers continued to harbor Lugardian attitudes toward missions. Given the autonomy conferred upon residents (and ultimately district officers) in the Lugardian years, those administrators had the latitude to

---

[140] Henry Farrant to (name of recipient illegible). SUM Northern Nigeria Collection University of Edinburgh (uncatalogued) (hereafter SUM N.N. Collection). See further Henry Farrant to Joseph Oldham August 11, 1931 CBMS/IMC/270 SOAS, Joseph Oldham to Henry Farrant (describing Cameron as a "real friend" to missions) CBMS/IMC/270 SOAS.

[141] Joseph H. Oldham, "The Educational Work of Missionary Societies," *Africa: Journal of the International African Institute* 7, no. 1 (1934): 47–59.

[142] At the meeting were H. R. Palmer, the lieutenant governor of Northern Nigeria, and the representatives of several missions.

[143] Minutes of Conference on Missionary Work in Northern Nigeria, Edinburgh House, October 6, 1927. CBMS/IMC/270 SOAS. Joseph Oldham to Missionary Societies in Northern Nigeria, October 21, 1927, CBMS/IMC/270 SOAS. See also Henry Farrant, *Northern Nigerian Opportunity* (undated) CBMS/IMC/270 SOAS.

[144] Joseph Oldham to Missionary Societies in Northern Nigeria, October 21, 1927, CBMS/IMC/270 SOAS

block missionary access. So powerful were residents in the Lugardian years that when the CMS Home Office had appealed to secretary of state for the colonies, Lord Crewe, in January 1909, Crewe had declined to intervene, citing "the repeated and unanimous opinion of all the responsible Residents ... that any extension of missionary enterprise ... would ... be undesirable and even dangerous."[145] That expansive authority of residents survived the Lugardian years, thwarting the efforts of Cameron and other senior administrators who sought to ease missionary restrictions.

Lugardians had lost the cultural argument about the better fit of Islam for Africans by the Cameron years. With that loss, the argument about the supremacy of Masu Sarauta religious liberty had become less convincing. Nevertheless, Lugardians continued to have a weapon in their arsenal: the demands of "order." These officials argued that to permit proselytization was to invite disorder. In a state that could not afford a standing army, the order argument caught the attention of senior administrators. When Thomson approved the long-desired CMS mission station in Kano, he conditioned the approval on two order-based factors. First, Thomson imposed a restriction on preaching in public areas by mandating an endorsement on the Certificates of Occupancy that in predominantly Muslim areas, missionaries would refrain from "preach[ing] in public places or carry[ing] out house to house visitations."[146] Second, the government sought to regulate missionary appointments. In particular, Thomson sought an undertaking that the CMS agree to withdraw Miller if that missionary was stationed in Kano and his activities became "in the least objectionable" to the emir, who had an "extreme distrust" of the missionary.[147] Miller's lack of popularity

---

[145] CMS Home Office to Lord Crewe, January 22, 1909. See also CMS Home Office to Lord Crewe July 21, 1909. CMS/OMS/A9 G3 L1 Cadbury Collections.

[146] Graeme Thomson to the CMS September 30, 1930. CO/583/181/5. See also The Acting Resident of Kano to the Governor, December 13, 1931. CO/583/181/5 NA, UK.

[147] Ibid. So much did the emir distrust Miller that he convinced the resident of Kano that, if permitted entry into Kano, Miller was sure to instigate intrigues against not only the emir, but also the resident and the district officers. While the emirs were suspicious of missionary work in general, they (especially the emir of Kano), had a particular aversion to Walter Miller and his sister, Ethel Miller, also a missionary. Part of the reason for this was the incendiary language used by Miller and his sister against Islam and Fulani rule, including in their pamphlet publications. Further, Miller's sister distributed these pamphlets in public, which raised the ire of both the emir and the colonial residents. For an account of Ethel Miller's sojourn in Northern Nigeria, see Shankar, *Who Shall Enter Paradise?*

was hardly secret; the missionary was regarded with disfavor due to his harsh criticism of Islam, and the Masu Sarauta.[148] Nevertheless, the CMS declined to accept the restriction and was thus precluded from proceeding with the Kano station. The order argument, therefore, continued to serve as an invaluable tool to pursue the agenda of Lugardians.

So powerful a hold did the "order" argument have that even Cameron would come to wield that notion. While the colonial governor continued to promote a vision of a Christianized Nigeria, he acknowledged that the process of educating emirs on "western ideas of religious toleration" "must necessarily be slow."[149] Cameron favored missionary liberty, but the practical demands of administration urged caution. Consequently, certain missionary restrictions existed during Cameron's tenure. Prior to granting missionaries authorization to preach in public, the governor had to be satisfied that there was "no active hostility ... apparent amongst the Moslems."[150] Further, public preaching near markets or mosques remained completely prohibited. House-to-house visitation, which missionaries preferred, continued to be prohibited in the Cameron years. However, that prohibition was not a blanket one as visitation was permitted upon "prior invitation."[151] Cameron's loosening of restrictions was itself reflected in the changed meaning of proselytization. While the Lugardian conception of proselytization encompassed all forms of missionary presence in Muslim areas and unrestrained missionary activity among adherents of Indigenous faiths, the Cameron conception was narrower. That understanding of proselytization centered on "preaching near marketplaces or mosques," "engaging in unwelcome house to house visitation," and "pressure brought to bear on another person to accept another faith."[152] The changed interpretation of proselytization loosened certain restrictions on missions.

---

[148] See generally Barnes, *Making Headway*, 127–129, 231.

[149] Records of Meeting, October 28, 1931, Kaduna, Northern Nigeria as reported on Colonial Secretary Lord Passfield to the CMS, December 3, 1931. CO/583/181/5 NA, UK.

[150] Ibid.

[151] Records of meeting dated October 28, 1931. CO/583/181/5 NA, UK. From 1950, these restrictions were endorsed on immigration certificates.

[152] The Agreement between the colonial government and the SUM for the operation of lepers settlements defined proselytization as "visitation from house to house for the purpose of teaching the Christian faith to any Mohammedan, teaching the Christian faith to any Mohammedan who has not of his own volition specifically asked for such teaching, or the bringing of any inducement or pressure to bear on any Mohammedan to accept the Christian faith or the distribution of tracts, pamphlets or other religious publication." See Clause 6, Agreement for the Operation

The new conception of proselytization was of particular benefit to missions in the domain of education and medical services in Muslim areas. However, missionary access to those fields was not unfettered. When a Sudan United Mission lepers' settlement was established in Maiduguri and a Church Missionary Society lepers' settlement was set up in Zaria, they were prohibited from proselytizing to Muslims and preaching publicly to anyone.[153] There were also restrictions in missionary provision of services. Further, the colonial government sought to insert a provision that Muslim parents could not consent to their children under 18 years receiving "religious instruction" and designating the emir as the only competent authority to consent to such religious instruction.[154] The colonial government was, however, compelled to reverse course when SUM attorney and secretary of the Annual Meeting of Representatives of Missions in Northern Nigeria, H. G. Farrant, compared the policy with the "spirit which in Germany and communist Russia has destroyed personal liberty and made the state the dictator of ideas."[155] The government then replaced the clause with another permitting either party to terminate the agreement by giving a notice of twelve months. The post-Lugardian sympathy with missions is also reflected in Section 21 of the 1952 Education Ordinance's conferment of a right of appeal upon the denial of applications to establish mission schools. The first appeal under this provision was brought by the Sudan United Mission with regard to its application to open a school in Mataszu, Katsina Province, a Muslim area. That case centered on the "right of a mission to establish a mission school in a Muslim area where existing educational facilities were still inadequate to meet the

---

of a Lepers Settlement (undated and unsigned prototype) agreement General Correspondence 1940–1942 Folder (uncatalogued), University of Edinburgh Center for the Study of World Christianity (hereafter Edinburgh Collections).

[153] Henry Farrant to Miss Gibson, October 20, 1936 CMS/IMC/ 271 SOAS. See further Minutes of meeting of Chief Commissioner of Northern Nigeria and H. G. Farrant April 11, 1940 CMS/IMC/ 270 SOAS.

[154] Algernon Edward Vere-Walwyn, Secretary of Northern Provinces to Henry Farrant, March 8, 1940. See further Henry Farrant to "All missionary organizations in Northern Nigeria," March 26, 1940, Algernon Vere-Walwyn, Secretary of Northern Provinces to Henry Farrant, Secretary of the Annual Meeting of Representatives of Missions in Northern Nigeria, March 8, 1940. Sudan United Missions General Correspondence 1940–1942 Folder (uncatalogued), Edinburgh Collections.

[155] Henry Farrant to Gilbert Dawson, March 27, 1940 Sudan United Missions uncatalogued materials, Edinburgh Collections.

needs of all children of school going age."[156] The Northern Region Board of Education decided the appeal in favor of SUM. Missionary proselytization, in sum, received a boost in the Cameron years.

Unlike Lugard's emphasis on the religious liberty of Masu Sarauta institutions to shield Muslims from proselytization, Cameron emphasized the state's neutrality on religious matters and was more inclined to grant missions access to the protectorate. However, not even Cameron's desire for an anglicized native population could eliminate restrictions outrightly. Ultimately, a census exercise conducted in the waning years of colonial rule would reveal that the missionary gains were limited almost exclusively to non-Muslims.[157] If the missionary project was not without gain, it was hardly the harvest missionaries envisioned when they set out for Northern Nigeria.

CONCLUSION

Imperial secularism was contingent on the career of indirect rule. The 1903 guarantee of noninterference issued to Muslim elites called for the embrace of Indigenous religious institutions as a vehicle for colonial governance. That adoption of indirect rule entailed two claims about the constitutional relationship between religion and the state. The first was religious liberty, that "all men had the right to worship God as they pleased," and the second was that the state would "not interfere with" religion, that is, state-religion separation. Neither commitment was principled. In fact, it was the varying sensibilities of colonial administrators that determined the tenor of imperial secular governmentality. Rooted

---

[156] Annual Report of the Education Department of Northern Nigeria, 1952–1953, 8. The official board members who were all colonial officials abstained from voting on the appeal.

[157] Muslims remained an overwhelming majority of the population at 73 percent, and the *magzawa* constituted 24.3 percent. Only 2.7 percent of the population identified as Christian. Nigeria, Federal Census Office, Population Census of the Northern Region of Nigeria, 1952–3 (Lagos: Census Superintendent 1953). This is not to uncritically accept the colonial records of religious affiliation. After all, there were important disincentives against identifying as a Christian convert during the census exercise particularly due to fear of a backlash in a society in which Lugardians continued to hold sway. See Barnes, "The 'Great Prohibition.'" However, even accounting for these inaccuracies, the census report appears to merely document a statistical fact that was commonly bemoaned by missionaries and commented on by observers of the missionary enterprise. See Sir Kenneth Grubb, "London Conference Faces Problems," *The Church of England Newspaper*, May 31, 1957.

in different attitudes regarding the means and ends of colonialism, and of the place of the missionary project in it, these administrative sensibilities determined on-the-ground policies on the contested question of missionary proselytization. With Lugard and Lugardians envisioning Muslims as the ideal colonized subject, and Cameron inclined to a vision of an ideal Christian subject, different imperatives of secularism came to be instruments wielded in furtherance of these positions. For Lugard and Lugardians, the emphasis was on religious freedom (of the Masu Sarauta) and the separation of the state from missions, while administrators leaning toward Cameron's approach stressed the separation of the state from caliphal institutions, and the religious liberty of missions. As administrative inclinations evolved, so too did the career of imperial secularism, and this mode of governmentality became an agenda rather than a coherent ideology.

The aphorism that "history, not jurisprudence, teaches the true principle" is true of the career of imperial secularism in Northern Nigeria.[158] Rather than stopping at the conclusion that imperial secularism is politics, however, a productive inquiry interrogates the sort of politics that mode of governmentality entailed – and its limits. The implementation of imperial secularism fielded the constitutional ideas of religious freedom and separation, with administrators wielding these notions to advance their inclinations on the missionary question. Missionaries savvily wielded the constitutional ideas deployed by colonial administrators to contest restrictions that threatened to frustrate their proselytizing ambitions. These efforts did not always cushion the blow to missionary expectations (as the practical necessity of maintaining a caliphal intermediary endured even beyond the Lugardian years); yet these notions of religious liberty and separation ultimately policed the boundaries of the discourse over missionary proselytization. Consequently, missionaries, like emirs and colonial administrators, were participants in shaping the trajectory of imperial secularism, and ultimately, in making the state. Colonial Northern Nigeria, therefore, became a site of intense struggle over the question of missionary proselytization. These struggles would endure, extending beyond the missionary question into other domains of contestation.

---

[158] Winnifred Fallers Sullivan et al., eds., "Introduction," in *Politics of Religious Freedom* (Chicago: University of Chicago Press, 2015), citing Georg Jellinek, *The Declaration of the Rights of Man and of Citizens: A Contribution to Modern Constitutional History*, trans. Max Farrand (New York: H. Holt, 1901), 97.

CHAPTER TWO

GOVERNING SHARI'A

As demonstrated in the preceding chapter, imperial secular governmentality was inextricably linked with indirect rule. Although that elaborate design relied on precolonial caliphate institutions and those of Indigenous religious groups, the colonial government gave an outsized influence to the colonial remains of the caliphate. That state intimacy with the Masu Sarauta gave rise to accusations of "Muslim sub-imperialism" by missionaries and other critics of the colonial arrangement.[1] These critics argued that rather than hinging on the separation of the state from all religions, colonial secular governmentality entailed the "unblushing bolstering up of Islam," thereby privileging the religious liberty of Muslims.[2] In fact, however, the indirect rule did not amount to an elevation or even preservation of the caliphal governance structures or the ideals on which they were built. Rather, indirect rule entailed the governance, and ultimately, the radical transformation of those institutions. Indirect rule was therefore not only governance through "Islamic institutions," it was, more importantly, governance *of* those institutions, a process that culminated in the making of a distinct British colonial Islamic law. This chapter traces that transformation as central to the career of imperial secular governmentality in the colony.

---

[1] See Jonathan Mamu Ayuba, "The Bible and Political Revolution: Religion and Minority Politics in Northern Nigeria, 1945–1957," *Journal of the Historical Society of Nigeria* 17 (2007): 145.

[2] September 27, 1917 Walter Miller to Miss Gollock. CBMS/IMC 271. School of Oriental and African Studies Special Collections, UK (hereafter SOAS).

Critical accounts of secularism have called attention to its tendency to entrench majoritarian norms and institutions.[3] Led by Talal Asad's *Formations of the Secular*, that body of work unsettles commonplace assumptions that secularism hinges on the state's separation from religion.[4] Moreover, these critical accounts suggest that the "sacred" and the "secular" are everywhere mutually constitutive, and that entanglement of the state and religion is the norm. This chapter underscores this reality of the state's intimacy with the Masu Sarauta, and consequently with Islamic law and institutions. At the same time, however, the chapter argues that apprehending the state's governance of Muslims and of Islamic law and institutions requires careful attention to the state's assertion of its separation from religion. Indeed, the modern state's intimacy with a faith does not leave that religions' norms and institutions unchanged; rather, secular governmentality renders those norms and institutions amenable to governance. In Northern Nigeria, the state's co-option of caliphal institutions for indirect rule produced a British colonial Islamic law through an unprecedented expansion of *siyasa* – the classical jurisdiction of political authorities over law.[5] That process

---

[3] Talal Asad, *Formations of the Secular: Christianity, Islam, Modernity* (Stanford: Stanford University Press, 2003); Saba Mahmood, *Religious Difference in a Secular Age: A Minority Report* (Princeton, NJ: Princeton University Press, 2015); Winnifred Fallers Sullivan et al., eds., "Introduction," in *Politics of Religious Freedom* (Chicago: University of Chicago Press, 2015); Brenda Cossman and Ratna Kapur, *Secularism's Last Sigh? Hindutva and the (Mis) Rule of Law* (Oxford: Oxford University Press, 2001).

[4] Asad, *Formations of the Secular*; Mahmood, *Religious Difference in a Secular Age*; Noah Salomon, *For Love of the Prophet: An Ethnography of Sudan's Islamic State* (Princeton, NJ: Princeton University Press, 2016); Sullivan et al., *Politics of Religious Freedom*; Cossman and Kapur, *Secularism's Last Sigh*; Ran Hirschl, *Constitutional Theocracy* (Cambridge, MA: Harvard University Press, 2011). Homi Bhabha, for instance, writes of "religious orthodoxy erupting within secularism, not simply in opposition to it." See "Secularism as an Idea Will Change," *The Hindu*, December 17, 1995, XIX in *Secularism's Last Sigh*; and Hirschl, *Constitutional Theocracy*. On the sacred underpinnings of modern secular law, see John L. Comaroff, "Reflections on the Rise of Legal Theology: Law and Religion in the Twenty-First Century," *Social Analysis* 53, no. 1 (2009): 193–216.

[5] Tamir Moustafa, "Judging in God's Name: State Power, Secularism, and the Politics of Islamic Law in Malaysia," *Oxford Journal of Law and Religion* 3, no. 1 (2013): 156. Scholarly work abounds on the emergence of British colonial versions of native law, including Islamic law across the empire. See, for instance, Iza R. Hussin, *The Politics of Islamic Law: Local Elites, Colonial Authority, and the Making of the Muslim State* (Chicago: University of Chicago Press, 2016). For British Hindu Law in India, see Dirk H. A. Kolff, "The Indian and the British Law Machines: Some Remarks on Law and Society in British India," in *European Expansion and Law: The Encounter of European and Indigenous Law in Nineteenth and Twentieth Century Africa and Asia*, eds. W. J. Mommsen & J. A. de Moor (Oxford: Berg Publishers, 1992), 201–235.

of appropriating the precolonial concept of siyasa to legitimate reform necessitated the state's entanglement with caliphal institutions. At the same time, however, the resulting transformation of siyasa and the ultimate emergence of an ahistorical colonial version of Islamic law dislodged precolonial caliphal practice. In tracing the contested emergence of this siyasa-authorized British colonial Islamic law, the following narrative lays bare the conditions under which the state could insist on separation from religion even as both were irretrievably entangled.

THE CALIPHAL ALLIANCE

Writing in May 1902 to Colonel Lugard, the head of the imperial army, the Sultan and Caliph of Sokoto was unequivocal about his perception of the British invasion as a religious confrontation.[6] Stating that the only interaction Sokoto could have with Britain was "war," Sultan Attahiru I declared that "Muslims do not consent to obey the Christians."[7] Attahiru's perception was widely shared among the ruling elites (the Masu Sarauta). Since indirect rule relied on these elites, early administrators were keen on assuring the Masu Sarauta of the primacy of Islam. As noted in Chapter 1, Lugard's first act upon conquering the territory was to guarantee "noninterference" in Islam.[8] To further reassure these elites, the new colonial government scripted the oath of office of the emirs to reflect a religious exemption: "I swear in the name of God well and truly to serve His Majesty King George V and his representative, the Governor of Nigeria, to obey the laws of Nigeria and the lawful commands of the Governor, and of the Lieutenant Governor, provided they are not contrary to my religion and if they are so contrary I will at once inform the Governor through the Resident."[9]

---

[6] The emirs were the sultan's subordinates who headed the provinces (emirates) of the caliphate. For the letter, see H. F. Backwell, *The Occupation of Hausaland, 1900–1904, Being a Translation of Arabic Letters Found in the House of the Wazir of Sokoto Bohari in 1903* (London: Frank Cass, 1969), 13. In June of the same year, the Sultan of Sokoto wrote a similar letter to Lugard.

[7] Backwell, *The Occupation of Hausaland*, 13; Mukhtar Umar Bunza, *Christian Missions among Muslims: Sokoto Province, Nigeria 1935–1990* (Trenton, NJ: Africa World Press, 2007), 22.

[8] See Chapter 1. Neville J. Brooke, *Report of the Native Courts (Northern Provinces) Commission of Inquiry Laid on the Table of the House of Representatives as Sessional Paper no. 1 of 1952* (Lagos, Nigeria: Federal Government Printer, 1952), i.

[9] Frederick John Dealtry Lugard, *The Dual Mandate in British Tropical Africa* (London: W. Blackwood, 1922), 212.

Taken publicly, that oath was intended to assure emirs that the state would not command them to carry out commands that would violate the state's guarantee of noninterference with Islam. It was, however, also targeted at the emirs' subjects – an assurance that colonial rule would not encroach into the sphere of religion. The assurance to emirs' subjects was crucial since the basis of emirs' legitimacy was their religious authority. These political rulers were regarded both by their subjects and colonial administrators as *amir-al mu'mineen*, meaning the head of the faith and leader of the Muslim community.[10] It was in this capacity that the state utilized these elites as its intermediaries in governing the colonial population.

The colonial government's alliance with the Masu Sarauta did not extend to all colonized Muslim subjects; the 1903 guarantee of interference applied only to the elites who became intermediaries of the colonial state and those who acceded to their authority. Indeed, the state's relationship with the Masu Sarauta was premised on a distinction between ideal Muslims and those Muslims regarded as dissident. The global and transnational historical process that witnessed the emergence of the good Muslim-bad Muslim dichotomy has received attention most notably in *Good Muslim, Bad Muslim* authored by Mahmood Mamdani.[11] As in the broader postcolonial process Mamdani describes, the dissident identity in colonial Northern Nigeria was contingent on the political contestations set in motion by imperial domination. Although the theological proclivities that came to be marked as dissident predated the colonial encounter, those identities were essentialized and the differences were deepened in furtherance of the political project of the state. In fact, the ideal versus dissident Muslim distinction was integral to the state's governance of Muslims.[12]

---

[10] Obaro Ikime, "The Establishment of Indirect Rule in Northern Nigeria," *Tarikh* 3, no. 3 (1971): 1–15. Lugard, for instance, states that the emir "commands allegiance as the 'Head of the Faith.' The Koran enjoins implicit obedience to his commands." Lugard, *The Dual Mandate*, 595.

[11] Mahmood Mamdani, *Good Muslim, Bad Muslim: America, the Cold War, and the Roots of Terror* (New York: Pantheon Books, 2004).

[12] See Jonathan Reynolds, "Good and Bad Muslims: Islam and Indirect Rule in Northern Nigeria," *The International Journal of African Historical Studies* 34, no. 3 (2001): 601–618. Like Reynolds, I use the ideal-dissident binary to illuminate the state's differentiation between Muslims allied with the Masu Sarauta and those seen as a threat to them. This book, however, situates that intra-Muslim differentiation within the broader imperial agenda of governing all faiths and managing religious difference.

PART I GOVERNING FAITH

In the colonial schema, ideal Muslims were those who acceded to Masu Sarauta rule, and to those elites' alliance with the state. On the other hand, administrators perceived opposition to the Masu Sarauta as dissidence. Although contingent on these political struggles, the distinction between ideal Muslims and dissident Muslims also took on an essentialized theological dimension to be eliminated by the Mahdi. The fact that the Masu Sarauta tended to affiliate with the *Qadiriyya Sufi tariqa* (the Qadiriyya Sufi order) provided a premise for this modeling of political differences onto theology. The Qadiriyya came to attain such a privileged status that one administrator even described the order as tantamount to "the established Church."[13] Since compliance of colonial populations was measured by association with the Masu Sarauta, tariqa affiliation came to determine dissidence.

Although other non-Qadiriyya tariqas were present in the colony, colonial administrators regarded the Tijaniyyah as particularly threatening and "lacking in moderation."[14] Tijaniyyahs were foremost critics of Masu Sarauta complicity in the colonial project; nevertheless, administrators' conflation of political resistance with Tijaniyyah theology was tenuous. The sustained critique of the Masu Sarauta alliance with the state that emerged from that group was hardly strictly rooted in theology. In fact, the demographic composition of Northern Nigerian Tijaniyyah already predetermined that group's political opposition. The group tended to draw members from merchant communities, which were traditional bastions of opposition to the Masu Sarauta due to precolonial tussles rooted in political and socioeconomic questions, including those involving taxation.[15] The Tijaniyyah's political

---

[13] Peter H. G. Scott, *A Survey of Islam in Northern Nigeria in 1952* (Nigeria: Government Printers, 1953), 1.

[14] The *Qadiriyya/Tijaniyyah* distinction was entrenched following the introduction of party politics in the late colonial years. Tijaniyyahs became allied with the Northern Elements Progressive Union, which was founded on a critique of Masu Sarauta monarchical feudalism. See Basa case infra and the discussion in Chapter 3. For records of the state's surveillance of the Tijaniyyah and NEPU, and its understandings of the connections between the two, see surveillance records in "Nigeria Tijaniyyah (Sufi Sect)." FCO 141/13699. National Archives United Kingdom (hereafter NA. UK).

[15] Certain emirs were Tijaniyyah, including at various points, emirs of Kano, Zaria, Katsina, and Argungu. These were, however, emirs who resisted the authority of the Sultan of Sokoto, who was the head of the precolonial Caliphate, the leader of the *Qadiriyya* order and, in the view of the state, "the fountain-source" of Islamic authority.

theology was influenced by these age-long contestations. Yet, the state's designation of the Tijaniyyah as an "other" of the "ideal" Muslim, and the consequent repression of that group, was the product of colonial governance rather than of preexisting differences.

The Tijaniyyah identity was the counterpoint to colonial imaginations of ideal Muslims until the late colonial years, but Mahdism occupied the attention of administrators in the early colonial period. Mahdism was the belief that the end of the world was near and that a messiah (*Mahdi*) had arisen or would imminently arise to reform Islam and eliminate corruption. The belief in the end of times itself stemmed from widespread belief among Muslims; however, what was distinct about colonial-era Mahdism was the conviction in the imminence of the Mahdi's arrival, or in many quarters, the belief that the Mahdi had already arrived. That conviction sprung from the perception that colonialism and the Masu Sarauta alliance with empire were the ultimate corruption. Because administrators tended to conflate anti-colonial resistance with Mahdist inclinations, they exaggerated the threat. In the 1903 annual report, for instance, Lugard noted that there were "four Mahdis and a rumor of a fifth."[16] Another official stated, "Wherever you look under every bush and tree, there is a Mahdi."[17] Because officials regarded Mahdism as deviant, the state responded with violence. A prominent example was the colonial expedition against Satiru, an alleged Mahdist-leaning village. As Burdon, the assistant resident, reported after the emir-supported British attack, "No wall or tree was left standing."[18] The colonial government tried the male survivors of the Satiru crackdown before the Sokoto Islamic Court and executed several of them.[19] Satiru was just one example; even in circumstances where the government was less inclined toward

---

[16] See Colonial Reports-Annual, o. 437, Northern Nigeria, 1903 (HM Stationery Office, 1904), 8.

[17] Asmau G. Saeed, "British Fears over Mahdism in Northern Nigeria: A Look at Bormi 1903, Satiru 1906 and Dumbulwa 1923," *Frankfurter Afrikanistische Blätter* 4 (1992): 34–46, and also in PPMS36 SOAS Special Collections, London.

[18] C0446/53. Lugard to C.O. March 14, 1906. One British soldier gave a "low estimation" of the casualty as five hundred. Goodwin to Lugard, March 11, 1906 – enclosed to Lugard's Letter to the Colonial Office. C0446/59 NA, UK. See Rowland Aderemi Adeleye, "Mahdist Triumph and British Revenge in Northern Nigeria: Satiru 1906," *Journal of the Historical Society of Nigeria* 6, no. 2 (1972): 193–214.

[19] Burdon's Sokoto Provincial Report, No. 29, March 31, 1906. Bormi, another alleged Mahdist village, was destroyed and its inhabitants displaced.

destroying entire villages, senior leaders and their core supporters were usually publicly executed, and their supporters deported.[20]

The ideal versus dissident Muslim dichotomy rendered Muslim minorities vulnerable to violence and repression. Intra-Muslim theological differences predated the colonial encounter. It was, however, colonial governance that infused these differences with unprecedented legal and political significance. Like the Muslim–non-Muslim distinction examined in Chapter 1, that intra-Muslim dichotomy became a crucial manifestation of the state's governance of religious difference. The colonial state entered into a pact with the Masu Sarauta to effectuate indirect rule; everyday colonial governance was not, however, a perpetuation of the Islamic faith or the precolonial caliphate, even in Lugardian years. Indeed, when the secretary to the colonial government, G. J. Lethem, wrote to colonial administrators on the need to crack down on dissent in a 1927 letter, Lethem described emirs as "secular chiefs" through whom the state governed.[21] Lethem emphasized that "the whole basis of the native form of administration is to place power and influence in the hands of secular chiefs and minimize the influence of leaders whose appeal is to religion."[22] Therefore, while the 1903 pact of "noninterference" might suggest a story of preservation, the chronicle of colonial governance is, in fact, one of the transformation of Islamic law and caliphal institutions.

SHARI'A GOVERNANCE: SIYASA AND THE MAKING OF A BRITISH COLONIAL ISLAMIC LAW

Although histories of the co-option of Islamic institutions by the British imperial legal project abound, the story of Northern Nigeria is considered unique.[23] Save for parts of the Aden Protectorate, only in

---

[20] Wallace, the acting high commissioner of Northern Nigeria, for instance, reports the execution of a Mahdi and the deportation of his followers in the 1906 Annual Report to the Colonial Office. See, for instance, Wallace, *Annual Report of Northern Nigeria, 1906*. See also Lugard, *Annual Report of Northern Nigeria, 1903*.

[21] G. J. Lethem, *Memoranda: Political Propaganda in Nigeria* (Colonial Office, September 29, 1927). K5521/4 PPMS60/2/1-7, 5 SOAS.

[22] PPMS36 SOAS. See also George John Frederick Tomlinson and Gordon James Lethem, *History of Islamic Political Propaganda in Nigeria* (Colonial Office, 1927).

[23] William Malcolm Hailey, *Native Administration in the British African Territories: West Africa: Nigeria, Gold Coast, Sierra Leone, Gambia* (London: HM Stationery Office, 1951); Charles L. Temple, *Native Races and Their Rulers* (Cape Town:

Northern Nigeria did Islamic law apply not just as personal law, but also as criminal law.[24] This presence of Islamic law in the criminal domain – the paradigmatic sphere of public law – was interpreted by critics as the colonial state's elevation of precolonial jurisprudence. Missionaries bemoaned what they regarded as the state's elevation of Islamic law and caliphal institutions, even under Governor Cameron's mission-permissive regime. This view was also prevalent among prominent scholars of Islamic law in the metropole.

Writing in 1955, J. N. D. Anderson, professor of Oriental laws at the University of London, observed: "At present, … Islamic law is more widely, and in some respects, more rigidly applied in Northern Nigeria than anywhere else outside Arabia."[25] Anderson further pointed out that Northern Nigeria's "orthodoxy" was occasioned not only by the precolonial caliphate's isolation but also by colonial legal practice.[26] Anderson was hardly alone in this view. In a study commissioned by the Institute of Colonial Studies in 1950, Joseph Schacht, foremost twentieth-century scholar of Islamic law and Oxford scholar, also criticized the colonial state for rigidifying Islamic law.[27] Schacht argued that the law frozen and elevated by the colonial state was the Islamic legal theory developed by jurists rather than historical Islamic legal practice. He noted that historical legal practice featured precolonial political authorities' (emirs) exercise of enormous influence over the administration of justice through their siyasa jurisdiction. Schacht further insisted that emirs' exercise of judicial powers – siyasa – had not

---

Argus, 1918); Margery Freda Perham, *Native Administration in Nigeria* (New York: Oxford University Press, 1937); Harry A. Gailey, *Sir Donald Cameron: Colonial Governor* (Stanford, CA: Hoover Institution Press, 1974); Reynolds, "Good and Bad Muslims"; Adamu Mohammed Fika, *The Kano Civil War and British Over-rule: 1882–1940* (New York: Oxford University Press, 1978); Walter Russell Crocker, *Nigeria: A Critique of British Colonial Administration* (London: Allen and Unwin, 1936); Kalu Ezera, *Constitutional Development in Nigeria* (Cambridge: Cambridge University Press 1960).

[24] In other British territories with significant Muslim populations, such as South (Western) Nigeria, India, Pakistan, Egypt, Indonesia, Malaysia, and Sudan, Islamic law applied only as "personal law," a new category which came into existence with the colonial encounter. For a history of "Islamic Personal Law," see Noel James Coulson, *A History of Islamic Law* (New Brunswick, NJ: Aldine Transaction, 2011).

[25] James Norman Dalrymple Anderson, *Islamic Law in Africa* (Oxon: Routledge, 2013), 219.

[26] Ibid.

[27] Joseph Schacht, "Investigation into the Application of Islamic law in Nigeria" (1951). CO 927/158/6 NA, UK.

been constrained by theoretical Islamic law as developed by jurists. Moreover, he pointed out that siyasa was at its most expansive in criminal law since states tended to exercise the greatest prerogative over that domain. The Oxford scholar accused the colonial state of privileging juristic theory with the consequence that emirs lost their siyasa powers and Islamic law became frozen.

There were important differences in Schacht and Anderson's understanding of the Northern Nigerian situation; nevertheless, both scholars regarded colonial law as synonymous with Islamic law.[28] Citing Northern Nigeria's religious diversity and sustained missionary criticism of the colonial condition, Anderson and Schacht called on the state to dissociate itself from Islamic institutions by adopting a vision of siyasa unconstrained by the juristic expositions of the Shari'a.

Schacht and Anderson's narrative continues to exercise tremendous influence.[29] Yet that account misses indirect rule's remaking of Islamic law particularly in the area that concerned commentators – the domain of criminal jurisprudence. This transformation, which began in the earliest days of colonial rule, was through the vehicle of siyasa.

Defined not only as the judicial powers of political authorities but also as "statecraft,"[30] "discretionary power of the ruler,"[31] "sharia governance,"[32] and even "politics,"[33] the scope and meaning of siyasa in Islamic scholarly discourse have not been free of debate. That debate has centered on the place of siyasa in the Shari'a and the relationship

---

[28] Although Anderson, unlike, Schacht, discerned traces of siyasa in emirs' jurisdiction, he was of the view that colonial-era siyasa was unduly restrictive. John Anderson, "A Survey of Islamic Law in Nigeria." PPMS 60/01/01, John Anderson Collection, SOAS, London.

[29] See Chapter 6. On the view that the transformation of Northern Nigerian Islamic law only followed Anderson and Schacht's prescriptions in the last decade of colonial rule, see for instance, Philip Ostien, "An Opportunity Missed by Nigeria's Christians: The 1976–78 Sharia Debate Revisited," in *Muslim-Christian Encounters in Africa*, ed. Benjamin F. Soares (Leiden: Brill, 2006), 221–255; and Matthew Hassan Kukah, *Religion, Politics and Power in Northern Nigeria* (Ibadan, Nigeria: Spectrum Books, 1993).

[30] Bernard Lewis, "Siyasa," in *Quest of an Islamic Humanism: Arabic and Islamic Studies in Memory of Mohamed al-Nowaihi*, ed. Arnold H. Green (Cairo: Cairo Press, 1984), 3.

[31] Moustafa, "Judging in God's Name," 156.

[32] Ebrahim Moosa, "Colonialism and Islamic Law," in *Islam and Modernity: Key Issues and Debates*, ed. Muhammad Khalid Masud (Edinburgh: Edinburgh University Press, 2009), 166.

[33] Lewis, "Siyasa"; Mervyn Hiskett, *The Course of Islam in Africa* (Edinburgh: Edinburgh University Press, 1994), 120–121.

between the political ruler and the jurist.[34] Positions ranged from considering siyasa as "satanic"[35] and opposed to *fiqh* (juristic expositions of the Shari'a), to regarding it as being harmonious with the Shari'a and as "serving the Sharia, alongside fiqh."[36] A strand of the latter position, which regards siyasa as *siyasa shar'iyya* (siyasa in accordance with the Shari'a), exerts influence on contemporary readings of classical Islamic governance.[37] Describing the classical constitutional structure, Ebrahim Moosa states that "the caliph ... was merely the steward of the law" and was obliged to "create an environment conducive to the application of Shari'a norms." Similarly, Wael Hallaq conceives of siyasa as conforming with the Shari'a as opposed to an "unfettered power of political governance."[38] Hallaq argues that siyasa exercise was limited to matters of public order and was exercised for the purpose of serving the public good. Hallaq, therefore, argues that restrictions imposed by siyasa shar'iyya meant that the executive ruler "stood apart" from the legislative authority as well as the juristic and judicial powers exercised by judges.[39]

---

[34] Ovamir Anjum, *Politics, Law, and Community in Islamic Thought: The Taymiyyan Moment* (Cambridge: Cambridge University Press, 2012), 106.

[35] Mamluk-era jurist, Al Maqrizi. Anjum, *Politics, Law, and Community*, 106.

[36] Asifa Quraishi-Landes, "Islamic Constitutionalism: Not Secular, Not Theocratic, Not Impossible," *Rutgers Journal of Law and Religion* 16, no. 3 (2015): 559. Examples of scholars who hold this view are Ibn al Jawzi, Al-Mawardi, and Ibn Taymiyyah. Each had a different answer to the question of the relationship between the ruler and the jurist. To Ibn al Jawzi, the authority of the ruler was subjected to that of the jurists – the authoritative expounders of the Shari'a. To Al-Mawardi, although the siyasa is encompassed within the Shari'a, rulers are not thereby subordinate to the jurists. See Frank Vogel, "Tracing Nuance in Māwardī's *al-Aḥkām al-Sulṭāniyyah*: Implicit Framing of Constitutional Authority," in *Islamic Law in Theory: Studies on Jurisprudence in Honor of Bernard Weiss*, eds. Reinhart and Gleave (Leiden: Brill, 2014), 339. Ibn Taymiyyah argues for "cooperation" between rulers, jurists, and the Muslim community. Anjum, *The Taymiyyan Moment*, 103–107. See also Kristen Stilt, *Islamic Law in Action: Authority, Discretion, and Everyday Experiences in Mamluk Egypt* (Oxon: Oxford University Press, 2011).

[37] See Moosa, "Colonialism and Islamic law"; Wael B. Hallaq, *The Impossible State: Islam, Politics, and Modernity's Moral Predicament* (New York: Columbia University Press, 2014); and Quraishi-Landes, "Islamic Constitutionalism."

[38] Hallaq, *The Impossible State*, 69. For a critique of Hallaq's account, see Lama Abu Odeh, "Review: *The Impossible State: Islam, Politics, and Modernity's Moral Predicament* by Wael Hallaq," *International Journal of Middle East Studies* 46, no. 1 (2014): 216–218.

[39] See Moustafa, "Judging in God's Name," 156.

The Shari'a-constrained notion of siyasa was held up as an ideal in the precolonial Sokoto Caliphate. That did not only constrain the legislative/regulatory powers of the rulers but also their judicial powers. To replace the unfettered siyasa in precolonial Sokoto, Uthman Dan Fodio, the leader of the revolution and founder of the Sokoto Caliphate, envisaged the exercise of supervisory jurisdiction over *alkalai* (judges, singular: *alkali*) by a chief judge appointed by the caliph/sultan.[40] The sultan, therefore, came to have restricted judicial powers. Emirs faced even more restrictions in their exercise of judicial functions, and, in many emirates, their judicial power was limited to boundary disputes.

To be sure, the founding leaders of the caliphate did not have a uniform conception of the scope of siyasa within the Shari'a. While Uthman Dan Fodio and his brother, prominent caliphal leader Abdullah Bello, evinced a restrictive view of siyasa within the bounds of the Shari'a, Fodio's son and immediate successor, Muhammed Bello, espoused a more expansive view. This latest Bello, who was the most engaged in practical administration of the three, argued that it was permissible to depart from the "letter of the sharia" in order "to relieve hardships and make life easier and better for the people."[41] To him, "if the letter of the sharia needs to be sacrificed to safeguard its spirit, so be it."[42] However, even Muhammed Bello's liberal construction of siyasa had Shari'i limits. Notably, Muhammed Bello stridently criticized unconstrained political power in his *Tanbih al-raqid*: "Rulers have dared to oppose the Sharia under the false apprehension that the policy of the Sharia is not capable of dealing with people and the best interest of the community. They overstep the limits ... and abandon the Sharia by rebelling in various ways and making innovations in government in a way that is not permitted." Consequently, siyasa was understood as siyasa shar'iyya in the constitutional discourse of Sokoto.[43]

In the prevailing intellectual thought in Sokoto, the Shari'a was discoverable in jurists' exposition of the law across the four schools

---

[40] Mervyn Hiskett, "Kitāb Al-Farq: A Work on the Habe Kingdoms Attributed to 'Uthmān Dan Fodio," *SOAS Bulletin* 23, no. 3 (1960): 558–579.

[41] Ibraheem Sulaiman, *The Islamic State and the Challenge of History: Ideals, Policies and Operation of the Sokoto Caliphate* (London: Mansell, 1987), 63.

[42] Ibid.

[43] Ibid., 73. See also B. G. Martin, "A Muslim Political Tract from Northern Nigeria: Muhammad Bello's *Usul al-Siyasa*," in *Aspects of West African Islam* (Boston: African Studies Center, Boston University, 1971), 63–86.

of Islamic jurisprudence. Maliki thought was favored; however, fiqh diversity was encouraged.[44] In his famed work, *Ihya' as-Sunnah wa Ikhmad a-Bid'ah*, for instance, Caliph Dan Fodio suggests that the administration of justice ought not be confined to Maliki thought. Instead, alkalai could draw on the jurisprudence of other schools. Dan Fodio, then, conceived of the role of the alkalai as that of a *mujtahid* (jurist), one free to exercise independent reasoning, both through the means of *takhayyur* (selecting opinions from different schools on different matters) and *talfiq* (amalgamating opinions of different schools with regards to the same matter).[45]

Within the scope of juristic expositions of the Shari'a, the ruler could make a wide range of judicial decisions/legislation/regulations as long as those were for the public good and with the motivation of "piety and support of Islam."[46] Yet, the ruler's judicial and legislative power was also constrained by subject matter. For instance, within the realm of criminal justice administration, the ruler's discretion was restricted to *ta'azir*: offenses against public order for which there are no fixed scriptural definitions or prescribed punishments. In practice, *ta'azir* also encompassed offenses "that do not warrant punishment" or for which "conviction could not be secured due to lack of evidence."[47] Within this realm, the ruler had the power to establish "equitable criminal procedure laws to deter criminals and protect the innocent."[48] The goal of executive power, here, was therefore that of deterrence and protection of society rather than punishment.

---

[44] Ahmed Beita Yusuf, *Nigerian Legal System: Pluralism and Conflict of Laws in the Northern States* (New Delhi: National Publishing House, 1982), 27.

[45] See Uthman Ibn Fuduye, *Ihya' as-Sunnah wa Ikhmad a Bid'ah*, trans. Abu Alfa Umar Muhammad Shareef Bin Farid (Sennar: Sankore, 1998); Musa Ali Ajetunmobi, *Shariah Legal Practice in Nigeria 1956–1983* (Ilorin, Nigeria: Kwara State University Press, 2018), 27. See further Ismail A. B. Balogun, *The Life and Works of Uthman Dan Fodio: The Muslim Reformer of West Africa* (Lagos: Islamic Publications Bureau, 1975).

[46] Sulaiman, *The Islamic State*, 68, citing Abdullahi Bello's *Diya al Hukam*.

[47] Sulaiman, *The Islamic State*, 69. See also Rudolph Peters, *Crime and Punishment in Islamic Law: Theory and Practice from the Sixteenth to the Twenty-First Century* (Cambridge: Cambridge University Press, 2006), 7–8. Beyond *ta'azir*, scholars set out two other categories of crimes: offenses which require as retribution a "divinely ordained punishment" (*huduud*), and those which call for talionic punishment (*qisas*). Christian Lange, "Crime and Punishment in Islamic History (Early to Middle Period): A Framework for Analysis," *Religion Compass* 4, no. 11 (2010): 698.

[48] Sulaiman, *The Islamic State*, 69.

The most striking transformation ushered in by imperial secularism was the "legal centralization of political power" in the state.[49] Siyasa governance shifted from its very limited role of enforcing the few laws aimed at maintaining public order in the precolonial caliphate to now encompass the extensive regulation of the lives of subjects. This concentration of the power to apply the Shari'a in the hands of the state – "Sharia statism" – was a fundamental legacy of colonial governance in Northern Nigeria.[50] Expanded beyond recognition, siyasa now manifested as state power,[51] with the state represented at different points by rulers, judges, colonial administrators, and ultimately, by the decade prior to Independence, by a central legislative council not unconnected to the old power structures. It was this statist arrogation of the power to determine Islamic law and the configurations and reconfigurations of authority it brought about that produced a British colonial Islamic law.

DISAGGREGATING THE COLONIAL STATE

Colonial governance of Islamic law was not monolithic; rather, it unfolded along the Lugardian-Cameron trajectory set out in Chapter 1. Lugardian native administration ideology was the perfect background for the commencement of reform through the expanded siyasa of emirs. That expansion reconfigured the roles of political and judicial authorities. There came to be a distinction between what alkalai conceived Islamic law to be and what they were ordered to do by the emir, who was in turn acting on the "instruction" of colonial administrators. Although siyasa was largely rooted in the emir in the Lugardian phase, the colonial administration had begun to arrogate power directly to itself by conferring supervisory jurisdiction over Islamic courts on European colonial administrators. The Cameron phase veered away from the Lugardian trajectory. Disapproving the valorization of native

---

[49] Quraishi-Landes, "Islamic Constitutionalism," 562; Moosa, "Colonialism and Islamic Law," 167.

[50] Brandon Kendhammer, *Muslims Talking Politics: Framing Islam, Democracy, and Law in Northern Nigeria* (Chicago: University of Chicago Press, 2016), 13–14, 52–54. Eltantawi argues that this statism was driven by the central colonial concern of "control." Eltantawi, *Shari'ah on Trial*, 121, 133. On Sudan, see Mark Fathi Massoud, *Law's Fragile State: Colonial, Authoritarian, and Humanitarian Legacies in Sudan* (Cambridge: Cambridge University Press, 2013).

[51] Quraishi-Landes, "Islamic Constitutionalism," 562, arguing that "state power has become today's *siyasa*." See also Hussin, *The Politics of Islamic Law*, 177.

institutions by the Lugardians, Cameron ushered in open reforms by creating an appellate bridge from native to English courts. With the Cameron reforms, siyasa power had moved from the emirs to the central state. Because Cameron, unlike Lugard, opposed the fusion of executive and judicial powers, he invested the power of reform not in colonial administrators, but in the hands of a judiciary staffed by European judges trained in English law. As with colonial policy on missionary proselytization, Cameron did not completely root out Lugardian ideas. Despite the sanction of the Colonial Office, his policy was never fully implemented, for there remained many Lugardians among those entrusted with effecting the reform, namely the residents and district commissioners. As a result, both Cameron's and Lugard's ideas on native judicial administration came to exist side by side in the last two decades of colonial rule. The complexity of colonial administration was not limited to the tensions between differing ideas and strategies of colonial administrators. The "tensions of empire"[52] extended to the relationship between the colonizers and the colonized as well as among the colonized. Rather than being a top-down imposition, the law and legal institutions were sites of contestations in which emirs, alkalai, colonial subjects, and administrators negotiated and renegotiated the state's governance of religion and religious difference.[53]

LUGARDIAN PHASE (1900–1930)

Central to Lugard's vision of Islamic institutions as a vehicle of indirect rule was a strong executive wielding both legislative and judicial powers. That vision, therefore, called for an unprecedented expansion of the siyasa of emirs. To be sure, some of Lugard's desire to glorify emirs and his rhetorical emphasis on Masu Sarauta religious liberty might have stemmed from his Orientalist fascination with these elites and his wish to maintain appearances of upholding his guarantee of noninterference. Yet, utilizing emirs for the state's reform project was also dictated by administrative exigencies, foremost among which

---

[52] Frederick Cooper and Ann Laura Stoler, eds., *Tensions of Empire: Colonial Cultures in a Bourgeois World* (Berkeley: University of California Press, 1997).

[53] Moosa, "Colonialism and Islamic Law," 177. See also Kendhammer, *Muslims Talking Politics*, 54. For an account mapping out the ways in which the varied responses of colonial subjects to colonialism were all justified in the language of the Shari'a, see Muhammad Sani Umar, *Islam and Colonialism: Intellectual Responses of Muslims of Northern Nigeria to British Colonial Rule* (Leiden: Brill, 2006).

was the severe manpower shortage in the colonial administration.[54] To administer the colony, the state depended on Islamic institutions and had to shore up not only their legitimacy but also their brute power. Lugard explains the mode of colonial rule in his Amalgamation Report of 1914: "The system of native administration ... [was] based on a recognition of the authority of the Native Chiefs. The policy ... was that these chiefs should govern their people, not as independent but as dependent Rulers. The orders of government are not conveyed to the people through them, but emanate from them in accordance ... with *instructions* received through the Resident."[55]

Hence, the Lugardian vision of a strong executive/administrator found its highest realization in the powers it granted to European colonial administrators, particularly residents. Residents' instructions, executed through the extended siyasa of the emirs, became the main vehicle of reform in the Lugardian phase. The other main vehicles of reform – the reorganization of the courts and the conferment of discretionary supervisory jurisdiction on the colonial administrators – closely relied on the logic of the siyasa-expansion tool. The content of the reforms set in motion by the state tended to be triggered sometimes by the ideas of the Lugardians on "good order," and sometimes by the advocacy of local missionaries, their international counterparts, and the Colonial Office.

Expanding Siyasa

Emirs' siyasa witnessed unprecedented expansion in the Lugardian years, serving as a foundation for the statist siyasa project that would commence in the Cameron era. The conclusion by academic experts like Joseph Schacht – that Northern Nigeria represented the "most spectacular instance of the self-effacement of siyasa as represented by the political authority" – therefore met with skepticism of administrators with knowledge of the everyday workings of the colonial legal system.[56] Notably, John Cornes, the Institute of Colonial Studies' supervisor of colonial services courses who had previously served as a Northern Nigerian administrator, pointed out that Schacht's reliance

---

[54] At the inception of colonial rule, there were one hundred British officers for Northern Nigeria, which had a size of 320,000 square miles and population of 8.7 million. *Annual Report, Northern Nigeria*, 1901. This manpower shortage would continue due to revenue constraints. Revenue was almost solely generated from taxes and 75 percent of this revenue was expended on administration.

[55] Emphasis added.

[56] Schacht, "Investigation into the Application of Islamic Law in Nigeria," 5.

on interviews had led to his mistaken conclusion.[57] Although emirs vehemently denied their exercise of siyasa when Schacht interviewed them, Cornes pointed to emirs' "tight hold over their *alkalai*" and exercise of both formal and informal control over judicial outcomes as evidence of their expansive siyasa.[58]

For Lugardians, emirs' extended authority was not an end in itself; rather, it was a tool for implementing colonial administrators' instructions. The process through which John H. Carrow, Resident of Kano Province, modified certain rules of evidence in alkalai courts is illustrative of the Lugardian approach to govern Islamic law. First, Carrow met with the emir's senior officials and spoke to them of "the necessity" of "adjusting ... to modern conditions."[59] To protect the emir from being "accused of failing in his faith," Carrow suggested that the governor issue an order mandating reform. Subsequently, Carrow met with the emir, who suggested that rather than issuing an order, the governor should write a personal letter "requesting" the changes. Upon receipt, the emir guaranteed that he would direct alkalai to comply. Such a strategy would ensure that "the whole matter is dealt with as discreetly and quietly as possible to avoid gossip and intrigue in Kano city."[60] Carrow agreed and did as the emir proposed.

When Lugard instituted reforms to eliminate the classical alternatives of compensation or forgiveness to criminal punishment, it was left to emirs to secure alkalai compliance. Therefore, in *Katsina NA v. Yakudi of Hababa and Dankoko of Renage*,[61] where the chief alkali discharged a defendant convicted of homicide in response to the request of the victim's family, the emir overturned the decision and sentenced the convict to death, citing "the instruction of the government" mandating punishment for criminal convictions.[62]

---

[57] John Cornes, Minutes on Joseph Schacht, "Investigation into the Application of Islamic law in Nigeria" (1951). CO 927/158/6 NA, UK.

[58] Ibid.

[59] "Rights of Non Mohammedans Before Mohammedan Courts," File no. 16032, Arewa House Kaduna in Umar, *Islam and Colonialism*, 48.

[60] Ibid.

[61] Anderson, "A Survey of Islamic Law in Nigeria." PPMS 60/1/12-17 SOAS Library Special Collections, London.

[62] Ibid. The abolition of the options of forgiveness or payment of diya (compensation) was particularly contested by alkalai, emirs, and even some colonial administrators due to the fear that insisting on the capital penalty would revive the practice of blood feud. Brooke, *Report of the Native Courts (Northern Provinces) Commission*, 186.

Alkalai sometimes contested this exercise of siyasa. In a case in Sokoto Province, the alkali refused to comply with the emir's directive on the basis that he "could not enforce a law made by an emir that is not in the Quran." Arguing that "Islamic law strictly commands obedience to those in authority," the emir overruled him.[63] The emir was, therefore, asserting that he was exercising siyasa shar'iyya. For emirs, retaining their authority in the face of their obligations to implement the wishes of their colonial overlords required clothing their commands in the language of the Shari'a. Since the state sought to preserve the authority of emirs in the eyes of the colonized population, administrators cooperated with emirs in justifying reform as siyasa shar'iyya.

Beyond alkalai resistance, emirs sometimes expressed hostility to this reform through siyasa project in the Lugardian years. Notably, the Advisory Council of Emirs passed a resolution in 1930 that "they were unable to suggest any departure from the strict letter" of Islamic law on the basis that, if they did so, "all their subjects ... would feel that they had abandoned their religion."[64] Thanking them for "their clear and unequivocal statement of their point of view," the lieutenant governor pointed out that their position was "entirely logical."[65] The lieutenant governor's response was, of course, entirely consistent with the Lugardian strategy of ostensible deference to emirs. Neither emirs' resistance nor the purported deference of colonial administrators halted reform. In these cases, Lugardians turned to the vehicle of supervisory jurisdiction over Islamic courts.

Reorganizing the Judiciary

The Lugardian reorganization of the judiciary was designed to expand the powers of emirs by setting up grades of courts and instituting a system of appeal. There were four grades of Islamic courts with the emirs' courts at the apex.[66] The emirs' courts had exclusive jurisdiction over homicide cases and were authorized to pronounce the death penalty, the execution of which was subject to the approval of the resident. Both residents and district officers had a right of access to the courts

---

[63] Anderson, "A Survey of Islamic Law in Nigeria."
[64] Brooke, *Report of the Native Courts (Northern Provinces) Commission*, 184.
[65] Ibid.
[66] Native Courts (Amendment) Proclamation (No. 10, 1908) (N.Nig.), 1911 and Native Courts Ordinance (No. 5, 1918) (Ng.).

and could "review, modify or suspend a judgment" or "order re-hearing" before the same court.[67]

Obviously, the expansion of the emir's jurisdiction had already increased the avenues through which the emir could exercise siyasa in the service of the state. Yet, colonial administrators' supervisory jurisdiction offered an alternative in situations where emirs resisted colonial directives. In the *Hassana of Fura* case, for instance, a defendant convicted of murder was forgiven by the parents of the victim. The emir discharged the defendant in line with Islamic law. The resident, however, insisted that a punishment of death ought to be imposed and complained to the governor who, in spite of his expressed desire not to offend the emir, imposed a judgment of five years imprisonment.[68]

By exercising supervisory jurisdiction over emirs' courts, political officers exercised judicial control without formal appellate jurisdiction. This design was informed by Lugard's conviction that it was "[un]desirable that there should be any formal right of appeal" but "essential that the duty of supervision and revision by the administrative staff be rigorously carried out."[69]

Operating parallel to the native courts were the protectorate courts. The Lugardian design, therefore, produced two systems of courts. On the one hand, there existed the native courts appeal system under the control of the administrators – the district officer, the resident, the high commissioner, and the governor, in that order. On the other hand, the English-style protectorate courts were under the control of the chief justice and applied local legislation, "English Common Law, doctrines of equity and Statutes of General Application that were in force in England on 1 January 1900."[70]

---

[67] Native Courts Proclamation.
[68] Brooke, *Report of the Native Courts (Northern Provinces) Commission*, 128.
[69] Frederick John Dealtry Lugard, *Political Memoranda, Revision of Instructions to Political Officers on Subjects Chiefly Political and Administrative 1913–1918* (London: Frank Cass, 1970), Memorandum No. 3.
[70] One of these was the 1916 English Criminal Code. The protectorate courts were of two categories: (1) the Supreme Court and (2) the provincial courts consisting of provincial courts and cantonment courts. See Protectorate Courts Proclamation of 1900 and Cantonment Courts Proclamation of 1902. Colonial administrators wielded immense power over both courts, especially the provincial courts since these were presided over by residents or a "fit and proper person" appointed by the High Commissioner (the provincial courts) or a Magistrate (the cantonment courts). The Supreme Court was the highest in the hierarchy with both supervisory

The relationship between the protectorate courts and Islamic courts was unclear.[71] This lack of clarity increased the discretion of colonial administrators. The question of jurisdiction could make a radical difference to the fate of a defendant. For example, a homicide may call for capital punishment under the Criminal Code applicable in protectorate courts, but the accused person could avoid the death penalty by paying *diya* (compensation) in Islamic courts. Also, a homicide may constitute manslaughter under the Criminal Code but be punishable by death in the Islamic courts.

In the Lugardian phase, the administrators did not transfer cases from the Islamic courts to the protectorate courts even though they had the power to do so. This attitude stemmed from the Lugardian impulse to preserve the appearance of strengthening the authority of emirs. The refusal to transfer cases left the vast majority of judicial work in the hands of emirs and alkalai under the supervision of the European administrators. Resident of Sokoto, E. Arnett, explains this disposition:

> A native judge may be less clever than an English one at analyzing a mass of evidence but he has two great advantages. His more intimate knowledge and understanding of native habits of life and thought and secondly, the greater weight attaching to an oath taken before a Mohamedan judge ... To take away this power from the native courts would seriously impair the authority of the emirs and the whole native administration.[72]

This did not prevent the exercise of judicial powers of supervision by the administrators in cases where these officials deemed it necessary. On the one hand, therefore, the Lugardian reforms increased the judicial powers of emirs as a vehicle for siyasa. On the other, the power of supervision provided a channel through which the state could directly determine judicial outcomes.

---

and appellate jurisdiction – appellate jurisdiction over the provincial courts and supervisory jurisdiction over cantonment courts and native courts if political officers transferred cases to it.

[71] Jurisdiction was determined by (1) Whether the accused person is a native/non-native; (2) Whether the alleged offence was committed within the boundary of an emirate and the case is investigated by the Nigerian police or the Native Authority police; and (3) Whether the resident or other officer *sees fit* to transfer the case from the native courts.

[72] Resident of Sokoto Province to the Secretary of Northern Provinces, "Delineation of Jurisdiction," Native Courts File #11454, 1915, vol. I, Kaduna National Archives (hereafter NA Nigeria) cited in Patricia C. Gloster, "The Evolution of Maliki Law in Northern Nigeria 1930–1960," PhD diss., (Columbia University, 1987), 137.

Judicial Reorganization: Jurisdiction over Non-Muslims

Consistently with Lugardian design, non-Muslims in both the Muslim emirates and areas with mixed religious populations[73] were subjected to Islamic criminal law and the jurisdiction of Islamic courts far beyond precolonial practice.[74] Besides the pervasive Christian missionary criticism that this arrangement violated "freedom of conscience,"[75] the status of non-Islamic customary law was highly contentious in disputes between Muslims and non-Muslims. In one case, a Muslim was accused of shooting and killing a *Maguzawa* (non-Muslim) whom he accused of attempting to steal his livestock. The victim's family, billed to testify before the court, insisted that custom forbade being in the presence of the accused person unless he "held a sheep in front of himself" and the next of kin of the victim, blindfolded, stabbed at the sheep until the animal's blood ran over the accused. The defendant declined to submit to the ritual. Holding that the death penalty could not be imposed in the absence of a key witness at the trial, the alkali ordered that diya be paid to the family of the deceased. The family of the victim declined to accept diya because it was forbidden by custom.[76]

While the complexities introduced by non-Islamic customary law posed challenges, the most criticized disadvantage of non-Muslims in the Islamic courts was in the area of evidence. Oaths not sworn to on the Quran, though admissible, had a lesser evidentiary value. This meant that the testimony of non-Muslims had lesser weight before the court. In Kano Province, introduced reforms had enabled Christians to swear on

---

[73] This was in spite of the Native Court Proclamation of 1900s, provision that the law applicable by a native court was native customary law prevailing in its area of jurisdiction.

[74] Colonial rule expanded the territory over which Islamic institutions exercised governance powers. Further, the ad hoc systems in which non-Muslims were tried before judges of the same ethno-religious persuasion (and customary law), was abolished. In *Reg v. Ilorin*, the Supreme Court upheld this colonial-era subjection of non-Muslims to the jurisdiction of Islamic criminal law on the basis of the argument that criminal law is territorial. The court further pointed out that in Northern Nigeria, there is no personal law in the sense in which the concept exists in India. Anderson, "A Survey of Islamic Law in Nigeria," 83.

[75] Christian Missionary Society General Committee III's January 26, 1916 Memorandum in which it urged the colonial government to conduct judicial and civil administration according to custom rather than Islamic law. Resolution by Subcommittee on Difficulties with the Nigerian Government, January 26, 1916. CMS/B/OMS/A3/CL/1916, University of Birmingham Cadbury Special Collections (hereafter Cadbury Collections).

[76] J. N. D. Anderson, *The Reform of Criminal Law Introduced by the British*, File 365205 PPMS 60/1/12-17, SOAS Library Special Collections, London.

the Bible in English and permitted "pagans" to swear using a knife. However, evidentiary restrictions against non-Muslims continued to exist in many provinces. In reaction, it was not uncommon for non-Muslim parties to agree to settle disputes informally outside of the legal system when a matter had not come to the attention of the authorities.[77]

Substantive Reforms

In keeping with the Lugardian valorization of Islam, the creation of the Lugardian idea of a colonial Islamic law largely relied on the procedural reforms described above. Overt substantive reform was rare. The most significant was the state's confinement of Islamic law to the jurisprudence of the Maliki school.[78] As noted earlier, although Maliki jurisprudence had been predominant in the precolonial Islamic state, judges had the latitude to apply the jurisprudence of other schools.[79]

Further confining jurisprudence was the narrow conception of Maliki law. In keeping with Lugard's prescription in *Political Memoranda*, many colonial administrators conceived of Maliki law "as a settled code which you look up in Ruxton."[80] Commenting on this, a colonial administrator admitted that he, like other colonial administrators, had "little idea of the number of points on which two or more orthodox Maliki views were possible."[81]

This narrow conception of Islamic law was most significant in the Lugardian policy on *hadd* penalties. In spite of the colonial policy that penalties must not involve "mutilation, torture or grievous bodily harm,"[82] the Lugardians largely upheld the univocal conception of Islamic law as contained in Ruxton. Hence, the restriction hardly meant anything in practice. For instance,

---

[77] Schacht, "Investigation into the Application of Islamic Law in Nigeria."
[78] Native Courts Proclamation (No. 2/1900) (N.Ng.).
[79] Yusuf, *Nigerian Legal System*, 27.
[80] Fitz Herbert Ruxton, *Mâliki Law: Being a Summary from French Translations of the Mukhtasar of Sîdî Khalîl: With Notes and Bibliography* (Wesport: Hyperion Press, 1916). Other texts used were Al Khairuwani Abd Allah Ibn Abu Zayd, First Steps in Muslim Jurisprudence, Consisting of Excerpts from Bakurat-Al-Sa'd of Ibn Abu Zayd, trans. Alexander David Russell and Abdullah Al-Ma'mun Suhrawardy (London: Luzac&Co., 1906); Khalil Ibn Ishak, Précis de jurisprudence musulmane ou principes de législation musulmane civile et religieuse selon le rite malékite, trans. M. Perron (Paris: mprimerie Nationale, 1848–52); Khalil Ibn Ishaq Al Jundi, Hedaya, trans. Charles Hamilton (London: W. H. Allen, 1870); and Napoleon Seignette, Code Musalman par Khalil. (Paris: Challamel aîné, 1878.). See Lugard, *Political Memoranda*, 92.
[81] Letter from official (name illegible) to Anderson. Anderson Collection, PPMS 60/01/16, SOAS Library Special Collections, London.
[82] Native Courts Proclamation Northern Nigeria (No. 2/1900).

Lugard expressly acceded to beheading and drowning as permissible penalties dictated by Maliki law. Yet, such punishments had become rare in Northern Nigeria before the advent of British colonialism.[83] If Schacht's thesis that the state upheld theory rather than practice was true, it was with regard to this confinement of Islamic law to a narrow conception of Maliki jurisprudence. Yet, Lugardian policy did not fully validate Schacht's thesis even in this regard. Irrespective of both theoretical prescriptions as contained in Ruxton's Maliki law and the practice of the courts, Lugard abolished restitution as a principle of criminal jurisprudence[84]; as a penalty for crimes, it did not, in his view, conform with "good order."[85]

In spite of these reforms, official rhetoric continued to valorize Islamic law. For instance, the stated purpose of the Native Courts Proclamation (No. 5) of 1900 was "better regulation and control" rather than the creation "of native courts." In Lugard's 1914 Amalgamation Report, he asserted that "the courts were served by judges erudite in Moslem law and fearless in its impartial application."[86] This was the situation when a distinct sensibility began to emerge in the colonial administration.

CAMERON PHASE (1931–1958)

In spite of the resistance that Cameron faced from rank-and-file Lugardians, the governor's governance design became so deeply embedded that no less a jurist than Taslim Elias regards Cameron as an "architect of Nigeria's postcolonial legal system."[87] At the core of Cameron's opposition to Lugardian design were the extensive powers granted to emirs in particular, and to the executive/administrators (native chiefs and political officers) in general. Cameron's criticism, therefore, centered on the fusion of executive and judicial powers, the increased siyasa of emirs, and the absence of an appellate channel from the native courts to the superior courts. To be sure, Cameron did not favor a complete departure from Islamic law and institutions.

---

[83] Alan Milner, *African Penal Systems* (London: Routledge, 1969). See also Eltantawi, *Shariah on Trial*, 121.

[84] Section 13 of the Native Courts Ordinance. See the *Hassane of Fura* case and *Katsina NA v. Yakudi of Hababa and Dankoko of Renage* above.

[85] Lugard, *Political Memoranda*, 93–94.

[86] Fredrick John Dealtry Lugard, *Report by Sir F. D. Lugard on the Amalgamation of Northern and Southern Nigeria, and Administration, 1912–1919*. London: H. M. Stationery Office, 1920. This was in contradiction to his derision for the courts of Southern Nigeria where customary (non-Islamic) law applied in personal law matters and where English procedure was utilized.

[87] Taslim O. Elias, *The Nigerian Legal System* (London: Routledge, 1963).

Indeed, he was cautious about reform, save for situations where it was "so flagrantly and dreadfully barbarous, so contrary to accepted standards of modern civilization or detrimental to the interest of others."[88] Cameron also argued in his "Principles of Native Administration and Their Application" that the purpose of colonialism was to make a "good African."[89] To an extent, therefore, Cameron subscribed to Lugard's essentialist view of Africans. Yet he, unlike Lugard, held Islamic law to the "modern standard of civilization" and "interest of others" standard. This went beyond Lugard's "good order" exception. Further, because Cameron neither valorized emirs nor made a show of idealizing Islamic law as Lugard did, he was willing to pursue reform openly, mostly through the courts. Since he, like Lugard, continued to utilize native institutions for the colonial enterprise, he had to engage in a balancing act between the need to maintain the efficacy of native institutions and the thirst for reform.

Despite their differences, Cameron's and Lugard's ideas on native administration both concentrated power over Islamic law in the hands of the state. If, for Lugard, Shari'a governance was largely through a state-directed, expansive emir's siyasa, for Cameron, it took the form of direct intervention of the state through the judiciary. Both converted the hitherto siyasa shar'iyya into an expansive statist siyasa.

Judicial Reorganization: Siyasa Recalibration

Cameron's judicial reorganization was designed to reduce the siyasa of emirs and administrative officers and shift power to a new locus – judges of the English courts. He set about doing this by curtailing the judicial powers of emirs through two channels – the creation of an appellate bridge to high courts[90] and the reduction of the jurisdiction of emirs' courts. Yet, Cameron's plan to depart from the Lugardian practice of curtailing emirs' siyasa could not go too far because the entrenchment of the Lugardian practice hindered radical transformation.[91]

---

[88] Donald Cameron, "Native Administration in Tanganyika and Nigeria," *Journal of the Royal African Society* 36, no. 145 (1937): 3–29, 23.

[89] Donald Cameron, *The Principles of Native Administration and Their Application* (Lagos, Nigeria: Government Printer, 1934), 4–5.

[90] The 1933 Native Courts Ordinance.

[91] For instance, although Cameron's initial plan was to strip all emirs' courts of jurisdiction over capital offenses, he acknowledged that "it is quite impossible to withdraw this power which they have exercised the full consent of the Government for over thirty years" and opted to reduce the number of emirs' courts with jurisdiction over capital cases from 23 to 16. Brooke, *Report of the Native Courts (Northern Provinces) Commission*, 186.

If the state no longer relied on emirs' siyasa in service of its reform project, the emirs and Masu Sarauta continued to find use for siyasa – with or without the state's consent. Indeed, siyasa would come to be an infamous tool utilized by the emirs and Masu Sarauta for repressing political opponents, particularly with the inception of party politics in the postwar period. The Northern Elements Progressive Union (NEPU), which was the primary challenger to the Masu Sarauta's Northern People's Congress (NPC) and drew many members from the Masu Sarauta's age-long rival – the Tijaniyyah – became the prime target. For instance, in the infamous *Basa* case in Yobe Province, the accused person, a member of NEPU, was charged with slandering the emir of Fika and some other political elites. Both the Native Authority police who proffered the charge and the chief alkali before whom he was tried acted under the direction of the emir. Basa was subsequently sentenced to eighty lashes of flogging, a sentence reviewed and confirmed by the emir himself. This sentence was executed by a "giant" who beat Basa so severely that he became disabled.[92] On appeal, Basa's conviction was overturned on the grounds that the offense was unknown to Islamic law; the sentence was improperly administered; and the emir of Fika had given judgment in his own case. The court awarded Basa compensation[93] and recommended that the chief alkali be disciplined.

Embarrassed by the publicity generated by the case, the government wrote to the emir, reprimanding him and expressing its intention to dismiss the chief alkali. On his part, the chief alkali expressed his displeasure with the government's decision and insisted that his judgment was justifiable since it was directed by the emir.[94]

---

[92] Muslim Court of Appeal decision, CNC/0101 Misc. KAD MIN JUS, in Gloster, *The Evolution of Maliki Law*, 230. See also Henry Willink, ed., *Nigeria: Report of the Commission Appointed to Enquire into the Fears of Minorities and the Means of Allaying Them* (London: HM Stationery Office, 1958), 69. See below for the appellate court, the Muslim Court of Appeal.

[93] The compensation awarded was twenty pounds; Basa had sought two thousand pounds.

[94] Testifying before the Native Authority Committee, the chief alkali said he had apprised Ali Basa of the alternative punishment (going around the town proclaiming that he lied against four important people), and Basa had chosen the lashing penalty. He had also explained to Basa the manner of execution of the sentence – that the person administering the penalty "would hold a tin under his arm as he administered the blows on Basa's back while he was sitting down." The tool to be used would be "a single thonged whip." The chief alkali further testified that he had warned the person administering the sentence to "avoid severe beating." See also Willink, *Nigeria: Report of the Commission*.

Colonial administrators could not always decisively reprimand the tendency of emirs to overreach. For instance, when the emir of Kano convicted five political opponents of "holding a political meeting without a permit," the resident, R. E. Gresswell, criticized the emir, pointing out that he had no power, save for offenses with fixed penalties, to award more than twelve strokes on a single person at a trial. He also informed the emir that he was at a risk of being ordered to pay damages if the defendants appealed. In response, the emir insisted that he had acted within his authority, citing *Tabsirat al-Hukam*, a Maliki text.[95]

Judicial Reorganization: Jurisdiction over Non-Muslims

Cameron moved to curtail the jurisdiction of emirs and alkalai courts over non-Muslims. Although this might have been partly due to his sympathy for Christian missionaries who vocally criticized the subjection of Christians to Islamic courts, the immediate catalyst was the *Eluaka* case. Victor Eluaka, a Christian in Plateau Province, had been whipped in execution of the judgment of an alkali court for refusal to pay land tax.[96] The case generated furor in missionary circles.[97] At the urging of the Church of England's Church Missionary Society, the Colonial Office waded into the matter. In response to Secretary of State Cunliffe-Lister's request for information, Cameron stressed that the flogging had been carried out without his knowledge or permission and assured the secretary that such would not happen again.[98] Cameron responded to the criticism generated by

---

[95] KSHCB, "Native Courts Policy and Instructions," June 29, 1956, in Jonathan Reynolds, *The Time of Politics (Zamanin Siyasa): Islam and the Politics of Legitimacy in Northern Nigeria, 1950–1966* (San Francisco: International Scholars Publications, 1998), 93.

[96] Eluaka had failed to pay a tax levied on his ownership of two plots of land in Bukuru, Plateau Province, a Type II area. Eluaka informed the native chief that he could not afford to pay the tax. Alongside three Muslim natives, he was charged to an alkali court. The alkali reported that during the proceedings, the four defendants did not "seem to take the alkali's warnings seriously," whereupon he (the alkali) issued a final warning: "If the four of them did not pay their taxes in six hours, he would have them arrested and publicly flogged." When they did not comply with the order, the four defendants were arrested, hauled to a public square, and flogged. Within a few hours, they paid their taxes in full. Public Record Office File, CO 583/190/1130 (1933), 2 in Gloster, "The Evolution of Maliki Law."

[97] See, for instance, "The Bukuru Tax Flogging Case," a June 24, 1933 account of *West Africa Magazine*.

[98] Not all administrators blamed the alkali. For instance, the acting secretary of the northern provinces, H. B. James, observed that the alkali had considered

the *Eluaka* case as well as the broader criticism on the situation of non-Muslims in alkalai courts by the creation of mixed courts, which applied the customary law of the parties to the dispute. They were presided over by appointees of emirs. Because mixed courts did not exist in every province and even where they did, the Native Authority police could still charge non-Muslims before Islamic courts, many non-Muslims continued to be subject to the jurisdiction of emirs and alkalai courts.[99]

Judicial Reforms

The legislation that embodied Cameron's reform of the judiciary was the 1933 Native Courts Ordinance. This legislation recalibrated the grades of courts.[100] The jurisdiction of the chief alkali was now as wide as that of the emir. However, emirs now exercised judicial powers infrequently.[101] At the same time, Cameron vastly curtailed the judicial powers of the colonial administrators.[102]

The most significant reform heralded by the 1933 Ordinance was its unification of the appellate system. As in the Lugardian phase, two sets of courts existed: the Islamic courts and the "superior" English-style courts. However, in a departure from the Lugardian design, there now existed a unified system of appeals; matters from

---

the sentence justifiable according to *al-Mukhtasar*, a Maliki text. Confidential Memorandum signed by H. B. James, Acting Secretary of Northern Provinces, No. 19062/26, April 4, 1933, Public Record Office File, CO 583/190/1130 (1933), 13.

[99] See *Effiong Ekpo v. Kano N.A* (1957) N.R.N.L.R 129 in which the High Court of Northern Nigeria held that contrary to the appellant's assertion that the emirs' court had no jurisdiction over non-Muslims, the emirs' court had jurisdiction to apply Islamic law "over all persons who are within the Native authority's jurisdiction and whose general mode of life while there is that of the general native community," 130. A latter Ordinance would seek to eliminate some evidentiary disabilities facing these persons before the Islamic courts. Ordinance No. 22 of 1958 mandated court officials to ask the accused person: "What is your religion?" as section 15A (1) provided. The response to this question would then determine what form of oath the accused person would take among other variations.

[100] Ordinances 44, 45, and 46 (1933).

[101] They usually referred matters back to the chief alkali except in land matters or in cases where the "Chief Alkali committed a flagrant crime" or if the case concerned a "Native Administration executive matter of a serious character" and needed attention.

[102] Political officers continued to exercise limited judicial power over certain appeals.

the Islamic courts were appealable to the superior courts – the High Court, the Supreme Court, and ultimately to the West African Court of Appeal.[103]

Although Islamic courts were now mandated to comply with the provisions of the Criminal Code, they continued to decide criminal matters according to Maliki jurisprudence and the demands of the emir's siyasa. Initially, the practice of the superior courts was to apply Maliki law (as interpreted by the Islamic courts) in determining appeals, although this contravened section 4 of the Criminal Code, which declared the code supreme in cases of discrepancies with native law.

This deferential attitude to the Islamic courts would not last. Cameron's reforms had not only empowered the judiciary, it also coincided with a change in its composition. The judges of the Lugardian era, although typically barristers-at-law, had usually started their careers in administrative positions and were thus more acquainted with native institutions. The judges of the Cameron years were different. According to the account of a prominent Lugardian, these Cameron-era judges not only lacked administrative experience in Northern Nigeria, they also "felt themselves out of sympathy with the people and their surroundings. They missed the company of fellow members of their own profession in this predominantly Muslim world and they disliked the relative austerity of living conditions."[104] By the years leading up to 1950, which culminated with the end of the Second World War, the new judges had abandoned the earlier posture of deference. The earliest sign of this shift was Justice Ames' dissent in *Magudama v. Bornu NA* where he stated:

---

[103] The significance of the reform was further heightened by the fact that lawyers were permitted to practice in these high courts though they remained barred from the Islamic courts. However, the right to appeal did not exist in some cases. In those cases, appeals remained subject to the district officer. Further, no appeals lay in personal law and family status cases; that is, matters related to "marriage, family status, and guardianship of children, inheritance, testamentary disposition or the administration of an estate." Cameron's reforms eliminated the provincial courts and replaced these with high courts. Further appeals lay to the Supreme Court (now united for the entirety of Nigeria), and then to the West African Court of Appeal.

[104] Bryan Sharwood Smith, Lieutenant-Governor, Northern Nigeria (1954–1957). Bryan Sharwood-Smith, *But Always as Friends: Northern Nigeria and the Cameroons, 1921–1957* (London: Allen and Unwin, 1969), 282.

Can it be the law of this large British protectorate that in any part of it, a man can be sentenced to death for what is shown by the evidence to be at most manslaughter and not murder? Mohammedan law has no privileged position. It prevails where it does prevail because it is the local law and custom.[105]

Ames' critique went beyond the refusal by the alkali court to comply with the 1933 Ordinance. It was a critique of what the superior court judges perceived to be an undue preference for Islamic law over other Indigenous legal systems.

One year later, in *Tsofo Gubba v. Gwandu NA*, the entire court adopted Ames' position. Chief Justice Verity declared: "where a native court exercises its jurisdiction to [sic] an act which constitutes an offence against the Criminal Code, it is required to exercise that jurisdiction in a manner ... in accordance with the provisions of the code."[106] Gubba had discovered the victim having intercourse with his wife and killed the victim in the ensuing fight. The alkali court convicted Gubba of homicide and sentenced him to death. The West African Court of Appeal overturned the conviction, holding that the facts of the case established the defense of provocation, a defense unrecognized under Islamic law.[107]

Emirs, alkalai, and scholars received the *Gubba* decision with shock. Although Cameron's departure from Lugardian practice had put them on notice, the initial deferential attitude of the superior court judges did not prepare them for the *Gubba* reversal. With this decision, the emirs concluded that the colonial government had reneged on the guarantee of noninterference. P. H. G. Scott records

---

[105] Anderson, *Islamic Law in Africa* citing *Magudama v. Bornu NA*, 1946 decision of the West African Court of Appeal, unreported.

[106] (1947) WACA, vol. 12. Prior to the openly confrontational approach adopted by the WACA in *Gubba*, Lugardian-minded administrators tended to adopt the approach of exercising supervisory jurisdiction to substitute alkalai and emir court decisions in cases where these administrators considered provocation to be a mitigating factor. See, for instance, *Kano N. A v. Isau Bansaki*, in which the criminal defendant killed the victim on the basis that the latter seduced his (traveling) son's wife. Kano Prof. File 2157. See further *Kano N. A v. Machido Dan Bakar Bibu and Dubo Dan Yammza and Dambatta* 1936 in Kano Prof. File No. 1808. NA Nigeria.

[107] Maliki jurisprudence makes no distinction between murder and manslaughter in terms of criminal penalty. However, whether a homicide is intentional or not makes a difference in the amount of blood money that would be levied if the family of the deceased is willing to accept diya in lieu of executing the penalty.

the story of the emir of Katsina Province who refused to try homicide cases in his own court due to the fear that the Supreme Court would overturn his decisions.[108] Instead, he transferred those cases to the High Court without acting on them. Several emirs and alkalai had a similar inclination.[109] This inclination to abstain from participating in the now open-reform enterprise was authorized by a pronouncement of three eminent jurists of the Kano Law School, issued nearly a decade before *Gubba*:

> The Shari'a is all sufficient and unchangeable. If after diligent search, no written guidance is found, judgment may be given in the spirit of the Law, but where the Quran prescribes a judgment, no other may be given ... Nevertheless, where for one cause or another, the whole government is not to be bounded by the Scriptures, it is better that those judges whose authority is founded upon the Shari'a should touch nothing in which the Shari'a may not be fulfilled. In Nigeria today, the alkalai profess that their authority is from the Shari'a, yet in many of their judgments they may not in certain matters which are brought before them pronounce the judgments prescribed by the Qur'an.[110]

The outrage was not merely a reaction to colonial interference in native courts, it was also rooted in the perception of Northern Nigerian political and judicial elites that English judges and Southern Nigerian lawyers were colluding to erode Islamic law and undermine their institutions. Even before the *Gubba* decision, emirs and alkalai with their Lugardian sympathizers already viewed the new class of judges with distrust. Not only did these judges openly disdain the ways of the North, they were also fastidious churchgoers. To make matters worse, they identified as professional peers of the mission-educated Christian barristers of Southern Nigerian origin. At this time, the Muslim areas of the North had not yet produced any native trained in English law. The emirs and alkalai were therefore deeply suspicious that the English

---

[108] Scott, *A Survey of Islamic Law in Northern Nigeria*.

[109] Some emirs and alkalai interviewed by Schacht in his 1950 study stated that since the government had chosen to contravene the guarantee of noninterference, it was preferable to abstain from exercising jurisdiction rather than applying "non-Islamic" law or being overturned on appeal. Stripping themselves of jurisdiction would take the matter "out of their conscience." Schacht, "Investigation into the Application of Islamic Law in Nigeria," 15.

[110] Memorandum by Annur Tingary, Bashir El Rayah, and Mohammed Swar El Dahab, "Extension of Jurisdiction of Native Courts," Kano Prof. File #2182, 41–43. NA Nigeria.

judges and the Christian Southern Nigerian barristers were colluding to erode the British government's guarantee of noninterference.[111]

The first legislative response to the protests that greeted the *Gubba* decision was the Native Courts Ordinance, No. 36 of 1948, which empowered the Islamic courts to try offenses in accordance with Islamic law even where such also constituted an offense under a statute. However, an appellate court was granted the discretion to choose any course available, even if the original decision was correct under Islamic law. Further, decisions in homicide cases were subject to review by a high court judge. Because the emirs and alkalai were not appeased by the 1948 Ordinance,[112] a latter ordinance enacted in 1951 sought to reassure them by abolishing the power of review of the High Court. However, the 1951 Ordinance also limited the punishment that native courts could impose. In practice, alkalai did not comply with these limits.

On their part, the judges of the superior courts were not induced by the post-*Gubba* legislation to turn back from their activist course. In *Fagoji v. Kano NA*,[113] the Supreme Court overturned the decision of the emir's court, holding that, although the 1948 Ordinance granted emirs' courts a "dispensation" from the obligation to try offenses under the Criminal Code, the High Court was bound by the code when considering appeals. The court further held that although the appellant had been properly convicted of homicide and sentenced to death under Maliki law, the facts of the case amounted to manslaughter under the code and did not warrant the death penalty. In *Maizabo v. NA*,[114] the Supreme Court went further by not only asserting appellate supremacy and the duty of appellate courts to comply with the code, but also by holding that the Islamic courts were obliged to comply with it.

---

[111] Sharwood-Smith, *But Always as Friends*, 282–284.

[112] The Acting Resident of Sokoto, A. T. Weatherhead, spoke with the sultan and his council about the 1948 Ordinance reforms. Relaying the discussion to Justice Hubbard, Weatherhead stated that the sultan and his council resented the restriction of their jurisdiction and the complexity introduced by the 1948 Ordinance. "The Sultan and his Council could not understand the provision that allowed a man who had confessed to murder in a Muslim court to plead 'not guilty' in the Supreme Court." Also, they neither understood nor accepted the substitution of the conviction of murder for manslaughter and the mitigation of the death sentence in cases where the "agnates of the deceased had demanded retaliation after the killing had been proved." Weatherhead to Justice Hubbard, March 6, 1950. SOK PROF 6887/10; Gloster, "The Evolution of Maliki Law," 120.

[113] *Fagoji v. Kano NA* (1957) NRNLR. 57 (S.C.).

[114] *Maizabo v. NA* (1957) NRNLR. 133 (S.C.).

Faced with the new activism of the superior courts and the measured resistance of emirs and alkalai, the colonial government assumed a mediating posture. Within three years of the *Gubba* decision, the administration commissioned three legal experts to conduct surveys on Islamic law. The first of these experts, Neville John Brooke, the chief justice of Nigeria, was to chair a commission charged with inquiring into native courts and making recommendations for reform. Although the Brooke Commission pointed out that Lugard's 1903 guarantee was not "a guarantee of immutability in the law," and predicted that Islamic criminal law in Northern Nigeria was bound to give way to codes of modern criminal law as "found elsewhere in Moslem countries," it recommended the retention of "Islamic criminal law" and Islamic courts.[115]

The other two experts, Joseph Schacht and J. N. D. Anderson, were mandated to situate their findings and recommendations within their own scholarly knowledge of Islamic law and Islamic societies. On his part, Schacht concluded that siyasa had been curtailed and this had frozen Islamic law theory. His core recommendation was that the state revive siyasa as a tool of reform while curtailing the jurisdiction of Islamic courts over non-Muslims and homicide matters.

Although Anderson's mandate was in the context of a wider survey of Islamic law throughout British African territories, his report would have the most far-reaching impact on Northern Nigerian colonial policy. Anderson was commissioned by a Colonial Office that had grown increasingly hostile to indirect rule especially in the "ultra-indirect rule" form it had come to take in Northern Nigeria.[116] His report validated senior colonial administrators' criticism of the Lugardian foundations of the colonial state.

Influenced by Sir Henry Maine (key thinker on the legal and administrative design of indirect rule),[117] Anderson considered Islamic criminal law through the lens of the "evolutionary-progressive" paradigm.[118]

---

[115] Brooke, *Report of the Native Courts (Northern Provinces) Commission*, 185. The Commission recommended that future alkalai be trained in customary law and apply it in matters involving non-Muslims. It also proposed the establishment of a Muslim Court of Appeal (created in 1956: Moslem Court of Appeal Law, No. 10, 1956). The emirs and alkalai remained unappeased because this court's decisions were appealable to the High Court.

[116] Margery Perham, "Preface to Lugard" in Lugard, *The Dual Mandate*, xl.

[117] Karuna Mantena, *Alibis of Empire: Henry Maine and the Ends of Liberal Imperialism* (Princeton, NJ: Princeton University Press, 2010), 177.

[118] John Anderson, "Homicide in Islamic Law," *Bulletin of the School of Oriental and African Studies* 13, no. 4 (1951): 811–812.

Although he considered its evolution salutary, he opined that Islamic criminal law had not evolved sufficiently to be adequate for twentieth-century Northern Nigeria. In his view, this inadequacy was marked by the inequality of treatment based, among other reasons, on religious difference.[119] Anderson argued that those features made Islamic criminal law unsuitable for a "contemporary state with a mixed-religious population such as future Nigeria."[120] He therefore called for immediate reform. As a "conservative evangelical" himself, Anderson was not immune from the advocacy of Christian missionaries for reform of the colonial Islamic legal system in Northern Nigeria.[121]

Citing the experience of other Muslim countries and arguing that "no realist would maintain that the Shari'a provides any adequate basis for criminal law in a modern state of mixed religious loyalties and progressive intentions,"[122] Anderson recommended stripping Islamic courts of jurisdiction and replacing Islamic criminal law with a code of English criminal law. He suggested two related vehicles through which this reform could be actualized. The first was an expanded emirs' siyasa, hints of which he already discerned in the workings of the state. Beyond the discretionary power of the ruler, however, Anderson argued that siyasa ought to encompass "a wider application of the principle that the Ruler may prescribe, in any point on which Muslim jurists have differed, which of the variant views is to be applied by the Courts."[123] In his view, this had been the basis of reform in Egypt and Middle Eastern countries.[124] Anderson therefore suggested a second vehicle of reform which he favored over the first: to convene a "conference of leading jurists to study the points concerning which uniformity or reform was desirable and to agree as to the rule which in each case is preferable, and then for instruction to be issued by appropriate authority that these decisions should be applied by the Courts."[125] While the first vehicle was rooted in the Lugardian idea of siyasa, the second involved the

---

[119] Ibid., 815.
[120] Todd Thompson, *Norman Anderson and the Christian Mission to Modernize Islam* (New York: Oxford University Press, 2018), 167, citing John Anderson's letter to Neville Brooke on April 6, 1951.
[121] Ibid.
[122] John Anderson to Neville Brooke on April 6, 1951, in Thompson, *Norman Anderson*, 168.
[123] John Anderson, "Islamic Law in African Colonies," Corona, the Journal of His Majesty's Colonial Service 3 (1951): 265.
[124] Ibid.
[125] Ibid.

exercise of siyasa by the state. In Northern Nigeria, the "appropriate authority" referred to by Anderson was the Legislative Council, which was comprised of not only colonial administrators, but also the class of elites appointed/elected under the new postwar party politics system yet still closely linked to the Masu Sarauta. As Anderson and certain officers in the Colonial Office's Africa Department[126] would note in a 1957 dispatch, "the difference therefore between the way in which criminal justice is administered in Northern Nigeria and other Muslim countries is not so much a matter of fundamental principle as of the way in which the siyasa jurisdiction of the state is exercised."[127] Anderson proposed that Northern Nigeria toe the path of these Muslim states. That proposal would ultimately form the basis of a reform exercise on the eve of Independence formally supplanting Islamic law with an English code in the domain of criminal law.

The following section of the book will dive into the making of the 1958 Penal Code as part of a broader consideration of the constitutional settlement of the religion question in the era of decolonization. As we will come to see, the 1958 Penal Code reform was consequential to the legal and political framework that constituted Independence. However, that reform was hardly the radical disjuncture from earlier colonial practice Anderson regarded it as, although Anderson's understanding of the reforms continues to dominate scholarly narratives.[128] In fact, viewed from the vantage of the series of reform processes that began since 1903, the adoption of the 1958 Penal Code was the culmination of the making of a British Islamic law rather than a radical transformation. Regardless of Lugard's guarantee of noninterference, colonial rule set in form a series of transformation that altered the essence of Islamic law, primarily through the means of siyasa. The freeing of siyasa from the constitutional boundaries set by the Shari'a – as espoused in jurists' fiqh – transformed Islamic law. This process was far from uniform across time; for Lugardians, the governance of Shari'a

---

[126] Robert Wray and Maurice Smith. Thompson, *Norman Anderson*, 180.

[127] "Draft Confidential Dispatch to the Governor Northern region, Nigeria, for Clearance SECRET AND PERSONAL by the Governor Before Issue," August 1957, London Private Collection of Ian Edge, Anderson papers cited in Thompson, *Norman Anderson*, 180.

[128] See Philip Ostien, ed., *Sharia Implementation in Northern Nigeria 1999–2006: A Sourcebook*, vol. 2 (Ibadan, Nigeria: Spectrum Books, 2007); Sam Scruton Richardson, *No Weariness: The Memoir of a Generalist in Public Services in Four Continents* (Wiltshire, UK: Malt House Publishing, 2001).

was through the vehicle of the expanded siyasa of their emir allies. For Cameron and those administrative and judicial officials who espoused his contempt for "native" institutions, governance of the Shariʿa shifted to administrators and judges. Since the state continued to pay lip service to indirect rule through Islamic institutions in those years, this meant not a displacement of siyasa, but rather a shift in its locus to the state. With that shift, the state was able to invoke Islamic law as the basis of governance while asserting an ever-expanding authority over its content and transforming its workings. In this way, imperial secularism enabled the state to claim fidelity to Islamic law and institutions while simultaneously authorizing the state's assertion of its separation from the religious institutions it instrumentalized for governance.

CONCLUSION

Departing from the received wisdom that secular governmentality hinges on the state's separation from religion,[129] a wave of critical scholarship posits that secularism entails the state's governance of, and hence, de facto entanglement with religion.[130] Led by Talal Asad's *Formations of the Secular*, these accounts disturb the religious-secular binary at the heart of separationist notions of secularism by suggesting that secular governmentality entails the state's construction and delineation of the categories of "religious" and "secular." Regardless of this de facto entanglement, however, states' *assertion* of a separation from religion is an ineluctable feature of modernity. These two manifestations of secularism – the assertion of separation of religion and the secular, and the reality of their entanglement – are not at odds as they might first appear. Indeed, it is the state, or more precisely, the actors who speak in its name, that construct the mutual opposition of the

---

[129] John Rawls, *Political Liberalism* (New York: Columbia University Press, 2005); Charles Taylor, "Modes of Secularism," in *Secularism and Its Critics*, ed. Rajeev Bhargava (New York: Oxford University Press, 1999), 31–53; Ackerman, *Social Justice in a Liberal State*; José Casanova, *Public Religions in the Modern World* (Chicago: University of Chicago Press, 2011).

[130] Asad, *Formations of the Secular*; Mahmood, *Religious Difference in a Secular Age*; Tamir Moustafa, *Constituting Religion: Islam, Liberal Rights, and the Malaysian State* (Cambridge: Cambridge University Press, 2018); Agrama, "Secularism"; Salomon, *For Love of the Prophet*; and Marc Galanter, "Secularism, East and West," *Comparative Studies in Society and History* 7, no. 2 (1965): 133–159.

sacred and the secular while simultaneously regulating the content of both in ways that inevitably defy the specious boundary between them.

Taking seriously the state's claim of its separation from religion even while it co-opted Islamic law and institutions allows one to discern the process through which the colonial state governed Islamic law. In co-opting "Islamic" institutions for the colonial enterprise, the state was not merely entrenching majoritarian norms and institutions. Beyond this, the state was remaking Islamic law and institutions in order to make them amenable to the colonial enterprise.[131] Emerging from a premise asserting religious-secular separation, this remaking of Islamic law took the form of the unprecedented expansion of the siyasa, first of the emirs, and eventually, its direct appropriation by the central state apparatus. From serving the Shariʻa alongside fiqh, siyasa came to dominate the field, casting a shadow over fiqh. This process not only altered the content of Islamic law, it also altered the relationship between Islamic law and the state, and reconfigured the roles of emirs, alkalai, and English jurists. It was in this way that imperial secular governmentality subverted the constitutional foundations of precolonial Islamic law.

---

[131] Catherine Adcock, *The Limits of Tolerance: Indian Secularism and the Politics of Religious Freedom* (Oxford: Oxford University Press, 2013), 25.

PART II

CONSTITUTING DIFFERENCE

CHAPTER THREE

THE CONSTRUCTION OF MINORITIES
Late Imperial Secularity and the Constitutional Politics of Decolonization

The decade following the *Gubba* case and the court's condemnation of Lugardian deference to Muslim elites witnessed a flurry of activity toward Nigeria's independence from the British Empire. Some of the momentum came from forces outside the colony: a wave of decolonization swept across the world in the years following the Second World War.[1] Beyond the broader international context, political changes within Britain began to set the tone, first for measured autonomy, and eventually, for independence of colonial territories. In 1946, the Labor Party came into power in Britain and Sir Arthur Creech Jones, an avid promoter of the idea of self-government for the colonies, was appointed secretary of state for the colonies.[2] That same year, the first step toward self-government was taken in the colony through the enactment of the Nigeria (Legislative) Order in Council, a constitution whose declared goal was "giving more room to greater participation of Nigerians in the administration of their country."[3] The constitutional politics of independence would

---

[1] See John Charles Hatch, *Africa: The Rebirth of Self-Rule* (Oxford: Oxford University Press, 1967); William Roger Louis, *The Transfer of Power in Africa: Decolonization, 1940–1960* (New Haven, CT: Yale University Press, 1982); John D. Hargreaves, *Decolonization in Africa* (London: Routledge, 2014); and Rudolf von Albertini, *Decolonization: The Administration and Future of the Colonies, 1919–1960* (Garden City, NY: Doubleday, 1971).

[2] See Anthony H. M. Kirk-Greene, *Principles of Native Administration in Nigeria* (London: Oxford University Press, 1965), 28.

[3] The Nigeria (Legislative Council) Order in Council 1946 was popularly referred to as the Richards Constitution after the name of the colonial governor at the time, Sir Arthur Richards.

unfold over the next fourteen years. Independence struggles featured actors from Northern, Western, and Eastern Nigeria and traversed a variety of questions. Yet, the pivotal issue was that of religion's place in state and society, and Northern Nigeria was at the center of the legal and political processes that sought to tackle that question.[4] Together, the three chapters in this section of the book ask: what was the consequence of imperial secular governmentality and the struggles it triggered for the Independence deal? Ultimately, the Independence deal on the thorny question of religion governance centered on three elements: the making of religious minorities, the constitutionalization of the human right to religious liberty, and the abolition of Islamic law from public law through excising Islamic criminal jurisprudence. This chapter unveils the legal politics of the construction of "religious minorities."

The religious minorities identity was the product of self-determination advocacy in the late colonial state. Advocacy to eliminate colonial restrictions on proselytization and to actualize the missionary dream of winning souls began to take the form of calls for self-determination in the decade leading to Independence. The call for self-determination was not unrelated to earlier missionary arguments for religious freedom and state separation from Islam; since the early days of colonial rule, missionaries had begun to seek autonomy for Indigenous faith populations from Muslim colonial intermediaries. It was, however, only in the decade leading to Nigeria's Independence in 1960 that those earlier calls for autonomy morphed into advocacy for self-determination through the creation of a state. Although the state-creation demand ultimately failed, the "group self" making the demand on the colonial state survived, coming to be a powerful force in decolonization struggles. That "self" was constructed and championed by Protestant missionaries and native converts. Nevertheless, the identity could not hinge exclusively on Protestantism; since Christians remained a "sprinkling" of the total population at 2.7 percent,[5] a state-creation demand

---

[4] As the Nigerian Working Group, a cohort of Colonial Office administrators tasked with crafting Nigeria's Independence Constitution, noted in an April 16, 1958 meeting, "most of our anxieties concern the Northern region"; yet the group pointed out that it was "desirable that the North did not feel it was being specially singled out for treatment." Nigeria Working Group, Minutes of Meeting. CO 554/1534. National Archives United Kingdom (hereafter NA, UK).

[5] See Kenneth Grubb, "London Conference Faces Problems," *The Church of England Newspaper*, May 31, 1957. Nigeria, Federal Census Office, Population Census of the Northern Region of Nigeria, 1952-3 (Lagos: Census Superintendent 1953).

without claim to legitimacy among adherents of Indigenous religions was bound to fail. To lay claim to representing other religious groups, Protestant advocates defined the "self" by reference to its overarching non-Muslim identity. The religious minorities identity was the outcome of that project.

Protestant advocates constructed the religious minorities identity to resist the colonial governance of religion; paradoxically, however, the making of that identity affirmed the classifications on which colonial governance was based. As noted in Part I, colonial indirect rule was predicated on the simplistic Muslim versus non-Muslim distinction. The unification of the diverse non-Muslim population into a single bloc was instrumental to the colonial policy of governing through "Islamic" institutions, a policy sharply criticized by missionaries as "Muslim sub-imperialism." By the last decade of colonial rule, however, as the country marched toward attaining formal autonomy from the British Empire, missionaries and converts to Christianity turned from critiquing the binarization to co-opting it for self-determination advocacy. By telling a story of the oppression of Christians and diverse Indigenous religious persuasions based solely on their status as non-Muslims, these Protestant advocates constructed an identity whose essence lay in its contrast to the Muslim identity. To capture the historical experience of these non-Muslim groups, the relations of power from which that experience emerged, and most importantly, to legitimate the self-determination being demanded of the state, Protestant advocates embraced the non-Muslim identity, wielding it to make claims on the colonial state. The self-determination project, therefore, came to assume the colonial binary and ultimately the colonial religion governance technique it originally envisioned itself as resisting.

The construction of minorities has received attention, including in colonial contexts. In *Define and Rule*, a seminal work on the subject, Mahmood Mamdani traces the genealogy of the colonial state's creation of the native as a political identity.[6] Mamdani's account foregrounds the invention of tribal and ethnic identities and of hierarchies in the colonial ideology of nativism. This book, however, suggests that the

---

[6] Mahmood Mamdani, *Define and Rule: Native as Political Identity* (Cambridge: Harvard University Press, 2012). See also Mahmood Mamdani, *Neither Settler nor Native: The Making and Unmaking of Permanent Minorities* (Cambridge, MA: Harvard University Press, 2020); Mahmood Mamdani, *Citizen and Subject: Contemporary Africa and the Legacy of Late Colonialism* (Princeton, NJ: Princeton University Press, 2018).

colonial state's making and unmaking of difference hinged on a religious governance agenda. With its departure from the civilizing-missionizing project following the Indian Revolt, empire turned to a secular governmentality that insisted on its separation from religion even as the design of indirect rule necessitated the colonial state's entanglement with religion. The construction of forms of religious difference and sameness, and the hierarchization of identities that arose from imperial secular governmentality, were at the heart of colonial governance in Northern Nigeria, precipitating colonial and decolonial struggles. This account therefore centers the processes of the construction of religious differentiation – and homogenization – in understanding colonial domination and the forms of resistance it predetermined and thwarted.

Rather than securing emancipation for the subjects on behalf of whom it claimed to act, the self-determination project bolstered the technique of imperial secular governmentality. In the bid to perform the non-Muslim identity that could claim self-determination, the construction of religious minorities reinforced the power of the colonial state to govern religious difference. Such projects, Saba Mahmood argues, bolster the power of the state to "serve as the arbiter of religious difference" as well as "to remake and regulate religious life while proclaiming its sanctity."[7] As with the state's creation of the Muslim and non-Muslim identity dichotomy, the religious minorities identity was not based on a predetermined demographic group. Rather, it produced "the kinds of subjects who [could] speak in its name," in the process, "transforming how religious differences [were] lived, recognized and contested."[8] Protestant advocates' making of the Muslim–non-Muslim identity went beyond the entrenchment of the colonial Muslim–non-Muslim distinction. Its aggregation of non-Muslims under the umbrella of a Protestant-led group of religious minorities entailed substantively repackaging and ultimately erasing the claims of the Indigenous religious groups it purported to represent. Moreover, the framing of the malady of the colonial circumstance as a struggle between Muslim sub-imperialists and non-Muslim minorities effectively excluded intra-Muslim minorities, who came to be labeled as a "dissident sect" rather than being recognized as religious minorities. The consequence of that designation was the inability to bring claims (self-determination

---

[7] Saba Mahmood, *Religious Difference in a Secular Age: A Minority Report* (Princeton, NJ: Princeton University Press, 2015), 32.
[8] Ibid., 33.

or otherwise) before colonial institutions, particularly the Sir Henry Willink-chaired Minorities Commission established to examine claims of marginalized groups in the colonial state. In seeking to produce the subject worthy of seeking redress, Protestant advocates, therefore, perpetuated the colonial state's exclusion, and elision of the exclusion, of Muslim minorities. If their self-determination project was intended to emancipate certain subjects, it inadvertently opened new doors to inequality.

The story that follows therefore grapples with the self-determination project, foregrounding its making of the religious minority identity, and interrogating the ways that project cemented the colonial legacy of defining, deepening, and hierarchizing religious difference.

RELIGION DIFFERENTIATION AND NATIONALIST POLITICS IN THE LATE COLONIAL YEARS

The politics of religious differentiation was central to Independence constitutional struggles. That contestation was already apparent with the first gesture of the colonial state toward self-government – the 1946 Constitution. The 1946 Constitution promised to foster representative politics; however, it preserved the old power order by granting the Masu Sarauta dominance in the bicameral legislature it created. One legislative chamber, the House of Chiefs, was comprised of emirs, Muslim chiefs administering mixed religious (Type II) areas, and elites administering the Indigenous religious (Type III) areas.[9] Further, emirs exercised influence over several appointments to the second legislative chamber, the House of Assembly, which was constituted by the colonial governor's designates.

Despite its perpetuation of the old relations of power, the 1946 Constitution nevertheless granted a new elite class separate from the colonial remnants of the precolonial aristocracy measured access to government positions. Several of these new elites were the product of missionary education, and an overwhelming majority were Christian. Chapter 1 has shown how the regime of restrictions on missionaries in Muslim (Type I) areas and parts of mixed religious

---

[9] Section 33(2) Richards Constitution. While all "first class chiefs," a group that was comprised exclusively of emirs, had seats in the House of Chiefs, not less than ten "second class chiefs" could be selected to serve in the House. These second-class chiefs were drawn from Type II and III areas. The governor had the prerogative to set the number of seats, and to stipulate the procedure for selecting the chiefs.

(Type II) areas severely restricted access to mission education. The few colonial government-owned schools in operation catered to Masu Sarauta allies, depriving most *talakawa* (commoners) of Western education.[10] On the other hand, the general population in Type III areas and in some non-Muslim parts of Type II areas had access to missionary education. Since missionary education tended to go hand in hand with proselytizing, it was commonplace for these mission-school attendees to convert.[11] The majority of Western-educated Northern Nigerians were therefore invariably Christian (Protestant) and lived in Type III areas and non-Muslim regions of Type II areas.[12] Several of these Christian elites became active in nationalist politics, and it was to that group that the governor turned to appoint representatives to occupy the six House of Assembly seats reserved for non-Muslims.[13] With this pegging of House of Assembly appointments to the Muslim versus non-Muslim colonial distinction, the House of Assembly became the site of conflict between the Masu Sarauta class and emerging Christian elites.

Tensions reached a boiling point in 1949 when a Muslim member of the assembly sponsored a bill to further tighten preexisting restrictions on missionary activity, an issue that remained the crux of Protestant critique of the colonial arrangement. The 1949 bill, which came on the heels of the widely publicized expulsion of missions from China, heightened Christian anxieties. The eventual defeat of the bill did not placate Protestants, and legislative proceedings came to be so tinged with religious rancor and bitterness that Sir Rex Niven, the colonial officer presiding over the House of Assembly, reported that "the most difficult part of his job had been to prevent the discussion of religion in

---

[10] This was the case even though much of the Masu Sarauta initially avoided enrolling their own wards in government schools. See Chapter 2. Billy J. Dudley, *Parties and Politics in Northern Nigeria* (London: Routledge, 2013).

[11] On the effect of missionary education on the formation of the Christian nationalist identity in Northern Nigeria, see Moses Ochonu, *Colonialism by Proxy: Hausa Imperial Agents and Middle Belt Consciousness in Nigeria* (Bloomington, IN: Indiana University Press, 2014); Yusufu Turaki, *The British Colonial Legacy in Northern Nigeria: A Social Ethical Analysis of the Colonial and Post-colonial Society and Politics in Nigeria* (Jos, Nigeria: Challenge Press, 1993); and Matthew Hassan Kukah, *Religion, Politics and Power in Northern Nigeria* (Ibadan, Nigeria: Spectrum Books, 1993).

[12] Ochonu, *Colonialism by Proxy*; Turaki, *The British Colonial Legacy*.

[13] These seats were designed to ensure representation for "interests and communities ... not adequately represented." See Section 33(4)(b)(ii) Richards Constitution. See further, Efiong Isaac Utuk, *Britain's Colonial Administrations and Developments, 1861–1960: An Analysis of Britain's Colonial Administrations and Developments in Nigeria* (Portland: Portland State University, 1975).

the House."[14] Describing another contentious legislative deliberation over a government grant to mission schools, Niven reports that the proceedings degenerated to a religious confrontation in which "Moslems speakers had attempted to attack Christianity and Christian members of the House ... had attempted in their replies to defend Christianity as such."[15] With the Muslim members of the assembly bent on restricting missionary activity and Christian elites interpreting the restrictions as the perpetuation of a colonial domination in the form of Muslim sub-imperialism, squabbles intensified not only within but also outside the assembly.

The Non-Muslim League (NML) emerged in 1949 as an immediate reaction to the 1949 anti-mission bill. Political organization by Protestant elites, however, predated the NML's creation. Notable among these efforts was a secret meeting convened in Bukuru in 1948 to deliberate over the condition of Christians in the late colonial state. The meeting resolved that churches raise the "consciousness" of congregants by "warning them of the dangers posed by Islam."[16] Another significant predecessor to the NML was the Berom Progress Union (BPU) founded in Plateau Province. Plateau, a mixed religious area, was a hotbed for contestation over state-religion relations, and was the setting for some of the greatest controversies of the colonial years, including the infamous *Eluaka* case discussed in Chapter 2. While earlier organizations such as the BPU were Christian in outlook and critics of state-Masu Sarauta rule, their founders nevertheless framed them as primarily cultural organizations in public discourse. The formation of the NML was a marked departure from these earlier forms of resistance. With its creation, the first political organization with a declared non-Muslim identity in Northern Nigeria emerged.[17] Its founder, Pastor David Lot, was a mission-educated clergyman with the support of the Sudan Interior Mission (SIM) and the Sudan United Mission (SUM).[18] Beyond Lot,

---

[14] Nigeria, "Political Situation in Northern Provinces." CO 554/372. NA, UK.
[15] Ibid.
[16] Mathew Hassan Kukah and Toyin Falola, *Religious Militancy and Self-Assertion: Islam and Politics in Nigeria* (Aldershot, UK: Avebury, 1996), 237. See also Jonathan Mamu Ayuba, "The Bible and Political Revolution: Religion and Minority Politics in Northern Nigeria, 1945–1957," *Journal of the Historical Society of Nigeria* 17 (2007): 142.
[17] For the genealogy of the Non-Muslim League, see Minutes of Proceedings of the Minorities Commission sitting in Jos on February 15, 1958. CO/957/5.
[18] Both were interdenominational but the most active of the SUM were the Danish Lutherans.

other clergy dominated the NML's leadership and Christians filled the group's ranks.

Missionaries remained in the background in party formation processes due to the continuing opposition of Lugardians among the rank and file of the colonial administration. Those officials argued that missionary involvement in politics constituted a threat to colonial rule by promoting disaffection to authority. Not even the newfound influence that missions had come to command in the Colonial Office—an influence that had only grown steadily since the inception of Governor Donald Cameron's tenure—could shield mission societies from sanctions against alleged political activity. Those sanctions included warnings, suspensions, and even deportations. For example, the Resident of Adamawa Province expelled two missionaries of the SUM on charges of being "implicated in political disturbances," a charge that was later altered to "being closely identified in the minds of persons living in the area with the forces of disorder."[19] Consequently, while missionaries remained principal critics of the colonial state and continued to wield political influence (including in the establishment of the NML), they made efforts to appear neutral in party politics. Even as they remained in the background, however, missionaries continued to hold sway, including in the NML's framing of late colonial struggle as one against Muslims. With the group's creation, missionaries and Christian converts together began to publicly challenge the political order of the colonial state.

As Protestant elites were venturing into party politics, the Masu Sarauta was similarly reconstituting itself into a political party. The same year the NML came into existence, the Masu Sarauta established the Northern People's Congress (NPC), a political party touting a slogan that sought to unite differences – "One North, One People Irrespective of Religion, Rank or Tribe."[20] Rather than seeing this as a reconciliation effort on the part of the NPC, Christian elites regarded the NPC slogan as an attempt to elide difference and perpetuate Muslim domination. Protestant advocates contended that the "one people" intended by the NPC was not neutral. Instead, it was based on a Muslim majoritarian identity and akin to the colonial government's policy

---

[19] The Commission of the Churches on International Affairs, "Religious Liberty in Nigeria," July 1956. BCC/DIA/7/3/4/3.
[20] Richard L. Sklar, *Nigerian Political Parties: Power in an Emergent African Nation* (Princeton, NJ: Princeton University Press, 2015), 338–349.

of defining the state as neutral while governing through Islamic institutions and Islamic law. As Doktori, a prominent Protestant elite, later noted during the 1958 Constitutional Conference, "it was the policy of the British and that policy was taken over by the NPC to assimilate the Middle Belt: under that system they would lose their identity."[21] Under these circumstances, Christian elites understood the project of sameness touted by the NPC as a perpetuation of the hierarchies set in motion by colonial governance.

The NPC sought to entrench the hegemony of the Masu Sarauta. To be sure, the party provided a pathway to political power for Western-educated persons who were not of the Masu Sarauta class. Most prominent of these was Abubakar Tafawa Balewa, who would become the first prime minister of an independent Nigeria. Nevertheless, even emerging elites required the patronage of the Masu Sarauta. In fact, Balewa, the poster child of NPC's supposed egalitarianism, himself reinforced the narrative of Masu Sarauta hegemony since his father, a district head, had enjoyed the patronage of the Masu Sarauta.[22]

The pedigree of the NPC's cofounder, Ahmadu Bello, only cemented the Masu Sarauta hold on the NPC. Bello was the great-grandson of Uthman Dan Fodio, the founder of the precolonial Islamic Caliphate, and a member of the Masu Sarauta class. Indeed, it was common for leading members of the NPC to hold traditional office simultaneously with elective positions. Ahmadu Bello himself keenly competed for the seat of the Sultan of Sokoto, and when that bid failed, he maintained an appointment on the Sultan's council holding the title of Sardauna (Head of the Sultan's Guards). Even those emirs and old political elites who did not hold elective offices held a "whip hand" over new political elites.[23] The NPC, therefore, marked Masu Sarauta entry into party politics, and Protestant advocates therefore regarded the NPC as an entrenchment of the old order of things.[24] In an age when Independence loomed on the horizon, these advocates perceived the NPC as

---

[21] Proceedings of the Resumed Nigeria Constitutional Conference, September–October 1958, vol. I. CO879/173 (Resumed Constitutional Conference, 1958), 305. NA, UK.
[22] Although district head appointments were hardly a sign of elite status, appointees tended to have considerable political clout since appointments required political patronage of an emir.
[23] Memo of Resident of Adamawa. Records of Willink Commission Sitting in Adamawa. CO/957/5. NA, UK.
[24] The 1951 Constitution brought about the advent of party politics.

PART II CONSTITUTING DIFFERENCE

a project to perpetuate the privileges conferred on the Masu Sarauta by their Lugardian friends who were by then described perjoratively as "Anglo-Saxon Fulanis."[25] That NPC members considered Ahmadu Bello to be a "divine leader ... a reincarnation of Shehu Othman Dan Fodio"[26] and that Ahmadu Bello himself traced his descent from the Prophet Muhammad[27] only served to heighten these fears of Christian political elites that the state would be "islamized" upon Independence.

Protestant elites were not alone in mounting an attack on the NPC's perpetuation of Masu Sarauta hegemony. One year after the NPC's formation, the Northern Elements Progressive Union (NEPU) emerged as a political party founded on a critique of the Masu Sarauta. Although NEPU was newly formed, the coalition that founded it emerged from the old Muslim opposition to the Masu Sarauta, long regarded by the colonial state as "dissident" and subjected to brutal repression.[28] Given the party's democratic socialist ideology,[29] it was clear from NEPU's inception that it would never match the political might of the NPC since it lacked the support of Masu Sarauta's age-long political architecture and extensive patronage network. Indeed, colonial officials mocked NEPU founder, Aminu Kano, as a "tame little revolutionary"[30] in reference to NEPU's little chance at political success. Yet, the colonial state repressed NEPU members in reaction to the party's

---

[25] See, for example, "Memorandum of the Northern Elements Progressive Union to the Minorities Commission in Kano." KA/1/5 CO/957/08.

[26] Alhaji Ladan Baki, House of Assembly Debates March 8, 1963, cited in Dudley, *Parties and Politics*, 184.

[27] This claim is questionable since Uthman Dan Fodio had strongly refuted claims of descent from the Prophet.

[28] See Chapter 2.

[29] NEPU's goal was to create a "Socialist Commonwealth." See Malam Aminu Kano's speech, broadcast on the Nigerian Broadcasting Service (and reported in *Nigerian Citizen*, December 16, 1954, 5) in Attahiru Jega et al., eds., *Mallam Aminu Kano: Selected Speeches and Writings 1950–1982* (Kano, Nigeria: Mambaya House, Bayero University, 2002), 188. Kano understood socialism not merely as an economic ideology concerned with improving the overall standard of living and attaining economic equality, but also as the maximization of individual freedom. See Address by Honorable Aminu Kano to the Opening Session of a Seminar on Socialism Held at the University of Lagos on October 17, 1969 in Jega et al., *Mallam Aminu Kano*, 240.

[30] See, for instance, Bryan Sharwood-Smith citing Margey Perham's impressions of Kano, Sharwood-Smith to Secretary of State, May 18, 1955, CO879/165: Nigeria Constitutional and Political, Correspondence 1955–1958, 27, Adam Mathews Digital Collection.

critique of the foundations of colonial indirect rule and the colonial state's governance of religion.[31]

As a political party, NEPU proceeded from the premise that the NPC, its Masu Sarauta foundations, and the socio-religious hierarchies it featured were un-Islamic.[32] Critiquing what it labeled as the NPC's "monarchical feudalism," NEPU argued that "Islam ... does not support the retention of hereditary parasites."[33] Rather, the party asserted that "the basic concept of the Islamic state is socialist-republicanism. ... The fundamentals of its constitution guarantee equal civil liberties to all subjects."[34] NEPU also staked a position in the debate over the status of non-Muslims by insisting that "All non-Muslims and religious communities have the right to get their own cases decided according to their own personal laws."[35] NEPU accused the Masu-Sarauta-allied NPC of deviating from the social democratic features of the precolonial caliphate by acceding to indirect rule. As the NEPU's founder, Aminu Kano, posited, "it [indirect rule] is the most exploiting system of colonial administration the world has ever known."[36] NEPU, therefore, regarded the problem plaguing colonial Nigeria as one that originated from indirect rule rather than one inherent in Islamic governance or the precolonial caliphate. Kano invoked several theological references to justify this position. Speaking at the 1953 Constitutional Conference, for instance, Aminu Kano reported that the Prophet Muhammad had "trembled with emotion while addressing the people from the pulpit to the extent that it was feared that he might fall while denouncing autocratic, tyrannical rulers."[37] In Kano's words, "he [the Prophet] did not say 'Render undo Caesar's those things that are Caesar's.' He said categorically: 'there are no Caesars.'"[38] Aminu Kano took this criticism of the Masu Sarauta further in a January 14, 1954 article for which he was charged with sedition. Kano argued in the publication that NEPU's opposition to the Masu Sarauta sprung from the

---

[31] See section titled "Judging Difference" below.
[32] Memorandum Submitted to the Minorities Commission in Kano (n.d.) KANO ka/1/5 CO/957/08, 14.
[33] Ibid. [34] Ibid. [35] Ibid.
[36] Aminu Kano, "Speech Made by Aminu Kano," July 31, 1933, Proceedings of the 1953 Constitutional Conference, 17. CO 879 159. NA, UK.
[37] Citing Al-Bukhari's Sahih Hadith collection.
[38] Aminu Kano, "Speech Made by Aminu Kano," July 31, 1933, Proceedings of the 1953 Constitutional Conference, 17. CO 879 159. NA, UK.

latter's refusal to "follow the laws of Islam ... [and] the teachings of the Prophet."[39] The NEPU founder pointed to European colonizers as the "greatest enemies" who have corrupted "religion."[40] Kano, a teacher who was extensively trained in Quranic sciences, was not himself disconnected from the elite class since his father had been a mufti in the alkali court in Kano. Nevertheless, Kano devoted his thought and political struggles to advancing the overthrow of Anglo-Masu Sarauta rule. It was therefore hardly surprising that NEPU drew its following from those Muslims subordinated by the state: the Tijaniyyah and, generally, the *talakawa*.

Regardless of their shared opposition to the Masu-Sarauta-allied NPC, Protestants and NEPU elites did not join forces. This was because religious difference had become so integral to political identity that it produced competing visions of emancipatory possibilities for both groups. Protestant elites founded the NML based on its distinction from Islam, and that vision would have been undercut by an alliance with Muslims even if those Muslims were unaffiliated with the Masu Sarauta. Moreover, although both the NML and NEPU mounted a critique on Masu Sarauta hegemony, there were important distinctions in their perception of the colonial malady. On their part, Protestant elites regarded the problem as Muslim overrule aided by British power. NEPU, however, diagnosed the malaise as entirely rooted in British imperial ambitions, and indirect rule's exploitation of Sokoto caliphal institutions. Therefore, NEPU posited that the colonial state had corrupted the precolonial caliphate with its egalitarian features, a starkly different position than the Protestant view that the colonial state perpetuated Islam and the precolonial state's illegitimate hegemony. Indeed, NEPU's critique of colonialism encompassed a criticism of missionary activity, and NEPU was unrestrained in its criticism of what it regarded as missionary interference in "domestic politics."[41] Under these circumstances, the fact that both NEPU and Protestant elites

---

[39] See Aminu Kano, "Europeans Have Degraded Our Religion and Self Respect" June 14, 1954, Daily Comet in PRO London CO 554/1069 as cited in Abba Alkasum, ed.,The Politics of Malam Aminu Kano (Lagos: Vanguard Printers, 1993), 93. See further Kano's 1950 letter of resignation written to the Bauchi Native Authority and which he subsequently published in the *Daily Comet*, November 11, 1950.
[40] Ibid.
[41] See, for example, an article by NEPU's founding member: Danbatta Magaji, "Religious Freedom Move Can Be Disastrous," *Nigerian Citizen*, June 20, 1956, 6.

found a common foe in the NPC and the Masu Sarauta did nothing to bridge the gap between their starkly different diagnosis of the colonial situation. The Protestant elites driving the NML would therefore pursue their political project independently of NEPU.

The United Middle Belt Congress: Ecumenism, Self-Determination, and the Making of "Religious Minorities"

The NML centered on Christian, and more specifically, Protestant ecumenism. To be sure, Protestant ecumenism dated further back to the 1922 formation of the Christian Council of Nigeria (CCN) as a Christian ecumenical body to contest colonial restrictions on missions. Although the CCN was Protestant, it described its advocacy project as a Christian effort.[42] That Christian ecumenical project, however, only assumed an overtly partisan political form with the creation of the NML. Through the NML, Protestant elites sought to fashion an ecumenical Christian identity based on its dichotomy with the "Muslim" identity and for the sole purpose of making political claims. Christian theology became instrumental to molding this political identity. Indeed, missionaries and Christian converts articulated their condition in the late colonial state as well as their reaction to it in theological terms. J. L. Maxwell, a prominent missionary with the SUM,[43] for instance, predicted that "Moslem members of the Government would greatly out-number the non-Moslems, so that the Christian minority would be hopelessly out-voted."[44] In order to prevent this, church preaching came to emphasize the necessity for Christian unity and participation in politics. Expressing the sentiments of missionaries across several denominations, Maxwell warned: "If they [Christians] do not stick together in these days ... when the executive and legislative work of Nigeria is being transferred to African hands, they may find themselves being exploited by the Moslem peoples of

---

[42] Not all Protestant missions were members of the Christian Council of Nigeria; however, even those who were not members of the CCN like the Sudan Interior Mission were allied with the CCN and cooperated with it. The Catholic Mission was, however, not allied with the ecumenical group. See discussion on Catholic position below. For a discussion of the Catholic Church's delayed embrace of global ecumenism, see Udi Greenberg, "Catholics, Protestants and the Tortured Path to Religious Liberty," *Journal of the History of Ideas* 79, no. 3 (2018): 461–479.

[43] The SUM and the SIM were particularly active within Indigenous religious communities.

[44] J. Lowry Maxwell, *Half A Century of Grace: A Jubilee History of the Sudan United Mission* (Westcliff-on-Sea, UK: Sudan United Mission, 1953).

the North. The only unifying force for the non-Moslems is the Christian church."[45] Maxwell, therefore, called for the centering of Christians' political identity on faith.

The Bible became a political text in building this unified identity. A detailed ethnography of the Bachama elite in Adamawa, a Type II area, shows how the Bible became a "political model."[46] For the Bachama and other Christian converts, the Bible became "a mirror, in which they [Christian converts] could see and understand their own history in a new way and make sense of their place in history."[47] It provided "a new language and a set of images, allegories, metaphors and symbols which made the politics of their time meaningful and at the same time, helped them to create a platform for political action."[48] Indeed, clergy advocated political action by making textual references to the Bible. Prominent among those references was the exodus metaphor through which missionaries and converts analogized the position of Northern Nigerian Christians to that of the oppression of Jews in Egypt. This analogy supposed that like the Jews, it was incumbent on Northern Nigerian Christians to take action to secure freedom.[49] The Matthew 5:13 reference to Christians as the "salt of the earth"[50] was another textual reference often cited by missionaries and converts. Building on that scriptural premise, Protestant advocates argued that Christians were the most fit to rule and urged political engagement.[51] Among the biblical accounts that provided legitimacy for political activism was also the Mark 11:15–17 account of Christ driving out sellers and buyers from the temple. Ultimately, these textual references became the basis for Protestant advocacy urging converts to "unite" the "political kingdom" and "the kingdom of God" into a Christian Kingdom.[52] Now necessitated by theology, Christian liberation called for an ecumenical vision of emancipation. That vision would center on the creation of a Middle Belt State autonomous from the Masu Sarauta.

---

[45] Ibid.
[46] Niels Kastfelt, *Religion and Politics in Nigeria: A Study in Middle Belt Christianity* (New York: Tauris, 1994).
[47] Ibid.   [48] Ibid.
[49] On a reading of "exodus politics" into revolutionary struggles, see Michael Walzer, *Exodus and Revolution* (Michigan: Basic Books, 1985).
[50] Matthew 5:13: "Ye are the salt of the earth."
[51] Kastfelt, *Religion and Politics*.   [52] Ibid.

The Protestant call for political autonomy was not novel; missionaries advocated for "political autonomy" of Indigenous religious groups from indirect rule through Muslim elites since the early colonial years.[53] As noted in an earlier chapter, that call for autonomy sought to advance a notion of missionary liberty by calling for the colonial state's excision of its ties with the Masu Sarauta. The self-determination claim that emerged in the last decade of colonial rule, circa 1950–1960, went far beyond the earlier demands for local governance autonomy. In that period, Protestant advocates began to call for the creation of an autonomous state within a broader federation. The Christian Council of Nigeria first tabled the proposal at a 1950 meeting with the chief commissioner of the Northern Region colonial government.[54] In response, the government secretary pointed out that Adamawa, the province in which the CCN sought to site the proposed Middle Belt State, comprised not only of Christians, but also other peoples of diverse religious, ethnic, and linguistic identities. The colonial government argued that in the absence of a common thread uniting those identities, there was no "group self" on behalf of whom a self-determination claim could be made, and the state-creation demand could not succeed. That government rejection of the CCN demand on the basis of the heterogeneity of non-Muslim faiths inspired a Protestant inclination to ally with adherents of Indigenous religions ultimately culminating in the "Non-Muslim religious minorities" political identity.

A series of events that unfolded over the next five years were integral to the creation of the religious minorities alliance. In 1951, the NML morphed into the Middle Zone League (MZL) not only to reflect the territorial aspirations over the Middle Belt, but also in response to widespread criticism that it was a Christian campaign for religious divisions. Although the MZL now directed its efforts beyond the earlier (NML) focus on Christians in Types II and III areas, these efforts did not translate into political gains when the first elections in Northern Nigeria were held in 1951. The NPC secured most seats in the regional

---

[53] For example, the Church Missionary Society argued in a 1915 Memorandum that subjecting non-Muslims to Islamic institutions (chiefs and courts) was a violation of religious toleration.

[54] Statement Submitted to the Civil Secretary of Northern Nigeria, April 20, 1955. CMS/OMS/A9/Alvarez. University of Birmingham Cadbury Special Collections (hereafter Cadbury Collections). See also The Commission of the Churches on International Affairs, Religious Liberty in Nigeria, July 1956. BCC/DIA/7/3/4/3. Church of England Record Center (hereafter CERC).

legislature since it enjoyed overwhelming support in Types I and II areas. Indeed, the NPC even recorded electoral gains in some Indigenous religious areas due to the party's patronage of Indigenous elites at odds with the Christian nationalist class. The NPC appointed three Christians into the government cabinet in 1953 in a bid to cultivate support outside of predominantly Muslim areas. Perhaps in pursuit of increasingly elusive electoral gains, the MZL tried the unprecedented move of forming a political coalition with the NPC in 1954. Although it was initially framed as an attempt to transcend the animosity between the two parties, that alliance was doomed from inception since MZL elites insisted on maintaining a distinct Protestant identity and continued to criticize Masu Sarauta complicity in the colonial order.[55] The MZL-NPC coalition crumbled within a few months. With the NPC's continued political dominance, the MZL turned to an official alignment with diverse Indigenous religious persuasions. Formed in 1955, the United Middle Belt Congress (UMBC) was the product of that new alliance.

The UMBC's mission was to "represent the minority groups of the region [Northern Nigeria] in the politics of independence" and its goal was "to actualize the creation of a Middle Belt State with its House of Chiefs and House of Assembly distinct from the Northern Region."[56] As put forth by the UMBC, what set the minority groups it represented apart from the rest of the population was its non-Muslim identity.

Like its predecessor organizations, the UMBC was championed by Christian elites. Nevertheless, the party strove to maintain the appearances of a non-Christian identity by asserting that it represented diverse Indigenous religions. That assertion was hardly consonant with practice since Christian converts dominated the echelons of the UMBC. Indeed, Christianity had a hegemonic hold on political discourse and participation of the many ethno-tribal groups who became a part of this Middle Belt project.[57] To be sure, certain ethnic groups sought to hinge their political claims on their ethnic identity. Indeed, one of the

---

[55] The Alliance between Northern People's Congress and Nigeria Middle Zone League (undated) exhibit attached to Minutes of Proceedings of the Minorities Commission Sitting in Jos on February 15, 1958. CO/957/5.

[56] Ayuba, "The Bible and Political Revolution," 145. See United Middle Belt Congress, *The Constitution of the United Middle Belt Congress* (Kaduna: Ola Moduro Press, 1955).

[57] See Kastfelt, *Religion and Politics* (tracing the ways in which Christianity became molded into the ethnic identity of ethno-religious communities, coming to shape their vision of resistance).

most sustained critiques against the colonial state was mounted by the Chambas of Adamawa Province, a Type II area.⁵⁸ So powerful was the Chamba call for autonomy that it culminated in the 1937 administrative reforms designed to grant the Chamba autonomy from the Muslim chief (titled *"lamido"*) of Adamawa, among other things. Although that reform was largely ineffectual due to the resistance of the Lugardian-backed Lamido, the Chamba remained a distinct bloc of resistance. Attempts by ethnic groups to pursue projects of liberation independent of—though not in opposition to—the Christian missionary project was a feature of struggles in earlier colonial years. However, with the onset of nationalist polities in the twilight colonial years, Christian converts among the Chamba and other ethno-religious groups had come to dominate the political elite class. In pursuit of their advocacy for the creation of a Middle Belt State, these Christian elites (who were at the forefront of the UMBC, and earlier, the MZL and NML), would construct a non-Muslim religious minorities identity.

The UMBC's claim of representing a Protestant-Indigenous faith alliance affirmed the Muslim–non-Muslim distinction on which colonial indirect rule was based. At the inception of formal empire, the colonial state created the binary Muslim versus non-Muslim distinction in furtherance of its governance agenda. While the stance of Protestant elites in the early colonial years was to contest this distinction due to the disadvantages it imposed, these elites shifted their position in the last decade of colonial rule. They now came to assert the difference of non-Muslims from Muslims on the basis of religion. At the same time, they asserted the sameness of all non-Muslims of diverse ethno-religious persuasions based on their common non-Muslim identity. By the time these Protestant advocates embraced the Muslim versus Non-Muslim classification, however, the colonial government sought to distance itself from that binary classification it had manufactured by insisting that there was no cohesive non-Muslim identity on which a self-determination claim could be based.

Neither was the claim for the creation of a Middle Belt State within a federal Nigeria unprecedented. As is discernible from previous chapters, federalist ideas were not new in the colonial state nor, for that matter, in British imperial Africa.⁵⁹ The colonial state's territorial

---

⁵⁸ See Ochonu, *Colonialism by Proxy*, 157–178.
⁵⁹ See Dan Juma, "The British Tradition of Federal Ideas: Kenya and Rhodesia in the Interwar and Postwar Years circa 1925–1960," PhD diss., (Harvard Law School, 2017).

religion-based classifications themselves evinced a federalist notion, a structural arrangement that was further reinforced by the 1946 Constitution's provision for regional autonomy for Nigeria's major geographical regions. The religious minorities coalition sought to crystallize the colonial classifications by carving out a subautonomous political formation for non-Muslim groups in the colonial state.

The UMBC presented the proposal for a Middle Belt State at the 1957 London Constitutional Conference, arguing that the continued existence of non-Muslims as a group in Northern Nigeria was detrimental to that group's interests. While the NPC was staunch in its opposition, the UMBC's demand was supported by NEPU and Southern Nigerian parties with which the UMBC had formed coalitions, foremost of which was the Action Group (AG). While the peculiar dynamics of the Northern Nigerian struggles over the politics and governance of religious difference remained, the struggles of decolonization necessarily featured cross-regional alliances across Nigeria.[60] Ultimately, a decolonized Nigeria was the goal of these parties, even if they had different visions of what the nationalist struggle for independence entailed. While Southern Nigeria activists imagined themselves to be seeking independence from a British colonial state symbolized by European overlords, the Protestant ecumenists championing the cause of religious minorities in Northern Nigeria sought independence from the Anglo-Masu Sarauta colonial state, and the self-determination move was a crucial step in that process.

When the UMBC presented its self-determination demand at the 1957 Constitutional Conference, secretary of state for the colonies, Sir Lennox Boyd, did not express his direct opposition. Nevertheless, Boyd effectively neutralized the demand by pointing out that the petition was bound to delay Nigeria's Independence. Boyd assured the conference that in the absence of such a time-consuming process as a self-determination claim entailed, Her Majesty's government would consider granting Independence to Nigeria. Boyd's connection of the state-creation demand with Independence was well calculated: unlike the Masu Sarauta, who were reluctant, even hostile to the idea

---

[60] At the time, all parties were regional. Dudley comments that these alliances were more likely efforts to curtail the dominance of the NPC since Northern Nigeria remained the most populous region in the country with over 50 percent of the country's population and NPC's dominance in that region translated to its dominance in national elections. See Dudley, *Parties and Politics*, 26.

of early independence, the UMBC, NEPU, and the parties of Southern Nigeria had begun to petition for Independence since the early 1950s. When Southern Nigerian party and UMBC ally Action Group had introduced a self-government motion before the National Parliament in 1953, the NPC had replaced the deadline in the draft motion: "1956" with "as soon as possible."[61] That redraft was hotly contested by the UMBC and other parties, but the numerical strength of the NPC ensured its passage. The ensuing public protests against the Masu Sarauta in Lagos, the seat of the Parliament, was followed by violence against Southern Nigerians in Kano who were overwhelmingly Christian. Regardless of the continuing hesitation of the Masu Sarauta, the UMBC and its AG ally remained committed to early Independence, and these groups abandoned the state-creation demand at the 1957 Conference in response to Boyd's conditioning of Independence negotiations on the absence of a state-creation demand at the 1957 Conference. To pacify these advocates, the conference instead set up a commission "to inquire into the fears of minorities and the means of allaying them." The commission, which was established in September 1957 and headed by Sir Henry Willink, Queen's counsel, was charged with ascertaining the "facts about the fears of minorities in Nigeria whether they are well or ill-founded."[62] Based on its findings, Willink and his colleagues were then required to make recommendations to allay the fears of minorities, including, if suitable, the creation of states.

GOVERNING RELIGION: THE WILLINK COMMISSION AND LATE IMPERIAL SECULARITY

The work of the Sir Henry Willink-chaired Commission to inquire into the fears of minorities and the means of allaying them has been the subject of many volumes on Nigerian constitutional history.[63] These accounts have tended to foreground the commission's work in

---

[61] Macpherson to Lyttleton on April 1, 1953. CO 554/260 NA, UK. See also John N. Paden, *Ahmadu Bello, Sardauna of Sokoto: Values and Leadership in Nigeria* (Zaria, Nigeria: HudaHuda, 1986), 161–162.

[62] Henry Willink, ed., Nigeria: *Report of the Commission Appointed to Enquire into the Fears of Minorities and the Means of Allaying Them* (London: HM Stationery Office, 1958) (hereafter Willink Report), iii. Other members of the commission were Gordon Hadow, Philip Mason, and J. B. Shearer.

[63] See generally Wale Adebanwi, "A Nation Betrayed: Nigeria and the Minorities Commission of 1957," *African Affairs* 111, no. 443 (2012): 335–337; Rufus Taiwo Akinyele, "States Creation in Nigeria: The Willink Report in Retrospect,"

the development of federalism. After all, the commission was a site for negotiating a constitutional structure and political arrangement to manage Nigeria's diversity. Elided in this focus on multiple axes of diversity has, however, been the commission's centrality to the struggles over religious difference in the late colonial state. This centrality is reflected by the circumstances that gave rise to the establishment of the commission; it is also revealed by the fact that the commission became a site for jousting over religious difference, not for the sake of religion, but rather in the quest for power and recognition in the late colonial state. Indeed, the convening of the commission became an epochal moment in the unfolding of the history of imperial secular governmentality. As the colonial state had done since its inception, the commission defined, deepened, and hierarchized religious difference. The commission perpetuated the colonial state's apprehension of religious difference on the basis of a Muslim–non-Muslim distinction and mapped this difference onto territorial formations. In fact, the commission produced the first religion map of Nigeria. By creating territorial maps of religion (see Map 3.1), the commission was not merely affirming religious identities asserted by religious adherents, it was also creating them permanently by affixing them to territory. In the process of perpetuating these colonial classifications, the commission was not only defining religion, it was also inevitably deepening and hierarchizing religious difference. As will be observed below, a critical reading of the Willink Commission's work, as of preceding decades of colonial governance of religious difference, destabilizes the classification of religions by revealing the labile legal and political processes through which religious identities were defined, not for their own sake, but for the purpose of positioning religions in opposition to each other. Those processes not only produced differentiation, they also created sameness and occluded diversity with consequences for the distribution of power and for notions of emancipatory possibilities. The analysis of the Willink Commission that follows therefore illuminates how an attempt to challenge colonial governance through a self-determination effort morphed to become the very object of its resistance.

African Studies Review 39, no. 2 (1996): 71–94; and Oluwatoyin B. Oduntan, "Decolonization and the Minority Question in Nigeria: The Willink Commission Revisited," in *Minority Rights and the National Question in Nigeria*, eds. Uyilawa Usuanlele and Bonny Ibhawoh (Cham, Switzerland: Palgrave Macmillan, 2017), 17–39.

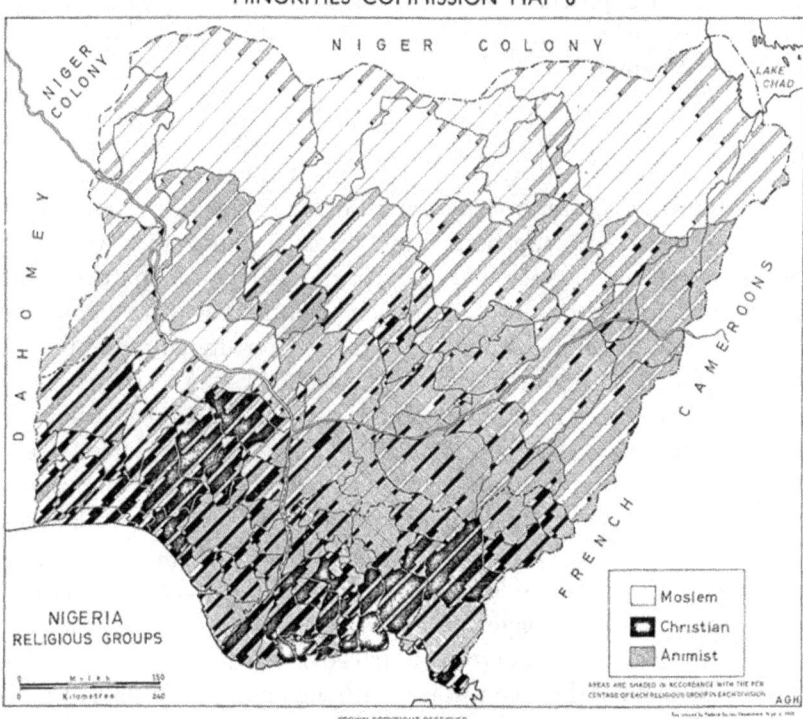

Map 3.1 Territorial map of religious affiliation by Willink Commission

Performing and Contesting Religious Difference
It was on behalf of "minorities of the Northern Region" that the UMBC petitioned for the creation of a Middle Belt State before the Willink Commission.[64] The UMBC's petition, which was supported by the Southern Nigerian Action Group political party, declared: "We desire that if and when the British will withdraw from Nigeria, we shall have strong and deep rooted democratic government ... but this will not take its effective place unless and until the country accepts the true principles of Federalism by granting the Middle Belt state."[65]

---

[64] United Middle Belt Congress, Memorandum to the Willink Commission, November 7, 1957 (hereafter UMBC Memo). CO 957/25. NA, UK.

[65] Ibid. The area to be covered by the state extended beyond the CCN's 1950 proposal and spanned Plateau, Kabba, Benue, Bornu, and Ilorin Provinces and parts of Niger, Zaria, Adamaw, and Bauchi. See also Nigeria Constitutional Conference 1957: Minutes of the Ninth Plenary Session, 125. CO 879/166. NA, UK.

PART II CONSTITUTING DIFFERENCE

By the time the proceedings of the commission commenced, the religious minorities identity on behalf of whom the UMBC brought the petition had emerged first through the NML, then the MZL, and ultimately the UMBC. It was, however, during the Willink Commission proceedings that that identity would be crystallized.

The petitioner (the UMBC) performed the religious minorities identity in the course of the commission's proceedings. That performance entailed weaving a common thread through the experience of diverse ethnic and religious groups; in the process, the petitioner produced a history of a united religious identity based on a common experience of disempowerment. The history of marginalization told by the petitioner was not merely intended to be a chronicle; that account was intended to lend credibility to the petitioner's expressed trepidation of a future in a Masu Sarauta-dominated Northern Nigeria. Consequently, as the petitioner narrated its history before the commission, so too did its vision of emancipation – one based on differentiation – unfold. That history and vision would survive the commission's proceedings and even the Independence deal to serve as a springboard for post-Independence struggles.

The NPC was the face of the colonial government's opposition to the UMBC demand at the commission. Although European administrators continued to control the levers of the colonial government and some even appeared before the Willink Commission, the regional legislative and executive councils were dominated by the Masu Sarauta-directed NPC by the time the commission convened. In responding to the petitioner's claim, the NPC had the backing of not only their Lugardian allies, they also had the support of administrators, who were generally sympathetic to missions. The latter officials were not opposed to toppling the privilege of the Masu Sarauta; however, they regarded the self-determination claim as a threat to the survival of empire's construct – Northern Nigeria. All administrators would, however, tread cautiously in their opposition to the state-creation claim. For one, the missionary backers of the demand had come to command tremendous influence in the upper echelons of the colonial administration by the late colonial years. Indeed, foremost global ecumenist championing the missionary interest and chair of the Commission of Churches on International Affairs, Sir Kenneth Grubb, had the ears not only of senior officials in the Colonial Office but also of Nigeria's colonial governor, James Robertson. In his visit to Nigeria during the commission's proceedings, Grubb had the benefit of private interactions with Sir Henry Willink, beside whose room Grubb and his wife were lodged in the deputy governor's residence.⁶⁶ Beyond the influence the UMBC demand commended through its missionary connections, events had begun to put a strain on NPC-Lugardian relations. While Lugardian administrators continued to declare full backing for Masu Sarauta proclivities in public, some of these administrators had begun to express their misgivings over the attitude of their allies in private. Writing a February 14, 1955 letter to Sir Lennox Boyd, the British secretary of state for the colonies, prominent Lugardian and Northern Nigerian governor, Bryan Sharwood-Smith, expressed his misgivings over the "acute religious intolerance" of senior NPC officials, fearing that it would "dangerously antagonize the non-Moslem elements in the Region."⁶⁷ The friction between Lugardians and their Masu Sarauta allies had begun to simmer in the aftermath of the 1947 *Gubba* decision. Although the *Gubba* judgment was an outcome of the Cameron reform project, it triggered distrust between Lugardians and their Masu Sarauta allies. Beyond the tensions that these earlier events generated, the disenchantment of certain Lugardians with the Masu Sarauta in the late colonial years was also kindled by the 1954 riots in Kano over the NPC-vetoed 1953 motion for self-government.⁶⁸ Smith was embarrassed by the riots which claimed several casualties and was widely denigrated by the Northern Nigeria non-Muslim coalition, NEPU, and Southern Nigeria parties.⁶⁹ Following these events, colonial administrators became measured in their objection to the state demand, abandoning the intractable posture they had assumed when the Christian Council of Nigeria first tabled the proposal in 1950. As a result, the NPC was left to champion the opposition to the UMBC proposal for an autonomous Middle Belt State in a federal Nigeria.

It was not the idea of federalism that the NPC opposed; after all, federalist ideas were integral to the colonial religion-territorial classification system.⁷⁰ Rather, it was the vision of federalism espoused by

---

⁶⁶ Kenneth Grubb, "Extracts from Report on Religious Liberty in Nigeria," December 13, 1957. CO 554/1534. NA, UK.
⁶⁷ Governor, Northern Region to Secretary of State on February 14, 1955, Nigeria Constitutional and Political Correspondence, 1955–1958. CO 879/165, 11–14. NA, UK.
⁶⁸ See account of George Padmore, "The Kano Riot: The Background," *West African Pilot*, May 29, 1953.
⁶⁹ Ibid.   ⁷⁰ See Chapter 1.

the petitioners that the NPC hotly contested. To the Masu Sarauta and their Lugardian allies within the administration, the territorial classifications in the colonial state and the regional autonomy granted by the 1946 Constitution were perfectly acceptable, even laudable. The creation of a Middle Belt State was, however, not acceptable to these political authorities. In a private meeting with the commission, Tafawa Balewa, NPC cofounder and future prime minister of Nigeria, rejected the federalist arrangement of autonomous states petitioned by the religious minorities. Balewa insisted that state creation was not the "answer to the problems of the minorities" and argued that "the push for state creation" was not reflective of the aspirations of the masses but was rather "ignited by the feelings that the politicians had lit in the people."[71] The thrust of the colonial government's argument was, therefore, the unity of Northern Nigeria as encapsulated in the NPC's "One North, One People" ideal.[72] The argument for unity was made not only in economic, social, or political terms; adopting the language deployed by the petitioners, it was also made in Christian theological terms. In fact, the Northern Region government headed its memorandum to the commission with a quote from Luke 11:17: "But He, knowing their thoughts, said unto them, every kingdom divided against itself is brought to desolation; and a house divided against a house falleth."[73] In a turn from the religious binarization that was the basis of the colonial state's religious governance project, the colonial government insisted that Northern Nigeria's identity was homogenous irrespective of "religion, rank or tribe." The colonial government's case before the commission would center on protecting that homogenized identity from the religious differentiation on which the religious minorities identity relied.[74]

The petitioner's performance of the religious minorities identity did not only hinge on rendering the history of the emergence of that identity, it also entailed distinguishing that identity from that of other Northern Nigerians. Chief counsel to the petitioners, Fani Kayode QC,

---

[71] Record of Private Discussions, November 1957–March 1958. CO/957/6. NA, UK.

[72] Submission by Sir Ahmadu Bello to the Minorities Commission, February 1, 1958. CO/957/4. NA, UK. See further NPC Memorandum to the Minorities Commission (signed by Muhammad Bello Adamawa, Provincial President, NPC Sokoto). CO957/36 NA.

[73] Government of the Northern Region of Nigeria, Memorandum to the Willink Commission. CO/957/27.

[74] Submission by Sir Ahmadu Bello to the Minorities Commission.

argued that the state-creation demand hinged on the "religious difference" of the minorities from "the Muslims of the far north.[75] Kayode pointed out that these non-Muslims were already regarded as a cohesive group in official and everyday discourse through the "contemptuous" reference to them as "pagans" or "kafiris" (unbelievers). Although this was true of official colonial discourse since the inception of colonialism as well as of social discourse by the late colonial years, it was hardly representative of the precolonial juristic status of and socio-linguistic reference to non-Muslim persons. Several of these groups were regarded as Amana or Dhimmah ("entrusted" or "protected" people) in recognition of their political and juridical autonomy.[76] Moreover, in the colonial years, the pejorative "pagan" label was used not merely by colonial administrators and the Masu Sarauta but also by Protestant advocates leading the self-determination claim.

Beyond citing the kafiri designation of non-Muslims in everyday discourse in support of their argument for the existence of a non-Muslim identity, the petitioners also argued that these groups had a distinct system of government marking them apart from Muslims. The petitioners charged that the long history of non-Muslims' unique and autonomous political organization had been violently truncated by the British imperial conquest, which placed non-Muslims under "Muslim emirs, by force of circumstance" and merely for the purpose of administrative convenience. Argued Kayode: "Now that Britain was on the threshold of voluntarily surrendering her sovereignty, it was incumbent upon her to create a system which could not leave these minority peoples at the mercy of the majority."[77] This claim regarding the distinct political organization of non-Muslims was intended to support the petitioner's case for the existence of a non-Muslim identity defined by its distinction from Muslims. Yet, that distinction on which the self-determination claim relied simultaneously reified the colonial territorial differentiation between the Muslim emirates and non-Muslim areas that advocates had hotly contested in earlier colonial years.

The petitioner did not only attempt to render a history that was inclusive of the experiences of the diverse non-Muslim peoples of Northern

---

[75] See Minutes of Proceedings of the Minorities Commission Sitting in Jos on February 15, 1958. CO/957/5.

[76] See Chapter 1. See further Mukhtar Umar Bunza, *Christian Missions among Muslims: Sokoto Province, Nigeria 1935–1990* (Trenton, NJ: Africa World Press, 2007), 7–13.

[77] See Record of Proceedings of the Minorities Commission Sitting in Jos on February 15, 1958. CO/957/5.

Nigeria, it also sought to weave a common thread through their experience of marginalization. The petitioner spotlighted the subordination of non-Muslim chiefs, invoking the fear that non-Muslim chiefs would be completely phased out upon Independence. The petitioner also pointed to the state's subjection of non-Muslims to Islamic law and alkalai courts, citing the fear that "Islamic courts would become a weapon of oppression" upon Independence.[78] In the process of rendering a common history of disempowerment for diverse religious groups who were not Muslim, the petitioner constructed a shared non-Muslim identity.

Despite the petitioner's efforts to connect the experiences of all non-Muslims as the basis for the state-creation claim, the grievance central to the petitioner's case was unique to the Christian experience. The question of missionary restrictions was central to the petitioner's account of the subordination of non-Muslims and the privileges of the Masu Sarauta. Moreover, the petitioner elided the experience of several non-Christian ethno-religious groups by excluding economic questions from the commission's proceedings. The petitioners argued that the grievances of religious minorities and the fears arising from them were religious, social, and political. UMBC elites dismissed insinuations that the petition for state creation was motivated by economic incentives. Speaking at the 1958 Conference, for instance, UMBC President Joseph Tarka asserted that the fears were far from economic; rather, Tarka argued that the overriding fear was that Northern Nigeria "could be turned into a Muslim state after Independence."[79] Even the commission echoed this position by contrasting the claims of Northern Nigerian minorities with those of minority-petitioners in other parts of Nigeria. While the claims of the latter centered on their economic disadvantages regarding infrastructure – schools, hospitals, roads, and other public services – the commission considered minorities in Northern Nigeria to be in a different position.[80] The commission pointed out that these minorities had greater access to infrastructure: "the presence of missionaries in the southern or minority areas led to far more being spent on both schools and hospitals than in the Muslim North, while the mileage of roads in proportion to the populations is also greater than in the South."[81] Indeed, this was an argument wielded by the NPC

---

[78] Ibid.
[79] Nigeria Constitutional Conference 1958. CO/879/174 NA, UK.
[80] The Willink Report, 58.   [81] Ibid.

against the state-creation demand; the NPC stressed that granting the minorities a separate state would have a devastating economic effect on Northern Nigeria. For instance, the NPC pointed to the fact that the civil service cadre was staffed primarily by mission-educated persons from Types II and III areas and argued that the loss of the expertise of these personnel would have a crippling effect.[82] The debate before the commission therefore excluded economic dimensions of the inequality engendered by imperial secular governmentality.

The exclusion of economic questions marginalized the experiences of the diverse religion-ethnic groups that the UMBC claimed to represent. In fact, the ethnic nationalities that the UMBC purported to represent under the religious minorities category had been vocal about the economic disempowerment imposed by colonial indirect rule through Muslim elites. For instance, in its submission to the Willink Commission, the Chamba alleged that its members were excluded from employment by the Native Authority for jobs due to their refusal to work on Sundays.[83] In addition, the Lokoja Improvement Union, representing the largely Indigenous minorities of Lokoja, hinged its submissions before the commissions on economic issues such as the need for more schools.[84] Moreover, when the Berom Progressive Union (BPU), a distant predecessor to the NML, had been founded in Plateau Province, a Type II (mixed religious) area, it was with the primary aim of securing compensation for the natives from the tin mining companies. At the core, these economic demands challenged the distribution of power in the colonial state. For instance, in the Berom Progressive Union case, the quest for compensation from the companies was not merely an economic campaign directed at expatriate companies; it was, fundamentally, a challenge of the political structure. The provincial chief, a Muslim, had jurisdiction over the grant of mining licenses, although

---

[82] As submitted to the commission, 61 percent of the junior grade of the civil service were natives of Kabba, Benue, and Plateau, three predominantly non-Muslim areas, and from Ilorin, classified as a Muslim area but having a considerable non-Muslim population. 20 percent of the senior cadre came from these areas and 20 percent were drawn from other predominantly non-Muslim areas. Given that Muslims constituted 73 percent of the Northern Nigerian population (according to the 1952 Census), those numbers were significant. CO/957/41.

[83] "Chamba Federation Separatist Movement," Report on the Chamba Subordinate Native Authority Submitted to the Willink Commission. CO 957/17. NA, UK.

[84] See also "Our Fears: Submission of the Alago State Union to the Willink Commission," November 12, 1957, tabling complaints of economic marginalization by people of Lafia. CO 957/32. NA, UK.

ultimate decisions over mining concessions were made by the residents and the district commissioners. The BPU therefore directed its campaign against the provincial political structure, an effort that had led to the appointment of Indigenous chiefs to the Native Authority in 1947. Besides these examples, clashes over land use between Fulani Muslim pastoralists and non-Muslim farmers were also an entrenched feature of the political struggles in Type II areas, particularly in the Plateau Province. In its focus on producing a coherent history of marginalization that centered Christian concerns, the petitioner erased the experience of several ethno-religious groups.

As the petitioner's claim rested on performing the religious minorities identity, NPC opponents sought to unravel that identity. Testifying before the committee, Ahmadu Bello, NPC cofounder and premier of the Northern Region, stated that the creation of new states in the Northern Region would "break the steady stabilizing influence which people in the North are convinced is the major role we have to play in forwarding the progress of [Nigeria]."[85] Pivoting from the state's construction of the Muslim versus non-Muslim distinction and ignoring the centrality of that distinction to the indirect rule design, the NPC contested the existence of a non-Muslim identity. Reminiscent of the colonial state's response to earlier Christian Council of Nigeria agitations, the NPC argued that any assertion of a united identity was false as the Middle Belt area comprised of several religions, two hundred ethnic groups, and over six hundred linguistic groups. The NPC insisted that it was impossible for such diversity to produce a united identity, stressing that only chaos could result from the creation of the proposed Middle Belt State. In response to the NPC, the UMBC argued that the diversity was not as varied as it seemed. The two hundred ethnic groups, they argued, were actually subidentities under four main ethnic identities: the Nupe Group, the Tiv Group, the Berom Group, and the Bachama. Nevertheless, for the colonial government and Northern Muslim elites, the commission was a theater for the performance of the "One North, One People, Irrespective of Religion, Rank or Tribe" project – a unity project designed to elide differences under the banner of state neutrality and impartiality.

The UMBC's performance was contested by some Indigenous religious groups. Attacking the coherent religious minorities identity the

[85] Ahmadu Bello, Speech to Willink Commission, February 5, 1958. CO/957/4. NA, UK.

UMBC claimed to represent, one Igala chief exclaimed: "It definitely verges on insanity for a human being of responsibility to suggest that the various tribes of the reverain area of the Northern Region have a common language."[86] As such, the non-Muslim identity was disputed not only by the colonial government opposing the state-creation claim, but also by some Indigenous groups whom the religious minorities claimed to represent.

Beyond its campaign for a unified Northern Nigerian identity, the NPC also challenged the religious minorities identity by arguing that it was not truly representative. The NPC argued that the ecumenical alliance behind the formation of the religious minorities identity was exclusionary as it did not include the Roman Catholic Church. Rather than join the petitioners, the Catholic Church had issued a declaration extolling its "cooperation and mutual understanding" with the government of Northern Nigeria.[87] The Church further noted its satisfaction with the government's guarantee that the Independence Constitution would include provisions on religious liberty.[88] The government seized on this opportunity to argue that the petitioner-championed religious minorities could not claim to represent all non-Muslims in its demand for a state. Moreover, the NPC contested the legitimacy of the state-creation demand by arguing that not all non-Muslims in the colonial state had a desire for such a state. In fact, the NPC called on chiefs from Type III areas to testify that there was no desire in their communities for the creation of a separate state. Some of these witnesses insisted that they did not suffer any discrimination under the present political and religious arrangement in the Northern Region.[89] The Kamuku and Gwari tribes, for example, charged the

---

[86] Memorandum of the Igala Union on the Creation of the Middle Belt State, November 11, 1957. CO/957/30.

[87] The Catholic Church in the Northern Province, The Catholic Church in Nigeria: Declaration (undated). CO/957/27.

[88] Ibid. The religious freedom described in the declaration was significantly different from the version that Protestant missions would come to champion as it did not include the right to convert or proselytize. See Chapter 5.

[89] For instance, the chief of Keffi Native Authority submitted a memorandum arguing against the creation of the Middle Belt Region. The reasons adduced by Keffi NA against the creation of the Middle Belt State were that funds were insufficient for the functioning of an additional state, "resultant taxation increases will bear hardly on the peasantry," and that there would be no sufficiently educated people to run the new state. See "The Joint Memoranda of The League of Northern Yorubas, Yagba Federal League and Egbe Irepo Yagba Before the Minorities Commission,"

PART II CONSTITUTING DIFFERENCE

UMBC petition for a Middle Belt State as "irresponsible" and lacking the "support of the indigenous people."[90] The chief of the Gwari tribe expressed his tribe's "wish" to remain in the Northern Region "until resurrection day."[91] Even if that chief's statement was exaggerated, his position and the sentiments of those political elites of tribes that had not converted to Christianity troubled the stability of the non-Muslim category on which the petitioner's claim relied.

In the end, the commission declined to recommend the creation of the Middle Belt State. It found restrictions on missionary activity, which was the foremost grievance, to be justifiable. To the extent that the commission sympathized with the petitioner's trepidation over the fate of the missionary enterprise after Independence, it pointed to a declaration of tolerance by Premier Ahmadu Bello's office as sufficient to address those fears. That declaration, which was issued in the course of the commission's proceedings, vaguely committed to protecting religious liberty.[92]

The commission also invoked that declaration in response to the grievances on the position of non-Muslims in Islamic courts; however, the reference to the Islamic law question was tangential to the commission's ruling since that issue was being examined by a separate body empaneled by the Colonial Office.[93] As with other questions, a faith-in-the-state approach also informed the commission's response to the fears regarding the subordination of non-Muslims. A key piece of evidence presented by the petitioners to establish non-Muslim subordination was the hierarchization of Indigenous chiefs and the conferment of special privileges on emirs. Dismissing the claim, the commission pointed out that the trend in the late colonial state portended the advent of a constitutional monarchy that would ultimately culminate in the decline of emirs' authority.

January 16, 1957, CO/957/30 (disputing the claims of discrimination). See also "Memorandum of the Igala Divisional Union Home Branch on the Creation of the Middle Belt State," CO/957/30; Memorandum on Minority Problems and Question of New States Submitted by Igbirra Tribal Union Before the Minorities Commission," (date illegible).

[90] Gwari and Kamuku Memoranda (undated). CO 957/32. NA, UK.
[91] Colonial Office: Commission on Minority Groups in Northern Nigeria Memoranda Submitted: Minna. CO 957/32. NA, UK.
[92] See "Religious Tolerance," Press Release from Northern Region Information Service: Kaduna, November 6, 1957, No. 2693. CO 554/1534. NA, UK.
[93] See Chapter 4.

THE CONSTRUCTION OF MINORITIES

Discounting the petitioner's claims, the commission concluded that the petitioner had failed to make a successful case for state creation. Moreover, the commission pointed out that state creation would only reproduce the same minority-majority divisions that plagued Northern Nigeria since it would create new minorities within the new political unit.[94] At the same time, however, the commission pointed out that "the sum" of the petitioners fears "is not to be disregarded" since it left an "impression of a genuine and not unreasonable alarm at what may happen when restraint and guidance are removed from the operation of the Northern system."[95] By doing so, the commission argued that the problem with the Northern Nigeria arrangement was not in the colonial governance arrangement but with the potential departure of colonial administrators. The commission, in essence, distorted the petitioner's demands by reframing the petitioner's case as an apprehension about an independent state free of imperial control.

Judging Difference

The Willink Commission's significance lies beyond its adjudication of the state-creation claim; in fact, for both the petitioner and respondent, the Willink Commission was an occasion to appraise the colonial state's governance of religious difference. The petitioner contended that the history it performed before the commission was an indictment of the design of indirect rule and the Muslim domination it engendered, and therefore, of the colonial governance of religious difference. The NPC, on the other hand, lauded the Lugardian legacy of indirect rule as a "service to mankind" and "great contribution to the subject of colonial administration."[96] Commenting on the Lugardian design in glowing terms, Ahmadu Bello reminded the commissioners that it was over the Lugardian work and legacy that the commission was "sitting in

---

[94] While the commission did not grant the statist demands of petitions submitted by groups from Western and Eastern Nigeria, in those cases, the commission declared the areas in which new states were sought "minority areas" entitled to "special protections" and recommended that "limelight should be focused on these areas and the normal sanctions of democracy be brought into play." The Willink Report, 97. However, it did not make a similar recommendation in Northern Nigeria because in its view, "it would be difficult to wield together all of those disparate areas of Northern Nigeria in order to make them one area." The Willink Report, 564.
[95] The Willink Report, 73.
[96] Ahmadu Bello, Speech to Willink Commission, February 5, 1958. CO/957/4. NA, UK.

judgment."[97] Far from limited to the narrow question of state creation for which it had been established, the commission therefore became a site for struggles that had commenced since the British Empire brought together disparate groups to constitute the Protectorate of Northern Nigeria in 1903.

The Willink Commission furthered the late colonial state's technology of religion governance by defining, deepening, and hierarchizing religious difference. The colonial state's act of creating the commission to adjudicate the claim of "minorities" itself presumed non-Muslims as a "group apart." Already premised on the Muslim versus non-Muslim dichotomy, the commission's work further perpetuated that dichotomy. Although the commission turned a blind eye to the claims of marginalization adduced by the petitioners in order to deny the state-creation demand, the commission embraced the petitioner's story of religion differentiation and sameness. The commission's proceedings did not merely provide an opportunity for the petitioner to perform the non-Muslim identity, the commission itself engaged in the legitimation of the petitioner's claim of a distinct religious identity founded in its dichotomy to the Muslim identity. As noted earlier, the commission produced the first religion map of Northern Nigeria, which mapped religious affiliation onto territorial space much as the colonial state had sought to do through its three-type area classification. Those processes of differentiation (based on the Muslim–non-Muslim dichotomy) and of homogenization of diverse non-Muslim faiths and cultures did not merely define religion and religious difference, they also deepened preexisting tensions among the colonized – Muslim, Protestant, and diverse adherents of Indigenous religions. These processes were hardly egalitarian; through the elision of non-Protestant experiences, the differentiation and homogenization processes that culminated in the religious minorities identity entailed the hierarchization of religion.

Perhaps nothing illuminates the commission's governance of religious difference more than its approach to an application by Tijaniyyah Muslims to bring claims as "minorities." As noted in previous chapters, the Tijaniyyah had long been an object of Anglo-Masu Sarauta ire and had been repeatedly subject to brutal repression by the colonial state. In ruling on the Tijaniyyah application, the commission assumed the prerogative to define who an ideal Muslim was, excluding the Tijaniyyah from that definition. According to the commission, religious minorities competent

[97] Ibid.

to bring claims for consideration did not include "a sect within a religious majority."[98] Such sects, the commission held, were "dissident sects" and did not qualify as a religious minority competent to bring claims before the commission.[99] By labeling the Tijaniyyah "dissident," the Willink Commission furthered the three governance techniques employed by the colonial state: defining, deepening, and hierarchizing religious difference. The commission defined "Islam" by casting the Tijaniyyah as being outside of "good" Islam and dissident to it. Moreover, the commission, in laying this boundary between what was inside Islam and what was resistant to it, deepened the difference between the Tijaniyyah and Qadiriyyas. Finally, by affixing the Tijaniyyah with the dissident label, the Willink Commission legitimized the good Muslim – bad Muslim distinction and hierarchy created by the colonial state.

Because the inception of party politics in the postwar period had entrenched the repression of Muslims critical of the Anglo-Masu Sarauta alliance, their exclusion from the Minorities Commission was particularly disempowering. As noted earlier, Post Second World War politics was intertwined with theology in the colony. With the NPC being allied with the Masu Sarauta-dominated Qadiriyya Sufi brotherhood and NEPU drawing a huge following from the Tijaniyyah, the repression of the latter intensified, manifesting in their prohibition from building mosques, among other abuses.[100] Arrests on charges of insulting political authorities among other tenuous charges were also common.[101] There was a tendency to deny bail, and offenders tended to remain in prison for lengthy periods before being availed of judicial processes, which were hardly independent and impartial given the colonial state's erosion of the precolonial constitutional separation of juristic and political authority. Torture, arbitrary assessment of taxes, and destruction of mosques also appear to have been rampant. The March 1957 attacks against the Tijaniyyah in Gusau was a prominent example. Based on the allegation that they were disobedient to constituted authority in contravention

---

[98] The Willink Report, 111.   [99] Ibid.
[100] See "Memorandum of the National Elements Progressive Union Submitted to the Minorities Commission" (hereafter NEPU Memo) (undated) CO 957/28. See further Willink Commission, Records of Private Discussions in Adamawa, February 23, 1958. NA. CO/957/5.
[101] See NEPU Memo. See also NEPU, Evidence to be Given Before the Members of the Minorities Commission Sitting at Kaduna, February 3, 1958. CO 957/27 and CO/957/5 NA, UK.

of the Islamic injunction (enjoining obedience to authority), Native Authority police attacked Gusau Tijaniyyah, destroyed their property, and burned several houses. Those attacks were widely believed to have been carried out with the backing of political elites. In fact, prior to those attacks, the Sultan of Sokoto had written a letter to district heads, ordering the "rough handling" of all Tijaniyyah arrested.[102] Variations in intra-Muslim theological inclinations had therefore not only resulted in political difference, it had also culminated in brutal oppression of marginalized Muslims. Nevertheless, the commission barred this group from bringing claims by declaring difference in theological inclinations and the politics attached to them as dissidence.

The commission was ultimately successful in barring Muslim minorities from tabling claims before it because it also excluded political minorities. Upon their exclusion from bringing a claim as a religious minority, Tijaniyyah could have brought the claim as a political minority through NEPU (since much of NEPU's following was drawn from the Tijaniyyah). Yet, the opportunity to pursue the claim through NEPU was frustrated by the commission's ruling that it would not "hear ... political parties in opposition except in so far as their evidence threw light on the condition of ethnic and religious minorities."[103] The commission's ruling effectively curtailed NEPU from making the nexus between religious identity and political repression.

Despite the commission's exclusion of these Muslim minority claims, NEPU's allegations of the state's persecution of its Muslim critics form part of the commission's archive. Particularly noteworthy is the experience of Madam Gambo Ahmed, leader of NEPU's Women Wing. Alongside forty other female members of the party, Ahmed had been arrested during a party gathering. When eventually availed of judicial proceedings, Ahmed was sentenced to a month in prison based on her party association. Three days after she completed her jail term, Ahmed was re-arrested for publishing an account of her experiences in a newspaper. She was thereafter sentenced to another month in prison and told to leave Kano, the city where the event had transpired. Subsequently, however, Ahmed would be imprisoned in Zaria, the city to which she had departed, on charges of abusing the premier of the Northern Region. Shortly after completing this prison term, Ahmed would again be sentenced to six

---

[102] See generally March 2, 1958 proceedings of the Willink Commission. CO/957/5. NA, UK.
[103] The Willink Report, 111.

months in prison and fined eighty-five pounds on charges of displaying the picture of Ahmadu Bello and questioning his commitment to good governance. The subsequent quashing of Ahmed's conviction on appeal to the English High court did not end her political travails.[104]

Despite the unsettling facts of Madam Ahmed's case and those of several other NEPU members who had experienced the repression of the Anglo-NPC machinery, the commission declined to consider NEPU's claims. This outcome is hardly surprising since the commission had not only held that NEPU's submissions were relevant solely to the extent that they illuminated fears of religious and ethnic minorities, but had also declared the Tijaniyyah to be a dissident group rather than a minority. By excluding NEPU's claims, the commission shut out NEPU's proposals on the appropriate response to the colonial situation.

For Ahmed and others repressed by the colonial state, NEPU sought not the structural federalist autonomy that the UMBC demanded, but rather the curtailment of the powers of the Masu Sarauta and fundamental rights protecting vulnerable persons in the state. To be sure, NEPU supported the UMBC's proposal for the creation of a Middle Belt State to redress the marginalization of non-Muslim persons. However, NEPU disagreed with the UMBC that federalism was the formulaic answer to the problem of hierarchization inherent to the colonial state's governance of religious difference. Indeed, NEPU argued that federalism was itself one of the legacies of the colonial rule through the colonial state's creation of a religion-territorial classification, a design that was foundational to indirect rule and the shoring up of Masu Sarauta power. Although NEPU was willing to support the UMBC's state-creation demand, it was opposed to the perpetuation of the colonial structure of governance that it feared federalism would bring. Besides, NEPU insisted that if federalism was to be the structure of governance, that determination had to be made through an inclusive grassroots democratic deliberation rather than through a colonial government-appointed commission.[105]

---

[104] See also the account of the six-month imprisonment of a Tijaniyyah leader for publishing "offensive" comments about the emir in the *Daily Comet* newspaper from November 21, 1949. See CO554/1534 folder and CO957/5 NA, UK. On repression of NEPU members, see Memo of the Colonial Office West Africa Department to the Minister of State, "Confidential Note for the Minister of State on the Arrest of NEPU Adherents," August 24, 1954, in which the department argues that NEPU had transnational communist links. CO 554/1069. NA, UK.

[105] See NEPU, "Views on the Nigerian Constitution Conference 1956," Rhode House Library, Oxford Ref. FCB 85/2 in Jega et al., *Mallam Aminu Kano*.

The commission's furtherance of the colonial technique of governing religion lay as much in the aspirations it frustrated as in the claims it allowed. The commission recommended rights as the panacea to the agitations of the religious minorities.[106] That rights recommendation was discordant with the commission's dismissal of the petitioner's fears and its absolution of the colonial state. At the same time however, the rights recommendation was consonant with the religious governance technique that was so central to the commission's workings. The commission's rights recommendation, which was notably distinct from the NEPU submission, was drawn from a Colonial Office proposal.[107] That proposal had been drafted in consultation with representatives of the Christian Council of Nigeria and the Christian Council on International Affairs, an international ecumenical body.[108] Although the scripting of the rights provision appeared to endow religious liberty regardless of religious affiliation, the origins of the provision and ultimately the vision of religion it sought to protect was markedly Protestant. A subsequent chapter will explore the ultimate constitutionalization of the right to religious liberty as a separate element of the Independence deal. It is sufficient here to note that in evaluating claims before it, the commission and the colonial state whose agenda it furthered were far from dispassionate arbiters of the question of religious difference. By recommending a rights provision that centered Protestantism and marginalized Indigenous faiths and Muslim minorities, the commission called for a vision of emancipation tied to religious difference and to a hierarchy of faiths. The Muslim–non-Muslim binary would therefore maintain a tenacious hold, occupying the horizon, and occluding alternative emancipatory possibilities.

CONCLUSION

The "construction of minorities"[109] is not novel. Although a range of social legal relations surely produce a circumstance that conditions a group as a minority, the marshaling of a "minority" identity to make

---

[106] The Willink Report, 101–102.   [107] See Chapter 4.
[108] Resumed Nigeria Constitutional Conference 1958 Fundamental Rights Brief No. 4, CO 554/1535, 2. Provisions for Safeguarding Religious Liberty and Declaration of Fundamental Human Rights. NA, UK. See Chapter 4.
[109] See André Burguière and Raymond Grew, eds., *The Construction of Minorities: Cases for Comparison across Time and around the World* (Ann Arbor: University of Michigan Press, 2001). See further Mamdani, *Neither Settler nor Native*.

political and legal claims necessitates both deliberate and inconscient choices over who to include and exclude. These choices are, in part, determined by the claims to be articulated. If the history of the non-Muslim identity in the colonial state was already exclusionary, the co-option of that identity by a group that had long criticized the identity only paved the way for further exclusions. Although it purported to represent both Christians and Indigenous religion adherents, the petition for self-determination before the Willink Commission centered Christian concerns. Further, the framing of the colonial malady as a Muslim versus non-Muslim problem necessitated the construction of a self primarily defined with reference to religion. The consequence was not only that the religious minorities identity would exclude intra-Muslim minorities but also that the non-Muslim identity was hardly representative of diverse non-Muslim concerns. Although envisioned as a resistance against the colonial state, the making of the religious minorities identity inherited the forms of difference – and sameness – bequeathed by colonial rule. The colonial state's Muslim versus non-Muslim differentiation, central to its imperial secular governmentality, therefore predetermined the nationalist vision of emancipation. The self-determination claim failed, but the religious minorities identity that was integral to that project survived. That identity became an entrenched part of constitutional politics, integral to the rest of the Independence deal and living on in post-Independence years.[110]

---

[110] See Chapters 4 and 5 below for the other two elements of the Independence deal – the abolition of Islamic criminal law and the turn to human rights.

CHAPTER FOUR

THE MAKING OF THE 1958 PENAL CODE

In the early hours of February 21, 1958, an elite delegation from Northern Nigeria arrived at Idris Airport in Tripoli, Libya. The delegation was led by Muhamadu Kobo, the emir of Lapai, and its secretary was Sam Scrutton Richardson, a Northern Nigerian district officer and Oxford graduate studying for the English bar. Other members of the delegation were Muhammad Sani, Chief Alkali of Kano; Haliru Binji, Maliki law scholar and recent graduate of the University of London; and Peter Achimugu, a Christian politician from Kabba (a Type III area) who was a minister in the Northern Region government and prominent member of the Northern People's Congress (NPC). The visit to Libya was at the behest of the colonial government. Following the recommendation of School of Oriental and African Studies professor John Norman Dalrymple Anderson, the Colonial Office tasked the delegates with studying Libya as a model of a decolonized Muslim state that had modernized by eliminating Islamic criminal law. Libya was only the first stop in the delegation's assignment; the same group would subsequently visit Pakistan, and another similarly composed delegation would undertake a similar assignment in Sudan.[1]

Two encounters were central to the delegation's work in Libya. The first was its meeting with Auni Dajani, barrister of the Inner Temple of

---

[1] See "Report of the Panel of Jurists Appointed to Examine the Legal and Judicial Systems of the Region," S.MOJ/12/S.1, vol. I, National Archives Nigeria, Kaduna (hereafter NA Nigeria).

England, and justice of the Libyan Supreme Court. Dajani was Palestinian and had been a high court judge of the British Mandate in Palestine before being appointed to the Libyan Supreme Court. It was not, however, Dajani's legal credentials that commanded the attention of the Northern Nigerian elites. Rather, what impressed them was Dajani's family pedigree: the jurist's lineage was the official custodian of "Islam's holy places" in Palestine.[2] Marveling at Justice Dajani's effect on the Northern Nigerian delegation, Sam Richardson, the delegation's scribe, described the "awe and respect" with which the Northern Nigerian elites listened to Dajani's expositions of Islamic jurisprudence.[3] For Richardson and the Colonial Office reformers he represented, Justice Dajani was a particularly effective choice for an expert to consult because they viewed jurist's position on Islamic law's place in the modern state as "measured and moderate."[4] The other expert to exert such influence on the delegation to the pleasure of Richardson and his Colonial Office superiors was the grand mufti of Libya, Mohamed Abulas'ad el-'Alem. Although they were initially wary of the grand mufti's association with Egypt's Al-Azhar University, where the jurist had studied, the colonial administrators later concluded that the grand mufti was not "a latter-day Muslim fundamentalist" as they regarded Al-Azhar scholars.[5] To the pleasure of the colonial officials, the Libyan mufti sanctioned the legality of Islamic criminal law's abolition in Northern Nigeria. Moreover, the mufti advised the delegation that in the absence of a direct conflict with the Quran, a "secular state" like Libya could legitimately abolish Islamic law from spheres other than personal law (marriage, divorce, inheritance, and guardianship) and the law governing worship (prayer, fasting, giving alms, and undertaking the pilgrimage).[6] Regulation of the spheres of criminal law, property, and land matters through a code legislated with no reference to Islamic jurisprudence was not merely compatible with Islamic law, it was, according to the grand mufti, required by the "secular" nature of the state.[7]

---

[2] Sam Scruton Richardson, *No Weariness: The Memoir of a Generalist in Public Services in Four Continents* (Wiltshire, UK: Malt House Publishing, 2001), 200. The two Islamic sites in question were in Jerusalem: King David's Tomb and the Cenacle, the room where the Last Supper is believed to have occurred, and which is said to be on an upper floor of King David's Tomb. For an account of the Dajanis, see Adel A. Dajani, *From Jerusalem to a Kingdom by Sea* (London: Zuleika Books, 2021).
[3] Richardson, *No Weariness*, 200.
[4] Ibid.   [5] Ibid.   [6] Ibid.   [7] Ibid.

PART II CONSTITUTING DIFFERENCE

For Richardson and the reformers at the Colonial Office, the Libyan visit achieved its purpose: it opened the eyes of Northern Nigerians to a leading example of what the role of Islam and Muslim jurists ought to be in a modern state. J. N. D. Anderson had since warned these colonial administrators in a 1951 advisory that "no realist would maintain that the Shari'a provides an adequate basis for criminal law in a modern state of mixed religious loyalties and progressive intentions."[8] Yet, this "modern," "progressive" state was what colonial administrators envisioned, and the visit to Libya was intended to convince the Northern Nigerian elites that a state could attain this vision primarily through eliminating Islamic criminal law.[9] The Libyan visit and the subsequent visits to Pakistan and Sudan were therefore intended to legitimate the impending plan to eliminate Islamic criminal law in the late colonial state. That legitimation project was central to the successful replacement of Islamic jurisprudence with an imperial code on the eve of Nigeria's Independence in 1960. Against the backdrop of stakeholders' contestations in the late colonial years, this chapter presents the final settlement on Islamic law – a codification project based on imperial law and justified in the name of Islamic law.

As is evident in the discourse of the 1958 processes, the Penal Code was legitimated by invoking Islam while also appealing to the late colonial ideal of disentangling the state from Islam and guaranteeing the liberties of non-Muslims. The code's Colonial Office proponents, Masu Sarauta (political elites), and alkalai (judges) legitimated the code as "Islamic" by citing the example of "modern" Muslim states like Sudan, Libya, Pakistan, and Egypt. At the same time, Anderson and other Colonial Office proponents insisted that the codification project was animated by a desire to reform law to meet the needs of Northern Nigeria's multireligious population. Anderson and others surmised that guaranteeing the religious liberty of non-Muslims required excising Islamic law from the public sphere by abolishing Islamic criminal law. They concluded that only such an emphasis on the state's separation from Islam could produce a twentieth-century secular state worthy of Independence from Britain.

The codes of Sudan and Pakistan, those Muslim states on which the Northern Nigerian Code rested, originated from imperial legislative

---

[8] J. N. D. Anderson to N. J. Brooke, April 6, 1951, PPMS 60. Anderson Collections, School of Oriental and African Studies (hereafter SOAS), London.
[9] Ibid.

processes. Their provisions drew from English Common Law and North American statutes, jettisoning Islamic jurisprudence. The Penal Code reform process did not only supplant Islamic jurisprudence with a code of Western law. To effect this substitution, it shifted the locus of lawmaking authority from the divine invocations underlying precolonial and early colonial expositions of the law – however rhetorical – to the late colonial state's legislative and executive officials. The remaking of Islamic law itself was not new; as shown earlier in this book, it commenced in the earliest days of colonial rule through the expansion of emirs' siyasa (discretionary jurisdiction of political authorities). If the early colonial project had transformed siyasa by altering its constitutional balance with fiqh (jurists' expositions of the Shari'a), what was distinct about the late colonial Anderson-led project was its radical disconnection of siyasa from its precolonial constitutional repository. Nevertheless, Anderson successfully argued that the late colonial state's direct assumption of power to abolish Islamic criminal jurisprudence was a legitimate exercise of siyasa jurisdiction and was consequently Shari'a compliant. Although this rationale ostensibly relied on the Shari'a to legitimate the 1958 Code, the essence of the reform project was to hinge Shari'a's legitimacy on the colonial lawmaking process itself. From the Shari'a legitimating siyasa, siyasa now began to legitimate the Shari'a. It was in this way that the making of the 1958 Penal Code climaxed the imperial transformation of Islamic law that commenced at the inception of colonial rule.

SHARI'A, SIYASA, AND THE MODERN STATE

The place of siyasa governance in the Shari'a continues to be a subject of much scholarly debate, some of which is explored in Chapter 2. Perhaps no question provides a more significant opportunity to explore these debates and what they reveal about the complexity of Islamic law's relationship with the modern state than codification. To be sure, the intellectual exercise of harmonizing juristic thought and rulings in different Muslim societies is far from a modern phenomenon. However, rather than codifying the corpus of Islamic legal jurisprudence across schools, premodern harmonization tended to be in the vein of "positivization": reducing abstract juristic postulations into rulings within individual schools of jurisprudence, such as the core Maliki jurisprudential text *Mukthasar Khalil* that is so influential across North and West Africa.

PART II CONSTITUTING DIFFERENCE

The Ottoman Tanzimat reform, particularly the Majalla Code, was prominent among the rare attempts at codification. In reducing Islamic legal jurisprudence to a set of "positive legal prescriptions" through the dual process of *takhayyur* (selection) and *talfiq* (harmonization) of conflicting juristic opinions, the Ottoman project pursued a vision of modernization modeled on European law.[10] However, another understanding suggests that the Ottoman codification project was designed to bolster Shariʿa's legitimacy in an irreversibly modernizing context.[11] Modernity, this second reading would assert, is not exclusively Western. Moreover, this position suggests that Islamic legal modernity can ground its authority exclusively in an Islamic legal paradigm even if it borrows its form and structure from Europe. The Tanzimat reforms continue to be an often-cited and invaluable reference point given the Ottoman Empire's place in Islamic legal history.[12] Yet, the Ottoman project is dissimilar to Northern Nigeria's 1958 reforms: for all of the Ottoman Majalla's cookie-cutter approach to fitting Islamic jurisprudence into the European form, the reservoir from which it drew much of the substantive principles was Islamic juristic texts. In its sourcing from the substance of European law, the Northern Nigerian Penal Code reform (and its counterparts in the Sudan and Pakistan Codes) was perhaps a little closer to the Egyptian Civil Code of 1949 drafted by Abdur-Razaq Sanhuri, albeit with the marked difference that the latter centered on civil law. Unlike the Egyptian exercise, the Northern Nigerian reforms expunged Islamic law from public law, particularly criminal law. Nevertheless, the focus of the Egyptian program on civil law (since the French legal reforms of 1883 had outrightly eliminated Islamic criminal jurisprudence) and the aversion of the Northern Nigerian reformers to the Egyptian reforms do not preclude the analytical gains of looking to the Egyptian example. As with the Nigerian Penal Code, the Egyptian Code laid claim to Islamic legitimacy despite its conscious modeling on Western law. Although Sanhuri based the

---

[10] Anver M. Emon, *Religious Pluralism and Islamic Law: Dhimmis and Others in the Empire of Law* (Oxford: Oxford University Press, 2012), 46; Samy A. Ayoub, *Law, Empire, and the Sultan: Ottoman Imperial Authority and Late Hanafi Jurisprudence* (Oxford: Oxford University Press, 2019).

[11] Ibid., 47. For a recent exposition of this position, see generally Ayoub, *Law, Empire and the Sultan*.

[12] See generally Ayoub, *Law, Empire and the Sultan*; Khaled Abou El Fadl, *Speaking in God's Name: Islamic Law, Authority and Women* (New York: Simon and Schuster, 2014); and Emon, *Religious Pluralism and Islamic Law*.

Egyptian Code on French law, the jurist insisted that the reform exercise did not discount the Shari'a. He cited the application of fiqh (jurisprudence) in matters on which the code was silent and when defining customary law – as long as the fiqh ruling did not contravene any of the code's provisions.[13] Manifesting in different forms, such efforts to legitimize the modern state's projects by invoking Islamic legal authority abounded in colonized Muslim societies.

These references situate the debates in colonial Nigeria in the longer history of the Muslim world; they do not, however, occlude the specificities of Northern Nigeria and the unique experiences catalyzed by its encounter with modernity. Even within a single context, legitimation projects were variable over time, starting, in the Northern Nigerian experience, from invoking emirs' siyasa as a basis of authority to shifting the locus of Shari'a governance to the late colonial state – while consistently invoking the Shari'a.

The jury is out on whether such colonial reform projects, often carried out in alliance with Muslim elites, amount to a disjuncture from the precolonial past. While conceding that such projects redefined the scope of the Shari'a, one view suggests that colonial reform of Islamic law did not amount to a radical transformation because the Shari'a has always been "positioned at the intersection of the law and the enterprise of governance."[14] In essence, the noted view of the seventh-century Islamic theologian Ibn Taymiyya that siyasa was bound within the confines of the Shari'a – "siyasa shar'iyya" – has always remained an idealized conception in Islamic legal history.[15] In fact, scholarship

---

[13] See Enid Hill, "Al-Sanhuri and Islamic Law: The Place and Significance of Islamic Law in the Life and Work of 'Abd al-Razzaq Ahmad Al-Sanhuri, Egyptian Jurist and Scholar, 1895–1971," *Arab Law Quarterly* 3, no. 1 (1988): 33–64.

[14] Emon, *Religious Pluralism and Islamic Law*, 248; see also Naveeda Khan, *Muslim Becoming: Aspiration and Skepticism in Pakistan* (Durham, NC: Duke, 2012); Noah Salomon, *For Love of the Prophet: An Ethnography of Sudan's Islamic State* (Princeton, NJ: Princeton University Press, 2017). See, however, Iza R. Hussin, *The Politics of Islamic Law: Local Elites, Colonial Authority, and the Making of the Muslim State* (Chicago: University of Chicago Press, 2016); Brinkley M. Messick, *The Calligraphic State: Textual Domination and History in a Muslim Society* (Berkeley: University of California Press, 1993); Wael Hallaq, *Shari'a: Theory, Practice, Transformations* (New York: Cambridge University Press, 2009); Tamir Moustafa, "The Judicialization of Religion," *Law & Society Review* 52, no. 3 (2018): 685–708; and Hikmet Kocamaner, "Regulating the Family through Religion: Secularism, Islam, and the Politics of the Family in Turkey," *American Ethnologist* 46, no. 4 (2019): 495–508.

[15] Emon, *Religious Pluralism and Islamic Law*, 248. See Taqī al-Dīn Ahmad Ibn Taymiyya, *al-Siyāsa al-Shar 'iyya fī Islah al-Rā'ī wa-al-Ra 'iyya* (Beirut: Dār -al

illuminating the extensive authority of political rulers over expositions of law confirms the existence of a constitutional boundary. A recent seminal work in this strand, Samy Ayoub's *Law, Empire and the Sultan*, demonstrates that late Hanafi jurists ascribed legal authority to Sultanic edicts, thereby challenging the notion that premodern jurists had sole legal authority over Islamic law.[16] Regardless of the context of Ottoman political transformations and the conditions of Western hegemony from which they sprung, projects such as the Majalla were not outside the Shari'a, as Ayoub's work shows. Instead, the codification project was, in Ayoub's words, "a Muslim response to modernity and its legal order, argued and justified from within the tradition."[17] In essence, rather than discount the Taymiyyan notion of siyasa as constrained by the Shari'a, works illuminating political authority over jurisprudence reinforce the acknowledgment of Shar'i constitutional boundaries by participants in struggles, even if only in discursive terms. If this was the case for the Majalla, it was even more true of both the process that birthed the 1958 Code in Nigeria and the code's substantive provisions. For all of its invocation of Islamic legal authority, including the practice of Muslim societies, the 1958 Penal Code reforms went beyond early colonial rule's disturbance of precolonial fiqh-siyasa constitutional balance. Instead, the political and legal processes of decolonization transformed siyasa from siyasa shar'iyya, as delimited by the Shari'a and as expounded by jurists, to a siyasa whose constitutional boundaries were determined by the modern state. Nigeria's Independence constitutional deal on Islamic law, therefore, sealed the state's prerogative to govern religion and religious difference.

THE TWILIGHT OF EMPIRE

Regretting the shift from the Lugardian ideals that marked early colonialism, Oxford scholar of British colonial rule in Africa and Lugard's biographer, Margery Perham, remarked in 1937: "how far is it our policy to use British law as an agent of civilization or, like the French, of imperial assimilation?"[18] If that civilization project was barely

---

Kutub al 'ilmiyyah, 1988). Ovamir Anjum, *Politics, Law, and Community in Islamic Thought: The Taymiyyan Moment* (Cambridge: Cambridge University Press, 2012).

[16] See Ayoub, *Law, Empire and the Sultan.*   [17] Ibid., 150–151.

[18] Margery Freda Perham, *Native Administration in Nigeria* (New York: Oxford University Press, 1937), 339. See further Margery Freda Perham, "Editor's

discernible when Perham published her *Native Administration in Nigeria* in 1937, it became patent with the colony's unmistakable march to Independence in the years following the Second World War. As noted in earlier chapters, in the years leading up to the *Gubba* decision, many at the senior levels of the colonial administration in Nigeria and key officials in the London Colonial Office became keen on veering away from what they understood as an undue deference to Muslim institutions. Early colonialism had not left the substance of Islamic law unchanged; yet the Lugardian tendency dominant in the early decades of colonial rule centered on covertly reforming it through expanding emirs' siyasa powers. The prevalent sensibility in the latter colonial years was markedly different. Rather than subscribing to Lugardian deference to the Masu Sarauta, these latter-day officials sought the active making of a colony "in which men are given the opportunity to grow to their full stature" – on the foundation of "Christianity and the rule of law."[19] The idea had become so popular within the colonial administration that by the time Perham revisited the issue she had raised eleven years earlier on the eve of *Gubba*, even she had a change of heart: "We have got to shift the basis of our empire still more from power to service, change it from a distant, half-forgotten affair which we leave to professionals, to officials."[20] Although Perham urged caution, declaring that "we may have to expect much from our colonies but not that they should change all their institutions, political habits and personalities overnight,"[21] the ardor for reform had been

---

Introduction to the Series," in Martin Wight, *The Development of the Legislative Council, 1606–1945* (London: Faber and Faber, 1946), 5; Andrew N. Porter, "Margery Perham, Christian Missions and Indirect Rule," *Journal of Imperial and Commonwealth History* 19, no. 3 (October 1991): 83–99; and Andrew N. Porter, "War, Colonialism and the British Experience: The Redefinition of Christian Missionary Policy, 1938–1952," *Kirchliche Zeitgeschichte* 5, no. 2 (1992): 273–274. For an account on Perham's influence in the colonial administration, see Kenneth E. Robinson, "Margery Perham and the Colonial Office," *Journal of Imperial and Commonwealth History* 19, no. 3 (October 1991): 185–196.

[19] See Harold Macmillan, "The Wind of Change Speech, Address by Harold Macmillan to Members of Both Houses of the Parliament of the Union of South Africa, Cape Town, 3 February 1960," accessed December 17, 2021, https://web-archives.univ-pau.fr/english/TD2doc1.pdf. See further Frank Myers, "Harold Macmillan's 'Winds of Change' Speech: A Case Study in the Rhetoric of Policy Change," *Rhetoric and Public Affairs* 3, no. 4 (2000): 555–575.

[20] Roland Oliver, "Prologue: The Two Miss Perhams," in *Margery Perham and British Rule in Africa*, eds. Alison Smith and Mary Bull (London: Routledge, 1991), 2.

[21] Perham, "Editor's Introduction to the Series," 12–13.

lit and would not be tempered in the hearts of senior administrators. The 1947 *Gubba* decision's reprimand of Lugardian tendencies and its declaration of the subsidiarity of Islamic law was merely the first step in this move toward reform. By the time the Colonial Office's foremost expert on Islamic law in Africa, J. N. D. Anderson, would advocate for sweeping Islamic legal reforms in his 1951 Survey for the Colonial Office, the Colonial Office would unreservedly embrace the proposal.[22] In Anderson, the Colonial Office had found a champion for the project to reform Northern Nigerian Islamic law.

Northern Nigeria was a thorny case, but the question of what to do with the legal systems of colonies upon Independence perplexed administrators all over the British Empire.[23] To deal with that question in British Africa, the Colonial Office convened a Judicial Advisers' Conference in 1953, which was chaired by Sir Roberts-Wray, the legal adviser to the Colonial Office and the Commonwealth Relations Office.[24] Convening at Uganda's Makerere University, the Judicial Advisers' Conference considered the problems posed by the existence of multiple legal systems in African colonial territories – the "Islamic," "Customary," and "English" legal systems – and deliberated over reducing the conflicts between those legal systems in preparation for Independence. In particular, the Makerere gathering of administrators, scholars, and jurists described Islamic law as posing "special problems"[25] and regarded the Northern Nigerian Islamic law question as uniquely peculiar given its odd retention of Islamic criminal law, which was unparalleled outside the British Aden Protectorate. While the conference considered Islamic law in other parts of the continent on a regional basis, the gathering treated the Northern Nigerian situation as a stand-alone case.[26] The administrators and jurists looked to Anderson for guidance on Islamic law in general and Northern Nigeria

---

[22] See J. N. D. Anderson, "The Application of Islamic Law in Northern Nigeria," May 8, 1957. CO 554/1941, 17E, 33. NA, UK.

[23] On the human rights angle to the legal reform project, see Charles Parkinson, *Bills of Rights and Decolonization: The Emergence of Domestic Human Rights Instruments in Britain's Overseas Territories* (Oxford: Oxford University Press, 2007).

[24] On the conferences, see Antony Nicholas Allott, "The London Conference on the Future of Law in Africa," *African Studies Bulletin* 3, no. 2 (1960): 13–15.

[25] *Native Courts and Native Customary Law in Africa: Judicial Advisers Conference 1953. A Special Supplement to the Journal of African Administration* (London: HM Stationery Office, 1953).

[26] Ibid., 33–36.

in particular.[27] The professor of Oriental laws maintained the position he had taken in his by-then acclaimed 1951 study, calling for the outright elimination of Islamic law from criminal law and invoking the precedent of modern Muslim states that had appropriated siyasa powers to curtail the domain of fiqh. Anderson attributed the retention of Islamic law in public law via criminal law to Lugard's 1903 guarantee of noninterference in Islam while also stressing that Lugard's words had been "quoted, honored and exploited to such a degree that make the original words appear innocuous in the extreme."[28] Relying on Anderson's expertise, the Makerere Conference recommended eliminating Islamic law from the domain of criminal law. Anderson, however, cautioned that change, although instantly desired, would be slow since efforts to reform had to remain "gradual ... for political and financial reasons."[29] The question of timing was therefore left unresolved even as Makere participants concluded on the abolition of Islamic criminal law.

While the question of Northern Nigerian Islamic law took a front seat in international deliberations like the Makerere Conference, the debate raged even more fiercely among stakeholders in the colony. For European Christian missionaries and their fledgling convert community, Islamic law remained the most sustained feature of the "Muslim imperialism" that marked colonial rule, and reform was imperative.[30] In theory, Islamic criminal law was still applicable to the entirety of the colonized populations, with the sole exception of those residing in Type III areas designated by the colonial state as Indigenous religious areas. That colonial governance had fundamentally reformed Islamic criminal law hardly mattered to those who regarded the presence of Islamic law in public law – even in form rather than substance – as a reminder of the privileges accorded to Muslim elites.

---

[27] Commenting on the selection of Anderson, Sir Roberts-Wray stated that Anderson had "first-hand knowledge and experience ... [and was] neither excessively conservative nor revolutionary," Minute, Kenneth Roberts-Wray, October 20, 1955. CO 955/20. National Archives United Kingdom (hereafter NA, UK).

[28] James Norman Dalrymple Anderson, "Conflict of Laws in Northern Nigeria: A New Start," *International & Comparative Law Quarterly* 8, no. 3 (1959): 442–443.

[29] *Native Courts and Native Customary Law in Africa*, 36.

[30] See J. Lowry Maxwell, *Half a Century of Grace: A Jubilee History of the Sudan United Mission* (Westcliff-on-Sea, UK: Sudan United Mission, 1953); Moses E. Ochonu, *Colonialism by Proxy: Hausa Imperial Agents and Middle Belt Consciousness in Nigeria* (Bloomington, IN: Indiana University Press, 2014).

Beyond changes in the substance of the law, the district officer had the administrative discretion to *sua sponte* transfer cases from alkalai courts to the English court system, thereby precluding the application of Islamic law. Regardless of the Lugardian leaning of many district officers, they often exercised that discretion usually due to the sustained advocacy of missionaries. Yet, the presence of that safeguard hardly alleviated the concerns of missionaries and Christian converts. In fact, that group argued that the administrative safeguard would be lost upon the departure of British officials following Independence, with the consequence that Christian converts would be tried before alkalai courts. To justify their fear, missionaries and converts alleged threats by Muslim elites to non-Muslims to "wait till the British go!"[31] Although the claims failed to convince the Willink Commission to grant self-determination, missionary calls for legal reform met a highly favorable reception with a Colonial Office now populated by critics of Lugardian policy and inclined to reverse the erstwhile ceremonial deference to Islamic law.[32] Senior administrators who were already sympathetic to missionary concerns and piqued by the barriers facing non-Muslims began to cite the alleged threats as a motivation for reforms. Notably, J. N. D. Anderson, who would be tapped by the Colonial Office to lead the reform project and had himself worked as a missionary in Egypt, not only found the allegations credible but also invoked them in justifying the ensuing reforms.[33] Drawing on this support it found in the upper echelons of the colonial administration, the now influential Christian constituency intensified calls for change that had begun in the early colonial years.

Christian advocates were hardly alone in calling for reforms as part of the Independence settlement of struggles over religion governance. A sustained debate over Islamic law played out among Muslims. Long repressed by Masu Sarauta-controlled courts and finding organized political representation through a political party – the Northern Elements Progressive Union (NEPU) – key Muslim intellectuals stepped up their critique of the Masu Sarauta and its version of Islamic law in the 1950s. The back and forth that ensued between NEPU, and the Masu Sarauta–allied Northern Peoples' Congress (NPC) became a tussle over competing visions of Islamic law in a modern world.

---

[31] Anderson, "Conflict of Laws," 450; Richardson, *No Weariness*, 209.
[32] See Chapter 3.   [33] Anderson, "Conflict of Laws," 449.

For NEPU elites, modernity necessitated the reform of Islamic law, and Egypt was the desired model. These activists cited Gamal Nasser's Egypt and, in particular, the Egypt Civil Code authored by Abdur-Razaq Sanhuri as the paradigm for determining the success of a progressive Muslim state.[34] For instance, in a 1955 newspaper publication, Mallam A. K. Metteden, a civil servant and prominent NEPU intellectual, called for Nigeria to follow Egypt's example and abolish Islamic courts.[35] Metteden charged that the rot in the administration of Islamic law in Northern Nigeria, like that in pre-reform Egypt, sprung from jurists' emphasis on law books and their departure from primary reliance on the Quran as the ultimate source of legal authority. Metteden's critique was not merely of the jurist class; it was an argument against legal tradition, especially in the form it had come to assume in the state. As a remedy, Metteden proposed the Egyptian model and, in particular, the Egyptian abolition of Islamic courts. Although Metteden conceded that the reformed Egyptian legal system did not derive from a direct reading of the primary source texts, he argued that the reforms had Islamic legitimacy primarily due to Egyptians' "Arabic language" and "Islamic heritage."[36] On the other hand, Metteden charged that Northern Nigerians were mere "converts"[37] to Islam and could not claim superior Islamic knowledge to Egyptians. Northern Nigerian revolutionaries championed the post-reform Egyptian model as the progressive vision of Islamic law while simultaneously insisting that the Egyptian example was the authentic version of Islamic law and jurisprudence. For NEPU intellectuals, therefore, decolonizing Northern Nigerian Islamic law meant turning to the Egyptian model.

The Masu Sarauta establishment hastened to take on the challenge. Retorting to Metteden, Nuhu Bamali, a prominent NPC elite, contested the idealization of the Egyptian model. Criticizing Metteden's association of Northern Nigerian Islamic law with corruption, Bamali pointed out that corruption afflicted all of modern society, including

---

[34] Alan Feinstein, *African Revolutionary: The Life and Times of Nigeria's Aminu Kano* (New York: Quadrangle, 1973), 189–190; Jonathan Reynolds, *The Time of Politics (Zamanin Siyasa): Islam and the Politics of Legitimacy in Northern Nigeria, 1950–1966* (San Francisco: International Scholar Publications, 1998), 98.

[35] John N. Paden, *Ahmadu Bello, Sardauna of Sokoto: Values and Leadership in Nigeria* (Zaria, Nigeria: HudaHuda, 1986), 205.

[36] Ibid., 206.

[37] See response by Idris Gana, "Not Necessarily," *Nigerian Citizen*, November 10, 1955, 8.

Muslim institutions: "I do not think it is Islamic law that is outmoded. It is justice, honesty and moral righteousness that are so."[38] To Bamali, therefore, the solution lay not in the reform of Islamic institutions as Egypt had chosen; instead, it lay in reforming society. With a sanitized society, Bamali argued, classical Islamic law and Muslim institutions remained the ideal model for administering justice even in modern times. Writing from London, Ali Akilu, another NPC elite and a former classmate of NEPU's Metteden, aligned with Bamali's view.[39] Shedding Bamali's reluctance to criticize Egypt directly, Akilu castigated the Egyptian model as an uncritical copying of Western law, pointing out that Western law was neither a single model nor a perfect one. Although the NPC elite acknowledged the defects in the administration of justice, he, like Bamali, sought to distinguish the administration of Islamic law from Islamic law itself. However, unlike Bamali's insistence on Islamic law's constancy and timelessness, Akilu conceded that Islamic law is "inadequate" and "does not envisage the complexity" of modern relationships.[40] Yet, the NPC intellectual argued that Islamic law needs "reinforcement" not "revolution," and with a barely veiled swipe at the Egyptian revolution, called for "reform by a sober evolutionary process and not by the dazzling, but often shaky success of revolutionary dictatorships."[41] The NPC elite was therefore opposed to the NEPU clamor for far-reaching reforms.

Not all NPC elites were opposed to the Egyptian model: a notable exception was Abdul G. F. Razaq, one of the ten English-trained lawyers practicing in Northern Nigeria in the 1950s. Razaq saw the Egyptian example as a possible model under the right circumstances.[42] The lawyer, however, argued that that model was not suitable for Northern Nigeria at the time due to the lack of sufficient personnel trained in Western law. Razaq went on to indicate his potential support for a similar measure in Northern Nigeria should the region have sufficiently trained personnel; yet, he stressed that the government had been successful in addressing challenges of the administration of justice in a manner suitable to local circumstances. Razaq's potential openness to Egyptian-style reforms remained a minority view on the NPC side of

---

[38] Nuhu Bamali, "Islamic Courts Must Remain," *Nigerian Citizen*, October 27, 1955, 9.
[39] Ali Akilu, letter to *Nigerian Citizen* dated November 4, 1955, 9.
[40] Ibid   [41] Ibid., 9.
[42] Abdul G. F. Razaq, "A Barrister Says North Is Not Ready to Do Away with Them," *Nigerian Citizen*, November 10, 1955, 8.

the debate; most NPC elites considered the Egyptian model a betrayal of Islamic values. The Masu Sarauta, therefore, remained strenuously opposed to the abolition of alkalai courts and the outright elimination of Islamic jurisprudence as acceptable outcomes of decolonization negotiations.

NEPU did not renege on its calls for reform. Its founder, Aminu Kano, joined the exchange through an article titled, "NEPU Would Not Do Away with Islamic Courts – But Sleepy Alkalis, Squatters and 'Go-Betweens' Must All Look Out."[43] Kano insisted that NEPU considered the Quran and Hadith as the primary texts regulating human affairs. At the same time, however, the principal critic of the Anglo-Masu Sarauta alliance and of indirect rule through the Masu Sarauta argued that Muslim minority intellectuals recognized the value of Western law and other external systems of law in providing ideas for tackling novel questions in Muslim societies. Kano, who was trained in the Islamic sciences, argued that early Muslim judges had engaged extensively with other systems of law, particularly at moments when Muslim societies encountered unique cultures and ways.[44] Kano declared: "Islamic law is not static and has not been so."[45] In particular, the NEPU founder cited *istihsan* (preferential reasoning),[46] arguing that the classical principle with strong foundations in the primary texts enabled modern societies to remain "alive to the changing conditions of life."[47] In Kano's philosophy, these decisions were not merely for the juristic class or political elites; the will of the masses had to be taken into consideration. Therefore, despite criticizing alkalai courts, Kano stressed that NEPU would adhere to the will of the masses and refrain from abolishing those courts if the electorate desired to retain them. Even in those circumstances, however, Kano insisted that a NEPU government would, at the minimum, overhaul those courts by eliminating the widespread ineptitude evidenced by the "go-betweens,"

---

[43] Aminu Kano, "NEPU Would Not Do Away with Islamic Courts – but Sleepy Alkalis, Squatters and 'Go-Betweens' Must All Look Out," *Nigerian Citizen*, November 10, 1955, 8.
[44] Kano argued that early jurists borrowed from Roman law and that the concepts of fiqh as jurisprudence, of the *faqi* as the lawyer, and of *ra'y* as opinion are borrowed from Roman law. He further argued that *istihsan*, *istihlas*, and *ijtihad* are simply the replica of *ra'y* adopted by the orthodox schools.
[45] Kano, "NEPU Would Not Do Away with Islamic Courts."
[46] Ahmad Hassan, "The Principle of Istiḥsān in Islamic Jurisprudence," *Islamic Studies* 16, no. 4 (1977): 347–362.
[47] Kano, "NEPU Would Not Do Away with Islamic Courts."

"the go and come back tomorrows," "the unnecessary squatters," "the sleepy alkalis," and court "presidents tottering with old age."[48] NEPU, therefore, regarded reform as imperative.

NEPU continued to criticize the colonial stultification of Islamic institutions and the Lugardian-enabled overreach of Masu Sarauta in the last decade of colonial rule. For instance, in a July 27, 1956 meeting with Ralph Grey, chief secretary of Nigeria, Kano requested that European district officers be retained after decolonization to guarantee the protection of Masu Sarauta critics from the abuses of Masu Sarauta-controlled alkalai courts.[49] Although abuses continued into the late colonial years, even critics were aware of the increasing impotence of Masu Sarauta and of their alienation from the Colonial Office in the twilight years of colonial rule. In fact, while NEPU continued to castigate the early Lugardian enablement of the Sarauta class as the malaise ailing legal system, it also viewed the post-*Gubba* shift of siyasa to state institutions as an anathema driven by imperial interests. Therefore, although NEPU called for short-term measures protecting marginalized populations such as those effected through the offices of the district officer, the opposition party's long-term vision of reforms was to modernize Islamic law in a decolonial fashion.

While the debate over the fate of Islamic law raged within the colony, the Colonial Office convened the second Judicial Advisers Conference in 1956 in Jos, Northern Nigeria.[50] As in Makerere, the Colonial Office nominated Anderson as its Islamic legal expert to the Conference. At Jos, the law professor departed from his 1953 posture in Makerere to adopt a tone of urgency: reforms confining Islamic law to personal law were not only necessary, they also had to be carried out without delay. Even the creation of the Muslim Court of Appeal, which was established to mollify emirs and alkalai in the aftermath of *Gubba*, did not escape Anderson's criticism. Anderson argued that the "Muslim" appellation of the court was itself a pointer to the special treatment Muslims enjoyed in the state. Anderson also regarded the Muslim Court of Appeal Law's classification of Islamic jurisprudence as an independent source of law separate from custom as ahistorical and argued that the distinction risked rigidifying

---

[48] Ibid.
[49] PRO, London, CO 554/1069; Ralph Grey to T. B. Williamson, July 28, 1956. See Alkasum Aba, ed., *The Politics of Mallam Aminu Kano* (Lagos: Vanguard Publishers, 1993), 138.
[50] On the conferences, see Allott, "The London Conference," 13–15.

Islamic law.[51] In sum, Anderson impressed on conference attendees the imperative of transformation chiefly by shrinking the domain of Northern Nigerian Islamic law. These submissions were met with a warm reception. Echoing Anderson's refrain upon the conclusion of the conference, Colonial Office legal adviser, Sir Roberts-Wray, expressed his dismay with the "anachronism, absurdities and injustices" occasioned by Northern Nigerian Islamic law.[52] Wray, like Anderson, argued that the path forward lay in borrowing a leaf from the modernizing developments elsewhere in the Muslim world. With a renewed determination to tackle the challenge raised by Northern Nigeria head on, the Colonial Office sought expert counsel, and Anderson was a natural choice.

In the report prepared for the Colonial Office, Anderson reiterated the ideas he had consistently expressed since his 1951 survey: Islamic law had to be expunged from public law, particularly from criminal law. This reform was necessary not only because of Northern Nigeria's multireligious population, but also because it was "the point of view of modern civilized opinion."[53] Moreover, Anderson argued that other Muslim states had fallen into step with this modern view by exercising siyasa powers to change the law. The genius in this mode of reform, Anderson argued, was that it was "procedural": by investing in a "Ruler or Legislature the right to confine and define the jurisdiction of the courts," modern Muslim states had been able to enact "substantive" reforms without having to formally declare the displacement of the Shari'a.[54] Conceding the Western origins of this model of lawmaking, Anderson stressed that states in the Near and Middle East had nevertheless adopted the model successfully. Crucially, Anderson argued that the code could be simultaneously Western and Islamic: to Islamicize the model, the lawmaking power could be justified as an exercise of siyasa jurisdiction but its locus would be shifted from political authorities with religious legitimacy (emirs) to a modern legislature or executive.

At the same time, the legislature or executive would seize on the discretion inherent in siyasa to enact wide-ranging reforms. As Anderson would put it in a latter memorandum: "the difference therefore

[51] Muslim Court of Appeal Law, 1956.
[52] Kenneth Roberts-Wray to T. B. Williamson, February 1957. CO 554/1941. NA, UK.
[53] See J. N. D. Anderson, "The Application of Islamic Law in Northern Nigeria," May 8, 1957. CO 554/1941, 17E, 33. NA, UK.
[54] Ibid.

between the way criminal justice is administered in Northern Nigeria and other Muslim countries ... is not so much a matter of fundamental principle as of the way in which the siyasa jurisdiction of the state is exercised."[55] Northern Nigeria would, therefore, find no dearth of precedent of Islamic legal modernization if it looked to other Muslim societies. Neither would Northern Nigeria be the first British colony where the state would expressly assume siyasa for this purpose: Warren Hastings had invoked the doctrine to assume authority to legislate Islamic law in India. Yet Anderson retained his earlier pessimism, just as he had despaired at the success of reforms at the Jos conference. Citing the obstacle of "persistent Muslim pride," he made clear in his Colonial Office report that he doubted the possibility of getting "the Muslims of the North to agree to any programme of reform."[56] Despite these misgivings, however, Anderson urged the Colonial Office to undertake the effort to reform. Anderson's academic conviction in the Mainean evolutionary development of societies had met with his reformist urge to accelerate the evolutionary process.[57]

Anderson's report received the unreserved approval of the Colonial Office; however, it ran into a stumbling block within Northern Nigerian colonial administration. Despite the disfavor with which Lugardian ideology had come to be viewed, certain Lugardians remained within the Northern Nigerian colonial administration in the waning years of colonial rule. The most infamous of these was David Muffet, a senior administrative officer and "self-appointed" "troubleshooter" of NPC founder, and Sir Ahmadu Bello, the premier of Northern Nigeria and sardauna of Sokoto. Muffet, who was "never seen as an impartial arbitrator in a factional fight" between the Masu Sarauta and any group (including colonial administrators), was among the ranks of "Young Turks," a group of administrators seeking to protect "the northern way of life" from what they perceived as an imposition by the Colonial Office.[58] So unrestrained was Muffet in his opposition to criticism

---

[55] "Draft Confidential Dispatch to the Governor Northern Region, Nigeria, for Clearance SECRET AND PERSONAL by the Governor Before Issue," August 1957, London Private Collection of Ian Edge, in Todd Thompson, *Norman Anderson and the Christian Mission to Modernize Islam* (New York: Oxford University Press, 2018), 182.

[56] Ibid.

[57] For the influence of Henry Maine's theory of evolutionary development on Anderson, see Chapter 2.

[58] Richardson, *No Weariness*, 214.

of the Masu Sarauta that in his testimony before the Sir Willink-led Minorities Commission, he had described the petitioner's complaints about the Masu Sarauta as "poppycock" to the consternation of reform-minded administrators.[59] Another Masu Sarauta ally was the attorney general of Northern Nigeria, Hedley Marshall, popularly called "dan kirki" for his closeness to Muslim elites.[60] Testifying before the Willink Commission, Marshall had pointed out that Islamic law was "inextricably mingled with the Moslem religion," insisting that reform would "upset the balance in relation to other parts" and "offend the susceptibilities and indeed the consciences" of Muslims.[61]

It was, however, a more restrained Lugardian, Sir Bryan Sharwood-Smith, governor of Northern Nigeria, who used his offices to convey opposition directly to the Colonial Office. Responding to Anderson's plan, Sharwood-Smith expressed concern at the appearance of British interference with Islam, which he argued would contradict the 1903 guarantee and also provoke revolt. As shown earlier in the book, Lugardians were not averse to reform per se: what these administrators found objectionable was the direct involvement of Europeans in reform processes.[62] Indirectly influencing changes through political elites was the acceptable method of reform in the Lugardian mode. Sharwood-Smith, therefore, urged the Colonial Office that reform, should it be desired, had to be effected "without ourselves appearing to be implicated."[63] Further, the longtime administrator questioned Anderson's expertise on Northern Nigeria, insisting that the latter's academic knowledge of Islamic law was not necessarily relevant to the Northern Nigerian experience. While calling it "theoretically fully justified," Sharwood-Smith nevertheless estimated Anderson's plan to be "supremely unconscious of the hard facts on the ground."[64] The governor then confidently declared: "I am sure that in its present form, Professor Anderson's summary would both offend and alarm Northern Moslem Ministers."[65] Governor Sharwood-Smith then suggested an alternative

---

[59] Ibid.
[60] Loosely meaning Marshall had perfected his relations with Hausa-Fulanis; Richardson, *No Weariness*, 212.
[61] The Attorney-General of the Northern Region of Nigeria, Memorandum Presented to the Minorities Commission, February 1, 1958. CO957/4. NA, UK.
[62] See Chapter 2
[63] Sharwood-Smith to John Macpherson, April 18, 1957. CO 554/1941. NA, UK.
[64] Ibid.
[65] Bryan Sharwood-Smith to C. G. Eastwood, May 30, 1957. CO 554/1941. NA, UK.

to Anderson's plan: rather than reform the Northern Nigerian legal system on the model of "modern Islamic countries," Sharwood-Smith proposed the study of "conservative" Muslim states that had modernized in unobtrusive ways.[66] Egypt was not, in Sharwood-Smith's view, an example in this mold; instead, he suggested studying "Pakistan or some similar country."[67] Further, Sharwood-Smith urged that the study should not be undertaken by a panel of European scholars of Islamic law as Anderson and the Colonial Office planned, but rather by "prominent" "moslem" "experts."[68]

Regardless of the opposition mounted by officials like Sharwood-Smith and Muffet, the Colonial Office and its expert adviser pressed ahead. In a dispatch authored by Anderson, Roberts-Wray, and Maurice Smith and sent to the Northern Nigerian regional government, the Colonial Office trio reiterated the case for Anderson's proposal: reform was imperative, and modern global practice was the acceptable standard.[69] Apart from Protestant advocacy, the Colonial Office trio invoked international law as a basis for reforms.[70] Anderson, Wray, and Smith argued that Northern Nigeria's application of Islamic law in criminal law was inconsistent with international legal protections for minority groups. Even the international legal provision cited by the dispatch as the global standard for safeguarding religious minorities from abuses – Article 9 of the European Convention of Human Rights – was not removed from the Nigerian struggles. In fact, Article 9 was an adaptation of Article 18 of the Universal Declaration of Human Rights, itself a product of sustained advocacy of global missionary ecumenists intimately familiar with and inspired by the Northern Nigerian experience.[71]

Sharwood-Smith, who was scheduled to retire later that year, knew that he could not continue to stave off the pressure from the Colonial Office. Describing the moment in a memoir of his times in Northern Nigeria, the colonial administrator laid out the stakes:

---

[66] Bryan Sharwood-Smith, *But Always as Friends: Northern Nigeria and the Cameroons, 1921–1957* (London: Allen and Unwin, 1969).
[67] Ibid.   [68] Sharwood-Smith to Eastwood, 18.
[69] "Draft Confidential Dispatch to the Governor Northern region, Nigeria, for Clearance SECRET AND PERSONAL by the Governor Before Issue," August 1957, London Private Collection of Ian Edge, Anderson papers, cited in Thompson, *Norman Anderson*, 180.
[70] Ibid.   [71] See Chapter 5.

besides the advocacy of non-Muslim minorities and their European missionary-advocates, "opinion abroad" had also become "critical."[72] Further, "all other Muslim states that valued world opinion had long since resorted to a Penal Code ... for the sake of reputation alone, the time had come for the North to undertake a thorough modernization of its entire legal system."[73] Yet, Sharwood-Smith was convinced that Anderson's plan was bound to run into unsurmountable opposition.

Against the background of the claiming and counterclaiming by Lugardians and reform-minded administrators, the final compromise included elements from both Anderson's and Sharwood-Smith's proposals. Sharwood-Smith successfully convinced two key figures – the reform-leaning governor of Nigeria, Sir James Robertson, and Northern Nigeria Premier Ahmadu Bello – to send a delegation to Sudan, Libya, and Pakistan to study the experience of these states. Faced with Robertson's approval of Sharwood-Smith's proposal, the Colonial Office could not dismiss it outright. Rather, the Colonial Office supplemented Anderson's plan with Sharwood-Smith's by deciding that, upon the conclusion of the foreign delegation's work, a panel would be set up along the lines proposed by Anderson. Accepting the proposal grudgingly, Sharwood-Smith nevertheless insisted that Anderson could not chair the panel, being "as much of a zealot in his own line as the Emir of Kano is in his."[74] In addition, Sharwood-Smith pointed out that Anderson's identity as a Christian and British was bound to challenge the legitimacy of the panel's work in the eyes of Northern Nigerians.[75] Although it conceded the strong possibility of a challenge to the legitimacy of an Anderson-chaired panel, the Colonial Office nevertheless insisted on Anderson's membership. Sir Robertson then went ahead to nominate his friend and chief justice of Sudan, Sayyed Mohammed Abu Rannat, as chair to deliberate on Northern Nigerian Islamic law following the delegations to Libya, Sudan, and Pakistan.[76]

---

[72] Sharwood-Smith, *But Always as Friends*.   [73] Ibid.
[74] Bryan Sharwood-Smith to John Macpherson, August 17, 1957. CO 554/1941, 37, NA, UK.
[75] Sharwood-Smith to Macpherson, 37; Anderson also acknowledges in "Conflict of Laws."
[76] Besides Justice Abu Rannat, the members of the Panel included Anderson; Justice Mohammed Sharif, the chairman of the Pakistan Law Commission; Shettima Kashim, the waziri (vizier) of Borno Province; Peter Achimugu, a prominent Christian politician in the ruling Northern People's Congress; and Sheikh Musa Othman, the chief alkali of Bida.

Sourcing "Modern" Islamic Law: The Delegations to Libya, Pakistan, and Sudan

Sharwood-Smith's proposal culminated in two delegations: one departed for Sudan, and the other proceeded to Libya and Pakistan to study the legal systems in those states. These delegations had a fairly similar composition: an emir, a serving alkalai, a jurist, a religious minority leader, and a colonial administrator. In keeping with Sharwood-Smith's goal of Masu Sarauta superintendence of the process, an emir led each delegation. At the forefront of the Libya-Pakistan delegation was the emir of Lapa, Muhamadu Kobo, and the delegation arrived at its first stop, Tripoli, on February 21, 1958, two days after its administrative secretary and colonial district officer, Sam Richardson, flew into Libya to prepare for its arrival.

Smith had proposed the Sudanese, Libyan, and Pakistani models due to what administrators perceived as the simultaneously Islamic and modern nature of these states; they had not engaged in Egyptian-style reforms condemned by administrators and the Masu Sarauta alike and, as such, were regarded as more likely to be accepted in Nigeria. Commenting on Libya, for instance, Richardson argued that it was ideal because it had "secularized" while simultaneously retaining Islamic jurisprudence in private law, particularly in personal and family matters.[77] However, convincing the Northern Nigerian delegation of this required arranging encounters with Muslim experts with solid credentials. Two of them would stand out: Supreme Court Justice of Libya and descendant of the lineage custodians of key Islamic sites in Jerusalem, Auni Dajani; and the grand mufti of Libya, Mohamed Abulas'ad el-'alem. As noted at the inception of this chapter, both Dajani and Abulas'ad el-'alem made a case for the compatibility of the Shari'a with the exclusion of Islamic jurisprudence from public law in the context of a modern state. The two jurists argued that the Libyan model was not only Islamic; they insisted that such a model was required by the nature of the modern state. 1958 Libya, Richardson surmised, provided "moderate, tolerant and politically acceptable answers to Northern Nigeria's legal and judicial problems."[78] That would equally be the conclusion of the emir of Lapai-led delegation in its subsequent visit to Pakistan, during which the delegation dined with Prime Minister Firoz Khan Noon and justices of the Pakistani

---

[77] Richardson, *No Weariness*, 199.   [78] Ibid., 201.

Supreme Court. As with the Libyan study, the Pakistani visit suggested to the Northern Nigerian delegation that reform was compatible with fidelity to Islam. Pakistan's governing elites, the delegation surmised, "were thoroughly westernized, albeit committed to a modern interpretation of a traditional Islamic way of life within Jinnah's concept of an Islamic republic."[79] The Pakistani and Libyan examples, therefore, represented a model of being Muslim in the modern world.

As the Pakistan-Libya delegation had done, the delegation to Sudan concluded that "the Sudanese believe and with a lot of justification, that there is nothing repugnant to Mohammedan Law in the Sudanese Penal Code" that had been introduced to replace Islamic criminal jurisprudence.[80] Chaired by Sir Kashim Ibrahim, the other members of the delegation were the waziri of Sokoto, Muhammadu Junaidu; and the wali of Borno, Muhammad Isa Ngileruma. Once more, Peter Achimugu, a prominent Christian politician in the ruling NPC, was the representative of non-Muslims. Senior crown counsel, Mamman Nasir, served as the delegation's secretary.[81] This elite delegation to Sudan reached a similar conclusion as the Pakistan-Libya group on classical Islamic law's encounter with modernity in those jurisdictions.

Having witnessed the melding of the "old" into the "new" in their travels, the delegations to Libya, Pakistan, and Sudan returned to Northern Nigeria.[82] The Muslim identity of those states commanded authority among the Northern Nigerian Muslim elites; yet it hardly imbued an unwavering conviction that Northern Nigeria had to toe the reform path those states had taken. For all their awe of the foreign examples, the Northern Nigerian elites had also encountered uncomfortable vignettes of what they interpreted as modern Muslim life during their visit: in Benghazi, Libya, they had been shocked to see casinos and dancers, and in Pakistan, they were shocked at women's open castigation

---

[79] Ibid., 205.
[80] "Report by the Delegation Appointed by the Government of the Northern Region of Nigeria to Study the Administration of the Sudan with Particular Reference to the Legal Systems," s.d., NA, CO 554/1942, p. 266, in Todd Thompson, *Norman Anderson*, 185.
[81] Ibid.
[82] Ahmadu Bello, "Speech to Assembly on Legal Reforms on December 12, 1958," in *Work and Worship: Selected Speeches of Sir Ahmadu Bello, Sardauna of Sokoto* (Zaria: Gaskiya Corporation: 1986), 221–223.

of polygamy.[83] Therefore, these elites worried that reforms, even those limited to the domain of criminal law, would put the "northern way of life" in "jeopardy."[84] Yet the onward march to reform, already covertly commenced before the despised *Gubba* decision, was irreversible.[85] No matter how much the Northern Nigerian political and judicial elites sought to stem the tide toward the celebrated overhaul contemplated by the Andersonians in the Colonial Office, the latter pressed forward. Indeed, the Colonial Office had made it clear that the Panel of Jurists recommended by Anderson to deliberate on the future of Islamic law in Northern Nigeria would sit regardless of the delegations' reports.

By the summer of 1958, pressure from the Colonial Office intensified. Under the influence of Anderson's allies there, the British government unequivocally staked a position: Independence of Nigeria would be contingent on the reform of Northern Nigerian judicial and legal system. Moreover, the British government suggested that the decision was not solely of its volition by reporting that the UN Trusteeship Council had expressed reservations about Nigeria's Independence in the absence of "radical" reforms of Islamic law in Northern Nigeria.[86]

It was against that background that Governor Gawain Westray Bell formally appointed the Panel of Jurists on July 29, 1958. The panel was constituted according to Anderson's recommendations, yet its terms of reference gestured to Sharwood-Smith's plan and aimed to reassure the Masu Sarauta of the legitimacy of the reforms. Sir Gawain, who had just been transferred to Nigeria from the Sudan, charged the panel to consider:

> whether in the light of the legal and judicial systems obtaining in other parts of the world where Moslem and non-Moslem live side by side, and with particular reference to the systems obtaining in Libya, Pakistan and the Sudan; and whether it was possible to avoid conflicts of law in Northern Nigeria between the three systems of law currently in force in that Region (English law, Islamic law and customary law), and to make recommendations as to how this could be achieved.[87]

---

[83] At a reception organized in honor of the delegation, women described Northern Nigerian delegates who admitted to being polygamous as "mad mullahs." See Richardson, *No Weariness*, 204.

[84] Anderson, "Conflict of Laws," 451.   [85] See Chapter 2.

[86] Richardson, *No Weariness*, 209.

[87] "Report of the Panel of Jurists Appointed to Examine the Legal and Judicial Systems of the Region," S.MOJ/12/S.1, vol. I, NA Nigeria.

By invoking Muslim societies, Sir Gawain framed the panel's work as grounded in Islamic precedent.

Alibis of Reform: The Panel of Jurists and the 1958 Codification Project

As envisioned by Sir Gawain's predecessor, James Robertson, Chief Justice Sayyed Mohammed Abu Rannat of Sudan chaired the panel. Despite their differences, senior administrators at the Colonial Office, intransigent Lugardian friends of the Masu Sarauta among the colonial administration, and the Muslim elites who were the subjects of the wrangling found it easy to agree on the choice of Abu Rannat. In the first place, Sudan was highly regarded as a center of Islamic learning and orthodoxy among Northern Nigerians. Crucially, it was not associated with the modernist reactionism that made Egypt so controversial among the Masu Sarauta. That Justice Abu Rannat himself was a Muslim was pivotal in establishing his credibility. Further, Abu Rannat's stellar juristic credentials also set him apart. At the Future of Law in Africa Conference, the landmark occasion to deliberate on African law and jurisprudence and the direction of its legal and judicial system, Justice Abu Rannat was a leading speaker, second only to master of the rolls, Lord Denning.[88] Abu Rannat would continue to enjoy continental and international acclaim long after his work on the Nigerian panel and past his tenure as Sudan's chief justice, serving on the UN Commission of Human Rights and on the International Commission of Jurists. And at home in Sudan, Abu Rannat had a reputation as an unequivocal liberal reformer, advocating for a Sudanese Common Law not bound to Islamic law.[89] It was this reputation that made Abu Rannat an attractive choice to the Colonial Office reformers. Given that their top choice, Anderson, had been rejected by Lugardians, Abu Rannat was an ideal replacement. As it turned out, Anderson and Abu Rannat were no strangers to each other. They had first met in Sudan

---

[88] Sayyid Muhammad Abu Rannat, "The Relationship between Islamic and Customary Law in the Sudan," *Journal of African Law* 4, no. 1 (Spring 1960): 16.

[89] Abu Rannat, "The Relationship"; Cliff F. Thompson, "The Failure of Continental Codes in the Democratic Republik of the Sudan – An Analysis," *Verfassung Und Recht in Übersee/Law and Politics in Africa, Asia and Latin America* 8, no. 3/4 (1975): 407–421. See also Abu Rannat's judgment in "Sudan Government v. Milton Thompson," *The Sudan Law Journal and Reports* (1963): 56–59, in which he held that the right to religious expression protected an accused person charged with blasphemy against Islam.

while Anderson was conducting his survey of Islamic law in Africa for the British government; motivated by their common ideas on liberal reform, they had struck a friendship since that initial meeting. That relationship would be invaluable in the 1958 reform process.

The strategy of hinging the legitimacy of the panel's work on its broad-based Muslim membership went beyond the choice of Abu Rannat as chairperson. S. S. Richardson, who had recently been admitted to the English bar and appointed as commissioner for native courts, recommended the appointment of retired judge of the Pakistani Supreme Court and chairman of the Pakistan Law Commission, Justice Mohammed Sharif, to the panel. Richardson, who would himself serve as secretary to the panel, argued that Sharif's choice would increase Muslim representation and, therefore, the panel's "credibility."[90] Having Sharif and Abu Rannat on the panel was thus crucial to legitimating the panel's work among the Masu Sarauta. Together with Anderson and Richardson, these Muslim jurists were the reformers that drove the panel's direction. Other members were Northern Nigerian elites: Shettima Kashim, the waziri of Borno Province; sheikh Musa Othman, the chief alkali of Bida; and Peter Achimugu, once again representing non-Muslims.

The panel assembled in Lugard Hall, Kaduna, on August 28, 1958 to begin its work. At its swearing in ceremony, Sir Gawain reminded panel members that they were following in the "footsteps" of Thomas Babington Macaulay, who had been appointed president of the Law Commission of India in 1834.[91] Macaulay, Bell noted, had been tasked with "[modernizing] the law of India" in order to "treat all people as equally as the diversity of India would allow."[92] Macaulay's goal – "uniformity of the law wherever possible, diversity only where necessary, but, in all cases, certainty" – was also to serve as a precedent for the Abu Rannat-led panel.[93] The panel recognized the similarities between their task and Macaulay's; however, they were also keenly preoccupied with the uniqueness of the Northern Nigerian situation and concerned that Northern Nigeria had failed to follow the reform trajectory of most Muslim societies. That the state had

---

[90] Richardson, *No Weariness*, 201.   [91] Ibid., 214–215.   [92] Ibid.
[93] Ibid. See David Skuy, "Macaulay and the Indian Penal Code of 1862: The Myth of the Inherent Superiority and Modernity of the English Legal System Compared to India's Legal System in the Nineteenth Century," *Modern Asian Studies* 32, no. 3 (1998): 513–557.

an Indigenous faith population and a "small but not inconsiderable Christian population" made this "stagnation" a particular a cause for concern.[94]

The panel, or more accurately, the quartet of reformers driving its direction, therefore began work with a premise: that Northern Nigeria's legal system featured "anomalies that seem contrary to natural justice and ... fundamental rights."[95] Reiterating the view that Anderson had advanced regarding the reification of Islamic law, these reformers stated that these "unsatisfactory features" of the Northern Nigerian legal system "can only be explained as a perpetuation, long beyond their time, of the traditional concepts and procedures for the application of Maliki law."[96] Completely ignoring preexisting colonial reforms, the reformers faulted the colonial administration for the "stagnation" of Islamic law, stemming from "a meticulous if exaggerated loyalty" to Lugard's 1903 guarantee.[97] If these reformers found the roots of stagnation in Lugard's guarantee, they traced its tenacity to Northern Nigeria's disconnection from the "currents of thought ... elsewhere in the Moslem world."[98] This had been the purpose of the delegations to Libya, Pakistan, and Sudan: to open the eyes of the government to Northern Nigeria's "backward state in comparison with the vastly greater part of the Muslim world," and to reveal how Northern Nigeria had become a "museum piece" when compared to these other societies.[99] There was only one path to bringing Northern Nigeria in step with the times: excluding Islamic law from public law, particularly criminal law, by introducing a code of criminal law.

Change was already in the air at the inception of the panel's proceedings. When it first convened, the London Constitutional Conference to deliberate on the terms of Nigeria's Independence was barely five weeks away. That conference and the restructuring it was expected to undertake as preparatory to Independence therefore loomed over the Abu Rannat panel's proceedings. As Anderson would comment on the timing of the panel's work: "the psychological moment was exactly right."[100] Not only did the London Conference create an atmosphere of expectancy of far-reaching reforms, it also created a sense of urgency

---

[94] Anderson, "Conflict of Laws," 443.
[95] "Report of the Panel of Jurists Appointed to Examine the Legal and Judicial Systems of the Region," S.MOJ/12/S.1, vol. I, 5. NA Nigeria.
[96] Ibid., 6.   [97] Ibid., 6.   [98] Ibid., 6.
[99] Anderson, "Conflict of Laws," 451, 456.   [100] Ibid., 456.

as the panel was required to submit its findings before the commencement of the conference. Indeed, a mere two weeks after the panel's inauguration, it would submit thirty-two proposals to the Northern Region government on September 10, the most significant of which was the reformers' ultimate goal of replacing Islamic criminal law with a code.[101]

Although the reformers on the panel were unequivocal as to their goal, the path to victory was unclear at the beginning, especially given the short timeframe. In fact, the first memorandum presented to the panel by Sir Ahmadu Bello and a group of political elites, with the support of Muslim elite members of the panel, opposed the proposed reforms completely. "Islam," these elites declared in the memorandum, is a "a total way of life" and to take away part of it, even in the domain of criminal law, would undermine the whole religion.[102] To move these elites from outright hostility to nonresistance in merely two weeks, the reformers embarked widely on informal consultations.

Even before the arrival of panel members, Richardson had consulted with Bello.[103] And once the panel convened, the reformers agreed that it was crucial to informally persuade prominent elites before unveiling any official proposals. As Anderson describes the process, the panel met with eminent personalities to convince them that the reform process was not an imposition but was rather to "enable them to put their own house in order and to administer their own affairs in the only way that would serve their basic interests."[104] Justice Abu Rannat took the lead in that effort. Relating Sudan's experience, Abu Rannat pointed out that colonial rule had provided the Sudanese with the luxury of not taking responsibility and "to blame anything that went wrong on the British administration," a situation that had changed upon Independence.[105] When Northern Nigerian elites tried to stall for time, Abu Rannat responded that reform was not only imperative but also urgent: to engage with the world, attract foreign investments, and join the UN, an independent Nigeria "must expect awkward questions and put themselves in a position to give satisfactory answers."[106] In sum, Abu Rannat argued that both Independence and progress were contingent on the reforms.

---

[101] Ibid., 454.   [102] Ibid., 451.   [103] Richardson, *No Weariness*, 213.
[104] Anderson, "Conflict of Laws," 452.   [105] Ibid.   [106] Ibid.

Abu Rannat's performance attracted praise. While Anderson commended the jurist for his "sagacity,"[107] Sir Gawain, the colonial governor, praised Abu Rannat for his handling of the emirs of Kano and Zaria, who had proved particularly intractable.[108] A. T. Weatherhead, who had been acting resident of Sokoto at the height of the post-*Gubba* backlash, praised Abu Rannat for the radical change of attitude among the Masu Sarauta, crediting the jurist for winning "the confidence of all by his absolute sincerity, simplicity and obvious desire to bring in a system which would not only suit this Region but give it credit internationally."[109] If Abu Rannat received the most public praise for his leadership role, the work of Anderson, Abu Rannat, and the other two reformers on the panel (Richardson and Sharif) was equally crucial to the actualization of the Colonial Office's vision of legal reforms.

Even in the light of Abu Rannat's (and the other reformers') acclaimed persuasive skills, the negotiations were not free of acrimony. Richardson, who would be known after the reforms as "mutum ya kasha maliki" (the man who killed Maliki law), described the negotiations as "torturous," admitting that he frequently despaired of reaching a consensus due to insistence that the reforms were not Islamic.[110] The discussion regarding the proposal to abolish diya, the payment of blood money in lieu of the capital penalty for unlawful killing, was particularly terse. For the reformers, this was nonnegotiable: the critique of diya was one of the central motivations for reform. Before the panel's proceedings, Anderson had published several searing critiques of the "inequalities" of the doctrine of diya:[111] non-Muslims had to be content with receiving diya and could not demand retaliation for a murder. Even in such cases, the diya due for the murder of a non-Muslim was not equivalent to that payable upon the unlawful killing of a Muslim: for Indigenous religious groups, it was limited to one-fifteenth of the sum payable upon the killing of a Muslim, and for Christians, this sum was limited to half. Further, among Muslims, there existed

---

[107] Ibid., 456.
[108] See Gawain Bell, Extract, December 12, 1958. NA CO 554/1943, 316.
[109] A. T. Weatherhead to C. G. Eastwood, September 12, 1958. NA CO 554/1942, 275.
[110] Richardson, *No Weariness*, 226.
[111] James Norman Dalrymple Anderson, "Homicide in Islamic Law," *Bulletin of the School of Oriental and African Studies* 13, no. 4 (1951): 811–812; James Norman Dalrymple Anderson, "Islamic Law in African Colonies," *Corona, the Journal of His Majesty's Colonial Service* 3 (1951): 265; Anderson, "Conflicts of Laws."

gendered disparities in calculating diya payable upon unlawful killing: a woman's unlawful killing gave rise to only half the diya payable for a man's. The inequities cited by Anderson were true of judicial practice and grounded in juristic interpretation. Yet, this was by no means the univocal position in Islamic criminal jurisprudence, especially because the discrepancies were not themselves based on express prescriptions of the Quran and Sunnah.[112] Besides these juristic contentions, diya's reign had been short-lived in the state; the compensation in lieu of capital penalty had long been drastically curtailed, albeit informally, even during the Lugardian years. For all the resistance of jurists, colonial administrators had insisted since Lugardian times that the response to crimes against the person was the prerogative of the state and that interpersonal resolution of such matters challenged imperial authority. Yet, this Lugardian guarantee and the peculiar form of indirect rule it entrenched had meant that statutory and, therefore, unequivocal elimination of diya remained elusive, even in the Cameron years. It was this unequivocal elimination of diya that the reformers sought during the 1958 negotiations – to the vehement opposition of emirs and alkalai.

In the lengthy negotiation that ensued, the panel did not make headway until it invited an expert with just the right credentials: the mufti of Sudan, Sheikh Mohammed Abul Gasim.[113] The mufti set to work to convince the Northern Nigerians, arguing that the preclusion of diya was permissible in Islamic law.[114] Invoking the Quran, Sunnah, and juristic works, the mufti argued that an imam's siyasa powers were sufficiently broad to envisage the compulsory imposition of

---

[112] See Mohammad Hashim Kamali, *Crime and Punishment in Islamic Law: A Fresh Interpretation* (Oxford: Oxford University Press, 2019), 215. Kamali cites the absence of the disparity in the primary source texts and the positions of Imam Ghazali and his commentator, Yusuf al Qaradawi, as well as in modern *ijtihad*, which argue that blood compensation is equal across gender and religious lines.

[113] The negotiations on diya went beyond even the initial panel visit: in the initial round of talks, the parties came to a tentative understanding that diya would be retained in circumstances where the prerogative of mercy was contemplated. This was the agreement reached in order for the panel to wrap up its work in 1958, but the question was such a sore one that it was revived again during the parliamentary debates in early 1959. It was at those deliberations that the mufti of Sudan was invited to the talks to once and for all settle the debates.

[114] Attorney General H. H. Marshall to the Panel of Jurists, September 10, 1958, S.MOJ/12/S.1, vol. I. NA Nigeria.

punishment in the interest of public security.[115] The mufti argued that under such circumstances, the preclusion of diya as an alternative was consistent with the Shari'a. Mufti Abul Gasim's argument therefore sprung from a similar premise from which Anderson justified the reform project: that in the context of a modern state, the state was in the place of the imam and wielded immense siyasa powers, including the ability to strip agnates of a victim of the right to demand diya, and to institute a criminal punishment in lieu thereof. Although framed as a compromise, the outcome of the discussions was the elimination of diya's essence in precolonial jurisprudence: diya was retained, not as an alternative to punishment as applied in precolonial jurisprudence, but rather as a justification for reducing a sentence in cases of homicide not amounting to murder. In cases of murder, the wish of the relatives of the victims to absolve the convict of criminal penalty could not lessen the penalty; the court was to record such a desire, which was only to become relevant in circumstances where the state was contemplating exercising its prerogative of mercy. Diya was, therefore, not a substitute for the state's punishment. Instead, it was "a means for readjusting the social equilibrium" upon the conclusion of a case on terms exclusively dictated by the state.[116]

It was not a coincidence that the Sudanese mufti's view hinged on an overhauled idea of siyasa. This re-envisioning, not only of the scope of siyasa, but also of the proper authority to exercise siyasa, had been central to Anderson's vision of reform of the Northern Nigerian legal system since his initial survey. In the new scheme first envisioned by Anderson and now proposed by the panel, siyasa was to be exercised by the central state apparatus, acting through its legislature and executive rather than the old emir-driven siyasa model. In fact, the panel recommended not merely the stripping of emirs' siyasa powers, but also the curtailment (and eventual abolition) of their judicial authority and their power to appoint alkalai.[117] The thrust of the 1958 reform project was therefore a reconceptualization of siyasa and, ultimately, the

---

[115] Ibid. See also Suleiman Ismaila Nchi and Samai'la Abdullahi Mohammed, eds., *Alhaji Sir Ahmadu Bello, Sardauna of Sokoto: His Thoughts and Vision in His Own Words: Selected Speeches and Letters of the Great Leader* (Makurdi, Nigeria: Oracle, 1999), 202–209.

[116] "Report of the Panel of Jurists," S.MOJ/12/S.1, vol. I, 7, NA Nigeria.

[117] The panel recommended that alkalai begin to receive formal legal education and training at the Institute of Administration, Ahmadu Bello University in Zaria, Nigeria.

transfer of emirs' siyasa powers, which had since been expanded capaciously by Lugardians to the late colonial state.

While resistance to the preclusion of diya from the code largely emanated from jurists, opposition to the elimination of emirs' siyasa powers was mounted by emirs. Long after the conclusion of the panel's work, Haliru Binji, the Maliki law jurist who served on the delegation to Libya and Pakistan, would remark that the elimination of diya by the 1958 reforms was "unIslamic."[118] Jurists were, however, largely silent on emirs' loss of siyasa powers, so infamous had the abuses that followed the Lugardian expansion of emirs' discretionary authority become. This left emirs alone to mount futile objections, a situation that would leave lasting tensions among the Masu Sarauta; emirs would blame the loss of their siyasa powers on the political elites that had emerged with the introduction of party politics. Although these political elites were a part of the Masu Sarauta, they simultaneously held office in the late colonial (and later postindependence) state institutions, such as the executive council and legislature, in which siyasa was now being vested. Foremost among these elites was Sir Ahmadu Bello, the premier of Northern Nigeria and sardauna of Sokoto. Reflecting on the elimination of emirs' siyasa powers years later, Abubakar Gumi, a prominent jurist on the committee that reviewed the 1958 deal and close confidant of Bello, pointed out that the elimination of emirs' siyasa powers soured relations between emirs and the sardauna. They understood the sarduana to have cooperated with the colonial administration, or at the least, to have failed to mount sufficient resistance against the colonial bid to strip them of their siyasa powers.[119] In fact, the sardauna's position in the colonial state was more akin to that of the emirs than the latter realized. Far from being in command as emirs imagined, Bello was in what anthropologist Max Gluckman describes as an "intercalary" position.[120] True, the premier had some clout in the state and was, in particular, a Lugardian favorite, yet any authority bestowed on the Muslim elite was ultimately in pursuit of colonial ends. Bello was subject to the authority of his colonial overlords while also striving to maintain his legitimacy before emirs and the general population. Consequently, in the deliberations over the 1958 reforms, Bello sought to

---

[118] Paden, *Ahmadu Bello*, 212. [119] Ibid., 84–92.
[120] Max Gluckman, "The Village Headman in British Central Africa: Introduction," *Africa: Journal of the International African Institute* 19, no. 2 (April 1949): 89–94.

appear loyal to emirate institutions and courts while also being keen to appear reform-minded to the colonial administration.

In the end, it was the precedent of Sudan, Libya, and Pakistan that made it possible for the sardauna and jurists like Gumi and Binji to accede to the reforms despite their lingering misgivings without losing face.[121] These jurists took comfort in the fact that the reforms had been accepted in Muslim societies that had not abandoned their fidelity to the Shari'a as they perceived Egypt to have done; looking to these "acceptable" examples, the jurists surmised that it was not inconceivable that Northern Nigeria's desire to maintain its adherence to the Shari'a could coexist with the reforms. The sourcing of the reforms from the model of modern Muslim states respected by these elites was therefore decisive.

The reformers on the panel did not merely cite abstract examples of model Muslim states to persuade the political elites and jurists; the key proposal was the wholesale replacement of Islamic criminal jurisprudence in Northern Nigeria with the Sudan Penal Code and Criminal Procedure Code. To eliminate Maliki law from public law, the reformers insisted that the law of crime had to be codified. Moreover, the reformers proposed the model of Sudan, citing its stellar Islamic credentials, its high regard in Northern Nigeria, and the Sudan Code's acceptance by "millions of Moslems" as evidence of the code's legitimacy and suitability.

Far from the Muslim-initiated legislation it was portrayed as in reform discussions, the Sudanese Code had traveled from colonial India. The 1860 Indian Penal Code itself had a colorful history: its provisions were inspired by statutes in England and North America, as well as by the common law, the Louisiana Civil Code, and the New York Code. Its origins were therefore no different from that of the Nigerian Criminal Code of 1916, the criminal law legislation that had existed alongside the Shari'a to govern criminal matters involving the British, and in certain circumstances, non-Muslims, since early colonial years. Widespread opposition of the Northern Muslim elite to the Nigerian Criminal Code had, however, made clear that the code had no chance of succeeding in the negotiations. Although it is unlikely that Northern elites knew of the long travels of the Indian Code, as other members of the panel, they were aware of its imperial origins and substantive

---

[121] See Abubakar M. Gumi's reflections on the reform in Paden, *Ahmadu Bello*, 210–211.

deviations from precolonial criminal jurisprudence. Regardless of this origin, Abu Rannat and his colleagues stressed the "Islamic" nature of the Indian Code and of its Sudanese and Pakistani derivatives.[122] Yet, the substance of the code was far from consistent with Northern Nigerian jurists' notions of Islamic criminal jurisprudence, even in those cases where the legislation ostensibly preserved Shar'i principles. As an example, while the code's preservation of the crime of adultery was ostensibly a nod to Islamic criminal jurisprudence, it instituted testimonial standards markedly laxer than the four-witness or confessional testimony that make principled adultery convictions nearly impossible to secure in Islamic law.[123] And although the code's institution of imprisonment and fines for the offense might have appeared to relax the stiff penalty under Islamic law, the execution of the classical prescription of capital penalty was itself an anomaly even in precolonial (eighteenth century) Northern Nigeria.[124] The punishment of adultery in the code was therefore, in the end, an expression of the old English crime of adultery, which itself found resonance in the North American legislation that informed the code's Indian predecessor. Nevertheless, Abu Rannat and Mohammed Sharif insisted on the code's Islamic credentials. At the same time, however, the jurists stressed that the code's acceptability was rooted in its "secular" nature since it applied "to the entire population without fear or favor toward any religious, tribal or sectarian group in the community."[125] The source codes were, therefore, simultaneously "secular" and "Islamic" in the discourse of the reformers.

Beyond the introduction of a Penal Code confining Islamic law to personal law, eliminating diya, and abolishing emirs' siyasa, the codification project encompassed several other proposals, some of which were intended to facilitate assent to the thrust of the reforms. Notably, the panel proposed that alkalai courts be merely "guided by" the new code for an unspecified interim period.[126] However, the panel stressed that the guidance period did not grant these courts liberty to ignore the new code; rather, the provision was directed to appellate English

---

[122] "Report of the Panel of Jurists," S.MOJ/12/S.1, vol. I, 7. NA Nigeria.
[123] Northern Nigerian Penal Code, subsections 387 and 388.
[124] See Sarah Eltantawi, *Shari'ah on Trial: Northern Nigeria's Islamic Revolution* (Oakland: University of California Press, 2017).
[125] Richardson, *No Weariness*, 215.
[126] "Report of the Panel of Jurists," S.MOJ/12/S.1, vol. I, 7. NA Nigeria.

courts to encourage those courts to adopt a "lenient and paternalistic attitude ... towards imperfect attempts [by alkalai courts] to apply" the code.[127] Another proposal codified the appellate hierarchy within the native court system whereby appeals lay to the High Court, thus preserving the judicial hierarchy that had made the *Gubba* decision possible.

The panel further proposed that the Shari'a Court of Appeal replace the Muslim Court of Appeal that had been created to pacify emirs and alkalai following *Gubba*. In response to Anderson's criticism that the court's "Muslim" title marginalized minorities, the reformers sought to substitute that word with "Shari'a."[128] While the Muslim Court of Appeal had been constituted on an ad hoc basis by alkalai taking a temporary leave from their own courts, the Shari'a Court of Appeal had permanent appointees – a grand khadi, deputy grand khadi, and two other khadis (judges) sitting as a bench of three.[129] The Shari'a Court of Appeal's jurisdiction was limited to appeals on "Muslim personal law and family law" emanating from "Muslim litigants," and its decisions were to be final.[130] The court's jurisdictional delineation consequently preserved the authority of Muslim jurists in the area of personal law.

Another proposal precluded legal representation in alkalai courts and other "native" courts. The reformers justified that proposal by arguing that alkalai lacked expertise in English law and by citing the Northern Nigerian distrust of lawyers encapsulated in the expression: *an yi mana lauya* (they did me over with a lawyer).[131] The proposal faced criticism from prominent Muslim jurists, especially Abubakar Gumi, who argued that the preclusion of legal representation deviated from the practice in Muslim societies, citing the example of Saudi Arabia.[132]

---

[127] Anderson, "Conflicts of Laws," 454.
[128] "Report of the Panel of Jurists," S.MOJ/12/S.1, vol. I, 19. NA Nigeria.
[129] Sudanese scholar, Sheikh Awad, who had been principal of the School of Arabic studies in Kano (renamed from the Kano Law School) would be the first grand mufti of the court. Two jurists involved in the 1958 negotiations would go on to serve on the court – Abubakar Gumi would serve as the first Nigerian grand khadi, and Haliru Binji would serve as Gumi's deputy.
[130] Other cases from new provincial courts ranked above the previous "A", and "A Limited" courts were to go to the High Court to be adjudicated by the native courts' appellate division of the High Court. In adjudicating such cases, the High Court was to be constituted by a panel of three judges: two High Court judges and the third, the Grand Khadi or another judge of the Shari'a Court of Appeal.
[131] Richardson, *No Weariness*, 210.
[132] See, however, Olu Odumosu, "The Northern Nigerian Codes," *The Modern Law Review* 24, no. 5 (September 1961): 612–615.

Gumi argued that Muslim aversion to the legal profession stemmed from its association with "Christianity" and "western paganism" through such symbols as a "dress of eagle form" (a reference to lawyers' robes).[133] Arguing that legal representation was permissible once such symbols were jettisoned, Gumi criticized the exclusion of lawyers from aklalai courts.

Regardless of criticisms such as those launched by Gumi, the reformers congratulated themselves on securing "substantial support" for the proposals.[134] Anderson and Richardson drafted the proposals within a few hours of the conclusion of the panel's nine-day proceeding, and the report was officially submitted to the Northern Region government. Two days later, on September 12, 1958, the Northern Region Executive Council accepted the proposals with two minor reservations.[135] The first reservation was with regards to the proposal of a learning/adaptation period during which alkalai courts would be "guided" by and not strictly bound by the letter of the new code.[136] While it agreed with the intent of that provision, the Executive Council expressed concern over the difficulty the provision would pose for legislative drafting. The second reservation touched on automatic appeals in homicide cases, a proposal the Executive Council found unnecessary since condemned persons seeking an appeal were already guaranteed the opportunity to do so.

The Northern Regional government formally endorsed the proposals with much fanfare at the Constitutional Conference in London. Governor Gawain Bell declared the reforms the "outstanding event of the Conference, from the point of view of the future stability of the North, and perhaps of the Federation as a whole."[137] In compliance with the legislative processes now put in place in the move toward self-government, the bill had to be put to the Northern Region House

---

[133] Memorandum of the Grand Khadi to the Panel of Jurists, May/June 1962, S.MOJ/12/S.1, vol. 1. NA Nigeria.
[134] Anderson, "Conflict of Laws," 453.
[135] Statement by the Government of the Northern Region of Nigeria on the Re-organization of the Legal and Judicial Systems of the Northern Region Laid on the Table of the Legislative Houses, December 1958, paras. 30, 55, in Philip Ostien, ed., *Sharia Implementation in Northern Nigeria 1999–2006: A Sourcebook*, vol. 2 (Ibadan, Nigeria: Spectrum Books, 2007), 50–56.
[136] Ibid.
[137] Gawain Bell, Extract, 12 December 1958, NA, CO 554/1943, p. 316, in Thompson, *Norman Anderson*, 187.

of Chiefs where it was passed into law in September 1959 as the Penal Code of the Northern Region of Nigeria.[138]

The reformers were hardly surprised by the success of the panel's report having laid sufficient groundwork for its victory. Given extensive prior informal consultations with political elites and jurists, none of the representatives of the Masu Sarauta class or jurists on the panel expressed dissent on the final outcome.[139] The reformers reveled in this unanimity. The Northern Nigerian members of the panel, Anderson pointed out, were, in fact, "eminently reasonable men" who had only been held back initially by concerns regarding public reaction.[140] The panel's report took care to preempt this general reaction, declaring "there is nothing in this Penal Code, which is contrary to the principles of Islam when it is properly understood."[141] However, the unanimity on the proposals was grossly overstated. Given the foregoing narration of the deliberative processes that culminated in the panel's recommendation, Northern Nigerian political and juristic elites were hardly the enthusiastic participants described by Anderson. Yet these elites' attempts to thwart the direction charted by the panel's reformers proved futile. Resigned to this, these elites seized on the alibi provided by the examples of modern Muslim states such as Sudan, Libya, and Pakistan to legitimize the code before their Northern Nigerian constituents.

No one bore greater responsibility than Northern Region premier, Ahmadu Bello, in this task of securing the legitimacy for the code. Mirroring the panel's declaration of the compatibility of the code with Islam, Bello introduced the Penal Code Bill on the floor of the Northern Region House of Assembly, asserting: "there is nothing in the [code] … that is in any way contrary to the tenets of our religion."[142] The premier then cited the code's origins in the Sudan and Pakistan Codes, "which have proved perfectly acceptable to the millions of Muslims among the populations of those countries." According to Bello, the goal was to "preserve the fundamentals of Islam for the Muslim majority" and to "allay the fears of the minorities." The reform, in his view,

---

[138] Northern Regional Legislature, Debates of the House of Assembly: Second Legislature, 3rd Session, 1959. POLI/1/4/21.
[139] Anderson, "Conflict of Laws," 454.
[140] Ibid., 452. See further Paden, *Ahmadu Bello*, 211.
[141] "Report of the Panel of Jurists," 7.
[142] Ahmadu Bello, "Speech to Assembly on Legal Reforms on December 12, 1958," in *Work and Worship*, 222. On Bello's oscillation between "reform" and "tradition," see Paden, *Ahmadu Bello*.

had succeeded in achieving these goals. Bello also found it crucial to emphasize that the code had won "admiration" of the Colonial Office and "business interests."[143] The reform process, Bello argued, had produced a legal system "combining the old and the new," "blending in the right proportions the traditional and the progressive," and consequently it would "achieve the ends of ... stability and contentment at home while commanding respect and admiration abroad."[144] Although Anderson lauded the premier and other members of the Sarauta class for their "goodwill, broadmindedness," "statesmanship," and "courage," the law professor simultaneously acknowledged the strain under which these elites acceded to the reforms.[145] In an article describing the panel's work, Anderson noted that this elite class was "under pressure from its opponents," and was anxious to "allay the fears of minorities" and show evidence of "tolerance and good will."[146] These factors, coupled with the speed with which the panel's work was carried out, was crucial to the success of its mission.

Christian missionaries wasted no time declaring the reforms as a victory. Immediately after the code came into law, it was translated into the Hausa language by Parsons, a Church Missionary Society (CMS) official in the proselytizing effort in Northern Nigeria. Parsons was assisted by Adamu, a Northern Nigerian student of Anderson at the school of Oriental and African studies, London. Nevertheless, the reaction from non-Muslims to the 1958 deal was by no means unanimously agreeable. J. S. Olawoyin, an Indigene of Offa (a mixed religious area) and Northern Region Parliament leader of the Action Group (a political party with a strong base in southwestern Nigeria and non-Muslim areas), embodied the non-Muslim opposition to the new Penal Code. Citing the efforts of the panel to court the Masu Sarauta during the negotiations, Olawoyin charged that it was clear that "serious attempts are being made to Islamize the whole of the Northern Region."[147]

---

[143] Bello, *Work and Worship*, 221, 223. In Bello's words, "[W]hen our proposals were first revealed in London at the time of the resumed Constitutional Conference they met with an exceptionally favorable reception not only from the Secretary of State and the conference but also from the commercial, industrial and banking interests." See also Paden, *Ahmadu Bello*; Northern Region House of Assembly session, December 12, 1958.

[144] Ibid. [145] Anderson, "Conflict of Laws," 456. [146] Ibid.

[147] Debates of the House of Assembly, Second Legislature, 3rd Session, August 12–19, 1959, column 501 in Ostien, *Shari'a Implementation in Northern Nigeria*, vol. 1, 5–6.

Olawoyin's opposition went beyond voting against the Penal Code Bill on the floor of the legislature; together with six other applicants, Olawoyin would go on to file a suit that successfully, though temporarily, ousted the khadis of the Shari'a Court of Appeal from the Native Courts Appellate Division of the Northern High Court – one of the key proposals of the 1958 reforms.[148]

Muslim minorities, represented by NEPU, oscillated between attacking the code and embracing its reforms. On the one hand, the Penal Code encapsulated key dreams of NEPU, particularly through its elimination of emirs' siyasa powers. By divesting these political elites of their broad discretionary powers in the administration of justice, NEPU officials had hope for an end to the persecution of religious and political dissent through the courts. Even though this reform did not rise to the level of the Egyptian model it idealized, NEPU nevertheless regarded it as an achievement. At the same time, however, NEPU elites were careful to avoid appearing to endorse de-Islamizing the legal system. As the party declared in a newspaper editorial: "Those who call for [a uniform legal code] insisted that they are not against Maliki law, but against crooked interpretation of the law. They want a uniform Code for all the courts in Northern Nigeria under the great umbrella of Imam Maliki."[149] Rather than displacing Islamic jurisprudence, NEPU stressed that its modernization vision was compatible with Islamic law and jurisprudence.

Although NEPU's position was now akin to the one the sardauna-led NPC had come to adopt since it realized the inevitability of the reforms, NEPU took great care to dissociate its reform discourse from that promoted by the Masu Sarauta. In particular, NEPU stressed that the Masu Sarauta was operating under the hegemonic colonial narrative of the supremacy of Western law, and that these elites had

---

[148] J. S. Olawoyin & Six Others v. Commissioner of Police (1961) (Supreme Court of Nigeria) 1 All N. L. R. (Part 2) 203. The Supreme Court ousted the khadis on the basis that the requirements for appointment as a khadi was inconsistent with the qualifications set out in the 1960 Constitution. The ouster was, however, temporary and reversed by a 1963 amendment to the constitution. Prior to joining the AG, Olawoyin had been involved in the Middle Belt Party and the United Middle Belt Congress – see Chapters 3 and 4. For more on this, see Abdulmalik Bappa Mahmud, *A Brief History of Shari'ah in the Defunct Northern Nigeria* (Jos, Nigeria: University of Joss Press, 1988), 39–40.

[149] Editorial, *Daily Comet*, June 22, 1960. The reference here is to Imam Malik, founder of the Maliki School of Jurisprudence, popular in the precolonial state and instituted as the exclusive source of Islamic jurisprudence by the colonial state.

tacitly acceded to colonial claims of the Shariʻa's barbarity. NEPU was therefore quick to respond when Emir Sanusi of Kano asserted (at the launching of an alkalai training course to promote compliance with the new code) that Islamic jurisprudence was insufficient to cater to the needs of modern Northern Nigeria. In an editorial titled "What Stops Islamic law from Being in Conformity with Modernity?," NEPU's Mohammad Danjani Hadejia declared: "I was highly disgusted when I read what his Excellency wrote. As far as I am concerned, uttering such words will make the followers of other religions think that the Islamic religion is not able to be modern like other religions."[150] It was the hegemonic hold of colonial notions of modernity, NEPU argued, that had led the Masu Sarauta to concede to a Penal Code that was "not strictly Islamic law."[151] Yet, the opposition party declared that the Penal Code legislation "can cover all aspect of ethics" even if it was not per se the Islamic law that the Sarauta class had sought to make it appear. NEPU, therefore, declared the making of the code as a victory: "We are happy. We are proud of our struggle. We achieved our objectives. In the future, no alkali will hide behind the smokescreen of Islam to cheat and oppress people and declare he is doing it in the name of Islam."[152] NEPU's critique of the colonial origins of the code would, therefore, come to coexist with its praise of the code's displacement of the old regime in which imperial law masqueraded as Islamic jurisprudence.

Scathing criticism of the code arose from English judges in the colony. In an article that became emblematic for this censure, Justin Price, British national and senior magistrate in the colony, charged that the reforms were designed to impose Islamic law on all Northern Nigerians through the back door.[153] Price argued that the Penal Code was a "retrograde legislation" designed to entrench the powers of the emirs and, therefore, the hold of Britain after Independence in a number of ways.[154] The first was the code's vesting of certain inquisitorial powers in magistrates, which Price insisted would undermine their independence by making them "official[s] of the executive," consequently boosting the powers of the emirs and the possibility of

---

[150] Mohammad D. Hadejia, Editorial, *Daily Comet*, April 27, 1960.
[151] Ibid.   [152] Editorial, *Daily Comet*, June 22, 1960.
[153] See Justin Price, "Criminal Law Reform in Northern Nigeria: Retrograde Legislation in Northern Nigeria?," *The Modern Law Review* 24, no. 5 (1961): 604–611.
[154] Ibid., 604–611.

"tyranny."[155] Further, the magistrate argued that the formal abolition of emirs' siyasa did not diminish their powers over the judiciary since they would continue to have control over alkalai, whom Price described as being of "poor quality."[156] What Price alluded to in his critique of the executive hold over the judiciary was that the party-politics system that produced the self-governing legislature in the last decade of colonial rule was based on the old power system. As such, several members of the Masu Sarauta continued to exercise both direct power (through membership of the legislative and executive councils) and indirect control (through patronage of political parties) over the pseudo-self-governing structure that would be the foundation of the impending independent state.[157] Under such circumstances, the transfer of siyasa to the state did not curtail the authority of those members of the Sarauta class who retained power and influence in the emerging state system. Consequently, Price suggested, the elimination of emirs' siyasa did not radically transform the distribution of power.

Reported by Southern Nigerian print media under the sensational headline, "Where Justin is, Justice shall be done!,"[158] Price's critique generated much controversy and renewed popular discussions about the tenacious hold of the Sarauta class in the administration of justice. In response, the handful of Nigerian English-trained lawyers practicing in Northern Nigeria mounted a defense of the reforms. Olu Odumosu, one of those lawyers, for instance, argued that far from being the "retrograde legislation" that Price labeled the code, "the legislation was only a little short of a revolution" given the state of the legal system in Northern Nigeria before the reforms.[159] Ahmadu

---

[155] Ibid., 606.
[156] Ibid. See Anderson's response in James Norman Dalrymple Anderson, "A Major Advance," *The Modern Law Review* 24, no. 5 (1961): 616–625. Defending the panel's work, Anderson argued that although the panel had–in deference to the Masu Sarauta–included certain provisions which may "outrage a lawyer trained in Anglo-Saxon notions of justice," the code was a "great advancement." For the response of a Northern elite, see "Reply to Mr. Justin Price's Attack," in Bello, *Work and Worship*, 225–232.
[157] Billy J. Dudley, *Parties and Politics in Northern Nigeria* (London: Routledge, 2013).
[158] Richardson, *No Weariness*, 223. Other reports that heightened tensions included an article published in *Daily Service*, a Southern Nigerian publication with widespread distribution in the North entitled, "The Light Goes Out in the North," critiquing the opting-out provision.
[159] Price, "Criminal Law Reform," 615.

Bello, himself, heatedly replied to Price's analysis.[160] In a newspaper rejoinder, Bello faulted Price's critique for making the English Common Law the sole "yardstick for justice," arguing that the Common Law was not "necessarily an ideal model for the rest of the world." Invoking Lord Denning's words in the *Nyali Bridge* case, Bello pointed out that the English Common Law was like the "English Oak ... you cannot transport it to the African Continent and expect it to retain the tough character it has in England."[161] Bello argued that regardless of the "careful tending" of English Common Law in its export overseas, it had been inflected by national peculiarities as was the case in Northern Nigeria where the relevant code was adapted to suit to local circumstances.[162]

These refutations of Price's criticism were forceful. Yet, Price's evisceration of the reforms had become so influential that even those jurists who had been on board with the reforms initially, such as Sir Algernon Brown, chief justice of the High Court of Northern Nigeria, began to question its validity. It would take the endorsement of two prominent British jurists, Lord Denning and Lord Diplock, the lord of appeal in the ordinary, to restore the faith of jurists like Sir Algernon in the reforms. Denning and Diplock issued the endorsement during a visit to Nigeria in preparation for the Denning-chaired Future of Law in Africa Conference to deliberate on Africa's legal systems.[163] Upon Denning and Diplock's approval of the Penal Code, Sir Algernon's restored faith became so deeply rooted that administrators would observe that he became "positively apostolic in his enthusiasm for the reforms."[164]

Although the 1958 reforms actualized the 1957 blueprint he presented to the Colonial Office, the Penal Code reforms did not go far enough for the "crusader" in Anderson that sought the total replacement of Islamic legal institutions, including the alkalai courts.[165]

---

[160] Ahmadu Bello, "Reply to Mr. Justin Price's Attacks on the Legal Reforms in Northern Nigeria," *Lagos Magazine*, October 28, 1961.
[161] Ibid.   [162] Ibid.
[163] Richardson, *No Weariness*, 224.   [164] Ibid.
[165] Richardson, *No Weariness*, 217; Matthew Hassan Kukah, *Religion, Politics and Power in Northern Nigeria* (Ibadan, Nigeria: Spectrum Books, 1993), 117. For an account of how Anderson's Evangelical Christian identity and ideas informed a "Christian Mission to Modernize Islam," see Todd Thompson, *Norman Anderson and the Christian Mission to Modernize Islam* (New York: Oxford University Press, 2018).

Nevertheless, the scholar and Oriental laws expert understood that the reforms had gone as far as was possible in 1958 Northern Nigeria. After much prayer and reflection in St. Christopher's Church, Kaduna, Anderson embraced the victories ushered in by the reforms.[166] For one thing, the situation of non-Muslim groups had vastly improved due to the abolition of emirs' siyasa, which "caused great uncertainty in the law and apprehension among minorities."[167] Above all, this had achieved the reform's primary goal: shifting the supreme lawgiver from a "divine" source to the legislature. In Anderson's view, the code de-Islamicized the law and secularized it. As he noted, "legislative authority became the basis of law without further seeking to root it in the Shari'a."[168] No longer could alkalai refuse to apply the law by invoking its inconsistency with the Shari'a. Neither could emirs invoke the Lugardian guarantee to oppose reform. The days of the intractable opposition that followed the *Gubba* decision were over, and the reformer and his colleagues could depart from the colony.

CONCLUSION

Late colonization of Islamic law took the form of codification. With the 1958 reforms, the late colonial state supplanted Islamic criminal jurisprudence with an imperial code of criminal justice. The transformation wrought by the codification project was not per se in the substance of the law; I have already shown in an earlier chapter that substantive reforms had begun to be implemented even in early Lugardian years. What was transformational about the 1958 reforms was its explicit location of the power to legislate in state institutions. The 1958 Penal Code reforms, therefore, completed the Donald Cameron-initiated process of transferring the locus of siyasa to the central state. While earlier reforms had been enacted through emirs and legitimated through the tenuous invocation of primary sources or juristic texts, the 1958 project vested lawmaking power in the legislature, consequently shifting the source of law from the divine claims legitimating emirs' authority to a human lawmaking body. Not even the alibi provided by precedents across the Muslim world could lessen the impact of this transformation.

---

[166] Richardson, *No Weariness*, 217.
[167] See also Anderson, "A Major Advance," 616–625.   [168] Ibid.

To be sure, premodern application of Islamic law was not in a vacuum; as several works show, human exposition of the Shariʻa has always straddled the realm of juristic labor and the enterprise of governance.[169] Significantly, the central governance apparatus or political authorities did not always consider themselves bound by the Shariʻa – as expounded by jurists' fiqh. Therefore, governments have always exercised influence over expositions of the law as it is applied in individual cases, even where it contradicts juristic preferences. Siyasa of the political authority was, in essence, not always necessarily siyasa sharʼiyya. Scholars making a case for this distinction cite Shafiʼi scholar Al-Juwayni. To illuminate the state's prerogative over the law, Al-Juwayni gives the example of a couple: while the husband adheres to the Hanafi school of thought, the wife is of Shafi'i persuasion and both are *mujtahid* (that is, both are equally capable of conducting expert legal reasoning in their respective schools' jurisprudence). Were the husband to pronounce divorce to the wife in a fit of anger, such a divorce would be invalid under Hanafi law but valid under Shafi'i law. Al-Juwayni submits that in the disagreement bound to ensue, the parties will table the dispute before a qadi whose decision becomes binding not because it accords with the ruling of either school of jurisprudence, but rather because the judicial institution is authorized – by the state.[170] As legal scholar Anver Emon notes, Al-Juwayni's analogy reveals that behind juristic doctrine "lies a host of background assumptions that link the Shariʻa's doctrines to the institutional and political framework within which those rules were intelligible."[171] This shows the influence of governance in the outcome of individual cases; nevertheless, in pointing out that government-appointed qadis determine which juristic opinion comes out ahead, Al-Juwayni reveals that the exercise of siyasa was understood as bound by the Shariʻa – however much jurists differed in their understanding of the Shariʻa. This is not to deny the existence of cases where extrajuristic considerations of governance and politics

---

[169] Emon, *Religious Pluralism and Islamic Law*; Khan, *Muslim Becoming*; Salomon, *For Love of the Prophet*; Ayoub, *Law, Empire, and the Sultan*.

[170] See Abu Al Ma'ala Al Juwayni, *Kitab al Ijtihad min Kitab al Talkhis*, ed. Abdul-Hamid Abu Zunayr (Damscus: Dar Al Qalam, 1987) in Emon, *Religious Pluralism and Islamic Law*, 10–11. See, however, Khaled Abou El Fadl, *And God Knows the Soldiers: The Authoritative and Authoritarian in Islamic Discourses* (Lanham: University Press of America, 2001), 60. See also Abou El Fadel, *Speaking in God's Name*, 161–162.

[171] Emon, *Religious Pluralism and Islamic Law*.

trumped juristic understandings of the Shari'a, including in precolonial Sokoto. Indeed, works such as *Wallahi Wallahi*[172] and *Tabbat Hakika*,[173] authored by the founder of the precolonial caliphate, Uthman Dan Fodio, were wistful musings on such abuses. If emirs' exercise of siyasa was not always faithful to juristic expositions of the Shari'a in precolonial times, Lugardian years witnessed an even greater betrayal of fiqh by emirs' siyasa. Yet emirs continued to invoke the Shari'a as the source of siyasa's legitimacy – however rhetorical this invocation was. Therefore, deviations from the constitutional boundary were regarded not as the norm, but rather as constitutional exceptions. With the 1958 reforms, however, the constitutional repository of siyasa changed from emirs and shifted to the late colonial state's legislature. Consequently, the vesting of siyasa in the state did not merely dissolve the constitutional boundaries of the siyasa; it, in fact, radically disconnected siyasa from its *fons et origo*. The 1958 reforms, in sum, shifted the seat of sovereignty to the political foundations of the state institutions now exercising siyasa.

In the end, the 1958 reforms were Islamic – only because the state declared them as such. This was the feat of imperial secular governmentality. Wielding the power to define and confine religion, the late colonial state could declare the 1958 Penal Code as Islamic while simultaneously supplanting Islamic jurisprudence with a code of Western law, and, even more importantly, altering the constitutional foundations of Islamic law and governance.

The relations of power set in motion by colonialism (in its early and late forms) meant that the 1958 reforms could not be the settlement of struggles over religious difference they set out to be. Far from resolving interreligious inequality and strife, the 1958 processes came to intensify the struggle over religious difference. The ensuing postcolonial contestation was already foreshadowed by the discontent that greeted the 1958 reforms. For all their rhetoric, the Masu Sarauta regarded the 1958 reforms as a loss to a late colonial abandonment of the 1903 guarantee and a mission-inspired passion to reform Islamic law along the lines of Western law. Even NEPU elites, ardent critics of the Masu Sarauta, continued to vacillate between criticism and embrace of the code. For all the desirability of reforms, they had fallen short of the

---

[172] Mervyn Hiskett, *The Sword of Truth: The Life and Times of the Shehu Usuman dan Fodio* (New York: Oxford University Press, 1973), 105.
[173] Ibid.

Egyptian vision idealized by NEPU, and even more objectionably to Kano and his NEPU comrades, the reforms had been championed by the colonial state. Christian missions rejoiced at the reforms, but while Indigenous converts welcomed the end to colonial Islamic law's reign in public law, they remained unconvinced that the state's religious hierarchies had been shattered. Most importantly, the reform was itself conducted with reference to religion – whether it sought to invoke it as an alibi for legitimacy or to frame it as the problem that the legal reform processes sought to resolve. By doing so, however, colonial law masked itself with religion, making the latter a continued currency of the debate that had emerged since the dawn of imperial rule and a source of enduring conflict.

CHAPTER FIVE

CONSTITUTING RIGHTS
Christian Religious Liberty in the Late Colonial State

The final element of the Independence deal on the governance of religion was the constitutionalization of the right to religious liberty. The outcome of a sustained global missionary effort, this turn to rights entailed the making of Article 18 of the Universal Declaration of Human Rights (the Universal Declaration), and the subsequent domestication of that international legal provision in Nigeria's Independence Constitution. Beginning at the 1910 World Missionary Conference in Edinburgh and ultimately reaching a crescendo in the years following the Second World War, international ecumenists championed a mission-permissive notion of religious freedom. Through that idea, ecumenists sought to liberate the missionary enterprise from the threats posed by a secularism that ecumenists regarded as antagonistic to Christainity and permissive to false orthodoxies such as Islam. The Protestant ecumenical vision of religious freedom emphasized two rights: the liberty of the proselytizer to preach, and of the target audience to convert. Article 18 of the Universal Declaration, which was adopted by the United Nations (UN) on December 10, 1948, was the outcome of that global ecumenical effort. Following the success of the ecumenical alliance at the UN, key leaders of the movement turned their attention to domesticating that international legal provision in late colonial Nigeria. The outcome was the triumph of a Protestant notion of religious liberty at Independence.

Histories of Article 18 tend to emphasize the provision's emancipatory character, presenting that provision and the Universal Declaration as a story of progress that ushered in the egalitarian guarantee of religious liberty following the horrors of the Second World War.[1] Other accounts have, however, interrogated Article 18 and, more broadly, the legal idea of religious liberty for its masked preferences.[2] To take an example, Saba Mahmood and Peter Danchin point out that "religious freedom often legitimates ... discriminatory practices of the state against religious minorities."[3] This critique of religious liberty goes beyond unveiling how that legal idea has benefited powerful constituencies and disfavored minorities. Indeed, critical accounts commonly situate the flaws of religious liberty in the downsides of the secularist notion of state-religion separation.[4] By interlinking the ideas of religious liberty and secularist state-religion separation, however, these narratives perpetuate the received accounts that they criticize.[5] Like received narratives, conventional accounts understand religious liberty to have emerged as part of a *harmonious* constitutional package featuring state-religion separation and religious liberty – even as they

---

[1] See Mary Ann Glendon, *A World Made New: Eleanor Roosevelt and the Universal Declaration of Human Rights* (New York: Random House, 2001). See, however, Samuel Moyn, *The Last Utopia: Human Rights in History* (Cambridge: Harvard University Press, 2012).

[2] Linde Lindkvist, "The Politics of Article 18: Religious Liberty in the Universal Declaration of Human Rights," *Humanity: An International Journal of Human Rights, Humanitarianism, and Development* 4, no. 3 (2013): 429, 440. Saba Mahmood and Peter G. Danchin, "Immunity or Regulation? Antinomies of Religious Freedom," *South Atlantic Quarterly* 113, no. 1 (2014): 129. See also Pritam Singh, "Hindu Bias in India's 'Secular' Constitution: Probing Flaws in the Instruments of Governance," *Third World Quarterly* 26, no. 6 (2005): 909–926, which critiques *Manohar Joshi v. Nitin Bhaurao Patil All India Reports*, 1996 SC 796, among other decisions. On the jurisprudence of the European Court of Human Rights, see Mahmood and Danchin, "Immunity or Regulation?" and Peter G. Danchin, "Islam in the Secular Nomos of the European Court of Human Rights," *Michigan Journal of International Law* 32, no. 4 (2011): 663. For commentary on a variety of contexts including the United States, see Winnifred Fallers Sullivan et al., eds., *Politics of Religious Freedom* (Chicago: University of Chicago Press, 2015); Winnifred Fallers Sullivan, *The Impossibility of Religious Freedom*, 2nd ed. (Princeton, NJ: Princeton University Press, 2018); Joan Wallach Scott, *The Politics of the Veil* (Princeton, NJ: Princeton University Press, 2009); and Hussein Agrama, *Questioning Secularism: Islam, Sovereignty, and the Rule of Law in Modern Egypt* (Chicago: University of Chicago Press, 2012).

[3] Mahmood and Danchin, "Immunity or Regulation?"

[4] Certain accounts link the critique of religious liberty and secularism by rooting the origins of both in "traditions associated with Christianity." Scott, *Politics of the Veil*, 92. See however José Casanova, "The Secular and Secularisms," *Social Research: An International Quarterly* 76, no. 4 (2009): 1049–1066.

[5] For a conventional account of secularism, see John Rawls, *Political Liberalism* (New York: Columbia University Press, 2015).

disagree over the merits of that package. This chapter unsettles that assumption by revealing the tensions between the concepts of religious liberty and state-religion separation during the making of Article 18 and its domestication in late colonial Northern Nigeria.

The narrative that follows reveals that Article 18 was the product of global ecumenical advocacy for a notion of religious liberty that would neutralize the secularist separation of the colonial state from Christianity and the missionary enterprise. Already, newer histories have begun to illuminate the Christian preferentialism inherent in the Article 18 project. Sam Moyn, for instance, argues that Article 18 was a Christian religious freedom project designed to marginalize secularism, understood by advocates as the state's separation from and alienation of Christianity.[6] That project, however, went beyond the shores of Europe as reflected in narratives such as Moyn's; it had important origins and manifestations in colonial territories, notably in Northern Nigeria. Besides "secularism," the other threat that preoccupied ecumenical discourse was what the movement understood as "Islamic orthodoxy." Northern Nigeria represented the unholy alliance between the threats of Islamic orthodoxy and secularism since the state governed through Islamic institutions while simultaneously invoking secularism. Far from contradictory, Islam and secularism were, in fact, characterized as complementary in ecumenical discourse. Ecumenists conceived of secularism as state separation from Christianity, not all religion, arguing that secularism's separation of the state from "true religion" had robbed the state and society of "its Christian glory."[7] Ecumenists, therefore, regarded secularism as a form of religion, albeit a false faith, compatible with questionable orthodoxies, prominent among which was Islam. Ecumenical leaders crafted the Universal Declaration's provision on religious freedom, Article 18, in response to that unchristian secularism. In sum, Article 18 sought to neutralize a secularism ostensibly allied with Islam in Northern Nigeria, that area of Africa that had long been of great attraction to the missionary project.

The story of Article 18 does not merely unsettle the historical assumption that the notions of secularist separation and religious freedom emerged in harmony. In revealing the tensions between both ideas during the making of Article 18 and in the constitutional negotiations

---

[6] Samuel Moyn, *Christian Human Rights* (Philadelphia: University of Pennsylvania Press, 2015), 140, 156.

[7] Miner Searle Bates, *Religious Liberty: An Inquiry* (New York: Harper Bros., 1945).

that imported that provision into Nigeria, this chronicle questions assumptions of the stability of the two concepts. Instead, this narrative reveals how both ideas take shape in specific contestations, and consequently makes the case for apprehending their workings through a close study of the struggles that galvanize them.

FROM EDINBURGH 1910 TO THE UNITED NATIONS

Gathering at the inaugural moment of modern global ecumenism in June 1910, the World Missionary Conference deliberated on the fate of the missionary enterprise.[8] For the ecumenists convened at Edinburgh, the project to spread the gospel to the "non-Christian world" – in many ways synonymous with the colonized world – was a primary obligation of the faith.[9] Yet, proselytization faced several hindrances in these territories, frustrating the missionary effort. As an unprecedented gathering of global ecumenists invested in the missionary enterprise, Edinburgh 1910 provided an opportunity to advocate for the removal of restrictions on missions.

Edinburgh ecumenists paid careful attention to assessing missionary restrictions in the Muslim world, particularly in the context of Africa. This was hardly surprising; as noted earlier in this book, the intersection of Africa and Islam piqued the missionary imagination.[10] Northern Nigeria occupied a particularly central place in the evangelization project, at par only with two other British Muslim territories – Sudan and Egypt.[11] The Edinburgh gathering was, however, disappointed with the trajectory of the missionary project in Northern Nigeria. The convener of the Edinburgh Conference, Joseph Oldham, was no stranger to the mission question in Northern Nigeria. Oldham, a Scottish missionary

---

[8] Brian Stanley, *The World Missionary Conference, 1910* (Grand Rapids: Eerdmans Publishing, 2009). Although earlier international ecumenical conferences had convened in 1898 and 1900, the 1910 gathering is regarded as the defining moment of Protestant ecumenism.

[9] World Missionary Conference, *Report of the World Missionary Conference Commission I: Carrying of the Gospel to All the Non-Christian World* (Edinburgh: World Missionary Conference, 1910).

[10] Thomas Prasch, "Which God for Africa: The Islamic-Christian Missionary Debate in Late-Victorian England," *Victorian Studies* 33, no. 1 (1989): 51–73.

[11] *Report of the World Missionary Conference Commission I*; World Missionary Conference, *Report of Commission VII. Missions and Governments: With Supplement: Presentation and Discussion of the Report in the Conference on 20th June 1910* (Edinburgh: Oliphant, Anderson and Ferrier, 1910), 113.

of the Church Missionary Society (CMS), was an ardent advocate for missions operating in that colony. Oldham's advocacy for Northern Nigerian missions was not limited to the CMS; because the global ecumenist was the brains behind the International Missionary Council (IMC) – the first international ecumenical Protestant group, and later the international ecumenical movement's division focused on global missionary affairs in Asia and Africa – he was active in advocating the removal of missionary restrictions on behalf of other mission groups in the Northern Nigerian mission field.

The Edinburgh Conference was convened only seven years after the declaration of Northern Nigeria as a British Protectorate. Even in those early years of colonial rule, imperial governance had begun to frustrate missionary ambitions. Lambasting the British Empire's inclination to ally with Islamic institutions in Muslim Africa while simultaneously restricting Christian missions, Edinburgh ecumenists declared it "a disgrace to British rule in tropical Africa that it should anywhere favor Islam and discourage the extension of Christian missions."[12] Edinburgh ecumenists consequently accused the British colonial government of enacting state-religion separation to the benefit of Islam and to the disfavor of Christianity. The misfortune in Muslim Africa was, therefore, not merely the British Empire's separation from Christian missions; it was also its alliance with Islam. In particular, Edinburgh 1910 delegates were concerned with the obstructive effect of the classical Islamic legal doctrine of *ridda* (apostasy) on missionary proselytization efforts.[13] Edinburgh ecumenists regarded the alliance between the colonial government and Muslim elites and institutions as going beyond a mere hostility to the missionary enterprise; it was, in their view, outrightly unchristian.[14] The ecumenists argued, in sum, that the colonial state's restrictions on missions amounted to an unchristian separation of empire from the missionary project.

Edinburgh provided an opportunity to critique unchristian separations and begin the task of envisioning a state-religion design that would

---

[12] See, for instance, *Report of the World Missionary Conference Commission I*, 209. Only in the cases of Sudan and Egypt did the colonial patronage of Islamic institutions and restriction on missionary proselytization receive as much missionary opprobrium as Northern Nigeria. *Report of the World Missionary Conference Commission I*, 113.

[13] See Chapter 1. However, that doctrine was hardly invoked in the discourse on missionary preaching within the colony itself.

[14] *Report of the World Missionary Conference Commission I*. See further Walter Richard Samuel Miller to Frederick Baylliss, September 5, 1902, CMS/G3/A9/01, Church of England Records Centre, London.

PART II CONSTITUTING DIFFERENCE

withstand challenges to the missionary enterprise. Perhaps nothing illuminates that vision more than the work of the Conference Commission VII. Charged by the conference with mission-government relations question, the commission's work reveals the beginnings of twentieth-century ecumenical thought on a normative state-religion design, particularly as it pertained to missions in the non-Christian world. Particularly noteworthy is the study prepared by the Reverend Professor G. Hausseleiter of the University of Halle, which became a part of the commission's report. Although it began from a premise that European governments were "Christian," the report insisted that the complete fusion of church and state is a feature of "non-Christian" states.[15] "Christ," Hausseleiter argued, "drew [a] distinction between the Kingdom of the Emperor and the Kingdom of God."[16] Nevertheless, this relationship between the two spheres was not one of separation; as ecumenical thought would come to make clear, Caesar's sphere is not free of God.[17] Therefore, while Edinburgh did not sanction a fusion of the state and church, it espoused a hostility to unchristian state-religion separation arrangements. In doing so, Edinburgh mounted a critique on the constitutional design of places like imperial Northern Nigeria, where the colonial assertion of state-religion separation was complemented by its utilization of Islamic institutions.

To be clear, ecumenists understood that Islam was not the only religion being privileged to the disfavor of missions. In fact, the missionary experience in India was also a matter of deliberation at the conference, and Edinburgh deliberations reflected a disapproval of all unchristian separations. Islam, however, remained central to this critique. Indeed, while the commission would eventually conclude that the jury was still out on the India case, it was unequivocal in its critique of Islam (especially in Northern Nigeria, Sudan, and Egypt), and emblematic of the unchristian separation promoted by the British government.[18]

To trump unchristian separations, the report advanced a view of the superiority of the principle of the "freedom of the church and mission." As Hausseleiter argued, freedom of the church and mission is "in the interest of the state" since both are the "conscience of the state."[19]

---

[15] *Report of the World Missionary Conference Commission VII*, 142.
[16] Ibid.
[17] This view would be fleshed out much more explicitly in the Oxford report discussed below: Joseph Houldsworth Oldham, ed., *The Oxford Conference: Official Report* (Chicago: Willett, Clark, 1937), 70.
[18] *Report of Commission VII*, 24.   [19] Ibid., 142–143.

Beyond this highlighted benefit to the state, the superiority of the freedom of the church and mission principle was also motivated by a suspicion of the state. Hausseleiter posited that if states are vested with the sole discretion to determine the place of the mission, they would invoke the principle of state-mission distance to "try everywhere completely to exclude the Mission."[20]

Edinburgh 1910 therefore commenced the process of crafting a notion of religious freedom that would aid the missionary effort. It was, however, the ecumenical efforts of the late transwar to early postwar period that would climax this effort. In those years, the ecumenical movement would finalize its religious freedom blueprint and champion the international legal and constitution-making processes that would actualize its vision.

Oxford 1937 and the Triumph of Protestant Religious Freedom

Edinburgh marked the inception of the ecumenical critique of unchristian separation as an imperial policy and colonial sensibility that had its roots in the intellectual idea of secularism. Nevertheless, the description of the abhorred state design as "secular" was more typically associated with colonial administrators in the Edinburgh years. Only sparingly did Edinburgh ecumenists deploy the term "secular"; the ecclesiastical brethren devoted much of their energies to describing the crux of the constitutional problem – unchristian separations – rather than naming it.[21] It was in the interwar years, those between the end of the First World War and the inception of the Second World War, that the ecumenical movement would put a name to the old "enemy" – secularism.[22]

---

[20] Ibid., 143.

[21] It was in the context of criticizing the colonial policy excluding Christian instruction in schools that the Edinburgh report features the term: "secular." See *Report of the World Missionary Conference Commission I*, 29.

[22] Scholars have explored the interwar roots of this ecumenical hostility to secularism. See Justin Reynolds, "Against the World: International Protestantism and the Ecumenical Movement between Secularization and Politics, 1900–1952," PhD diss., (Columbia University, 2016). See also Udi Greenberg, "Protestants, Decolonization, and European Integration, 1885–1961," *Journal of Modern History* 89, no. 2 (2017): 314. Greenberg, for instance, argues that following the First World War, ecumenical Protestants understood the spirit of nationalism that inspired the war and the rise of ideologies like Bolshevism to be rooted in "secularism." Greenberg, "Protestants, Decolonization, and European Integration," 328. Further, ecumenists understood secularism to be a false ideology replacing Christianity as "Europe's spiritual center," leading to a "horrendous spiritual decline," Greenberg,

As first described by the 1928 gathering of the International Missionary Council Conference in Jerusalem, secularism was not the absence of religion, it was a comprehensive belief, a "system of life and thought."[23] Secularism amounted to paganism, and both, ecumenists argued, were in "defiance of God's sovereignty."[24] By asserting "human self-sufficiency," secularism culminated in moral, political, and economic systems based on the "deification" of the "world" as well as the "self."[25] Unchristian separations were, consequently, not the cause of secularism; they were a symptom. Ecumenists further argued that secularism was a malady afflicting the entire world and threatening Christianity everywhere.[26] The challenge to the missionary enterprise abroad by supposedly Christian empires was already a reflection of this threat. The problem was, therefore, not merely the violent repression of the church by Soviet Communism and German National Socialism; even in those Western European states that did not feature this intense hostility, ecumenists were concerned with the increased disempowerment of churches and the decreased salience of Christianity in the lives of European populations.[27] In a 1929 lecture to the Dutch Missionary Conference titled "The Christianizing and Unchristianizing of the World," Joseph Oldham would declare that "the demonic attempt to put the world or the self in the place of God ... has stricken at the heart of Europe."[28] Ecumenists were convinced that it was the marginalization of Christianity that produced the imperial policy alienating Christian missions abroad.

"Protestants, Decolonization, and European Integration," 328, 329. Although Greenberg's account situates late interwar ecumenical opposition to colonialism within the broader ecumenical critique of secularism, it fails to uncover the earlier roots of this critique of imperial secularism in the experience of missionary restrictions in colonies, especially in Muslim Africa.

[23] Reynolds, "Against the World," 114–117, 158.   [24] Ibid., 161.

[25] Ibid., 161, 173, and 176. See Emil Brunner, "Secularism as a Problem for the Church," *International Review of Mission* 19, no. 76 (1930): 498.

[26] See Brunner, "Secularism as a Problem," 64. Note of a Meeting of the British Members, March 18, 1927, 2 (WCC, 260.001, folder 01), in Reynolds, "Against the World," 135.

[27] Terrence Renaud, "Human Rights as Radical Anthropology: Protestant Theology and Ecumenism in the Transwar Era," *The History Journal* 60, no. 2 (2017): 493; Keith Robbins, *England, Ireland, Scotland, Wales: The Christian Church 1900–2000* (Oxford: Oxford University Press, 2008).

[28] Joseph Oldham, "The Christianizing and Unchristianizing of the World," (1929), Joseph Oldham Papers, folder 2, box 15, New College Archive, Edinburgh University, cited in Greenberg, "Protestants, Decolonization and European Integration," 314–354.

Capturing this ecumenical alarm at the dechristianization of the world, William Temple, rector at St. Paul's Piccadilly and future archbishop of Canterbury, declared: "the world has gone pagan."[29] The question on the mind of ecumenists then was: "what is a Christian to do?"[30]

By the late interwar period, the ecumenical movement went beyond this initial concern: it began to regard the struggle with secularism as a threat to the "very existence of the church."[31] Articulating this crisis in Faeno, Denmark in August 1934, the Universal Christian Council's Life and Work Movement set out the broad outlines of a conference to deliberate on the church-state question and respond to the challenges posed by the new paganism.

Reflecting this recognition of secularism's connections with "false" religion, the theme of Oxford 1937 was "the life-and-death struggle between Christian faith and the secular and pagan tendencies of our time."[32] The Oxford Conference of the Life and Work Movement, regarded as the most significant event in twentieth-century ecumenism, called on the church to dismantle constraints on Christianity in Europe and abroad with the idea of "freedom of religion." In its report, "The Universal Church in the World of Nations," the conference affirmed the centrality of "freedom of religion" in a "better international order." According to the conference, church advocacy was in pursuit of "freedom of conscience" of both Christians and non-Christians. The conference asserted: "we do not ask for any privilege to be granted to Christians that is denied to others. While the liberty with which Christ has set us free can neither be given nor destroyed by any government, Christians, because of that inner freedom are both jealous for its outward expression and solicitous that all men should have freedom in religious life."[33] The conference was careful to condemn socioeconomic

---

[29] William Temple, *Papers for War Time: Christianity and War* (Oxford: Oxford University Press, 1914), 3.

[30] Ibid.

[31] See Renaud, "Human Rights as Radical Anthropology."

[32] Joseph H. Oldham, "Introduction to Oxford Conference Report," *The Oxford Conference*, 2. For an account of Oxford 1937, especially from perspective of US ecumenists and their project of Christian internationalism, see Michael G. Thompson, *For God and Globe: Christian Internationalism in the United States between the Great War and the Cold War* (New York: Cornell University Press, 2015).

[33] The International Missionary Council, "The Universal Church in the World of Nations, 1937." BCC/DIA/7/3/4 Church of England Record Center Collections (hereafter CERC).

privileges granted to European Christians in some imperial territories; it affirmed: "We deprecate any attempt by Christians to secure under the shelter of the power or prestige of their nations any privileges in other countries in such matters as civil status, the holding of property, or the language of education."[34] Yet, this caution was not a call for the disestablishment of the church, a point that the conference would make clear in its other report, "The Church and State."

Issued by the conference section chaired by Max Huber, the renowned Swiss churchman and judge of the Permanent Court of International Justice, the Church and State report is particularly significant for the insight it provides into the ecumenical movement's thought on church-state relations. As a structural matter, Oxford 1937, like Edinburgh 1910, insisted that the biblical analogy of Caesar-God separation did not support the church-state separation evinced by secularist tendencies. As the report put it, "it is God who declares what is Caesar's."[35] This inclination toward establishment was, however, conditional. The report suggested that the ultimate relationship between church and state ought to be determined by the nature of the state. Where the state fails to live up to its God-given duty of "upholding law and order," "ministering to the life of the people united within it,"[36] and becomes an "instrument of evil,"[37] the church ought to take on a position of "criticism or opposition" since the church is "not the lord" but rather a mere "servant of justice."[38] Not only was ecumenical approval of establishment contingent on the nature of the state, it also hinged on a particular religion: Christianity.[39]

Oxford 1937 ecumenists were gravely concerned with the effect of secularization on state and society. Secularization, conference delegates concluded, had "robbed" the state of its "religious glamor," leading to absolutist tendencies and hostility toward the church by the state. This hostility manifested not only in the visible repression of the church resembling "pre-Constantine conditions,"[40] but also in the less obvious phenomenon of favoring the church not as an intrinsic good, but for the benefits it could offer the state.[41] Within

---

[34] "Report of the Section on the Universal Church and the World of Nations," in Oldham, *The Oxford Conference*, 168–169.
[35] "Report of the Section on Church and State," in Oldham, *The Oxford Conference*, 70.
[36] Ibid., 66.   [37] Ibid., 67.   [38] Ibid.   [39] Ibid., 66.   [40] Ibid., 233.   [41] Ibid., 231.

"society," conference delegates pointed out, secularization had given rise to materialism.[42] Although secularism had dechristianized the state and society, the conference was careful to emphasize that the state's claim of being devoid of religion was increasingly tenuous. To fill the spiritual vacuum left by Christianity, both the secularized state and secularized humanity had, in fact, turned to "new forms of faith," made "new idols," and rediscovered "old religion."[43] This old religion, according to the conference, was the quintessential sin of human glorification. Therefore, ecumenists did not imagine that secularism of the state and secularization of society had eradicated religion; rather, they were convinced that false gods and secularism could, in fact, coexist. American-English poet T. S. Eliot's 1940 work, *The Idea of a Christian Society*, encapsulates ecumenists' equation of secular constitutional arrangements with false orthodoxy.[44] Eliot jointly founded a "conservative think-tank" with Joseph Oldham, and in the book, which emerged from Eliot's lectures during and after Oxford 1937, he equated a "neutral society" with a "pagan society."[45] In the context of this broader ecumenical understanding of secularism as a comprehensive, albeit "false" belief, the Islamic and secular features of places like colonial Northern Nigeria were not only compatible, but in fact complementary.

To counter this slide into paganism, Eliot and his ecumenical brethren at Oxford called for the making of a Christian society.[46] Although Oxford ecumenists were enthralled by the benefits of the Christian church's establishment, the conference, nevertheless, recognized that establishment did not always correlate with the freedom of the church.[47] Ecumenists, therefore, cautioned that where establishment would deprive the church of certain freedoms, the church has a duty to free herself and retrieve the freedoms "even at the cost of disestablishment." These freedoms of the church, which were crucial both in establishment and non-establishment regimes, included the freedom to determine its faith and creed; freedom of public and private worship;

---

[42] Ibid., 227. [43] Ibid.
[44] Thomas Stearns Eliot, *The Idea of a Christian Society* (New York: Harcourt, Brace, 1940). For more on Eliot's place in the ecumenical critique of secularism, see Greenberg, "Protestants, Decolonization and European Integration," 341. See further, Thomas Stearns Eliot, "Catholicism and International Order," in *Essays Ancient and Modern* (New York: Harcourt, Brace, 1936), 113–136.
[45] Eliot, *The Idea of a Christian Society*, 5.
[46] Ibid. [47] Ibid., 255.

preaching and teaching; freedom from any imposition by the state; of religious ceremonies and forms of worship; and freedom of Christian service and missionary activity both at home and in foreign lands. Expectedly, Oxford 1937 was preoccupied with the question of evangelization. As the Oxford Church and State report stressed in its concluding lines: "The one thing that matters is that it [the church] should be free to proclaim the good news of Christ, without let or hindrance, in accordance with the commission given to the church by its Lord."[48] When the International Missionary Conference would reconvene the following year in Tambaram, India, it would put the issue of proselytization at the center of its agenda, listing these as part of the "most essential" rights.[49]

The Oxford Conference's most far-reaching decision was its establishment of the World Council of Churches (WCC) with the specific goal of working toward the making of an international legal provision on religious liberty. The WCC would go on to establish the Commission of the Churches on International Affairs (CCIA) to achieve this goal. Specifically, the rights conception to be advanced by the WCC was rooted in the idea of "Christian personalism": that "the human being [is] a theological person in community with others and in partnership with God."[50] Although universal, the personalist notion of humanity was therefore rooted in Christian theology and the firm missionary conviction that all men were potential Christians.[51] Although Oxford 1937 had resolved that it was incumbent on the church to defend universal humanity regardless of nationality, race, or class, this universal mandate was to be molded by Christian personalism and the primacy of religious freedom as the foundation

---

[48] "Additional Report of the Section on Church and State," in Oldham, *The Oxford Conference*, 255 (citing Matthew 28:18–20).

[49] Other rights set out in the India 1938 report were similar to those in the Oxford 1937 Church and State report. See BCC/DIA/7/3/4/3 CERC.

[50] Samuel Moyn, "Personalism, Community, and the Origins of Human Rights," in *Human Rights in the Twentieth Century*, ed. Stefan-Ludwig Hoffmann (Cambridge: Cambridge University Press, 2011), 85 (citing Jacques Maritian and Charles Malik as influential in this project); Samuel Moyn, "The First Historian of Human Rights," *The American Historical Review* 116, no. 1 (2011): 58. For an account of the theological foundations of the idea of personalism, see Renaud, "Human Rights as Radical Anthropology"; and Reynolds, "Against the World."

[51] Renaud, "Human Rights as Radical Anthropology," 497; Reynolds, "Against the World," 29.

for all rights. As the WCC would declare several years later at a 1949 Chichester meeting:

> a peaceful and stable order can only be built upon foundations of righteousness, of right relations between man and God and between man and man. Only the recognition that man has ends and loyalties beyond the State will ensure true justice to the human person. Religious freedom is the condition and guardian of all true freedom.[52]

This notion that religious freedom was the foundation of human rights had been advanced by the famous Six Pillars of Peace issued by the John Foster Dulles-chaired American Federal Council of Churches' (FCC) Commission to Study the Bases of a Just and Durable Peace in 1943. Dulles had himself been a platform speaker on international affairs at the Oxford Conference and was actively involved in the conference's Universal Church and the World of Nations report. Six Pillars of Peace not only called for an international bill of rights, but it also advocated for religious liberty as its "essential linchpin."[53] The FCC and the American Protestants it represented were immersed in this project of internationalizing a personalist notion of rights and considered religious freedom to be its foundation.[54] Indeed, this missionary campaign for the centrality of religious freedom to postwar international order had begun to gain political traction even before the FCC's Six Pillars. For instance, President Franklin D. Roosevelt had outlined religious liberty as part of the four basic freedoms in his famous address to Congress in 1941.[55]

---

[52] Renaud, "Human Rights as Radical Anthropology," 515; George K. Bell, *The Kingship of Christ: The Story of the World Council of Churches* (Middlesex: Penguin Books, 1954), 85, 124–128. See also W. A. Visser't Hooft, *Memoirs of W. A. Visser't Hooft* (Philadelphia: Westminster Press, 1973), 219.

[53] Samuel Moyn, *Christian Human Rights* (Philadelphia: University of Pennsylvania Press, 2015). For the text of the six pillars, see John F. Dulles, *A Just and Durable Peace: Discussion of Political Propositions (Six Pillars of Peace)* (New York: Commission to Study the Bases of a Just and Durable Peace, 1943). See further Anna Su, *Exporting Freedom: Religious Liberty and American Power* (Cambridge, MA: Harvard University Press, 2016); O. Frederick Nolde, *Free and Equal: Human Rights in Ecumenical Perspective with Reflections on the Origin of the Universal Declaration of Human Rights* (Geneva: World Council of Churches, 1968).

[54] For an account of how American Protestantism took on the mantle of internationalized human rights, see Gene Zubovich, "The Global Gospel: Protestant Internationalism and American Liberalism, 1940–1960," PhD diss., (University of California, Berkeley, 2014).

[55] Franklin D. Roosevelt, "Annual Message to the Congress" (January 6, 1941), S. Doc. No. 77-188, at 86–87 (2nd Session, August 12, 1942).

When the Atlantic Charter subsequently concluded between Roosevelt and Winston Churchill of the United Kingdom failed to explicitly reference the freedom of worship, Roosevelt would come under such intense criticism from the Protestant coalition that the American president would be prompted to submit to Congress: "it is unnecessary for me to point out that the declaration of principles includes of necessity the world need for freedom of religion and freedom of information. No society of the world organized under the announced principles could survive without these freedoms which are a part of the whole freedom for which we strive."[56]

It was therefore unsurprising that American Protestants came to be at the forefront of harnessing international ecumenical thought on religious freedom into a concrete international legal provision. CCIA's inaugural director and architect of Article 18 was Otto Frederick Nolde, dean of the Graduate School at the Lutheran Theological Seminary in Philadelphia. Prior to his time at the CCIA, Nolde had served as spokesman of the Joint Committee on Religious Liberty (JCRL) established in partnership by the FCC and the Foreign Missions Conference in North America in 1942. Like the CCIA, the aim of the JCRL was the crafting of an international legal provision on religious freedom.[57] Further, the JCRL, like the CCIA, made the freedom to proselytize and convert a crucial element in this envisaged international legal provision.[58]

---

[56] Quoted in Quincy Wright, "Human Rights and the World Order," *International Conciliation* 21 (1943): 238. On the UN Charter, see Ruth B. Russell, "A History of the United Nations Charter: The Role of the United States 1940–1945," 975 (Appendix B) (1958) (reproducing H. Doc. 358/77C1/1941). See also Malcolm D. Evans, *Religious Liberty and International Law in Europe* (Cambridge: Cambridge University Press, 1997), 174.

[57] Nolde also served as an associate in the FCC's advisory group to the US delegation to the UN charter talks. The task of the group was the promotion of human rights in the charter negotiations.

[58] The Joint Committee on Religious Liberty's statement on religious liberty provides: "Religious liberty shall be interpreted to include freedom of worship according to conscience and to bring up children in the faith of their parents; freedom for the individual to change his religion; freedom to preach, educate, publish, and carry on missionary activities; and freedom to organize with others and to acquire and hold property, for these purposes." "Statement on Religious Liberty," adopted in 1944 by the Federal Council of Churches (April 12) and the Foreign Missions Conference (March 21), and quoted in Linde Lindkvist, "The Politics of Article 18: Religious Liberty in the Universal Declaration of Human Rights," *Humanity* 4 (2013): 429, 440.

A useful lens through which one might understand the JCRL's postwar vision of religious liberty is its report, *Religious Liberty: An Inquiry*, published in 1945 and authored by Miner Searle Bates, Baptist missionary and professor of history at China's Nanking University.[59] Overlooking the horrors of the Holocaust, *Religious Liberty* found the most extreme cases of denial of religious liberty in Soviet Russia, Franco's Spain, and "Moslem Countries." Indeed, the report considered the restrictions on religious freedom by Soviet Russia as not only the action of a totalitarian state, but really as evidence of the "profound incompatibility" of religious liberty and the secularism espoused by communism.[60] While Russia, therefore, represented extreme hostility to religion, the report argued that Spain's problem lay in the monopoly of the Roman Catholic Church and the resulting infringement of religious liberty of people of other religions.

In the case of "Orthodox Islam," the report found it to be "contrary of religious liberty" that "finds no room for the concept as developed in Western lands."[61] This assessment was based on restrictions on Christian missions in Muslim territories, which arose both from direct legal and administrative proscriptions on evangelization as well as indirect constraints on the missionary enterprise such as the classical Islamic legal prohibition on apostasy. Although Bates and the JCRL were concerned with the restrictions on Hindu-Christian conversions in India, they considered Islamic restrictions and particularly the doctrine of *ridda* to be the most egregious violation of religious liberty. Bates stressed that Iraq, Palestine, Lebanon, and Northern Sudan were the only Near East countries with an established and recognized procedure regarding conversions from Islam, changes which he attributed to influences external to Islam. Even in these cases of permitted conversions, converts were, in Bates' account, subject to disadvantages in issues concerning inheritance and employment, among others. Beyond Islamic legal constraints on conversion, Bates found certain context-specific restrictions on missions as springing from the fierce intolerance of natives (British Somaliland), the machinations of colonizers (Mussolini's Tripoli), constitutional text and politics (Egypt), as well as nationalism and authoritarianism (Turkey),

---

[59] Miner Searle Bates, *Religious Liberty: An Inquiry 1945* (New York: Harper Bros., 1945).
[60] Bates argued that communism was in some ways akin to religion, though "without the name, providing for men, a conviction of destiny, a bond of emotion and action, prophets and saints of authority if not actual saviors, an ethic systematically inculcated, a message and program of salvation for the multitude." Bates, *Religious Liberty*, 3.
[61] Ibid., 9.

among others. Even the classical status of *ahl-al kitab* (People of the Book), which guaranteed communal protection for Christians and Jews in Muslim territories, did not escape Bates' critique.

Bates argued that this legal status merely permitted these religions "to continue in quiescent communities, on sufferance as long as they do not challenge the dominant Islamic society." The religious liberty agenda to be advanced by the ecumenical movement was targeted at addressing "the socio-religious-political pressures for uniformity in the Mohammedan societies."[62]

Religious Liberty adopted a remarkably generous tone in its assessment of the allied West. Beyond its identification of paganistic secularism and the consequent subjugation of religious liberty with the East, the report was careful to not implicate Western colonial powers in its critique of Islamic orthodoxy. In analyzing the case of Northern Nigeria, for instance, the report centered its critique solely on Islam. Minimally commenting on British indirect rule's propensity to co-opt precolonial religious institutions in the territory, *Religious Liberty* praised Britain's tradition of tolerance as a potentially positive influence on orthodox Islamic practices in Northern Nigeria. In Egypt, the report blamed Islamic orthodoxy's co-option of constitutional text and politics, and in Turkey, the culprit was the meeting of the faith with nationalism and authoritarianism.[63] Indeed, condemnation of colonial powers' culpability in the restrictions on religious liberty was limited to Roman Catholic European powers, particularly in Mussolini's Africa.[64] The report was therefore emphatic in its location of the problem of religious liberty elsewhere – in Muslim territories and the East. The former raised no eyebrows in the ecumenical movement, but the latter ran contrary to ecumenical attention to the ravages of secularism everywhere, at least since Jerusalem 1928. This attitude among key JCRL elites (as well as certain British ecumenists) to regard religious liberty as an Eastern, and not a Western problem, would come to be a source of intra-ecumenical disagreement.[65]

---

[62] Ibid., 305.
[63] However, the report found laicist Ataturk Turkey was "tending towards" religious liberty in a remarkable progress from the prerevolution period. Bates, *Religious Liberty*, 14.
[64] For the argument that anti-Catholic attitudes of US Protestants influenced JCRL thought and advocacy, see John Nurser, *For All Peoples and All Nations: The Ecumenical Church and Human Rights* (Washington, DC: Georgetown University Press, 2005), 82–83.
[65] Of these British ecumenists was Anglican layman and editor of the WCC's periodical, *The Ecumenical Review*, Martin Wight. Wright argued that it was in the West's

For now, it is important to acknowledge the points of contact between *Religious Liberty* and general ecumenical thought. Like the Oxford report and the thought espoused at Edinburgh 1910, *Religious Liberty* was not averse to the establishment of Christianity and did not regard it as a threat to religious freedom. Indeed, *Religious Liberty* was effusive in its praise for the British tradition of establishment of the Church of England, arguing that it featured a "high degree of religious liberty" and a "tradition of social tolerance."[66] Although the report acknowledged that the British constitutional arrangement tied key political appointments to members of the Church of England and granted Parliament authority over forms of worship,[67] it regarded these features as insignificant.[68]

Religious Liberty's sanction of the intermingling of church and state was also apparent in its analysis of US constitutional practice. Besides England, the US was the other beacon of religious liberty highlighted in Bates' report. Importantly, the report did not consider US religious liberty to be the necessary product of church-state separation. As Bates pointed out, the First Amendment to the US Constitution was not intended to prescribe church-state separation but was rather designed to prevent the federal government's interference with the church-state entanglements that existed during the making of the First Amendment. US national policy on religion, according to Bates, was "separation of state from church, but not from Christianity."[69] Citing Christian prayers at government events, Sunday's work-free status, holidays with Christian roots, and blasphemy laws based on Christian ideas, Bates pointed out that these features of the US state-religion arrangement amounted to "informal support of Christianity"[70] and protected the

---

struggle against the Soviet Union "that the demonic concentrations of power of the modern neo-pagan world have their clearest expression." Martin Wight, "The Church, Russia, and the West," *The Ecumenical Review* 1, no. 1 (1949): 30, in Jonathan T. Reynolds, *The Time of Politics (Zamanin Siyasa): Islam and the Politics of Legitimacy in Northern Nigeria, 1950–1966* (San Francisco: International Scholar Publications, 1998), 292.

[66] Bates, *Religious Liberty*, 111.
[67] For instance, the amendment to the Church's Book of Prayers in 1934 required the endorsement of the Parliament. Bates cites Cecilia M. Ady, *The Church of England and How It Works* (London: Faber and Faber, 1940).
[68] The report labeled such issues "minor." Bates, *Religious Liberty*, 86.
[69] Citing Isidore Goldstick, "Where Jews Can't Pray," *Contemporary Jewish Record* 6, no. 6 (1943): 587.
[70] Bates, *Religious Liberty*, 94.

"Christian standards of the majority."[71] Nevertheless, Bates stressed that these manifestations of the entanglement of the church with state did not amount to restrictions on religious liberty, pointing to the "popular American view that entire religious liberty had been secured" and the approval, "even … envy," of European scholars for US religious liberty.[72]

Although Bates conceded that church-state separation might sometimes correlate to a higher degree of religious liberty than church-state union, he insisted that the evidence was not conclusive. Church-state separation, Bates argued, may be a mere manifestation of secularization, rather than the "triumph of free religion" that is the true goal of religious liberty.[73] Secularization was, in Bates' formulation, the separation of religion from community life and not compatible with religious freedom. Rather, *Religious Liberty* advocated for "friendly separations," which it described as church-state arrangements permitting "little or much voluntary cooperation between Church and State as the citizens may desire and agree upon."[74]

These "friendly separations," which Bates found to be based on a fundamentally Christian idea,[75] charted the middle course between the extremes of "state-implemented religion" and "individualistic religion" and would permit the triumph of the free religion advocated by the report. Marking out the uniqueness of Protestant thought on religious liberty, Bates argued that the mainline-Protestant position was the most favorable to religious liberty, taking great care to compare it to the Islamic position (which he dismissed) and the Roman Catholic approach (which he argued was marked by the exaltation of the liberty of the church rather than that of the individual).[76] Hence, *Religious Liberty*'s approval for establishment was not absolute, as it condemned both the "Islamic Orthodox" and Spanish arrangements. Neither did *Religious Liberty* imagine that the secularization of state and society held the answer, since secularization was named as a key culprit in the infringement of religious liberty.

Ultimately, the report emulated Oxford 1937 by recommending the adoption of an "International Bill of Rights" or "International Charter of Liberties"[77] to tackle constraints on religious liberty. As with Oxford, prominent among the provisions in this bill were to be rights

---

[71] Ibid., 91. [72] Ibid., 90. [73] Ibid., 385. [74] Ibid., 432.
[75] Ibid., 2. [76] Ibid., 387. [77] Ibid., 569.

to worship, convert, preach, and teach. Nevertheless, the JCRL report indulgently chided the "unrealistic efforts" in ecumenical circles to center the advocacy for these rights on the movement's Christian personalist notions. Consequently, while the report advanced the proposals of ecumenical groups,[78] it, at the same time, put forth the proposal designed by the American Law Institute's (ALI) Committee of Advisors on Human Rights. The committee, which drew representatives from the United States, Britain, Canada, China, France, Germany, Italy, Latin-America, Poland, Soviet Russia, and Syria, had been commissioned by the Council on American Law Institute. Unlike the ecumenical proposals cited in *Religious Liberty* and forming the crux of its rights charter plan, the proposal of the ALI Committee did not provide for the right to convert or proselytize.[79] Although both the JCRL and the US FCC as well as their global ecumenical colleagues would continue to insist on these core rights, the inclusion of the ALI Committee proposal was reflective of the outlook of the American ecumenists. The American Protestant elites, particularly Dulles and Nolde, were in fact criticized by global ecumenical counterparts, including the Swiss jurist Max Huber, as attempting to "translate" the Protestant project of "personhood" into "a legal idiom with broad appeal to people of goodwill whether or not Christian."[80]

Like other JCRL elites, Nolde regarded *Religious Liberty* as a key achievement. Reviewing the report in *The Annals of the American Academy of Political Science*, Nolde stressed that its significance lay in its contribution to the "urgent" global imperative of securing human rights.[81] The JCRL spokesman then commended the report to those striving to actualize that goal. Three years later, Nolde would become the inaugural director of the CCIA. In that capacity, Nolde would not only have the opportunity to actualize the JCRL vision, but he would also come to be integral to the formulation of the international charter

---

[78] Ibid., 321–323, 570. These statements were issued by the Joint Committee on Religious Liberty (1944), British Commission of the Churches for International Friendship and Social Responsibility (1939), and an "informal group" of American Protestants and Roman Catholics.

[79] Ibid., 570. See also Committee Representing Principal Cultures of the World, "The Statement of Essential Human Rights," *The American Law Institute*, December 10, 2018, www.ali.org/news/articles/statement-essential-human-rights/.

[80] Reynolds, "Against the World," 414.

[81] O. Frederick Nolde, "Review: *Religious Liberty: An Inquiry*, by M. Searle Bates," *The Annals of the American Academy of Political and Social Science* 243, no. 1 (1946): 150.

that *Religious Liberty* proposed.[82] Acknowledging Nolde's work in the crafting of the Universal Declaration, Eleanor Roosevelt, chair of the UN Commission on Human Rights, pointed out that Nolde was the most active Non Governmental Organization (NGO) delegate to the negotiations and drafting proceedings of the instrument.[83] The ecumenical movement's participation was not limited to the NGO delegation. Charles Malik, prominent Lebanese member of the CCIA, was rapporteur of the UN Commission on Human Rights, and Dulles was actively involved in the San Francisco drafting and negotiation proceedings that produced Article 18.[84] Nevertheless, Nolde is credited with actualizing the ecumenical movement's goal. In Malik's words, Article 18, the Universal Declaration's provision on religious liberty, was "principally his [Nolde's] fashioning."[85] For the ecumenical brethren, Article 18 was the core of the rights provisions in the Universal Declaration since they had always held fast to the view that religious liberty was the foundation of all rights.[86] As Malik would admit:

---

[82] On the global Protestant ecumenical origins of Article 18 of the Universal Declaration and on the work of the CCIA and Nolde in particular, see Linde Lindkvist, *Shrines and Souls: The Reinvention of Religious Liberty and the Genesis of the Universal Declaration of Human Rights* (Lund, Sweden: Bokbox förlag, 2014); Pamela Slotte, "Whose Justice? What Political Theology? On Christian and Theological Approaches to Human Rights in the Twentieth and Twenty-first Centuries," in *International Law and Religion: Historical and Contemporary Perspectives*, eds. Martti Koskenniemi, Mónica García-Salmones Rovira, and Paolo Amorosa (Oxford: Oxford University Press, 2017), 210 (arguing that human rights work was "a Christian task"); Matti Peiponen, *Ecumenical Action in World Politics: The Creation of the Commission of the Churches on International Affairs 1945–1949* (Helsinki: Luther-Agricola-Society, 2012); and Moyn, *Christian Human Rights*. For an account of how CCIA came to be granted a formal consultative status within the United Nations Human Rights Council, see Peiponen, *Ecumenical Action in World Politics*, 232.

[83] See Eleanor Roosevelt, "Introduction," in *Freedom's Charter: The Universal Declaration of Human Rights*, ed. O. Frederick Nolde (New York: Foreign Policy Association, 1949), 3.

[84] For diverse perspectives on Malik's human rights work, see Lindkvist, *Shrines and Souls*; Johannes Morsink, *The Universal Declaration of Human Rights: Origins, Drafting, and Intent* (Philadelphia: University of Pennsylvania Press, 1999); Glenn Mitoma, "Charles H. Malik and Human Rights: Notes on a Biography," *Biography* 33, no. 1 (2010): 222–224; Glendon, *A World Made New*, 222–232; and Makau Mutua, *Human Rights: A Political and Cultural Critique* (Philadelphia: University of Pennsylvania Press, 2002), 154–155.

[85] Charles Habib Malik, "The Universal Declaration of Human Rights," in Nolde, *Free and Equal*.

[86] See Renaud, "Human Rights as Radical Anthropology."

though I cared for every word in the Declaration, I felt that if we should lose this Article on freedom of conscience and religion ... my interest in the remainder of the Declaration would considerably flag. ... Without the full and unimpaired right to think and believe freely, the value of these other rights pales into relative insignificance.[87]

In its final form, Article 18 would capture the thrust of ecumenical concerns: "Everyone has the right to freedom of thought, conscience and religion; this right includes freedom to change his religion or belief, and freedom, either alone or in community with others and in public or private, to manifest his religion or belief in teaching, practice, worship and observance."[88] Article 18's protection of conversion, and by implication, the right to proselytize, were crafted to address the challenges Islamic orthodoxy posed to missionary activity in places such as Northern Nigeria. By affirming the right of the proselytizer to evangelize and the right of the target to accept the message, Article 18 aimed to override the legal and administrative constraints on missionaries seeking to spread the gospel.

Nigeria was not represented at the Article 18 proceedings. Of the infamous trio identified at Edinburgh 1910 – Sudan, Northern Nigeria, and Egypt – only Egypt was present at the Article 18 deliberations since much of Muslim Africa, including Nigeria, had not attained independent statehood at the time. Together with Saudi Arabia, Egypt mounted a critique on Article 18's provisions on conversion and proselytization.[89] The states challenged Article 18 as the product of an empire-missionary alliance intended to further the European missionizing project and cited instances where missionary activity had stirred unrest and religious conflict, which had paved the way for imperial expansion.[90] Jamil Baroody,

---

[87] Malik, "The Universal Declaration of Human Rights," 11.
[88] Scholars like Malcom Evans point out that the broader postwar turn to human rights was due to the failure of the minority rights regime of the interwar period. See Evans, *Religious Liberty*; Mark M. Mazower, "The Strange Triumph of Human Rights, 1933–1950," *Historical Journal* 47, no. 2 (2004): 379. Nevertheless, there is no doubt that ecumenical experience, discourse, and advocacy was crucial to the crafting of Article 18 and for these influential ecumenists, religious liberty was the core of human rights. See Peiponen, "Ecumenical Action in World Politics," 226–228.
[89] Saudi Arabia voiced its objections during the debates in the Human Rights Commission while Egypt expressed its disapproval when the proposal was tabled before the United Nations General Assembly. See John Kelsay, "Saudi Arabia, Pakistan and the Universal Declaration of Human Rights," in *Human Rights and the Conflict of Cultures: Western and Islamic Perspectives on Religious Liberty*, eds. David Little, John Kelsay, and Abdulaziz A. Sachedina (Columbia: University of South Carolina Press, 1988).
[90] Linde Lindkvist, "The Politics of Article 18." See also Lindkvist, *Shrines and Souls*, 120.

Saudi Arabia's representative, pointed out that "throughout history, missionaries had often abused their rights by becoming the forerunners of political intervention, and there were many instances where peoples had been drawn into murderous conflict by the missionaries' efforts to convert them."[91] Yet, Muslim opinion was by no means unanimous. Unlike Saudi Arabia and Egypt, Pakistan supported the freedom of conversion provision, arguing that freedom of religion is intrinsic to Islamic law. *Ridda*, Pakistan argued, was a "spiritual offence" and therefore not the subject of worldly penalties. In the words of Zafrullah Khan, the Pakistani delegate, "however condemnable [apostasy] is a spiritual offense and entails no temporal penalty. This is the essence of the freedom to change one's religion. The Quran is explicit on it."[92] On the other hand, opposition to the freedom of conversion and proselytization was not limited to Muslim majority countries. Sweden and Greece, both states with an intimate relationship with a specific religious denomination, raised significant opposition to the provisions. In what was framed as an effort to "protect individuals who have religious beliefs different from the officially recognized religion, or who have no religious belief whatever, against manifestations of religious fanaticism," the Swedish delegate proposed a proviso to Article 18: "that this does not interfere unduly with the personal liberty of anybody else."[93] Sympathizing with the Swedish proposal, the Greece representative was concerned with whether the freedom to manifest religion "'might not lead to unfair practices of proselytizing' and felt that 'while, admittedly, every person should be free to accept or reject the religious propaganda to which he was subjected, ... an end should be put to such unfair competition in the sphere of religion.'"[94] The (failed) opposition of these states was, therefore, concerned with the public order effects of proselytization and was markedly different from the imperial criticism that undergirded the Saudi-Egypt critique.

---

[91] 3rd Session, Third Committee, 127th and 128th Meetings, 1949 (A/C.3/SR.127-128) 391–392, 396, in Evans, *Religious Liberty*, 187. Zafrullah Khan, *Islam and Human Rights* (Islamabad: Islam International Publications Ltd., 1967).

[92] Khan, *Islam and Human Rights*, 117; Malik, "The Universal Declaration of Human Rights," 10, 45.

[93] 3rd Session, Part I, Third Committee, 127th and 128th Meetings, 1949 (A/C.3/SR.127-128) in Evans, *Religious Liberty*, 186.

[94] Evans, *Religious Liberty*, 137.

Article 18 survived these challenges and made it into the Universal Declaration. The critique from some ecumenical quarters that the JCRL-led international human rights project had blunted some of the Christian personalist elements for the sake of broad appeal remained. Yet, the adoption of Article 18 was widely acclaimed as a triumph. The success of the religious liberty campaign was, without doubt, a high point of twentieth-century ecumenism. In two years, Article 18 would find its way into the European Convention on Human Rights.[95] The CCIA would then embark on a successful campaign to domesticate the international legal provision into national constitutions, devoting particular attention to Nigeria, the territory that had long attained infamy in ecumenical circles.[96]

DOMESTICATING ARTICLE 18 IN NIGERIA

After the adoption at the United Nations of Article 18, the CCIA, the British Council of Churches on International Development, and the Christian Council of Nigeria (CCN, the Nigerian ecumenical body) began to invoke that provision for unrestricted access to Northern Nigeria. And once plans got underway to convene a conference to deliberate over the terms of Nigeria's Independence, these ecumenical partners began to advocate for the domestication of Article 18 in the impending Independence Constitution. When the CCN officially presented the Article 18 proposal in April 1955, the Colonial Office rejected the plan, citing the opposition of the Masu Sarauta and that of the colonial secretary, Sir Oliver Lyttleton. The ecumenists were hardly surprised by the Colonial Office's reference to Masu Sarauta opposition; after all, that group had spent the colonial years opposing missionary efforts to proselytize. To introduce a notion of religious liberty that positively supported the missionary enterprise would undercut the position the Masu Sarauta had espoused since the dawn of colonial rule. With regards to the secretary of state, Sir Oliver Lyttleton, his opposition stemmed from his general aversion to bills of rights. In fact, Lyttleton had made clear his distaste for bills of rights when he vehemently opposed a proposal to constitutionalize a comprehensive bill of fundamental rights at the 1953 Constitutional Conference.[97]

---

[95] Article 9, European Convention of Human Rights, 1953.
[96] The earliest successes recorded were in India, Pakistan, Indonesia, and Sudan.
[97] There is some indication from the list of the rights and the language of the provisions that the proposal was influenced by the Universal Declaration of Human

Among other rights, that bill of rights proposal encompassed a range of rights including the right to religious liberty, although the latter provision was crafted broadly rather than in the missionary-specific language of Article 18. That comprehensive rights proposal was, in fact, sponsored by a broad coalition of nationalists, namely two Southern Nigerian parties in a pact with Northern Nigerian non-Muslims – the National Council of Nigeria and the Cameroons (NCNC) and the Action Group (AG) – and the party representing the Muslim opposition to the Masu Sarauta, the Northern Elements Progressive Union (NEPU). In spite of that broad-based support, Lyttleton opposed the rights proposal for two reasons. The first was the colonial administrator's conviction that rights guarantees are "meaningless" since rights only exist to the extent that they do not infringe on the rights of others.[98] The second was Lyttleton's commitment to adhering to the "tradition" of the British Commonwealth, which rarely featured a bill of fundamental rights in written constitutions. He pointed out that the existence of a bill of rights in India's Constitution was an exception that proved the superiority of the general rule. The Indian experience, Lyttleton argued, made clear that the insertion of fundamental human rights in a constitution was an insufficient guarantee of its protection.[99] By invoking Lyttleton's formalist opposition to the bill as well as the potential objection of emirs, the colonial government claimed that its opposition to the Article 18 project did not stem from an ideological opposition to religious freedom. Rather, the colonial government insisted that its hands were tied by Lyttleton's objection and more significantly, by the Masu Sarauta.

The shift in colonial rhetoric – from its earlier jousting of a Muslim-centered notion of religious freedom against the freedom of missionaries, to invoking administrative and bureaucratic constraints – was not merely strategic. As noted in earlier chapters, Governor Donald Cameron's tenure had heralded a gradual turn from the Lugardian attitude to the mission question. Just as with the Islamic law question discussed in an earlier chapter,[100] the late colonial years saw the rise of anti-Lugardian views in the central colonial administration, and several senior colonial administrators, both in Lagos and London, became

---

Rights. See Records of the Proceedings of the 1953 Constitutional Conference. CO879/159. Adam Mathews Digital Collection (hereafter A. M. Collection), 100.
[98] Ibid.   [99] Ibid.   [100] See Chapter 4.

more inclined to loosening restrictions on missions. However, since the colonial government not only continued to rely on the Masu Sarauta, but much of the lower cadre of the colonial bureaucracy also continued to be staffed with officials who adulated these aristocrats, an abrupt reversal of the long-standing colonial policy was inexpedient.

Missionary ecumenists, therefore, took the hint when the Colonial Office cited Lyttleton and the Masu Sarauta as the reason for its opposition. The CCN began to argue that Article 18 protections were intended to safeguard the liberties of minorities not from intrusions by the colonial government, but from the whims of the Masu Sarauta after Independence. Writing to the deputy chief secretary of colonial administration on September 13, 1955, the secretary of the CCN asserted: "we are thinking of the future. Such a clause [on religious freedom] if put into the constitution at a fairly early stage in the progress towards complete self-government would be more likely to stay in future constitutions." The CCN secretary also cited the examples of states who had domesticated Article 18 – India, Pakistan, Indonesia, and Sudan – pointing out that Christian minorities in those countries "have found the safeguard of value."[101] Sounding sympathetic to the proposal, the chief secretary of Northern Nigeria assured the CCN that he had relayed the proposal to the Colonial Office but pointed out that it was preferable for "natives" to champion the proposal and that the matter "is not one in which the interests which you properly seek to serve would be served by action of the Government of the Federation." On its part, the Colonial Office suggested a religious freedom provision similar to that of Ceylon.[102] However, CCIA chair Sir Kenneth Grubb demurred and suggested that even if the Ceylon provision was adopted, Article 18 ought to be incorporated into it. To achieve this, Grubb proposed adding the following to the Ceylon provision: "to ensure sufficient guarantee for religious and educational freedom in Nigeria"; and "however, Parliament shall not make any law or enactment which would prohibit and/or restrict the free enjoyment of the rights embodied in the Declaration of Human Rights of the United Nations."[103] Grubb's opposition to the Ceylon

---

[101] Secretary of the CCN to the Deputy Chief Secretary of the Federation, September 13, 1955. BCC/DIA/7/3/4/3. CERC.
[102] Section 29, Ceylon Constitution Order in Council, 1946.
[103] British Council of Churches International Department, "Nigeria: Human Rights, July 1956." BCC/DIA/7/3/4/3. CERC. For more on Grubb's role in the ecumenical movement and his work of Article 18, see Kenneth George Grubb, *Crypts of Power: An Autobiography* (London: Hodder and Stoughton, 1971).

proposal stemmed from the fact that the Ceylon provision protected neither the right to convert nor the right to proselytize. Consequently, the CCN and the CCIA opposed that proposal for a substitution and insisted, instead, on an Article 18-type provision.

For the ecumenical partners, the watershed moment came on July 16, 1956, when an ecumenical delegation called on Lord Perth, minister of state for colonial affairs, to advocate for the inclusion of religious freedom in the constitution.[104] The ecumenical delegation comprised of Sir Kenneth Grubb and other prominent members of the ecumenical movement including William Godfrey, bishop of Liverpool; Canon Forster, the secretary of the Nigerian Council of Churches; and other representatives of the International Department of the British Council of Churches. At the meeting, which the participants resolved to keep secret,[105] the ecumenical representatives made the case for the insertion of Article 18 of the Universal Declaration in the impending Nigerian Constitution, stressing that this was necessary to protect religious minorities. Specifically, the delegates identified Christians and Indigenous religious groups as those minorities in need of protection from Muslim hegemony. This, of course, excluded any reference to Muslim minorities who had suffered pervasive restrictions in the colony.[106] The religious freedom mandate of the delegates, therefore, centered on Protestants and a group they regarded as potential Protestants.

Lord Perth was convinced by the submissions of the delegation both regarding the situation of minorities and the necessity for Article 18. Yet, the Colonial Office's embrace of the ecumenical position might not have been so encompassing without the active support the ecumenical alliance enjoyed among the ranks of the colonial administration. In Nigeria, CCIA's Sir Kenneth Grubb had cultivated the friendship of the colonial Governor James Wilson Robertson and

---

[104] Colonial Office, "Nigeria Constitutional Conference 1957: Provisions for Safeguarding Religious Freedom and Declaration of Fundamental Human Rights, No. 14, Briefs for the Secretary of State," April 1, 1957. CO 879/164. A. M. Collection.

[105] The exception, they agreed, would be if the secretary of state specifically decided that it was "useful" to disclose it to the public.

[106] The delegates also made reference to southeastern Nigeria, arguing that the minorities in need of protection in that region were Protestants who were being subordinated by Roman Catholics. Ecumenical concern with Roman Catholic domination in colonial territories was not limited to Nigeria; the situation in Malta was also of immense concern to the movement.

usually resided at the latter's residence during his visits to Nigeria. Further, Grubb was a childhood friend of Tom Williamson Esq., head of the Nigerian Group within the West Africa Department, a friendship that would prove crucial in paving the way to the Colonial Office's embrace of the ecumenical proposal to domesticate Article 18.[107] Williamson's approval of the ecumenical proposal was not supported by unequivocal legal advice; indeed, when Williamson called for legal advice on the issue from the lawyers in the legal department, he received conflicting advisories. While one legal officer, D. C. Gordon Smith, argued in favor of the desirability of entrenching a protection for religious freedom in the constitution, the other, James McPetrie, argued against it. Williamson would ignore McPetrie's position to uphold D. C. Gordon Smith's counsel. Williamson's support for the ecumenical proposal predated Lord Perth's official declaration of support for the proposal; even prior to the ecumenical delegation's visit to the Colonial Office, Williamson had begun to advocate for the constitutionalization of the ecumenical vision of religious liberty. Given the support that the ecumenical alliance already enjoyed among senior colonial administrators in Nigeria and in the West Africa Group of the Colonial Office, the official endorsement of the secretary of state for the colonies during the July 1956 visit was all that was required to seal Colonial Office support for – and adoption of – the ecumenical alliance's religious freedom project.

Because it realized the opposition that was bound to emanate from the Masu Sarauta, the Colonial Office began to strategize on how to convince Northern Nigeria Muslim elites at the impending constitutional conference. In a brief prepared for the secretary of state for the 1957 Constitutional Conference, officials of the Nigeria Working Group set up by the West African Department to work on the religious freedom constitutional project[108] argued that the proposal for religious freedom was not completely new as it had an antecedent in Lugard's

---

[107] Kenneth Grubb, "Extracts from Report on Religious Liberty in Nigeria," December 13, 1957. CO 554/1534. National Archives United Kingdom (hereafter NA. UK). See further Charles Parkinson, *Bills of Rights and Decolonization: The Emergence of Domestic Human Rights Instruments in Britain's Overseas Territories* (Oxford: Oxford University Press, 2007), 142–145.

[108] Members of the group were Chris Eastwood (head), Aaron Emanuel, Ian Watt, E. C. Burr, and Maurice Smith. These were all non-lawyers. The Colonial Office had decided to have these area experts draft the provisions which would be subsequently vetted by lawyers in the legal department.

1903 guarantee to the emirs of Northern Nigeria that "All men are free to worship God as they pleased."[109] The argument, of course, contradicted earlier colonial interpretation of the 1903 guarantee of freedom of worship and of noninterference in Islam – that it required restrictions on missionary activity in deference to the religious liberty of Muslims.[110] Neglecting this history, the brief argued that inserting the freedom into the constitution would merely constitutionalize a preexisting protection rather than create a new one. By framing religious liberty as a preexisting liberty, the brief presented the move to constitutionalize Article 18 as a formality rather than a novel move inspired (or worse, pressured) by the ecumenical alliance.

Conviction in the necessity of constitutionalizing Article 18 was not enough. The Nigeria Working Group knew that successfully selling the idea to the 1957 Constitutional Conference depended on avoiding appearing to favor missions. Just as this required asserting that religious freedoms had existed from the commencement of formal empire, it also necessitated introducing religious freedom as just one of several rights to be proposed at the constitutional conference. The rights package that would come to be presented at the constitutional conference therefore emerged from the advocacy for the right to religious freedom. This strategic attitude of the Colonial Office lawyers was markedly different from the attitude of international ecumenists toward fundamental rights other than religious freedom. As noted earlier, that group conceived of religious freedom as the foundation from which all other rights emerged. Yet, in advocating for the domestication of Article 18 in Nigeria, ecumenists devoted their energies to religious freedom with no mention of other fundamental rights. It was the Nigeria Working Group that devised the strategy of presenting the religious freedom provision as part of a broader rights package to avoid appearing to collude with the ecumenists. It was in this way that advocacy for the inclusion of religious freedom led to the eventual constitutionalization of a corpus of fundamental rights. So intent were officials on publicly distancing themselves from the ecumenical project that they advised the UK delegation to the 1957 Conference to initiate the discussions on rights only in the unlikely event that no Nigerian representative tabled such a proposal.

---

[109] See Colonial Reports-Annual, No. 409, Northern Nigeria, 1902 (HM Stationery Office, 1903), 16.

[110] See Chapter 1.

The 1957 Constitutional Convention

As the Colonial Office predicted, the rights proposal was resubmitted by its 1953 proponents when the constitutional convention was convened on May 23, 1957. Titled "fundamental rights," the proposal not only prohibited the "establishment" of religion and the imposition of "religious observance," it also called for the protection of "free exercise."[111] Although this vaguely worded free exercise proposal was poles apart from the Protestant-flavored Article 18, Lord Perth seized the opportunity to pursue the ecumenical agenda. Over the objections of the emir-allied Northern People's Congress (NPC) that constitutionalizing a religious freedom guarantee would threaten public order and renege on Lugard's 1903 guarantee to the Masu Sarauta, Perth convinced the conference to agree that fundamental rights, including religious freedom, be included in the constitution. He further persuaded delegates to resolve that the rights provisions be drafted by the legal advisers to the secretary of state and debated at the 1958 Constitutional Conference proceedings.

Drafting the provision went hand in hand with negotiating the NPC, which was its key opponent. Opposition to the ecumenical-inspired rights provision was not, however, limited to the Masu Sarauta or their political party, the NPC. The Northern Elements Progressive Union (NEPU) was also unequivocal in its opposition to the Article 18 proposal. In an article titled "Religious Freedom Move Can Be Disastrous," Dambatta Magaji, founding member of NEPU and prominent critic of the Masu Sarauta, warned of the dangers of a religious freedom provision driven by European missionaries: "I am not opposed to religious freedom as such. Indeed, I like it ... I am trying to draw attention to ... the fear that by writing a clause about religious freedom in our constitution we are causing the elimination of that freedom, inviting unrest."[112] Indeed, Magaji and several other NEPU elites' trepidation about the domestication of Article 18 did not hinge on the constitutionalization of rights since NEPU had itself sponsored rights proposals.

---

[111] See Obafemi Awolowo, "Fundamental Rights: Revised Memorandum by the Action Group," Proceedings of the Nigerian Constitutional Conference, May–June 1957, vol. II Conference Memoranda. CO879/167 A. M. Collection, 554. The bill also prohibited religious tests for office with the exception of the judge of Muslim courts (see section 1.2).

[112] Dambatta Magaji, "Religious Freedom Move Can Be Disastrous," *Nigeria Citizen*, June 20, 1956, 6.

The challenge, as these elites saw it, was with constitutionalizing what they regarded as an imperialist notion of religious liberty.

Regardless of NEPU's concerns, it was the NPC who, as the defender of the status quo, mounted the most sustained opposition to Article 18, and it was to this group of elites that the Colonial Office directed its negotiation efforts. In an attempt to placate the missionary alliance and forestall constitutional negotiations, the regional government, which was controlled by the NPC and sympathetic colonial administrators, issued a proclamation declaring its neutrality to religion and endorsing religious liberty "subject only to the requirements of law and public order."[113] Indeed, Ahmadu Bello, premier of the Northern Region, had issued a Christmas Day message in 1957 in which he addressed the question of religious difference, urging people of the Northern Region to "forget their differences and keep in mind only the brotherhood of man before God."[114] Addressing Muslims and Christians directly, Bello stressed that "our diversities may be great, but the things that unite us are stronger than the things that distinguish us." Bello's message and the government's proclamation were far short of the reassurances sought by the ecumenical alliance. It therefore failed to satisfy these advocates or

---

[113] Subject only to the requirements of law and public order, the Regional Government has no intention of favouring or advancing any religion at the expense of another. All persons in the Region are, as they have always been, absolutely at liberty to practice their beliefs according to their conscience without fear or favour, let or hindrance, within the limitations outlined above. If however, religious observances of any denomination or sect are conducted in such a manner that they cause or appear likely to cause, apprehension or concern to the majority of the people living in a particular area, or if a breach of the peace or outbreak of violence seems likely to result from them, then, the Regional Government will unhesitatingly take action to restore order and in doing so, may find itself compelled to prohibit or curtail the freedom of individuals in that area to conduct themselves in the manner that they desire.

With regards to proselytization and missionary activity amongst all shades of denomination in the religious groups, which make up the Region, the Regional Government has demonstrated time and time again ... that it welcomes vigorous and extensive enterprise in the educational and social fields. Subject only to the considerations referred to previously, the Regional Government does not intend to place any curb on the religious activities of missionaries or on their right to receive converts from amongst other religions.

See "Religious Tolerance," Press Release from Northern Region Information Service: Kaduna, November 6, 1957. No. 2693. CO 554/1534. NA, UK.

[114] Ibid.

their champions at the Colonial Office. In an effort to convince the Masu Sarauta, lawyers of the Colonial Office referenced religious freedom provisions in the constitutions of many former British colonies, especially those of Muslim majority states like Pakistan and Sudan.[115] At the same time, they insisted that Article 18 of the Universal Declaration (as transplanted into Article 9 of the EU Convention) was the yardstick to be adopted. In particular, lawyers of the Colonial Office, like the ecumenical advocates, were keen that the right to change religion uniquely provided for in Article 18 be contained in the Nigerian religious freedom provision, although this was not included in the constitutions of other former colonies cited by the Colonial Office.[116] These lawyers were not naive about the strength of Masu Sarauta feelings on the conversion and proselytization proposals. Indeed, in a June 23, 1957 internal memo to the secretary of state, these lawyers worried that the Masu Sarauta would "explode" at the inclusion of the proposal for conversion and proselytization.[117] As predicted, the proposal ignited strong feelings among the Masu Sarauta. NPC representatives argued that the constitutionalization of a religious freedom would violate Lugard's 1903 guarantee and in fact threaten public order.[118] Much of Masu Sarauta energies were targeted at opposing the conversion and proselytization elements of the proposal; in fact, once NPC leaders realized that senior colonial administrators were unwilling to withdraw the proposal, they counter-proposed a religious freedom provision devoid of protections for conversion and proselytization. In particular, Prime Minister Tafawa Balewa of the NPC proposed a Sudan-type provision as an alternative to Article 18. This proposal was, however, not acceptable to the Colonial Office and ecumenical advocates precisely because the Sudan provision did not include the freedom to proselytize and to change religion. NPC resistance was therefore futile; dismissing

---

[115] Ghana, Sudan, India, Pakistan, Sri Lanka, Malta, and the Carribbean Federation. In particular, the Colonial Office made much of the inclusion of religious freedom provisions in the constitutions of Pakistan and Sudan in order to convince the Northern Nigeria delegates.

[116] None of the other constitutions cited by the Colonial Office contained this right to change religion.

[117] June 23, 1957, Memorandum to the Secretary of State. CO 554/1535. NA, UK.

[118] For an article typifying the understanding (both of the Masu Sarauta and the general public) that the religious liberty provision defeated Lugard's 1903 guarantee of non-interference in Islam, see "Fundamental Rights May Be Started in 1959," *Nigerian Tribune*, August 11, 1958, 4.

the opposition, the Nigerian Working Group of the Colonial Office proceeded to draft the bill of rights, modeling its religious freedom provision on Article 18.

Non-ecumenical proposals did not make it into the draft, although the Working Group insisted that it carefully considered the recommendation. Responding to the proposal by Indigenous religious minority groups for the inclusion of a clause prohibiting the state's establishment of religion, for instance, the Working Group insisted that it was "unnecessary."[119] The Working Group concluded that the non-establishment of religion was not crucial to the guarantee of religious freedom – the goal of the constitutional proposal. The establishment provision would, therefore, not make it into the final draft.[120] Instead, the wordings of the draft bill's religious freedom protections were drawn solely from the text of Article 18 and the input of the ecumenical alliance. Upon completing the draft, the Working Group circulated that document to legal advisers in the Colonial Office and senior colonial administrators.[121]

The Resumed Convention
When the convention resumed in 1958, the religious freedom issue was the first item on the agenda. The draft presented by the Colonial Office's legal team to the conference encapsulated the dream of the ecumenical advocates.[122] Indeed, the draft produced by the Colonial Office was more comprehensive than Article 18. Unlike the latter's indirect guarantee of the right to proselytize, this draft proposal expressly included the right to do so.[123] It was clear to Muslim elites

---

[119] See the proposal above.

[120] Brief No. 4, "Fundamental Rights, Briefs for the Secretary of State: Resumed Nigeria Constitutional Conference 1957." CO 554/1535, CO 554/2594, and CO 879/176.

[121] See August 27, 1958 letter to Eastwood [addressor unclear]. "Provisions for Safeguarding Religious Freedom and Declaration of Fundamental Human Rights." CO 554/1535. NA, UK.

[122] Rather than cite the Universal Declaration as the source of the draft, the lawyers cited Article 9 of the European Convention of Human Rights as the basis for the proposed provision. Apart from a limitation provision, Article 9 of the EU Convention is identical to Article 18 of the Universal Declaration. Besides the EU Convention, the legal draftsmen identified another source of the draft provision – the Constitution of Pakistan, a reference targeted at convincing the NPC delegation.

[123] Note that the initial memorandum submitted on behalf of the Action Group included the right to "disseminate religion." See F. R. A. Williams, Fundamental

and the few colonial administrators who remained allied with them that the Colonial Office was determined that the religious freedom provision become a reality. Yet, the NPC would not give up without one last fight. Its representatives conditioned their agreement to the proposal upon the insertion of a limitation clause. Beyond the limitations of "public order," "public safety," "public morality," "public health," and "the rights and freedoms of others" inspired by the European Convention, NPC proposed subjecting religious freedom to another limitation – "rights and freedom [of others] to observe and practise their religions without the unsolicited intervention of members of other religions."

The proposal of this additional limitation clause sought to respond to the draft bill's protection of the right to proselytize. If Muslim elites had come to resign themselves to the religious conversion provision, they were still hostile to the protection of religious propagation. To these elites, if Lugard's 1903 guarantee was to mean anything at all, it ought to at the minimum shield Muslims from missionary proselytization. The premier of Northern Nigeria, Ahmadu Bello, argued at the convention that the provision's right to propagate directly violated Lugard's undertaking to limit missionary proselytization to non-Muslim areas.[124] The NPC delegation also insisted on another amendment to the proposed draft. In place of the draft's clause subjecting religious freedom to "limitations necessary in a democratic society,"[125] the delegation proposed a lesser standard – a restriction of limitations to those "reasonably justifiable in a democratic society."[126] These proposals hardly constituted a menace to the Article 18 project and would be included in the final draft to mollify the defeated Masu Sarauta.

Rights Proposal by the Action Group Delegation, June 20, 1957, Proceedings of the Nigerian Constitutional Conference, May–June 1957, vol. II Conference Memoranda. CO879/167 A.M. Collection, 431 (section 1.c). For reasons that are not apparent, however, the Action Group withdrew that memo within three days and substituted it for a revised one that excluded the right to "disseminate" religion. See Obafemi Awolowo, "Fundamental Rights: Revised Memorandum." CO879/167, 554.

[124] Records of the 2nd Plenary Session, Proceedings of the Resumed Constitutional Conference, September 30, 1958, vol. I, CO879/173. A. M. Collection, 38.

[125] This had been borrowed from Article 9 of the EU Convention.

[126] "Rights Concerning Religion." Memorandum by the Northern People's Congress Delegation, Proceedings of the Resumed Nigeria Constitutional Conference, September-October 1958, vol. II. CO 879/174. A. M. Collection, 174.

The output of the negotiations was Section 23 of the 1960 Independence Constitution, a provision that not only entrenched all the guarantees of Article 18 but even offered more extensive protections for the missionary enterprise by explicitly protecting the right to proselytize. The provision declared:

23.---(1) Every person shall be entitled to freedom of thought, conscience and religion, including freedom to change his religion or belief and freedom, either alone or in community with others, and in public or in private to manifest and propagate his religion or belief in worship, teaching, practice and observance.
(2) No person attending any place of education shall be required to receive religious instruction or to take part in or attend any religious ceremony or observances if such instruction, ceremony or observances relate to a religion other than his own.
(3) No religious community or denomination shall be prevented from providing religious instruction for pupils of that community or denomination in any place of education maintained wholly by that community or denomination.
(4) Nothing in this section shall invalidate any law that is reasonably justifiable in a democratic society –
   (a) in the interest of defence, public safety, public order, public morality or public health; or
   (b) for the purpose of protecting the rights and freedom of other persons, including their rights and freedom to observe and practise their religions without the unsolicited intervention of members of other religions.

It was in this way that a Protestant notion of religious liberty found a foothold in Nigeria's Independence Constitution.

CONCLUSION

Ostensibly participatory, the constitutional making processes that domesticated Article 18 consolidated the late colonial state's power to determine what forms of religious beliefs and expression were worthy of protection. Religious freedom projects such as Article 18 are inextricable from the regulation of religion that is so intrinsic to secular governance. As Saba Mahmood points out, the legal idea of religious freedom secures the modern state's "prerogative ... to serve as the arbiter of religious differences, to remake and regulate religious life while proclaiming its sanctity."[127] While such projects promise to resolve religious tensions, they "[intensify] interreligious inequality and conflict" through "the valuation of certain aspects of religious lives over others."[128] The Article 18 project sought to protect Protestants rather than all marginalized religious groups who had been rendered particularly vulnerable by the relations of power set in motion by colonialism. Not only did the Article 18 vision of emancipation center on advancing the cause of the Protestant missionary enterprise, it in fact sought to overturn, rather than dismantle, religious hierarchies in the late colonial state. With missionaries glorious at victory and Muslim elites smarting from defeat and perceiving the outcome as the victory of "Christian human rights,"[129] Article 18's triumph not only escalated religious tensions in the late colonial years, it also foreshadowed postcolonial contestations.

Revisionist accounts of religious liberty illuminate the failings of that legal idea; nevertheless, these narrtives err in their historical assumption that religious liberty emerged in harmony with the idea of secularist separation that is so integral to their understanding of secularism.[130] As this chapter shows, postwar advocacy for religious freedom aimed to neutralize the secularist separation of the state from Christianity. As utilized in ecumenical discourse, secularism (used interchangeably by ecumenists with secularist separation) was the state's dissociation from Christianity and its alliance with false orthodoxies. These false orthodoxies varied with the result that secularism manifested as communism, Nazism, and the deification of self-desires in different parts of Euro-America. Moreover, secularism manifested as Islam in colonial Muslim Africa, especially in Northern Nigeria.

The essence of this chronicle of Article 18 is not merely to trouble the genealogical links between secularist separation and religious freedom in the period after the Second World War. In Nigeria, the clash of both ideas had been simmering since empire's turn to governance through Islamic institutions at the beginning of the twentieth century. As earlier chapters show, missionary advocacy in earlier

---

[127] Saba Mahmood, *Religious Difference in a Secular Age: A Minority Report* (Princeton, NJ: Princeton University Press, 2015), 15.
[128] Ibid.
[129] I borrow this phrase from Sam Moyn. See Moyn, *Christian Human Rights*.
[130] Mahmood and Danchin, "Immunity or Regulation?"; Danchin, "Islam in the Secular"; Scott, *The Politics of the Veil*.

colonial years had centered on calls for the state to separate itself from caliphate institutions rather than on the notion of state separation from all religions. Just as ecumenists expressed enthusiasm for church establishment in their transwar and postwar discourse, they were open to empire's return to its nineteenth-century alliance with missions in the colony. Neither was the Article 18 project intended for all religions. Like missionary calls for freedom of conscience in early colonial Nigeria, the religious freedom espoused by Article 18 sought to protect the liberty of missions to preach and the freedom of the target audience to convert. That this Protestant idea of religious freedom would be waged against a secularism perceived as hostile to Christianity in the postwar period was, therefore, hardly unexpected. This story of the triumph of Protestant religious freedom ultimately shows that neither religious freedom nor its ostensible rival, secularist separation, are fixed. Rather, both ideas take their shape in the course of specific contestations and are embedded in particular relations of power.[131]

In fact, the Independence deal would be revisited seventeen years later on the site of the first postindependence constitutional conference in 1977. Seeking to undo their defeat at Independence, the new Masu Sarauta would seek the establishment of a Federal Sharia Court of Appeal with exclusive jurisdiction over Muslims in personal law matters. Ironically, they would defend this demand by invoking the constitutional provision on religious freedom they had opposed at Independence. In a reversal, those who would oppose the demand for rights in the postindependence period would be the successors to the Christian missionaries – the Christian converts. Strikingly, their opposition to the Shariʻa proposal would be made in the language of secularism, understood as the separation of the state from religion. In an abrupt reversal from their position during the Independence negotiations, they would oppose the religious freedom claims of the Muslim elites and argue that religious freedom was at best secondary to the demands of secularism. That group articulated its opposition to the Muslim court proposal as a defense of secularism, the idea their global ecumenical forebears had opposed. Moreover, the Christian camp now understood secularism as mandating the separation of the state from all religions, a reversal of the "unchristian separation" they had attributed

---

[131] See Winnifred Fallers Sullivan et al., eds., "Introduction," in *Politics of Religious Freedom* (Chicago: University of Chicago Press, 2015).

to secularism in the colonial years. By this time, however, the camp advocating the Shariʿa court had not only come to embrace religious liberty, it had also come to adopt the colonial-era ecumenical discourse on secularism. In a move that was reminiscent of the earlier global ecumenical argument that secularism was hostile to Christianity, the Shariʿa court proponents argued that secularism was objectionable because it marginalized Islam. The next chapter will zoom in on this postindependence constitutional moment.

PART III

IMAGINING THE PAST

CHAPTER SIX

THE 1977 CONSTITUTIONAL CONFERENCE AND BEYOND

On October 6, 1977, Nigeria's first constitutional conference since the nation's Independence in 1960 was held, with 223 delegates gathering in Lagos for the meeting. The 1977 gathering offered the opportunity to renegotiate the framework of the state free of formal imperial dominion. Its mandate spanned formulating the structural allocation of power among the component units of the federation, fashioning the state's economic outlook between the competing global visions of capitalism and socialism in a cold war context, and designing the proper relations between religion, the state, and society. It was, however, an issue of religion, the "Shari'a question," that came to dominate the constitutional discussions, eclipsing all other issues. As one delegate to the 1977 Conference aptly put it, "Once the Sharia issue was disposed of, one could say the work of the Assembly was virtually over."[1] The 1977 debates centered on a proposal to establish a Federal Sharia Court of Appeal (FSCA) with jurisdiction over Muslims in personal status matters. The demand was hardly radical: it was, in fact, a proposal to revive a court that had been an integral element of the late colonial state's reform of Islamic law and, by extension, the broader constitution deal negotiated in the waning days of imperial rule.

As set out in Part II, that deal comprised of three elements. The first was the recognition of the Protestant-dominated non-Muslim bloc as "religious minorities" in constitutional discourse. That recognition did not itself culminate in the creation of the state sought by Protestants;

---

[1] *The New Nigerian*, April 1978.

nevertheless, the religious minorities identity became entrenched in constitutional discourse. Wielded by its Protestant champions, it exercised tremendous impact in the constitutional politics of Independence. A second element of the Independence deal was the constitutionalization of the right to religious liberty. That aspect of the constitutional settlement took the form of domesticating Article 18 of the Universal Declaration of Human Rights, the brainchild of global missionary ecumenists in the 1960 Independence Constitution. Complementing the recognition of religious minorities and the constitutionalization of their right to religious liberty was the third element of the deal and the one most implicated in the 1977 debates – the elimination of Islamic law from public law, especially in the domain of criminal law. The Islamic law component of the deal was therefore premised on an ahistorical distinction between criminal and civil branches of Islamic law, which was then followed by the replacement of the former with a Penal Code rooted in imperial law. Integral to that reform exercise was the establishment of Sharia courts to exercise jurisdiction over those aspects of Islamic law retained, namely personal status matters concerning Muslims as well as certain civil law matters. At the top of that hierarchy of Sharia courts had been the Northern Region Sharia Court of Appeal. The call for the revival of that court, which had become defunct when Northern Nigeria was broken down into component states, was the essence of the 1977 proposal. As a proposal to revive a court that was one of the key legacies of colonial rule, the proposal was hardly an anti-colonial move. Nevertheless, the Shari'a question, as the debate over the court would be known, came to play out as a struggle over the colonial legacy of state-religion contestations.

The debate over the Sharia Court of Appeal was framed in terms of opposition to the idea of secularist separation of the state from religion. Proponents of the court, who overwhelmingly identified as Muslim, framed the proposal as an effort to counter the "secularism" bequeathed by the colonial state.[2] "Secularism," they argued, was a constitutional idea of state-religion separation that had been introduced by the empire to exclude Islamic institutions and disempower Muslims. Moreover, they insisted that secularism was not neutral because it covertly privileged Christian civilization, consequently giving Christians the

---

[2] "Proceedings of the Nigeria Constituent Assembly: Official Report 1977," Volume I and II (Lagos: Federal Ministry of Information, 1977) (hereafter Proceedings of the Constituent Assembly).

upper hand in constitutional politics.³ Springing from this memory of secularism's intimate connection with colonial subordination, the postcolonial case for the court became a struggle against secularism.

The framing of the Shariʿa project as an anti-secular campaign was mirrored by the opponents of the court proposal. Visibly championed by a coalition of Christian groups, their opposition to the court proposal was framed as a defense of "secularism," which they understood to entail the state's separation from all religions.⁴ Like Muslim proponents of the court, the Christian opposition marshaled the memory of the colonial state in defense of its position. Insisting that the colonial experience had been one of disempowerment for them, they blamed it on the absence of "secularism" and the reification and protection of Islam in the past. The Christian coalition understood "secularism" to have been attained only in the Independence deal, and therefore considered it critical to defend that idea of ordering state-religion relations.

With the constitutional debate thus conducted in the shadow of the legacy of a colonial state that both camps claimed disempowered them in mutually exclusive ways, 1977 became an opportunity to transcend that colonial legacy. Consequently, the postcolonial contestation came to be framed in apocalyptic terms with the pro-Shariʿa camp proclaiming that "Sharia ... is everything"⁵ and the anti-Shariʿa camp asserting that the Shariʿa was an "instrument of oppression."⁶ Through the lens of postcolonial constitutional confrontations, particularly at the 1977 Constitutional Conference, this chapter reckons with the legacy of colonial contestations on state-religion relations.

The postcolonial debate saw parties to colonial-era struggles switch positions. While the Muslim camp's forebears had been allied to a colonial state that insisted on its secularity, the postcolonial Muslim project hinged on a critique of imperial secularism. That critique bore an uncanny similarity to the charge leveled against the colonial state by Christian missionary ecumenists – that the state was covertly allied with a competing religion. If Islam was the "secular" that colonial-era missionary ecumenists deplored, Christianity was the new "secular" that postcolonial Muslim critics abhorred. The heirs to the

---

[3] Ibraheem Sulaiman, "Conflict of Values in Nigeria: A Background to the Encounter between Islam and Western Civilization" (paper presented at the Conference on the National Question, Abuja, 1986), 4.
[4] Toro Kachia, Proceedings of the Constituent Assembly, 1765.
[5] Alhaji Ibrahim Dasuki, Proceedings of the Constituent Assembly, 74.
[6] Mr. Ogaba Ede, Proceedings of the Constituent Assembly, 355.

Northern Nigeria 1952 Census (%age)

Religion	Population	Percentage
Muslims	12,289,975	73
Christian	454,561	2.7
Pagan	4,091,046	24.3

Northern Nigeria 1963 Census (%age)

Religion	Population	Percentage
Muslims	21,342,866	71.7
Christian	2,880,112	9.7
Pagan	5,540,302	18.6

Nigeria 1952 Census

Region	Muslim	Christian	'Pagan'	Total
Northern Nigeria	12,289,975	454,561	4,091,046	16,835,582
South-Eastern Nigeria	24,032	3,610,781	1,922,155	7,215,251
South-Western Nigeria	2,083,491	2,346,826	3,580,438	6,352,472
Total	14,397,498	6,412,168	9,593,639	30,403,305
Percentage	47.4	21.1	31.6	

Nigeria 1963 Census

Region	Muslim	Christian	'Pagan'	Total
Northern Nigeria	21,342,866	2,880,112	5,540,302	29,763,276
South-Eastern Nigeria	29,964	9,573,622	2,790,878	12,394,463
South-Western Nigeria	4,565,388	6,388,700	1,847,599	12,801,687
Total	14,397,498	6,412,168	9,593,639	54,959,426
Percentage	47.2	34.3	18.5	

Figure 6.1 Religious affiliation as measured by 1952 and 1963 censuses

missionaries – the postcolonial Christian coalition – did not miss a beat in abandoning the critique of secularism invented by their forebears. The irony did not end there. Significantly, the weapon of choice deployed by the postcolonial Muslim coalition in contesting what they understood to be a Christian preferentialist secularism was religious liberty, a notion their predecessors had vehemently (and unsuccessfully) opposed at the Independence constitution negotiations. Just as with the discourse on secularism, the Christian coalition deserted the religious liberty preference of its missionary predecessors to now hold up secularism as the fundamental constitutional principle. As secularism's old detractors became its vanguards, the religious freedom project jumped ship (Figure 6.1).

STRUGGLES IN TRANSITION: BETWEEN INDEPENDENCE AND THE 1977 CONSTITUTION CONFERENCE

By the time the 1977 Constituent Assembly convened for the first constitution-making exercise since the end of formal imperial dominion in 1960, much had transpired on the national political scene. On the night of January 11, 1966, a group of young Nigerian army officers, overwhelmingly Christian and of Eastern Nigerian extraction, executed a coup d'état, assassinating prominent political elites.[7] An overwhelming majority of these elites were Northern and Muslim, and the most prominent was the premier of Northern Region and sardauna of Sokoto, Ahmadu Bello, who was shot together with his wife, Hafsah, in their Kaduna home.[8] The coup plotters, led by Major Chukwuma Kaduna Nzeogwu, justified their actions as a patriotic effort to rid the state of "corruption."[9] Crucially, these officers understood this corruption to manifest in, among other things, the efforts of Northern Nigerian elites, particularly Bello, to "islamize" Nigeria.[10] These allegations of an Islamization agenda were not limited to Nzeogwu and his comrades; fear of an "islamization" agenda was widespread among Northern Nigerian Christian minorities and the broader national Christian community.[11] These fears were especially

---

[7] Anthony H. M. Kirk-Greene, *Crisis and Conflict in Nigeria: A Documentary Sourcebook, 1966–1969*, vol. 1 (New York: Oxford University Press, 1971), 124.

[8] Ibid.; Abubakar Gumi, *Where I Stand* (Ibadan, Nigeria: Spectrum Books, 1992), 92.

[9] Chukwuma Kaduna Nzeogwu, "Radio Broadcast by Major Chukwuma Kaduna Nzeogwu – Announcing Nigeria's First Military Coup on Radio Nigeria, Kaduna on January 15, 1966," *Vanguard*, September 30, 2010, www.vanguardngr.com/2010/09/radio-broadcast-by-major-chukwuma-kaduna-nzeogwu---announcing-nigeria's-first-military-coup-on-radio-nigeria-kaduna-on-january-15-1966/.

[10] See Gumi, *Where I Stand*.

[11] See, for example, Matthew Hassan Kukah, *Religion, Politics and Power in Northern Nigeria* (Ibadan, Nigeria: Spectrum Books, 1993), 117; Iheanyi M. Enwerem, A

ignited by Muslims' proselytization efforts. Following Independence, Bello had begun to conduct widespread conversion tours across Northern Nigerian non-Muslim communities, especially to those *Maguzawa* areas that had resisted Christian proselytization.[12] Those conversion tours not only received intense media coverage, they also appeared to have been successful with accounts suggesting the conversion of entire villages. Further stoking fears were Bello's foreign visits to predominantly Muslim states in pursuit of his declared aim of healing rifts and uniting Muslims globally.[13] If Bello framed these efforts as a spiritual goal, Christians understood it as an agenda to "islamize" the state. Commenting on Bello's work, Reverend Matthew Hassan Kukah, prominent Christian Northern Nigerian critic, for instance, charged that Bello utilized "the apparatus of modern democracy" to do all he could to transform Northern Nigeria into a "modern caliphate."[14] Regardless of these attempts to rationalize the coup, the narrative that the bloody overthrow of government had been motivated by the patriotic desire to free the state from factionalism and usher in good governance failed to gain traction among Muslims, especially those of Northern Nigeria. Citing the bloodiness of the coup, the Northern Muslim identity of most of its targets, and the Christian identity of the coup plotters and coup-imposed leadership, the Muslim (Northern) narrative and memory of the experience would be of a Christian crusade against Islam. That Sardauna Bello was declared "a martyr who had been killed in the cause of the religion" by no less a jurist than the grand khadi of the Sharia Court of Appeal, Abubakar Gumi, and that the sardauna was consequently buried according to rites for martyrdom, only intensified widespread fears that Muslims were under an onslaught.[15] The abolition of alkalai courts across

---

Dangerous Awakening: The Politicization of Religion in Nigeria (Ibadan, Nigeria: IFRA-Nigeria, 1995); and Hypolite A. Adigwe, *Nigeria Joins the Organisation of Islamic Conference, OIC: The Implications for Nigeria* (Archdiocesan Secretariat: Catholic Archdiocese of Onitsha, 1986).

[12] See Kukah, *Religion, Politics and Power*; Enwerem, *A Dangerous Awakening*; and Ousmane Kane, *Muslim Modernity Postcolonial: Nigeria: A Study of the Society for the Removal of Innovation and Reinstatement of Tradition* (Leiden: Brill, 2003).

[13] Moses E. Ochonu, *Colonialism by Proxy: Hausa Imperial Agents and Middle Belt Consciousness in Nigeria* (Bloomington, IN: Indiana University Press, 2014), 194; Kane, *Muslim Modernity*, 83.

[14] Kukah, *Religion, Politics and Power*, x.

[15] Gumi, *Where I Stand*, 115–116.

Northern Nigeria by a military decree four days after the coup further served as evidence for this narrative of an anti-Muslim onslaught.[16] That narrative would withstand the revival of those alkalai courts within a few days of their abolition once the new military government realized that English-style magistrate courts could not cope with the caseload. It was, however, the abolition of the Gumi-headed Sharia Court of Appeal that would ultimately lead to a constitutional confrontation over Muslim demands to reinstate the court beginning at the 1977 Constitutional Conference. The abolition of the court was not the result of direct legislative action; it became defunct following the division of Northern Nigeria into six component states by a military decree.[17] Neither was the military decree promulgated by the government brought into power by the January 1966 coup that eliminated key Northern Muslim elites; the 1967 States (Creation and Transitional Provisions) Decree was promulgated by a military government ushered into power by a July 1966 coup that sought to neutralize the January 1966 revolt. The new military head of state was of Northern extraction, and to critics, his Christian faith hardly mattered in a context in which de facto and de jure Muslim elite control was understood by its critics to be furthered by a Muslim alliance with a handful of Christian elites. The brutal transfers of power in those early years of Independence let loose violence on the streets including, significantly, the widespread killing of Eastern Nigerians living in major Northern Nigerian cities. Eventually, Eastern Nigeria would announce its secession from the rest of the nation, ushering in a brutal three-year civil war.[18]

The story of the Nigerian Civil War is intricate, and its reverberations continue to resound, but for the purpose of this narrative, that event was significant for the role it played in shaping the postcolonial alignments in the struggles over religion and religious difference.

---

[16] Musa Ali Ajetunmobi, *Shariah Legal Practice in Nigeria 1956–1983* (Ilorin, Nigeria: Kwara State University Press, 2017), 50; Gumi, *Where I Stand*.

[17] North-Eastern State, North-Western State, Kano, Kaduna, Kwara, Benue-Plateau. These six states were further broken down into twelve in 1976: Abuja (FCT) was carved out of Niger State, North-Western State was divided into Sokoto and Niger, and North-Eastern State was divided into Borno, Gongola, and Bauchi. Benue-Plateau was separated into Benue and Plateau.

[18] Samuel Fury Childs Daly, *A History of the Republic of Biafra: Law, Crime, and the Nigerian Civil War* (Cambridge: Cambridge University Press, 2020).

The events leading to the civil war and its aftermath played a crucial role in nationalizing those struggles. From the colonial-era framing of the struggle as one between Masu Sarauta-allied Muslims and a non-Muslim position dominated by Christians, the tussle became nationalized as one between Muslims and Christians. To be sure, the nationalization of the Christian interest predated Independence; as I have shown earlier, negotiations leading up to Independence featured strategic alliances between Northern Nigerian Christian-led minority parties and Christian-dominated parties in Western and Eastern Nigeria. Even more importantly, earlier chapters reveal the formation of the Christian Council of Nigeria in 1923 as a national ecumenical body of Protestant missions to contest the state's restrictions on missionary activity in Northern Nigeria. Yet, these interregional connections hardly coalesced the Christian position into the national form it took in the postindependence years. Significantly, Eastern Nigerian missions, which were overwhelmingly Catholic, were largely missing from the ecumenical alliance of the colonial years. Even in its limited presence in Northern Nigeria, the Catholic Church abstained from ecumenical efforts to contest colonial restrictions. Far from being allied with national and global Protestant ecumenical efforts, the Catholic Church was a target of Protestant advocacy; ecumenists argued that the Catholic Church frustrated Protestant missionizing, including in Eastern Nigeria (and elsewhere such as Malta) and deployed Article 18 to counter what was understood as Catholic hegemony.[19] Much had, however, changed by the late 1960s. Internationally, the Catholic Church had embraced ecumenism in 1965 following the Second Vatican Council's abandonment of the Church's opposition to the Christian religious liberty project.[20] That shift in the Church's attitude on the international stage would find fertile ground in an Eastern Nigeria reeling from the power tussle with the Muslim-controlled North. The Eastern Nigerian Catholic Church would consequently ally with the Christian Council of Nigeria, which had indigenized following the departure of European missionaries, to form the Christian Association of Nigeria (CAN) in 1976.

[19] Bastiaan Bouwman, "From Religious Freedom to Social Justice: The Human Rights Engagement of the Ecumenical Movement from the 1940s to the 1970s," *Journal of Global History* 13, no. 2 (2018): 255.

[20] Udi Greenberg, "Catholics, Protestants and the Tortured Path to Religious Liberty," *Journal of the History of Ideas* 79, no. 3 (2018): 461–479.

CAN's establishment in 1976 was in preparation for the looming 1977 constitutional confrontation over the Sharia Court of Appeal.[21] Since that court's 1967 elimination under the circumstances described above, calls for its reinstatement had already begun. Those calls only got louder as the events leading up to and following the civil war intensified the competition – and animosity – between Christian and Muslim groups. CAN emerged as a response to the court proposal, which was widely regarded in Christian circles as a manifestation of the deceased Bello-inspired plan to "islamize Nigeria."[22] Moreover, that Islamization agenda was understood as an attack on the state's secularism. CAN consequently set as its objectives: "the continued assurance of Nigeria's secularity; the prevention of islamization and the gain of power and resources for the Christian constituency."[23] CAN's understanding of secularism, which it stood ready to defend from all attacks, was of the separation of religion from politics. Elucidating this idea, CAN president and Catholic archbishop, Olubunmi Okogie asserted: "your religion ... is a private affair between you and your God."[24] Yet, this call for separation was hardly unconditional. Reenacting Joseph Oldham's insistence at the 1937 Oxford Conference that Caesar's sphere is not free of God, prominent Christian clergy insisted that "all of life is an offering for God."[25] The postcolonial inheritance of the missionary project was unmistakable. Yet, the postcolonial Christian agenda was far from a straightforward continuation of the earlier missionary discourse. While colonial-era missionaries had based their critique of the state on a secularism that they understood as state-religion separation and sought to neutralize that separation with a Christian notion of religious liberty, their postindependence successors did the opposite. These advocates of the postcolonial church mounted a defense of secularism, understood as separation, and regarded religious liberty claims as, at best, secondary to the primacy of separation.

---

[21] See also Ebenezer Obadare, *Pentecostal Republic: Religion and the Struggle for State Power in Nigeria* (London: Zed Books, 2018).
[22] Hypolite A. Adigwe, *Nigeria Joins the Organisation of Islamic Conference, OIC: The Implications for Nigeria* (Archdiocesan Secretariat: Catholic Archdiocese of Onitsha, 1986).
[23] Toyin Falola, *Violence in Nigeria: The Crisis of Religious Politics and Secular Ideologies* (New York: University of Rochester Press, 2001), 110.
[24] Interview in *Monthly Life*, December 1987, 9.
[25] Matthew Hassan Kukah and Toyin Falola, *Religious Militancy and Self-Assertion: Islam and Politics in Nigeria* (Aldershot, UK: Avebury, 1996), 11.

PART III IMAGINING THE PAST

On the other side of the 1977 struggles and spearheading the proposal for the court was the Nigerian Supreme Council for Islamic Affairs (NSCIA). Formed in 1973, the NSCIA's mission was "to promote the Shari'a and to defeat secularism."[26] The organization did not only frame the Shari'a and secularism in oppositional terms, it regarded secularism as "an attack on Islam," a "disease of the mind," and leading the state to "untruth and misery."[27] The NSCIA was the nationalization of the Muslim position on state-religion relations. The organization emerged from the union of Northern and Southern Nigerian Muslim organizations – the Western State Joint Muslim Organization, representing Southern Nigerian Muslims, and the Jama'atu Nasril Islamiyyah (JNI) of Northern Nigeria. Both organizations featured intelligentsia promoting the Shari'a project and articulating the critique of secularism, but JNI elites undoubtedly played a leading role. As an organization, the JNI understood secularism as intrinsically opposed to religion, declaring that "secularism is a system of social teachings or organizations which allows no part for religion."[28] Although the JNI had originally been founded to facilitate the Ahmadu Bello-led conversion campaigns, its elites became key players in the anti-secularism, pro- Shari'a project.

No one was more prominent in immersing the JNI in the constitutional debates than Abubakar Gumi. Undoubtedly the most active jurist from the colonial era involved in the postcolonial constitutional debates and a founding member of the JNI, Gumi sometimes deviated from the JNI position, criticizing the organization's elites for their complicity in the colonial project and their deviation from Islamic orthodoxy. Indeed, Gumi had first come to the limelight in the colonial years when he criticized the sultan of Sokoto for his practice of paying homage to the English monarch in his sermons following Eid prayers. Alongside his membership in the JNI, Gumi would simultaneously become active in the reactionary Izala, the Jama'atu Izalatil Bid'ah Wa Iqamatus Sunnah (Society of Removal of Innovation and

---

[26] Stated missions of the organization include the "the observance of Islamic morality" and ensuring "that the ideals of Islam as laid down in the Glorious Qur'an and the Sunnah of the Holy Prophet Muhammad (P.B.O.H) are adhered to by all Muslims in Nigeria." "About," Nigerian Supreme Council for Islamic Affairs, accessed January 7, 2023, www.nscia.com.ng/about.

[27] Nigerian Supreme Council for Islamic Affairs, "What We Stand For," *New Nigerian*, January 23, 1987, 12.

[28] Jama'atu Nasril Islamiyyah, *New Nigerian*, June 1, 1987.

Reestablishment of the Sunnah), a group founded as a conscious critique of traditional political and legal authority. Given this inclination, it was therefore hardly unexpected that Gumi would abandon the traditional restraint that marked the JNI's interventions into political discourse by unreservedly launching a critique on secularism and the Christian opposition: "I have made several appeals before for a government founded on religion. Man is not a mindless animal whose only object in life is to eat, mate, sleep and die. Secularism, therefore, as the policy of operating government outside God's control, is alien to civilized human existence."[29] Calling instead for an intimate relationship with the state, Gumi declared, "siyasa ta fi muhimmanci da salla" (politics is more important than prayer).[30] This was not a denigration of acts of worship; rather, Gumi sought widespread participation of Muslims in politics to ultimately transform the state to one fundamentally based on religion. Politics, in Gumi's view, had priority solely because it would ultimately facilitate religion and the upholding of "sacred law."[31] In insisting that the secular model held out by CAN was "atheist," Gumi deployed the argument that had been advanced by global ecumenists in the making of Article 18, and its subsequent constitutionalization at Nigeria's Independence. Secularism was therefore, in Gumi's account, not the absence of religion: it was the alliance between a false faith and a constitutional structure that sought to displace true religion. Consequently, secularism could never truly be neutral; instead, it could be – and was being – deployed by its ally, Christianity, to exclude and disempower Muslims in the state.

For all the widespread attention Gumi's fiery rhetoric received, the jurist was hardly the most distinctive voice in the postcolonial Muslim coalition. In fact, the marked feature of that coalition was its inclusion of a new intellectual class. Typically educated in both Islamic and English law, several of these scholars were trained simultaneously in traditional madrasah and colonial educational institutions in Nigeria or the United Kingdom. The Institute of Administration, Zaria, which had been established in 1957 to train judges and judicial officers implementing the late colonial legal reforms, became a hub for these

---

[29] Gumi, *Where I Stand*, 127.

[30] Allan Christellow, "Three Islamic Voices in Contemporary Nigeria," in *Islam and the Political Economy of Meaning*, ed. William Roff (Oakland: University of California Press, 1987), 234–235.

[31] For a comparison between Gumi's views and those of the Islamic jurist, Al Mawardi, see Christellow, "Three Islamic Voices," 236.

intellectual drivers of the Muslim critique of secularism. "Secularism," argued Ibraheem Sulaiman, a prominent scholar and faculty at the Institute of Administration, "is hostile to Islam. It seeks to undermine Islamic values, supplant Islamic laws with those of its own and deface the sanctity of the Muslim society."[32] This critique of secularism was based on the memory Sulaiman and his comrades had of the colonial experience. Writes Sulaiman: "the organic integrated structure of Islam has been sacrificed, and Islam itself is subjected to continuous definition to allow secularism to gain a foothold in the domain of Islam, and to accommodate a philosophy and an order of life imposed on us by the Euro-Christian civilization."[33] As another academic, Musa Ali Ajetunmobi, argued in a widely influential book, "christian missionaries ... left no stone untouched to christianize Nigeria. They were aided by the British colonizers and the English law, which is Christian in orientation – a tool with which they actually christianized the Nigerian judiciary. Their sympathizers continued with hostility to Sharia legal practice in Nigeria till this day."[34] By remembering the colonial project as a secularizing and Christianizing venture carried out by a cohort of Christian missionaries and colonial officials, these postcolonial Muslim elites projected the CAN's dalliance with secularism to the colonial years.

Crucially, these Muslim critics of secularism understood the postcolonial experience of disempowerment, which was rooted in the Independence deal, as one that spanned the colonial years. Colonial rule, in this interpretation, therefore, had always disempowered Muslims by deploying secularism. Writing the introduction to an edited volume on Islamic law authored by postcolonial Muslim intellectual elites, Syed Khalid Rashid, head of the department of Islamic law at the University of Sokoto, asserted that "the present truncated form of Islamic law in Nigeria, and the overall attitude toward it is the product of colonial tyranny."[35] In the foreword to the same volume, the vice chancellor

---

[32] Sulaiman, "Conflict of Values in Nigeria," 4.

[33] Ibraheem Sulaiman, "Islam in Nigeria," *New Nigerian*, March 27, 1988. For more on Sulaiman's thought, see Kukah, *Religious Militancy*, 26–28. See also Christellow, "Three Islamic Voices," 236. See also Roman Loimeier, *Islamic Reform and Political Change in Northern Nigeria* (Evanston: Northwestern University Press, 2011), 67.

[34] Ajetunmobi, *Sharia Legal Practice*, 240.

[35] Syed Khalid Rashid, ed., *Islamic Law in Nigeria: Application and Teaching* (Lagos: Islamic Publications Bureau, 1988), 181.

of the same university, Professor Mahdi Adamu, argued that "one of the most far-reaching consequences of Nigeria's colonial experience was the imposition, by our British colonizers, of the English Common Law, which has now largely supplanted ... the Shari'ah ... The contempt and antagonism with which the English Common Law holds the Shari'a has meant that Islamic legal practice was, and still is, relegated to civil matters and other personal issues ... What an injustice!"[36] Even while it imagined itself to be targeting earlier global ecumenists and their postcolonial descendants, the postcolonial Muslim critique essentially regurgitated the earlier ecumenical critique of secularism. Secularism was not the separation of the state from religion that CAN insisted it was. Rather, in the hands of the colonial state and the powerful postcolonial Christian constituency, secularism was infused with Christian values – in service of the subordination of Muslims. Noted Muslim jurist and grand khadi of the Bauchi State, Abdulmalik Bappa Mahmud, for instance, argued that the colonial state deployed the idea of state-religion separation in service of its mission to exclude Islam from the public sphere. Mahmud further argued that this hostility toward Islam was the basis of the different attitudes of colonial administrators on state-religion relations in different parts of Nigeria, with the colonial state's insistence on "secularism" in Northern Nigeria and not in Southern, Christian-populated areas.[37] The colonial state, Mahmud argues, subordinated Muslims and Islamic law through its deployment of secularism while simultaneously privileging Christians.

Not only European colonizers and Christian missionaries were implicated in this narrative of the secularization and subordination of Islamic law; these intellectuals blamed Muslim elites for their complicity in the colonial project. As Sulaiman charged: "the Muslim intelligentsia has, to a considerable extent, betrayed the cause of Islam. This betrayal has had a spillover effect even in the secular pretensions of the elite. Give them a state to manage, they will turn it into Hollywood."[38] The new intellectual class represented by Sulaiman and his colleagues blamed the Masu Sarauta for conceding to the Independence deal, which they insisted finalized the project of secularizing, and therefore, Christianizing Nigeria. The challenge mounted by these intellectuals revived

[36] Mahdi Adamu, "Foreword," in Rashid, *Islamic Law in Nigeria*, vii.
[37] Abdulmalik Bappa Mahmud, *A Brief History of Shari'ah in the Defunct Northern Nigeria* (Jos, Nigeria: Jos University Press, 1988), 5.
[38] Loiemeier, *Islamic Reform*, 367.

colonial-era Masu Sarauta insecurities. Realizing that their painstaking promotion of the 1958 deal to their constituents had foundered, those among the old elites who survived the turbulence of years following Independence saw the 1977 Conference as an opportunity for redemption.

As in the colonial years, a third minority position existed. This group shared the critique of the hegemonic hierarchies that defined the discourse of the colonial-era Aminu Kano-led Northern Elements Progressive Union (NEPU) as featured in earlier chapters. Kano, who lived several decades after Independence, continued to call for internal reform of Islam and the displacement of hierarchies. Yet, the colonial-era firebrand steered away from the Shari'a court debates even as he was a delegate to the constitutional conference. With Kano in the shadows, the postcolonial manifestation of the NEPU position was led by historian and self-described Marxist Yusufu Bala Usman. This minority group, mostly of university academics, argued that the debate over the Shari'a and secularism was a "systematic manipulation" of religion for the ends of capital and as a ploy to "divert attention" from crucial economic questions and the "harsh conditions of existence."[39] This view was also expressed by a handful of delegates during the constitutional conference proceedings.[40] Nevertheless, this opinion remained in a minority position in broader constitutional discourse. The framing of the struggle as pivoting on secularism attained dominance both in the imagination of the parties to the postcolonial contestations and in scholarly literature.[41]

The foregoing reveals that it is impossible to tell the story of postcolonial struggles over state-religion relations in isolation of the new alliances that the politics of decolonization and the memory of the colonial experience brought to the question of such relations. These postcolonial alliances were not a straightforward continuation of the colonial-era positions set out in previous chapters. Regardless of these

---

[39] Yusuf Bala Usman, *The Manipulation of Religion in Nigeria 1977–1987* (Kaduna, Nigeria: Vanguard Press, 1987).

[40] Proceedings of the Constituent Assembly, 130–131.

[41] See, for instance, Austin Metumara Ahanotu, ed., *Religion, State, and Society in Contemporary Africa: Nigeria, Sudan, South Africa, Zaire, and Mozambique* (New York: Peter Lang, 1992); Falola, *Violence in Nigeria*; Kukah and Falola, *Religious Militancy and Self-Assertion*; and Vincent O. Nmehielle, "Sharia Law in the Northern States of Nigeria: To Implement or Not to Implement, the Constitutionality is the Question," *Human Rights Quarterly* 26, no. 3 (2004): 730–759.

transformations, postcolonial adversaries framed their positions and identities with reference to the colonial-era Muslim versus non-Muslim contestation, and consciously evoked the colonial experience in the struggle to advance their projects – even when they deployed it in incongruous ways from their colonial-era forebears.

RENEGOTIATING THE INDEPENDENCE DEAL: THE SHARI'A COURT DEBATE AND THE 1977/78 CONSTITUTIONAL CONFERENCE

The framing of the constitutional debate over state-religion relations as a binary between Christian vanguards of secularism and a Muslim camp defending the Shari'a was on full display from the moment Constituent Assembly delegates convened on October 6, 1977. Starting from that inaugural sitting, the debate was overwhelmingly conducted in sectarian terms – the vast majority of Muslims spearheaded by the NSCIA supported the proposal and the Christian coalition championed by CAN opposed it. The Muslim coalition came to the 1977 Conference with a sense of victimization. Armed with a memory of the "humiliation" of Islamic law and Muslims, this camp saw the reversal of fortunes as contingent on the success of the court proposal.[42]

For the Christian delegates espousing the CAN defense of secularism against claims of the Shari'a, fear was the overriding emotion. These delegates invoked the existence of the "psychological fear"[43] that the Shari'a proposal would reintroduce the subordination of non-Muslims that they remembered to have pervaded colonial policy. Even the Shari'a proponents acknowledged the existence of this fear based on the Christian memory of the colonial experience, although that hardly amounted to their agreement with the Christian version of history. Noting that the members of the secular Christian coalition were "blinded by some historical feedbacks and personal experiences or allegations of unfair treatment in the past," one delegate argued that the Christian opposition to the Shari'a project was "simply a means of displaying anger against what they consider to be the wrong

---

[42] Mahmud, *A Brief History of Sharia*, 45.
[43] Rev. Dr. Joseph Agbowuro urged the assembly to set aside a "suitable length of times to dispel the psychological fear emanating from the experience of the activities of the Islam community in the country ... the minority has not been adequately protected." Proceedings of the Constituent Assembly, 55.

PART III IMAGINING THE PAST

done to them in the past."[44] This Christian memory of disempowerment in the colonial era then became the basis for understanding the 1977 demand for the Sharia Court of Appeal as an attempt by Muslim elites to retain their historical stranglehold on the state by "entrenching a theocratic institution"[45] The Christian coalition's response was to insist that "the secularity of Nigeria is not negotiable."[46] On the other hand, Muslim proponents of the Sharia Court of Appeal argued that "there is no virtue in having a secular state. Nigeria is a state of religions."[47] "Secularism" therefore became the language of debating the court proposal.

Acknowledging the polarizing effect of the court proposal in his opening address to the Constituent Assembly, chairman of the Constitution Drafting Committee (CDC) and prominent lawyer, Rotimi Williams, QC, declared: "it is an open secret that many of us have come to this Assembly with our minds made up on the provisions of the Draft constitution relating to the Federal Sharia Court of Appeal. My personal view is that a very simple and straightforward problem has been converted by extremists on all sides into an explosive and seemingly intractable problem."[48] Williams' framing of the court proposal as a "simple and straightforward problem" reflected the view of a group of English-trained Nigerian jurists who saw the court proposal as a mere technical fix for the state's judicial design. No less a body than the All Nigerian Judges Conference expressed this view at its 1972 gathering.[49] The gathering of judges recommended the creation of a Federal Sharia Court of Appeal (FSCA) to replace the defunct Sharia Court of Appeal of the Northern region.

As noted earlier, the Northern Region Sharia Court of Appeal's jurisdiction had been limited to personal law;[50] moreover, that court's decisions had not been final. In the judicial hierarchy, the court had ranked at par with the High Court, the court of first instance applying English law, and its appeals had laid directly to the Supreme Court. Further, in determining appeals, the Supreme Court could empanel judges without

---

[44] Alh A. Ibrahim, Proceedings of the Constituent Assembly, 794.
[45] Dr. Omo Omoruyi, Proceedings of the Constituent Assembly, 644.
[46] Toro Kachia, Proceedings of the Constituent Assembly, 1765.
[47] Alhaji Adamu Ciroma, Proceedings of the Constituent Assembly, 203.
[48] Proceedings of the Constituent Assembly, 44.
[49] "Item 7 All Nigeria Judges Conference Communique," cited in Mahmud, A Brief History of Sharia, 40.
[50] See Chapter 4.

regard to whether or not those judges were learned in Islamic law.[51] Therefore, not only was the defunct Sharia Court of Appeal's stature minimal and its jurisdiction narrow, its decisions were liable to be set aside with no expert engagement with Islamic jurisprudence. This was the position of the court when it became defunct following a 1967 military edict's division of the Northern Region into states and the resulting states each created their own Sharia courts of appeal. Although those courts continued to engage with Islamic jurisprudence, they hardly produced uniform results even when adjudicating similar questions. Moreover, the absence of an appeal channel to a higher court of Islamic jurists meant that jurisprudence regarding Muslim personal law remained diverse and unstandardized. The 1972 All Nigeria Judges Conference regarded the lack of uniformity as an anomaly in the broader design of Nigeria's court system which otherwise does not tolerate conflicting judgments in similarly situated courts across states. Consequently, the All Nigeria Judges Conference recommended the creation of the FSCA as a replacement of the defunct Northern Nigerian Sharia Court of Appeal to "harmonize" decisions across state Sharia courts of appeal and align the Sharia Court system with the rest of Nigeria's judicial design.[52]

Like the 1972 jurists, the CDC of the 1977 Constitutional Conference was convinced of the technocratic justification for the creation of the Federal Sharia Court of Appeal. Chaired by Williams, the CDC consisted of government-appointed experts and was charged with drafting proposals that would form the basis of the deliberations of the more representative Constituent Assembly, also to be moderated by Williams. The CDC proposal for the FSCA went a step beyond the All Nigerian Judges Conference's recommendation: Williams and his colleagues sought the establishment of a court to be staffed by Islamic law experts and to serve as a final court for all Islamic personal law matters without further appeals to the Supreme Court.[53] Williams and his colleagues intended that the FSCA would harmonize Islamic jurisprudence by presiding over appeals from state Sharia courts of appeal. In the words of Williams, the proposal was targeted at ensuring "that there

---

[51] In any event, appeals to the Supreme Court from the Sharia Court of Appeal were very rare since these appeals were as "of right" (rather than by leave) only in a few circumstances.

[52] Nigeria's judicial system follows the German model and conflicting judgments in similar courts from state to state were otherwise unheard of.

[53] An exception would be where a state legislation provided for appeals to the Supreme Court.

are no embarrassing conflicts of judicial decisions as to what Islamic law is on any particular point as interpreted by the Sharia Court of Appeal from state to state."[54] If this design varied from the All Nigerian Judges Conference proposal, it sought, like that earlier plan, the technocratic goals of uniformity and harmonization.

These goals of uniformity and harmonization were in service of the state's governance of Islamic law rather than rooted in an internalist effort to revive classical Islamic law in the postcolonial state. In fact, the lack of uniformity and harmonization that arose following the demise of the old Sharia Court of Appeal is hardly an anomaly in Islamic law. Diversity in jurisprudence and, therefore, in case outcomes, was an everyday feature of classical Islamic jurisprudence and, to an extent, in later forms that aspired to the classical model, such as the precolonial caliphate. Asifa Quraishi-Landes points out that the acceptance of diversity was premised on the recognition of human fallibility. Fiqh was a human effort to arrive at God's law, the Shari'a, and hence it was imperfect and prone to errors.[55] Not only was juristic diversity consonant with classical Islamic legal practice, the absence of an appellate channel to harmonize diverse decisions was congruent with the design of classical courts.[56]

Drawing from this knowledge, certain opponents of the court proposal momentarily deviated from the secularism-based opposition to

---

[54] Proceedings of the Constituent Assembly.

[55] Regardless of this possibility of error, human effort is commendable. For instance, a report of a hadith narrates the Prophet to have said that the one who does *ijtihad* (this effort of legal interpretation) and arrives at the right answer will receive two heavenly rewards, and the one who does *ijtihad* and arrives at the wrong answer will receive one reward. Second, diversity is inherently commendable, an idea that finds basis in another hadith. See Asifa Quraishi-Landes, "Who Says Shari'a Demands the Stoning of Women? A Description of Islamic Law and Constitutionalism," *Berkeley Journal of Middle Eastern and Islamic Law* 1, no. 1 (2008).

[56] Martin Shapiro explains this absence of appeals by the lack of a need for "hierarchical control" through the judges. He notes: "The Shari'a courts did not need to be mustered in a hierarchical fashion to achieve the secular tasks of territorial rulers, since those rulers enjoyed a second legal and administrative system for such purposes. Moreover, they did not need to be hierarchically organized to support the hierarchical structure of the religious community because no such structure existed in the religious community. The religious fragmentation of Islam is a part of its more general fragmentation. Although political institutions such as the caliphate and the Ottoman Empire often claimed centralized authority, in practice Islam was usually divided into a large number of independent territorial states." Martin Shapiro, "Islam and Appeal," *California Law Review* 68, no. 2 (1980): 350–381.

argue that the demand for an appellate court was not consonant with Islamic law. Several opponents of the court proposal not only argued that Islamic law does not permit appeal, they also contended that establishing appellate Shari'a courts would contravene the Shari'a by creating room for appealing a supposedly divine law. Crucially, opposition to the proposal on the basis of its inconsistency with classical Islamic legal practice was not limited to Christians; a handful of Muslim delegates from Southern Nigeria opposed the proposal on the same basis, although that position was hardly dominant.

In response, proponents of the court argued that appeals are consistent with Islamic law. As one faculty member of the Institute of Administration argued before the Assembly, the proposed Sharia Court of Appeal was to serve as the "Nazir-al-Muzalim" – "a redresser of wrongs," a role played by precolonial emirs' courts.[57] Since emirs had lost all judicial power with the 1958 reforms, there was a need for a final court capable of reexamining the decisions of qadis.[58] According to the court's proponents, appeals could not detract from the divinity of Islamic law since "an appeal merely questions the judge's interpretation; it does not question the law itself."[59] An appeal, they argued, is not "an appeal against the sharia itself."[60] Rather, it is an appeal against the "human mind who sits on the chair and delivers judgment in that case."[61] Invoking these justifications, these delegates made a case for the FSCA.

Neither the reference to the dissimilar Nazir-al-Muzalim, which operated in a more executive pardon capacity, nor the technical rationale for an appeal system masked the FSCA proposal for the power contestation that it was. Framing the debate as one of inclusion, Muslim proponents of the court argued that, since other Nigerians had the right to appeal decisions to higher courts, the establishment of the FSCA for Muslims in their personal law matters was a question of equality and inclusion. As one delegate asked: "why should a Muslim be restricted from raising an appeal if he disagrees? ... if this arrangement is not made, I will feel

---

[57] Dr. Yusuf of the Institute of Administration, Proceedings of the Constituent Assembly, 255. For a discussion of the appeals system in precolonial caliphate system, see Ajetunmobi, *Sharia Legal Practice*, 54.

[58] Dr. Yusuf of the Institute of Administration, Proceedings of the Constituent Assembly, 255.

[59] Dr. I. Abubakar, Proceedings of the Constituent Assembly, 276.

[60] Alhaji Yusuf, Proceedings of the Constituent Assembly, 347–348.

[61] Ibid., 348.

that I am not being protected because you are leaving me at the mercy of the state court."[62] Another delegate insisted: "I would like to see that I am given the necessary protection so that if the ... [the State Sharia Court of Appeal] took a decision on my case and I am not satisfied then I have somewhere to go." The call for an appellate court was therefore justified by the need for oversight of state-level Sharia courts of appeal by a higher federal court staffed with experts in Islamic law. This call for oversight was intimately coupled with demands for harmonization of Islamic jurisprudence – on a similar basis as the operation of the English Common Law and statutory law applicable to non-Muslim Nigerians. Postcolonial Muslim elites' pursuit of the court project was, therefore, paradoxical. On the one hand, the crux of these elites' campaign was a critique of the colonial state, including its bequest of the 1958 deal. On the other hand, their Sharia Court of Appeal proposal sought to revive an institution established by that state. Even more incongruously, the goal of harmonization promoted by these elites was strikingly similar to the colonial state's abolition of eclecticism in Islamic jurisprudence.[63] At its crux, however, these intellectual elites' pursuit of the court project was rooted in the context of a polarized constitutional struggle in which Muslim victory was essential. Under these circumstances, the ironies of the court proposal, even if apparent to its advocates, hardly mattered.

Even those Muslim intellectuals who admitted that the court proposal was hardly the substantive redress of Islamic law's subjugation that they desired nevertheless supported the demand. Notably, the director of the Institute of Administration and law professor, Dr. Sule Kumo, openly mocked the "self-congratulatory exultation" of Muslim political elites at the acceptance of their proposal by the CDC. Kumo pointed out that, contrary to the Masu Sarauta's "song and dance" about "their achievement in getting the Sharia accorded a fitting place in the judicial scheme, ... their only achievement ... is essentially the name of the Court: the form and not much substance."[64] Kumo nevertheless threw his weight behind the proposal not only because it would

---

[62] Alhaji Turu Muhammadu, Proceedings of the Constituent Assembly, 75.
[63] See Chapter 3.
[64] Sulaiman Kumo and Abubakar Aliyu, eds., *Issues in the Nigerian Draft Constitution: Report Conference Held at the Institute of Administration, Ahmadu Bello University, Zaria, 21st-24th March 1977* (Zaria, Nigeria: Ahmadu Bello University, 1977).

harmonize Islamic jurisprudence – itself a worthy goal to court proponents – but also because the Shariʿa court debate had by that time come to be synonymous with the broader constitutional struggle for the soul of postcolonial Nigeria. For the Muslim intellectual elite class represented by Kumo, the broader agenda was to transcend the tragedy of colonial – and postcolonial – domination and renew Islamic law.

It was the suspicion that the court proposal was a step toward the renewal of Islamic law that intensified Christian opposition to it. For that camp, the Shariʿa plan was not merely an agenda to revive Islamic law for Muslims, it was rather suspected to be a stealth plan to "islamize" Nigeria. As one delegate representing Makurdi (a colonial-era Type III area) warned, the proposal was "geared at ultimately replacing English law with sharia law."[65] Although the court proposal sought to maintain the personal law boundaries to which Islamic law had been formally confined by the Independence deal, the Christian coalition argued that the court proponents would never be satisfied with personal law. One delegate, for instance, cited a Nigeria Supreme Council for Islamic Affairs declaration that "in Islam, the law, both criminal and civil, are part and parcel of our religion. The application of Sharia in all is aspects will go a long way in bringing discipline, morality and unity in this country."[66] Raising the specter of a stealth Shariʿa plan, another delegate cautioned: "I am worried more by what the supporters of the Federal Shariʾa Court of Appeal have left unsaid, and, also, by what has been said outside of this Assembly, than by what they have said within this Assembly."[67] That delegate further went on to note that "when one reads critically the reports of seminars and symposia held on the question of the Sharia and examines closely arguments advanced by Islamic theoreticians who have their cell at the Institute of Administration in Zaria, then, you will agree with me that what the supporters of the Sharia are after is a dull society along Sharia Laws."[68] Another delegate warned that "the most frightening thing about Sharia is the fact that the crusade is a way of life. If Sharia is a way of life, that means that it will govern the political life, the economic life, the social life ... to create any government institution in this country above the state level on the basis of religion is going to be very dangerous for

---

[65] See also J. O. Aghimien, Proceedings of the Constituent Assembly, 235.
[66] Oyagbola, Proceedings of the Constituent Assembly, 913–914.
[67] R. B. Adewunmi, Proceedings of the Constituent Assembly, 490.
[68] Ibid.

peaceful co-existence of this country."⁶⁹ If the Muslim proponents of the court understood the situation that gave rise to the demand of the court as one of colonial and postcolonial disempowerment, the Christian coalition opposed to the proposal charged Muslims with attempting "to use Sharia as a vehicle to getting to political power."⁷⁰ Under these circumstances, resisting the court proposal was a mere front in a broader constitutional battle the Christian coalition was determined not to lose.

Regardless of these broader constitutional dynamics, the two sides to the 1977 constitutional debate were resolute in articulating their positions in terms of a binary view on state-religion relations. The Muslim proponents of the FSCA maintained its critique of secularism's marginalization of Muslims and put forth "religious freedom" as the fundamental constitutional principle. On the other hand, Christian opponents of the court proposal insisted that religious liberty was, at best, secondary to the demands of secularism.

Muslim delegates' invocation of religious freedom was in the language of rights and federalism. Although their forebears had deplored the missionary-inspired constitutionalization of religious freedom (at Independence) as a violation of the colonial guarantee of noninterference in Islam, the postcolonial Muslim coalition passionately wielded that provision in support of its position.[71] As a Northern elite argued at the conference: "if we agree to freedom of religion, there is no need truncating my freedom, I must be given the chance to do it fully. If I am not subject to the Shari'a, I will regard myself as not having freedom of religion."[72] Another delegate pointed out that "to deny Sharia which governs the life of millions of its adherents is like passing a bill in parliament or enacting a law in the constitution suspending all Christians in the country from attending Sunday worship."[73] Court proponents also hinged their religious liberty claims on the argument that the state had a federalist obligation to accommodate religious diversity. As one delegate passionately put it: "If we really believe in unity and diversity, if we really believe in live and let live, if we really believe in

---

[69] John Pam, Proceedings of the Constituent Assembly, 950.   [70] Ibid.
[71] Like the Independence Constitution, both the draft constitution debated by the 1978 Constituent Assembly and the resulting 1978 Constitution entrenched religious freedom as a constitutional right.
[72] Alhaji Adamu Ciroma, Proceedings of the Constituent Assembly, 201.
[73] Alhaji Abdu Mashi, Proceedings of the Constituent Assembly, 666.

mutual coexistence, if we really believe in respect and accommodating lawful and legitimate peculiarities of each other, there is no reason why the Sharia Court of Appeal should not be established throughout this country."[74] Analogizing the Nigerian situation to a marriage, another delegate claimed: "the Nigerian union is like a marriage and must take the needs of all, including the Muslims into consideration."[75] Delegates further argued that this accommodation was crucial for the state's federalism to be truly representative. As a delegate asserted: "if Nigeria is going to be a true federal system we shall have a weaker federation if the sharia is not represented at the top."[76] These federalism arguments were ultimately claims for inclusion. One delegate declared: "I am not part of the federation because I cannot make an appeal to the federation."[77] For these delegates, therefore, the religious liberty argument for the court found justification in both an individual and group-based rights claim.

Opponents of the court proposal who were overwhelmingly Christian responded by calling for the creation of corresponding courts for Christians and adherents of Indigenous religions. However, as Williams pointed out, this was not a "concrete demand."[78] In fact, rather than pursue this claim for the creation of courts serving other religious groups, opponents of the FSCA proposal argued that creating any courts to cater to a religious group was harmful to national unity. Several delegates described the situation that would result from the creation of the Federal Sharia Court of Appeal as "judicial ... apartheid,"[79] arguing that the Shari'a court proposal for a dual legal system was inconsistent with the popular desire for a united nation-state. Stressing this point, one delegate added: "what I literally dread is a situation where in all legal matters, the Muslims have their separate courts, followers of various traditional religions will have their separate courts ... if we do arrive at such a situation then we might as well apportion to every religious and non-religious group its own territory which will mean the end of Nigeria as we know it."[80] Rather than such a legal design, this

---

[74] Alhaji Yahaya Gusau, Proceedings of the Constituent Assembly, 663.
[75] Chief M. K. O. Abiola, Proceedings of the Constituent Assembly, 261.
[76] Mr. Gani, Proceedings of the Constituent Assembly, 454.
[77] Ibid.
[78] Proceedings of the Constituent Assembly, 44.
[79] John Pam noted that a dual legal system will result in apartheid "that would make what obtains in South Africa a child's play," Proceedings of the Constituent Assembly, 950.
[80] Fasanmi, citing Chris Abashiya, Proceedings of the Constituent Assembly, 519.

camp opposing the proposal argued that the state ought not to permit any or all religion into legal institutions since religion ought to remain in the private sphere. This exclusion of religion from law and legal institutions was, in that view, the essence of secularism.

These proponents of secularism insisted that separation of the state from religion is a fundamental norm of the modern polity. As Toro Kachia, a delegate from Kaduna, a colonial-era Type II area, put it, "in catering for our religious diversities, ... this should in no way be at the expense of our national unity because the secularity of Nigeria is not negotiable."[81] Consequently, the Christian camp argued that the validity of religious freedom claims depended on their compatibility with secularism. At the same time, however, this coalition suggested that the Muslim understanding of religious liberty was mistaken, arguing that, when invoked correctly, religious freedom was consistent with secularism since the essence of secularism was the protection of all – including religious minorities. These critics of the FSCA proposal pointed out that regardless of the limitation of the jurisdiction of existing state Shari'a courts to Muslims at Independence, those courts continued to exercise jurisdiction over a number of non-Muslims due to a variety of factors including the lack of access to reasonable alternatives. Although court proponents cited this anomaly as evidence of the popularity of Shari'a courts, the Christian coalition invoked it as evidence of repression and argued that non-Muslims continued to suffer colonial-era disadvantages in these courts. These included the nonrecognition of the oaths of non-Muslims, and the related lesser weight assigned to non-Muslims' judicial testimonies, particularly in the absence of corroborating evidence. Citing this judicial practice, the FSCA opponents concluded that the Shari'a court system not only violated secularism's requirement of non-adoption of religion, it also violated the religious freedom of non-Muslims.[82] As one delegate representing a colonial-era Type III area argued, "there is no basis at all to even discuss the probability of providing a court structure or system which by definition is a religious court and use federal funds to maintain

---

[81] Toro Kachia, Proceedings of the Constituent Assembly, 1765.
[82] Although the state Sharia Court of Appeal's jurisdiction was mandatory over Muslims only, it does appear that non-Muslims frequently appeared before the courts. While Muslim delegates argued that the appearance of Muslims before the court was based on consent of these parties and reflective of the popularity of the court, Christian delegates cited the same fact as reflective of the coercive nature of the courts.

such a court in a basically secular state."[83] "The Sharia Court system," another delegate proclaimed, "runs counter to the political objectives and the social order on which we seek to build our nation."[84] The court proposal's requirement that the court judges not only be "learned in Islamic law" but also be "Muslims" further bolstered these arguments. As a delegate asked rhetorically: "can the use of public funds to hire Muslims be interpreted in any other way but entrenching a theocratic institution?"[85] Concluding that the proposal was an attempt to establish an Islamic theocracy, the Christian camp opposing the proposal stood ready to defend its view of a secular state.

Muslim proponents of the court contested this vision of the state, arguing that "there is no virtue in having a secular state."[86] Insisting that "Nigeria is a state of religions,"[87] this group put forth a vision of a multireligious state that recognized religion in public institutions. To be sure, there was a minority of delegate proponents of the court who did not express aversion to secularism and regarded the proposal as compatible with that constitutional idea. That group acknowledged the need for limits on the entanglement of the state and religion to protect religious minorities. Yet, the few delegates who fell into that camp insisted that minority protection ought not to be at the expense of the majority. According to this view, an inclusive view of religious liberty was wholly consistent with secularism's vision of tolerance and neutrality. For all its attempts at moderation, this group's position was, therefore, still at odds with that of secularism's vanguards since the latter insisted on the exclusion of all religions from public institutions.

The Muslim response to the Christian defense of secularist separation was not limited to their disagreement with the normative idea of separation; Muslim delegates and the intellectuals of this coalition questioned the neutrality of Nigeria's secularism. In particular, Muslim delegates argued that the Nigerian state, as inherited from British colonizers, was not neutral given the Christian foundations of the English Common Law that formed the basis of the Nigerian legal system. The "Common Law," these critics of secularism insisted, "is part of a Christian culture."[88] Even the CDC chair, otherwise sympathetic to the court

---

[83] Paul Unongo, Proceedings of the Constituent Assembly, 1215.
[84] Ibid., 1215, referring to Sections 9 and 11 of the draft constitution.
[85] Dr. Omo Omoruyi, Proceedings of the Constituent Assembly, 644.
[86] Ibid.   [87] Ibid.
[88] Adamu Ciroma, Proceedings of the Constituent Assembly, 203.

proposal, objected to this categorization of Nigerian law. Williams not only insisted that the colonial state-bequeathed English Common Law was sourced from Germanic and Roman law, the jurist also maintained that the identity of the law giver – the British colonizer – was "secular."[89] Neither of these arguments dissociating Nigeria's received English Common Law from Christianity convinced the Muslim coalition. One Muslim delegate scoffed in response: "You can tell that to the marines."[90] These delegates argued, in sum, that the secularist arrangement of the state favored Christianity at the expense of other religions. If this argument was strikingly reminiscent of the critique colonial-era ecumenical missions leveled against imperial secularism, it failed to ring a bell to its postcolonial Muslim reinventors.

(Non)Resolution

With both sides putting forward irreconcilable visions of the state's proper relationship to religion and insisting on "secularism" as the faultline – even as the meaning of that constitutional idea was hardly apparent – tensions escalated in the Assembly. In the end, the CDC was swayed by the arguments in support of the court proposal. Making a federalism-based argument for religious liberty, Williams argued that the state was obliged to not "do anything, which is calculated to impose a system of laws associated with a particular religion upon a people who do not believe or practice the faith, which is the basis of that religion."[91] The CDC chair stressed that "accommodat[ing]" the court proposal would not Islamize Nigeria. Williams further argued: "those who do not want the Islamic law system will not have it. Anybody who feels that this country is being turned into a Muslim state is simply being mischievous."[92] At the same time, Williams cautioned that the "give and take" spirit equally applied to the court's proponents. In an indirect reference to the Muslim intellectuals of the Faculty of the Institute of Administration, Williams referenced persons arguing that "the creation of the court did not go far enough to ensure the development of Islamic law" and said of such persons: "I suspect that ... [they] are not prepared to make the kind of compromises which are essential to the formulation of a Federal constitution and indeed, to

---

[89] Proceedings of the Constituent Assembly, 51–52.
[90] M. K. O. Abiola, Proceedings of the Constituent Assembly, 262.
[91] Proceedings of the Constituent Assembly, 47–52.   [92] Ibid.

the survival of Nigeria as a united country."[93] Williams and the CDC therefore aligned with the religious liberty argument but vehemently opposed demands by postcolonial intellectual elites for a wholesale renewal of Islamic law. However, not even the CDC's support for the court proposal was sufficient to ensure the success of the proposal to insert a declaration of the state's "secularity" into the constitution. As Bola Ige, lawyer and CDC member who would go on to serve as attorney general, reported of the CDC deliberations, "it was suggested that Nigeria should be a secular state. Immediately our Muslim colleagues heard this, they raised an objection, saying that a secular state is a godless state. In spite of the heated debate the members of the CDC had on this, the word had to be deleted."[94] In the end, the CDC draft that was ultimately ratified by the Constituent Assembly replaced the term "secular" with what the jurists on the CDC regarded as the essence of that constitutional idea: the prohibition of the "adoption of religion" by the state.[95]

Regardless of the CDC's recommendation that the Federal Sharia Court of Appeal be established, the Christian Association of Nigeria-coordinated opposition drew on its majority in the Constituent Assembly to throw out the proposal. Instead of an appellate court dedicated to the Shariʿa, this group resolved that the preexisting Federal Court of Appeal would consider appeals arising from the decisions of the state Sharia courts. In considering an appeal arising from these courts, the Federal Court of Appeal would be constituted by a panel of persons "learned in Islamic law."[96] Such experts did not have to be Muslims as sought by the Sharia court proponents. Neither was the Islamic legal training required defined, leaving open the possibility that persons with only modest exposure to Islamic law might be regarded as satisfying the requirement. The Assembly also gestured to the concern over the Islamic legal education of judges presiding on appeals from state Sharia courts by addressing the composition of the Supreme Court, which was the apex court in the appellate hierarchy. The provision ratified by the Assembly enjoined presidents to "be mindful of the

---

[93] Ibid.
[94] Ige Bola, "Religious Freedom and the Modern Constitution," cited in Kukah, *Religion, Politics and Power in Northern Nigeria*, 228.
[95] Section 17 of the draft Constitution, which would become Section 10 of the 1979 Constitution, provided that "The Government of the Federation or of a State shall not adopt any religion as State Religion."
[96] Section 226 (a), 1979 Constitution.

need to ensure that they include persons learned in Islamic personal law" in Supreme Court justices.[97] Without mandating the appointment of Islamic law experts, this alternative left open the possibility that the Supreme Court would preside over Islamic law matters with no expertise. This arrangement failed to pacify the Sharia Court of Appeal proponents. In the first place, the alternative fell short of the demand for a designated court entertaining appeals from the state Sharia courts and presided over by Muslims learned in Islamic law. Even more importantly, the Muslim coalition, and in particular, postcolonial Muslim intellectual elites, proposed the Federal Sharia Court of Appeal not as an end in itself, but rather as a means of reversing colonialism's displacement of the Shari'a. To lose the proposal was, therefore, to suffer a stinging loss in a broader constitutional struggle for power. In protest of the inevitable defeat of the proposal, Muslim delegates staged a walk-out from the conference.

Left only with delegates opposing the creation of the FSCA, the Assembly proceeded to formally vote against the proposal. Muslim delegates eventually returned to the conference assembly upon the urging of the Federal Military Government. Further resistance was, however, futile since the defeat of the court proposal was, by then, irrevocably sealed. The assembly proceeded to submit its report to the Federal Military Government on August 29, 1978 with the proposal for the Federal Sharia Court of Appeal glaringly absent from its recommendations of provisions for the 1979 Constitution.

BEYOND 1978

The debate did not end at the 1977–78 Constitutional Conference. The defeat of the court proposal heightened the Muslim's coalition's sense of marginalization, a feeling that only intensified with the events that followed the conference. Notable among these events was the 1981 *Ado and Rabi v. Dijah* decision.[98] In that case, which began as an inheritance dispute, the presiding High Court sat with two judges of the High Court and one of the Sharia Court of Appeal. That composition was consistent with the court's practice in cases concerning

---

[97] Section 252, 1979 Constitution. These provisions survived subsequent constitutional (re)making processes.
[98] Ado and Rabi v. Dijjah, Ado v. Dije, 2 Federation of Nigeria Law Reports 213 (1983) (FCA/K). See Mahmud, *A Brief History of Sharia*, 43.

Muslim law as required by Section 63(1) of the High Court Law of Northern Nigeria. Counsel for the appellant, J. B. Majiyagbe, however, raised a constitutional objection to the presence of the Sharia Court of Appeal judge, a move reminiscent of an objection by a Christian Nigerian minority following the 1958 reforms. The appellant argued that by stipulating that Sharia Court of Appeal judges sit on High Court panels considering Islamic law cases, the High Court Law was inconsistent with Section 238 of the 1979 Constitution, a product of the 1977–78 constitutional debates. That argument was hardly compelling. The constitutional provision cited by the appellant provided that "the High Court of a State shall be duly constituted if it consists of at least one Judge of that Court." On the face of it, this hardly invalidated the High Court Law's provision for the court's sitting with an additional high court judge and a third from another court – the State Sharia Court of Appeal. Nevertheless, in its much-anticipated decision, the Federal Court of Appeal held the High Court Law provision to be unconstitutional.

The *Dijah* case received widespread attention with attorneys general of several Northern Nigerian states submitting amicus briefs and Muslim jurists received the court's decision with dismay. Commenting on the decision, Kadi Abdulmalik Bappa Mahmud, for instance, charged that the judgment put "Islamic Law ... to such humiliation the like of which it had never experienced in the hands of colonial masters who defeated and conquered the country."[99] Mahmud linked the decision with the identity of the presiding judges who were "Christians from the South" (albeit with the complicity of some Northern Nigerian legal practitioners solely trained in English law). The effect of the decision, Mahmud pointed out, was to "put determination of appeals or cases decided under Islamic law in the hands of Judges who are not conversant with Islamic law and most of whom are non-Muslims who are from the South."[100] This was because judges staffing the high courts were predominantly Christian and of Southern Nigerian origin. The non-Muslim composition of those courts was due to the inadequate number of English law-trained Northern Nigerian legal practitioners who met the requirements for High Court appointments. The invalidation of the practice of a Sharia Court of Appeal judge joining High Court panels deciding issues of Islamic law, therefore, made it all

---

[99] Mahmud, *A Brief History of Sharia*, 45.   [100] Ibid., 45.

but certain that "non-Muslims" would determine appeals on Islamic law.[101] These circumstances only deepened the sense of victimization of Northern Nigerian Muslims.

Further intensifying the controversy, the Federal Court of Appeal followed its *Dijah* pronouncement by another decision curtailing the jurisdiction of the Sharia Court of Appeal even more narrowly than the 1958 deal. That latter case was *Umary Fannami v. Bukar Sarkiu*[102] and the legal provision in question was Section 11(e) of the Sharia Court of Appeal Law. Section 11(e) vested the State Sharia Court of Appeal with jurisdiction over appeals from upper area court decisions in civil law matters (other than personal law) where parties consent. To consent to the court's jurisdiction, the parties did not have to be Muslim.[103] The *Sarkiu* decision only heightened fears of a concerted effort to eradicate Islamic law. Kadi Mahmud lamented the trend: "if we continue at this rate, what will follow next will be the closure of all these courts applying Islamic law and of course an end to Islamic law in what was once the Caliphate of Sheikh Usman Dan Fodio and Kanem Bornu Empire."[104] Mahmud then hastened to invoke divine help to avert such a situation: "Hasten the success of your Sharia, of its followers and of those who adore it, amen."[105] Mahmud and other prominent elites therefore understood the judicial developments that came on the heels of the 1977–78 Conference as heightening the precarity of Islamic law and Muslims in the postcolonial state.

The polarizing discourse on the Shari'a was not merely intellectual; as a broader constitutional debate, it had come to suffuse popular discourse. Indeed, by the time former colonial administrator and architect of the 1958 Islamic law reforms popularly known as "mutum ya kasha maliki" (the man who killed Maliki law), Sam Scrutton Richardson, visited Northern Nigeria in 1983 to deliver a lecture at Institute of Legal Studies, Zaria, he was confronted by thousands of protesters. That throng comprised not only of students and academics but also imams, journalists, and average citizens, many of whom had traveled from distant locations around Northern Nigeria.[106] Together, these protesters denounced

---

[101] Ibid., 45.
[102] Umary Fannami v. Bukar Sarkiu (1985) 1 Sharia Law Reports of Nigeria 94 (No. CA/3/16S/84) (FCA/K).
[103] Mahmud, *A Brief History of Sharia*, 47.
[104] Ibid.   [105] Ibid., 48.
[106] Sam S. Richardson, *No Weariness: The Memoir of a Generalist in Public Services in Four Continents* (Wylye: Malt House, 2001), 200.

the colonial state for foisting the 1958 Penal Code to get rid of Islamic law.[107] For that group, just like the intellectual elites championing the project, it hardly mattered that the demands being made of the postindependence state hinged on the reinstatement of colonial-era institutions, especially those created by the much-abhored 1958 reforms.

If the outrage that greeted Richardson in 1985 indicated the ferocity of the Shari'a debates, the contestation only intensified in the coming years. By the time the next constitutional conference was convened in 1988, the military head of state attempted to douse tensions by insisting on the maintenance of the 1977 status quo. Inaugurating the 567 members of the 1988 Constituent Assembly, General Ibrahim Babangida warned Assembly members not to engage in "the fruitless exercise of trying to alter the agreed ingredients of Nigeria's political order, such as ... the non-adoption of any religion as State Religion."[108] This warning was futile and the debate over the proposal for a Federal Sharia Court of Appeal once again took the center stage as it had at the 1977 debates. So contested was the 1988 Conference that it came to be known in constitutional history as "the Great debate."[109] Chair of the 1988 Constituent Assembly and Justice of the Supreme Court, Mr. Aniagolu, observed about the proceedings: "We saw this country totter helplessly almost to the point of collapse by reason of religious confrontation in the Constituent Assembly over the vexed issue of the Sharia Court of Appeal."[110] So polarized was the Assembly that the composition of Committee XXIV, the State Judicature Committee that was charged with deliberating on the Sharia Court question, itself generated intense dispute. The disagreement centered on the religious affiliations of committee members. Following much disagreement, the Assembly eventually set the religious composition of the committee as nineteen Christians and eighteen Muslims, including the chairman. The initial dispute had, however, set the tone

---

[107] Kukah, *Religion, Politics and Power*, 117–118.
[108] General Ibrahim Babangida, "Inaugural Address to Members of the Constituent Assembly," May 11, 1988 in Kola Olugbade, "The Nigerian State and the Quest for a Stable Polity." *Comparative Politics* (1992): 293–316, 302.
[109] Walter Ibekwe Ofonagoro, Abiola Ojo, and Adele Jinadu, eds., *The Great Debate: Nigerian Viewpoints on the Draft Constitution* (Apapa-Lagos, Nigeria: Daily Times Publication, 1989); Maurinius Iwuchukwu, *Muslim-Christian Dialogue in Post-Colonial Northern Nigeria: The Challenges of Inclusive Cultural and Religious Pluralism* (Berlin: Springer, 2013), 87.
[110] Anthony Nnaemezie Aniagolu, *The Making of the 1989 Constitution of Nigeria* (Ibadan, Nigeria: Spectrum Books, 1993), 254.

for what was to come.¹¹¹ Hopelessly polarized along religious lines, the committee failed to reach a consensus and eventually resorted to a majority vote authorizing completely expunging all Sharia courts, including state Sharia courts, from the constitution. This measure reversed even the 1978 gesture that the Muslim camp had found insufficient. The result was chaos in the Assembly and violent altercations on the streets. Eventually, on November 28, 1988, the Federal Military Government stepped in. To douse the tension, the government instructed the Constituent Assembly to exclude any discussion about the constitutional debates and to maintain the status quo set by the 1979 Constitution.¹¹²

The gag order imposed by the military government at the 1988 debates did not dispel the Shariʿa debates following the conference. By the time Nigeria transitioned from the second era of military rule into a third democratic republic eleven years later, in 1999, the Shariʿa project had morphed into a demand for a total reversal of the colonial legacy on Islamic law. As noted earlier, the pre-1999 demand for a revival of a court that was a key legacy of empire rested uneasily with the critique of the colonial Independence deal from which it sprung. The intellectual elites driving the postcolonial Muslim agenda were not blind to this reality; they pursued the FSCA project as a step toward challenging the postcolonial hierarchies that the Independence deal had set in motion. The intense partisan opposition mounted by CAN against the tame court proposal in the years between 1977 and 1999 only substantiated these allegations of the postcolonial subordination of Muslims. The 1999 agenda sought to displace the entirety of the legal reforms bequeathed by empire. By doing so, authors of the post-1999 project sought to challenge the 1958 constitutional deal, the colonial domination that produced it, and the postcolonial hierarchies that it set in motion.

Replacing the pre-1999 agenda of reviving a colonial-state-bequeathed court with jurisdiction confined to personal status/civil law matters, the post-1999 project challenged the colonial separation of Islamic law into criminal and civil law itself. The post-1999

---

¹¹¹ Committee XXVI was the largest of the twenty-three committees of the 1988 Constituent Assembly.
¹¹² Note, however, that the 1989 Constitution reinstated the pre-1979 provision that the jurisdiction of the Sharia Court of Appeal was once again over the questions of civil law in cases between Muslims; the 1979 Constitution had restricted the jurisdiction of the court to cases involving personal law.

agenda primarily took the form of reintroducing Islamic criminal law. Pioneered by Zamfara State, twelve Northern Nigerian states, which correlated with colonial-era Types I (Muslim majority) and II (mixed religious) areas, enacted Shari'a Penal Codes between 1999 and 2000.[113] The broader agenda, however, transcended criminal law. The revival of Islamic criminal law was merely one element of what these states designed as a broader Islamic renaissance project. Therefore, beyond the enactment of Sharia Penal and Criminal Procedure Codes to be applied in relation to Muslims, the renaissance project consisted of several elements. These states established new Sharia courts unrestrained by the colonial-era civil law/personal status boundaries and with jurisdiction to apply all aspects of Islamic law in matters involving Muslims. With their jurisdiction now unlimited, these courts had the authority to preside over all appeals from lower courts. The states also embarked on enacting a broad range of legislations and regulations targeted at reorienting society toward the Shari'a. These legislations were directed at "social vices" like the "consumption of alcohol,"[114] "gambling,"[115] "prostitution,"[116] "unedifying media,"[117] and "corruption," including but not limited to financial dealings.[118] Institutions were established to effectuate this societal reform project, the most prominent among which was the *hisbah* – the morality police. The *hisbah* was responsible for apprehending offenders and charging them to court as well as mediating and conciliating disputes. Other institutions included state Shari'a commissions, public complaints and anti-corruption commissions, councils of *ulama* (jurists), and *zakat* (alms) collection boards.

The drivers of the post-1999 agenda, a coalition of Muslim intellectual and political elites with a popular following among the general Muslim population, understand the post-1999 project to be a

---

[113] These were Bauchi, Borno, Gombe, Jigawa, Kaduna, Kano, Katsina, Kebbi, Niger, Sokoto, Yobe, and Zamfara.

[114] See, for instance, Niger State Liquor Law (as amended 2001).

[115] See, for instance, Borno State Repeals and Savings Provisions Law (2000), and Giwa Local Government (Kaduna State) by-law on liquor, gambling and prostitution (1999).

[116] See, for instance, Kano State Prostitution and Other Immoral Acts (Prohibition) Law (2000).

[117] See, for instance, Kano State's State Censorship Film Board Law (2001).

[118] See, for instance, Zamfara State Anti-Corruption Commission Law (2003). For a comprehensive sourcebook compilation of the laws relating to various aspects of the legal reforms, see Philip Ostien, ed., *Sharia Implementation in Northern Nigeria 1999–2006: A Sourcebook*, vol. 3 (Ibadan, Nigeria: Spectrum, 2007).

continuation of the 1977 and 1988 struggles. As before, the NSCIA and JNI feature as prominent advocates; players involved in the earlier debates who lived on to witness the 1999 agenda seized the opportunity, and new intellectual descendants steeped in the history of the earlier struggles joined in advancing the cause. For all the striking expansion of the earlier agenda, the post-1999 project was therefore framed in the same terms as the 1977 and 1988 debate: as a postcolonial critique of the secularism bequeathed by the colonial state. That critique continues to wield the idea of religious liberty against a secularism that it accuses of being unneutral, and to advance a Shariʻa agenda that aims to transcend the colonial legacy.

On the opposing side remains the Christian Association of Nigeria. For CAN, the Shariʻa renaissance project is as anti-secular as the older agenda to create the Federal Sharia Court of Appeal. Further, CAN, continues to regard that agenda as an effort to revive colonial-era hierarchies. It, therefore, views its mandate as the defense of secularism against religious liberty claims that advance what it regards as the stealth theocratic goals of the Shariʻa project. As parties continue to insist on the language of secularism and religious liberty as the language of the debates, dueling imaginations of the colonial past and its postcolonial legacy continue to define the character of the struggles.

CONCLUSION

For all the critique of the colonial experience from which it emerged, the postcolonial agendas of both the drivers of the Shariʻa renaissance and their Christian critics are not liberated from that history. This inheritance is not only visible in the rehashing of the ideas of secularism and religious liberty against which the forebears of the postcolonial contestants contended, it is also apparent in the projects that postcolonial contestants seek to advance. Both sides seek the governance of religion in the manner of the colonial state they despise. For the postcolonial Christian respondents to the Shariʻa renaissance project, the decolonizing agenda has entailed an insistence on a secularist, separationist design. As in its colonial manifestation, that design has been hardly neutral. Rather, it is one that governs religion and deepens religious difference through the hierarchies it perpetuates in constitutional politics. Hence, the Christian memory willfully ignores Christian missionaries' decisive influence on the Independence, and ultimately, postcolonial constitutional arrangement. The coalition also ignores the Christian roots of the English Common Law that was bequeathed by empire as the neutral, nonreligious law in the patchwork that is the Nigerian legal system.[119] Crucially, the Christian position continues to advance the application of Islamic law and other religious customary law by state courts, which it perceives to be the neutral arbiter. In doing so, the notion of the secular advanced by the Christian coalition is far from separate from the sacred as it claims; rather, the construction of that category – the secular – is already deeply entangled with the religion.

Just as the secular advanced by the Christian coalition is entwined with the sacred, the Shariʿa renaissance agenda is also embroiled with the secular project in a way that reenacts the colonial experience. Commenting on the Shariʿa renaissance project, Sarah Eltantawi maps out the disconnect between the "idealized Sharia" held up as the vision of the renaissance project and the "political Sharia" that emerges from the reform efforts.[120] What this distinction elides is that the idealized vision of the Shariʿa held out by the renaissance project has been the mode of engaging in politics in the postcolonial state.[121] To transcend the subjugation of the (post)colonial experience, the drivers of the postcolonial agenda (especially in its post-1999 version) hold up a vision of a precolonial caliphal model as an ideal.[122] Rather than understanding the precolonial polity for the aspirational and "complex … polity ordered around the religious mission of its founders"[123] that it was, the postcolonial renaissance project sees the caliphate ideal through the lens of the state midwifed by colonial modernity. This lens, which Hussein Agrama refers to as an "objectification lens," results in the "state-fication"[124] of Islamic law and institutions. The sacred agenda is, in sum, already constituted by the secular in spite of contestations

---

[119] See John Marshall Gest, "The Influence of Biblical Texts Upon English Law," *University of Pennsylvania Law Review and American Law Register* 59, no. 1 (1910): 15–38.

[120] Sarah Eltantawi, *Shari'ah on Trial: Northern Nigeria's Islamic Revolution* (Oakland: University of California Press, 2017), 14–15.

[121] See generally Mark Fathi Massoud, *Shari 'a, Inshallah: Finding God in Somali Legal Politics* (New York: Cambridge University Press, 2021).

[122] Mervyn Hiskett, *The Sword of Truth: The Life and Times of the Shehu Usuman dan Fodio* (Oxford: Oxford University Press, 1973), 54–55.

[123] Brandon Kendhammer, *Muslims Talking Politics: Framing Islam, Democracy, and Law in Northern Nigeria* (Chicago: University of Chicago Press, 2016), 54–55.

[124] Hussein Agrama, *Questioning Secularism: Islam, Sovereignty, and the Rule of Law in Modern Egypt* (Chicago: University of Chicago Press, 2012), 54.

to the contrary. The consequence is that the postcolonial renaissance agenda becomes the very model of governance that it critiques.

This is apparent in all the paraphernalia of the Shariʿa governance structure. For all its opposition to imperial, secularist governance that it understands colonial governance to be, the renaissance project calls for the regulation of the Shariʿa by the state bequeathed by colonial modernity. While the 1977 proposal for the Sharia Court of Appeal was a call for "religious freedom," it was also a demand for increased state regulation of the Shariʿa. The same is the case for the '99 affirmation of Islamic criminal law – an affirmation of Islamic law's supremacy by the abolition of the personal status/criminal matters distinction on the one hand, and a call for statist direction through codification, appeals, and federal institutional regulation on the other. Within the judicial system, the result of the statist codification of classical Maliki jurisprudence without the juristic license to grapple with source texts has culminated in a situation Ghislaine Lydon refers to as "kadijustiz without qāḍīs," flipping Webber's well-known denigration of Islamic judging.[125]

Perhaps the most well-known cases demonstrating the incongruity of the postcolonial claim to renewal have been the adultery cases prosecuted in the post-1999 renaissance movement. Take the widely cited *Amina Lawal* case[126] in which the defendant was tried and convicted for the offense of *zina* (engaging in sexual intercourse outside of wedlock) by the Sharia Court of Bakori, Katsina State. The evidence relied on by the Katsina State's *hisbah* corps for Lawal's arrest was her pregnancy out of wedlock. Invoking Maliki thought, which is atypical (compared to other schools of Islamic jurisprudence) in allowing the circumstantial evidence of pregnancy to ground adultery convictions, the court convicted Lawal and sentenced her to death. Lawal's trial, which attracted much international condemnation, was more a product of the imperial, Islamic law governance-inspired mode than the Shariʿa renaissance vision held up by Shariʿa reformers. In the first

---

[125] Ghislaine Lydon, "Inventions and Reinventions of Sharia in African History and the Recent Experiences of Nigeria, Somalia and Mali," *Ufahamu: A Journal of African Studies* 40, no. 1 (2018): 100.

[126] See records of the proceedings of the *Amina Lawal* case in Philip Ostien, ed., *Sharia Implementation in Northern Nigeria 1999–2006: A Sourcebook*, vol. 1 (Ibadan, Nigeria: Spectrum, 2007), 52–107. See also Carina Tertsakian, "Political Shari'a: Human Rights and Islamic Law in Northern Nigeria," *Human Rights Watch* 16, no. 9a (2004).

place, the court's limitation of its juristic efforts to Maliki thought has its roots in the colonial state's governance of Islamic law. In a shift from the precolonial practice of eclectism and in furtherance of the goal of legibility and predictability, the colonial state mandated Maliki thought as the sole mode of jurisprudence applicable in courts. That legacy has continued into the postcolonial renaissance moment. Even more importantly, the apprehension of Amina Lawal was a product of the colonial state-inspired postcolonial machinery of regulation. The policing machinery that led to Lawal's apprehension and prosecution, the mode of judging that secured her conviction and, ultimately, the appellate hierarchy that led to Lawal's liberation[127] are all part of the postcolonial statist design governing Islamic law. Therefore, for all its critique of colonial governance, the postcolonial renaissance project could not shake off the imperial legacy. The state, in the renaissance mode as in its old colonial form, continues to assume the authority to "constitute" religion and religious law.[128]

Postcolonial Muslim critics turn from the tenuous alliance of colonial-era predecessors with the "secular" colonial state to now invoke the religious liberty spurned by those forebears in furtherance of a religious renewal agenda. On the other hand, however, the renaissance project finds expression in a governance design that defeats the emancipation sought – one that continues to allocate disproportionate authority to political authorities to define, confine, and regulate religion. As shown earlier, this irony also afflicts the postcolonial Christian coalition that resists the Shari'a renaissance agenda by championing the idea of secularist separation that their missionary forebears abhorred and critiquing the expansive notion of religious liberty that their predecessors advanced. This paradox in modern struggles over religion and religious difference reflects what Saba Mahmood describes as the "promise" and "peril" of secular governmentality.[129] Inherent in this ineluctable mode of governance, Saba Mahmood argues, is the "possibility of prejudice

---

[127] The Katsina State Sharia Court of Appeal overturned the lower Sharia court's decision based, among others, on the "sleeping fetus" principle in Maliki thought. This principle stipulates that a pregnancy conceived by an unmarried woman within seven years of the end of valid marriage is not evidence of adultery. See Amina Lawal Bakori v. The State, in Ostien, *Sharia Implementation*, 103.

[128] Tamir Moustafa, *Constituting Religion: Islam, Liberal Rights, and the Malaysian State* (Cambridge: Cambridge University Press, 2018).

[129] Saba Mahmood, *Religious Difference in a Secular Age: A Minority Report* (Princeton, NJ: Princeton University Press, 2015), 21.

and equality" that draws subjects to "often contest ... discriminatory practices ... through the same legal instrument that enshrine majoritarian privilege."[130] Hence, contestants in Nigerian struggles invoke ideas of religious liberty and separation to advance their projects even while they critique the imperial secular governmentality with which it is implicated.

To end this chapter with Mahmood's observation would, however, be to slip into representing the power relations that galvanize these struggles as unchanging. Instead, the narrative in this book reveals that contestants switch their allegiance to ideas of religious liberty and secularist separation and deploy those ideas in shifting ways. This lays bare the instability of those ideas and the elusiveness of a conceptual resolution of the struggles. Even more importantly, however, it shows that secularism, or secular governmentality, within which all these ideas can be subsumed, is not an unchanging mode of domination. It is a domain of contestation.

[130] Ibid., 176.

CONCLUSION

The story of religion and political power in colonial Northern Nigeria is one of sustained entanglement. The British Empire's embrace of secular governmentality called for a rhetoric of state separation from religion. At the same time, however, the ideological underpinnings and administrative exigencies of indirect rule translated into the co-option, regulation, and transformation of religion and religious institutions. In the end, therefore, imperial governmentality – in its varied, spatial, and temporal manifestations – entailed the uneasy coexistence of the rhetoric of state-religion separation with the everyday intimacy of religion and state authority.

Regardless of the continuing legacy of that history of entanglement, postcolonial constitutional debates over the proper relationship between the state and society on the one hand and religion on the other remain locked in a binary frame. Contestants inevitably present their struggle in terms of a mutually exclusive allegiance to the "sacred" or the "secular."[1] That framing also defines prominent scholarly accounts.[2] Take Lamin Sanneh's celebrated volume, *The Crown*

---

[1] See generally Nigeria Constituent Assembly, *Proceedings of the Nigeria Constituent Assembly: Official Report 1977*, vol. 1 and 2 (Lagos: Federal Ministry of Information, 1977).

[2] See, for example, Lamin Sanneh, *The Crown and the Turban: Muslims and West African Pluralism* (New York: Routledge, 2018); Austin Metumara Ahanotu, *Religion, State, and Society in Contemporary Africa: Nigeria, Sudan, South Africa, Zaire, and Mozambique* (New York: Peter Lang, 1992); Toyin Falola, *Violence in Nigeria: The Crisis of Religious Politics and Secular Ideologies* (Rochester: University of Rochester Press, 2001).

and the Turban.³ Sanneh's account is premised on a supposed clash between Muslims and Western secularism and places that confrontation at the heart of constitutional struggle over Shari'a renaissance projects.⁴ However, this is at odds with the historical processes through which the "sacred" and the "secular" were not only constituted but also *re*-constituted. Far from evolving separately, these labile categories emerged in a dialectic, and were together co-constitutive of the colonial and lately, the postcolonial state.

When Talal Asad published his seminal *Formations of the Secular* in 2003, he advocated a paradigm shift from the sacred-secular binary prevalent in both scholarly accounts and in public constitutional discourse.⁵ Asad called, instead, for an interrogation of the historical processes through which these categories emerge. Asked Asad: "How, when and by whom are the categories of the sacred and the secular defined?"⁶ Not a few have since taken up his invitation to unmask the legal and political processes that have culminated in the formation and delineation of the "sacred" and the "secular" in different contexts.⁷ These accounts have offered a corrective to received understandings of modern liberal secularism. Yet, they typically overlook a crucial fact: that the "sacred," and the "secular" are not merely formed by relations of power but are also periodically *re*-formed during constitutional struggles. The consequence is that narratives of secularism treated as an unchanging tool of domination abound in the critical tradition.⁸

By illuminating shifts in the making and remaking of the "sacred" and the "secular" – especially at moments of upheaval – this book shows that the construction of secularism is constantly shifting. Lugardian

---

³ Sanneh, *The Crown and the Turban*.   ⁴ Ibid., 1.
⁵ Talal Asad, *Formations of the Secular: Christianity, Islam, Modernity* (Stanford: Stanford University Press, 2003).
⁶ Ibid., 200.
⁷ See, for example, Saba Mahmood, *Religious Difference in a Secular Age: A Minority Report* (Princeton: Princeton University Press, 2015); Tamir Moustafa, *Constituting Religion: Islam, Liberal Rights, and the Malaysian State* (Cambridge: Cambridge University Press, 2018); Winnifred Fallers Sullivan et al., eds., *Politics of Religious Freedom* (Chicago: University of Chicago Press, 2015); and Hussein Agrama, *Questioning Secularism: Islam, Sovereignty, and the Rule of Law in Modern Egypt* (Chicago: University of Chicago Press, 2012), 54.
⁸ See, for instance, Mahmood, *Religious Difference in a Secular Age*; Saba Mahmood and Peter G. Danchin, "Immunity or Regulation? Antinomies of Religious Freedom," *South Atlantic Quarterly* 113, no. 1 (2014): 129–159; and Joan Wallach Scott, *The Politics of the Veil* (Princeton, NJ: Princeton University Press, 2009).

governance entailed the making of a *colonial version* of caliphal institutions as the "secular," shoring up the state's Muslim intermediaries by invoking ideas of religious liberty. At the same time, Lugardians construed other faiths as "religion," calling upon religion-state separation to exclude and subordinate these groups. In a struggle to defend their proselytization project, European Christian missionaries denounced Lugardian entanglement with caliphal institutions. Oblivious to the radical transformation of Islamic institutions that commenced in the Lugardian years, these missionaries sought to neutralize what they described as the state's "bolstering up of Islam" by advancing a notion of separation conducive to Christian missionizing.[9] The missionary cause came to find sympathy in later colonial years among Cameronians, those senior colonial administrators averse to Lugardian deference to the colonial remains of caliphal institutions. Their inclination to raise the Lugardian "curtain" shielding Muslims from missionary access produced a shift in constitutional discourse and governmental practice. Ultimately, at Independence, missionaries and Christian converts would draw on Cameronian support to counter what they regarded as the "secularist" Muslim threat with a notion of religious liberty favorable to Christian evangelism. Markedly Protestant, that idea of religious liberty hinged on an exclusionary notion of religions worthy of protection. In doing so, it excluded the most vulnerable groups in the state – the so-called dissident Muslims and Indigenous non-Muslim faith groups.

Given the triumph of mission enthusiasts at Independence, the postcolonial state unsurprisingly saw a reversal in the construction of the "sacred" and the "secular," and with it, in the deployment of the notions of religious liberty and secularist separation. The Christian coalition descending from colonial-era missions now defined demands by Muslim groups, even those far removed from precolonial caliphal practice, as essentially "religious" claims and hence in violation of the sacrosanct separation of the state from religion. For its part, the postcolonial Shariʻa camp has essayed a statist vision of the Shariʻa, defending that project on the grounds of religious liberty and critiquing what it understands as the Christian secularist threat. The history of the unfolding of imperial secularism in Northern Nigerian is a chronicle of contestation over the *longue durée*.

---

[9] Walter Miller to Miss Gollock. September 27, 1917 CBMS/IMC 271. School of Oriental and African Studies Special Collections, UK.

CONCLUSION

Regardless of the mutual imbrication of the sacred and the secular revealed throughout this book, constitutional struggles continue to center on the incessant though tenuous delineation of those categories. Those involved present the "secular" and the "sacred" as neutral, a priori concepts that precede constitutional debates. In fact, however, constitutional argument pivots on their making and unmaking. Moreover, their shifting deployments have had immense consequences for the distribution of power and liberties. With the colonial (and postcolonial) state and its ever-shifting superintendents ascribing the "secular" to itself and deeming what was outside it as the "religious," politically and legally salient hierarchies ensued. The ultimate casualty was and continues to be equality.

Hierarchies have, in sum, been an enduring feature of the constitutional politics of religious difference in the colony and postcolony. Those hierarchies have, however, been far from stable. Instantiated by changing power relations, themselves authorized by shifting legal ideas, those hierarchies have shifted at moments of constitutional transformation. Tragically, however, the oscillation of those hierarchies has not been inspired by emancipatory projects geared at ushering in egalitarian constitutional politics. Rather, they have been informed by efforts to overturn the status quo, making yesterday's subordinated today's dominant, and entrenching the inequality and contestation that is the legacy of imperial secularism.

The archive of struggle recorded in this book is unmistakably one of power. In this light, one might wonder whether the story of imperial secularism is merely one of brute politics. Does the law have any place in this account beyond being a strategic tool used by disputants in their pursuit of dominance? As if to assert just this, the Nigerian Supreme Court has remained eerily silent in the name of the law on the protracted postcolonial constitutional debate. The most obvious opportunity for the court to have intervened arose in 2001, in *A. G. Kano v. A. G. Federal Republic of Nigeria*.[10] In that case, Northern Nigeria's Kano State sought a judicial declaration of the constitutionality of the *hisbah*, the police corps established by the state in 2000 to enforce Shariʿa criminal law as part of its broader Shariʿa renaissance project. Kano had instituted the suit in response to the inspector general of police's arrest of senior officers of Kano's *hisbah* corps. That arrest had come on the heels of the inspector general of

---

[10] A. G. Kano v. A. G. Federal Republic of Nigeria (2007) 3 SC.

police (and the federal minister of information's) allegations of the unconstitutionality of Kano's criminal law regime. Beyond alleging that Kano's establishment of the *hisbah* violated the exclusive constitutional allocation of police powers to the federal government, these federal officials also stressed that Kano's institutionalization of a religion-based criminal law violated the 1999 Constitution's prescription of secularism. Like the expressed legal edicts of the colonial state before it, the 1999 Constitution made no explicit reference to "secularism." Nevertheless, that Constitution, like previous ones, prescribed the conventional elements of secularism as espoused by classical political theory.[11] The Constitution prohibits the government from adopting any state religion, thereby invoking the notion of distance, if not separation of the state from religion.[12] It also provides for religious liberty.[13] In being asked to declare the *hisbah* corps constitutional, the Supreme Court was, in essence, invited to wade into the controversy over religion's place in the postcolonial state.

The Supreme Court declined to exercise jurisdiction, holding that the proper respondent in the case was the inspector general and not the federal government. Its rationale was peculiar since the inspector general's actions are attributable to the federal government by law. Nevertheless, the court drew a tenuous distinction between the two, arguing that it had jurisdiction over the latter but not the former, thus to avoid pronouncing on *hisbah*'s constitutionality and, more broadly, on the secularism question.[14]

---

[11] John Rawls, *A Theory of Justice* (Cambridge: Harvard University Press, 1971); Bruce Ackerman, *Social Justice in the Liberal State* (New Haven: Yale University Press, 1980); and Donald Eugene Smith, *India as a Secular State* (Princeton, NJ: Princeton University Press, 2015).

[12] Section 10, Constitution of the Federal Republic of Nigeria, 1999.

[13] Section 38, Constitution of the Federal Republic of Nigeria, 1999.

[14] The Supreme Court similarly avoided pronouncing on the "secularism" question in a later case, Lagos State Government and others v. Asiyat Abdulkareem and others (Suit SC 910 2016, delivered on June 17, 2022). That case involved the Lagos State government's restrictions on pupils' wearing of the Muslim headscarf in state-owned and operated schools. Although Lagos is in southern Nigeria, the headscarf question raised the specter of the secularism debate that had emerged since the 1977 Constitutional Conference, revealing the nationalization of the debate along Muslim versus Christian lines. The Supreme Court held the ban incompatible with the constitutional provision on religious liberty. Ignoring the inextricability of the issue of religious liberty from the persistent secularism debate, the court framed its

CONCLUSION

The court's refusal to entertain the question has left the debate in the political sphere, where it has surfaced at intense moments of contestation – especially during constitutional conferences. In that context, contestants have deployed shifting ideas of religious liberty and state-religion separation to limn tenuous binaries of what constitutes the sacred and the secular, and ultimately to advance their agendas. Nonetheless, it would be mistaken to view imperial secularism, in its colonial and postcolonial forms, as purely an expression of politics. Law may always be political, but it is never reducible to politics or to the relations of power that it (re)produces. After all, law can be a prisoner of its own rhetoric.[15] The colonial state deployed secularism as a technique for managing local populations and for defining, confining, and regulating religion. At the same time, however, that mode of governmentality provided concrete tools for colonial subjects.[16] Far from being passive receptors, those subjects deployed imperatives inherent within imperial secularism, notions of religious liberty and state-religion separation, to advance their agendas. Law, as it emerged from the colonial encounter, was never a mere tool of domination.[17] At the same time, however, the reality of the relations of domination that colonial law enabled meant that it was hardly an exclusive instrument of resistance either. Rather, law, both colonial and postcolonial, is simultaneously an instrument of domination and a repertoire of tools that may be harnessed for contestation.

The contestation narrated in this book has unfolded against a background of power relations unique to the history of Nigeria. However, that (post)colony is not singular in its encounter with colonial modernity. Indeed, to think productively about the legacy of colonialism for postcolonial constitutional contestation is necessarily to adopt a global lens. That lens illuminates the ways in which postcolonial debates across the world are part of the "unfinished nature" of

---

decision in reference to religious liberty, and declined to comment on the question of secularism.

[15] Edward Palmer Thompson, *Whigs and Hunters: The Origin of the Black Act* (New York: Pantheon Books, 1975).

[16] John Comaroff, "Colonialism, Culture, and the Law: A Foreword," *Law & Social Inquiry* 26, no. 2 (2001): 305–314. See further Mark Fathi Massoud, "Islamic Law, Colonialism, and Mecca's Shadow in the Horn of Africa," *Journal of Africana Religions* 7, no. 1 (2019): 121–130.

[17] See Martin Chanock, *Law, Custom, and Social Order: The Colonial Experience in Malawi and Zambia* (Cambridge: Cambridge University Press, 1985).

the colonial past.[18] It also unearths the ways in which the legacy of colonialism reverberates globally, defying boundaries that once divided the colonizer from the colonized.[19] As ubiquitous debates over religion continue to inhabit the history of colonial liberal modernity, the Northern Nigeria constitutional experience offers enduring lessons on the law and politics of the modern state's governance of religious difference.

---

[18] Gayatri Chakravorty Spivak, A Critique of Postcolonial Reason (Cambridge, MA: Harvard University Press, 1999).

[19] See Jean Comaroff and John L. Comaroff, Theory from the South: Or, How Euro-America Is Evolving Toward Africa (New York: Routledge, 2015); Rabiat Akande, "Neutralizing Secularism: 'Religious Antiliberalism' and The Twentieth Century Global Ecumenical Project," Journal of Law and Religion 37, no. 2 (2022): 284–316.

BIBLIOGRAPHY

ARCHIVAL MATERIALS

National Archives, Kaduna, Nigeria
ACC 230 Vol. S. 6
Acc 344 Constitutional Conference
AS/II 613
Draft Constitution – 1/5/A66
Facts about N. Nig – GX/D4(14/2/D4)
Facts about N. Nig – The Legacies Vol. 1 no. 1, Feb., 2009
Federal Parliamentary Debates (uncatalogued)
Kano Prof File 95
Kano Prof. File 1808
Kano Prof File 2059
Kano Prof. File 2157
Kano Prof File 2182
Kano Prof. File 2874
Kano Prof. File 4011
Kano Prof. File 4867
Laws of the Federation 1948
Legislative Council Debates (uncatalogued)
LK 794
LK 836
LK 1102
LK 1106
LK 1108
LK 1286
MIA R2255
Minfor 11 Vol. 1
Northern Nigeria Law Reports
Northern Nigeria Supplementary Gazette, 1958
EAP535/1/2/25/12
Pol 1/1
POLI/1/4/21
S. MOJ/12/s.1/1
SMOJ 51

S. MOJ51 Vol. 12
SNP 6–17
SOK PROF 6887/10
SPE 1/3/2
Speeches of the Premier (uncatalogued)
Yola Prof/C778/9

National Archives, United Kingdom
CO 583
CO 446
CO 927/158
CO 927/171
CO 957
CO 879
CO1071/292
FO371/113500
DO/186/6
CO 554/372, 1321, 1864, 2496
CO 587
Fco141/13699
CO 554/1534
CO 554/1535
CO 554/1285
CO 554/1941
CO 879/173
CO 879/165
CO879 159
CO 879/176
CO 957/25
CO 554/2594
CO/957/5
CO 957/32
CO 975/75
CO 955/20
CO 554/1943
CO 554/1942
CO/957/08

Special Collections, School of Oriental and African Studies (SOAS), University of London
CBMS/IMC 270
CBMS/IMC/BOX 271
IMC-CBMS/01

PPMS36
PPMS 60/01,10,11,16
PPMS 74/25/105
PPMS 73/02/18
PPMS 60/2/1–7, 5
PPMS 60/01/16

University of Birmingham Cadbury Research Library Special Collections
CMS/B/OMS A9
CMS/B/OMS A2
CMS/B/OMS A3
CMS/A3/L5/1898

Center for the Study of World Christianity, University of Edinburgh
Sudan United Missions (Nigeria) Collections (uncatalogued)

Lambeth Palace Library
MC/OV/AFRICA/5
MEC/MISS/SOC/3
MS3122
Bell 97
Tait 127, 137, 152, 159
Ramsey 91, 105, 109, 123, 141, 148, 149, 150, 195
Ramsey 150
Ramsey 105
Davidson 179
Fisher 250

Church of England Record Center
BCC/DIA/7/3/4/3
MC/OV/AFRICA/5
MEC/MISS/SOC/3
CERC PB 023
CCIA11X/8

Adam Mathew Digital Collection
Confidential Print Series: CO 879 & DO 201

University of Illinois Urbana-Champaign (Digitized Books Initiative)
Annual Reports of the Colonies, Nigeria 1897–1938

PUBLISHED BOOKS, ARTICLES, AND REPORTS

Aba, Alkasum, ed. *The Politics of Mallam Aminu Kano*. Lagos: Vanguard Publishers, 1993.

Abd Allah Ibn Abū Zayd, Al Khairuwani. *First Steps in Muslim Jurisprudence: Consisting of Excerpts from Bakurat-Al-Sa'd of Ibn Abu Zayd*. Translated by Alexander David Russell and Abdullah Al-Ma'mun Suhrawardy. London: Luzac & Co., 1906.

Abou El Fadl, Khaled. *And God Knows the Soldiers: The Authoritative and Authoritarian in Islamic Discourses*. Lanham: University Press of America, 2001.

——— *Speaking in God's Name: Islamic Law, Authority and Women*. New York: Simon & Schuster, 2014.

Abu Odeh, Lama. "Review: Wael Hallaq, the Impossible State: Islam, Politics, and Modernity's Moral Predicament by Wael Hallaq." *International Journal of Middle East Studies* 46, no. 1 (2014): 216–218.

——— "The Relationship between Islamic and Customary Law in the Sudan." *Journal of African Law* 4, no. 1 (1960): 16.

——— "Sudan Government v. Milton Thompson." *The Sudan Law Journal and Reports* (1963): 56–59.

Ackerman, Bruce. *Social Justice in the Liberal State*. New Haven: Yale University Press, 1980.

Adamu, Mahdi. "Foreword." In *Islamic Law in Nigeria: Application and Teaching*, edited by Syed Khalid Rashid. Lagos: Islamic Publications Bureau, 1988.

Adcock, Catherine S. *The Limits of Tolerance: Indian Secularism and the Politics of Religious Freedom*. Oxford: Oxford University Press, 2013.

Adebanwi, Wale. "A Nation Betrayed: Nigeria and the Minorities Commission of 1957." *African Affairs* 111, no. 443 (2012): 335–337.

Adebanwi, Wale, and Ebenezer Obadare., eds. *Democracy and Prebendalism in Nigeria: Critical Interpretations*. New York: Palgrave Macmillan, 2013.

Adeleye, Rowland Aderemi. "Mahdist Triumph and British Revenge in Northern Nigeria: Satiru 1906." *Journal of the Historical Society of Nigeria* 6, no. 2 (1972): 193–214.

Adigwe, Hypolite A. *Nigeria Joins the Organisation of Islamic Conference, OIC: The Implications for Nigeria*. Archdiocesan Secretariat, Catholic Archdiocese of Onitsha, 1986.

Ady, Cecilia M. *The Church of England and How It Works*. London: Faber and Faber, 1940.

Agrama, Hussein. "Secularism, Sovereignty, Indeterminacy: Is Egypt a Secular or a Religious State?" *Comparative Studies in Society and History* 52, no. 3 (2010): 495–523.

——— *Questioning Secularism: Islam, Sovereignty, and the Rule of Law in Modern Egypt*. Chicago: University of Chicago Press, 2012.

Ahanotu, Austin Metumara, ed. *Religion, State, and Society in Contemporary Africa: Nigeria, Sudan, South Africa, Zaire, and Mozambique.* New York: Peter Lang, 1992.
Ajetunmobi, Musa Ali. *Shariah Legal Practice in Nigeria 1956–1983.* Ilorin, Nigeria: Kawara State University Press, 2017.
Akande, Rabiat. "Neutralizing Secularism: 'Religious Antiliberalism' and the Twentieth Century Global Ecumenical Project." *Journal of Law and Religion* 37, no. 2 (2022): 284–316.
Akande, Rabiat, Wendell Marsh, and Ann McDougall. "The Making of the Islamic World: Islam at a Crossroads in West Africa." Ottoman History Podcast, January 13, 2021, www.ottomanhistorypodcast.com/p/the-making-of-islamic-world.html
Akinyele, Rufus Taiwo. "States Creation in Nigeria: The Willink Report in Retrospect." *African Studies Review* 39, no. 2 (1996): 71–94.
Al-Azami, Muhammad Mustafa. *On Schacht's Origins of Muslim Jurisprudence.* Oxford: Oxford Centre for Islamic Studies, 1996.
Al Jundi, Khalil Ibn Ishaq. *Hedaya.* Translated by Charles Hamilton. London: W. H. Allen, 1870.
Al Juwayni, Abu Al Ma'ala. *Kitab al Ijtihad min Kitab al Talkhis.* Edited by. Abdul-Hamid Abu Zunayr. Damscus: Dar Al Qalam, 1987.
Alkasum, Abba, ed. *The Politics of Malam Aminu Kano.* Kaduna: Vanguard Printers, 1993.
Allott, Antony Nicholas. "The London Conference on the Future of Law in Africa." *African Studies Bulletin* 3, no. 2 (1960): 13–15.
Allyn, David Edley. "The Sabon Gari System in Northern Nigeria, 1911–1940." PhD diss. University of California, Los Angeles, 1976.
An-Nai'im, Abdullahi Ahmed, ed. *Proselytization and Communal Self-Determination in Africa.* Eugene: Wipf and Stock Publishers, 2009.
Andersen, Casper, and Andrew Cohen, eds. *The Government and Administration of Africa, 1880–1939: Recruitment and Training.* London: Routledge, 2017.
Anderson, James Norman Dalrymple. "A Major Advance." *The Modern Law Review* 24, no. 5 (1961): 616–625.
"Conflict of Laws in Northern Nigeria: A New Start." *International & Comparative Law Quarterly* 8, no. 3 (1959): 442–443.
"Homicide in Islamic Law." *Bulletin of the School of Oriental and African Studies* 13, no. 4 (1951): 811–828.
Islamic Law in Africa. Oxon: Routledge, 2013.
"Islamic Law in African Colonies." *Corona, the Journal of His Majesty's Colonial Service* 3 (1951): 265.
Aniagolu, Anthony Nnaemezie. *The Making of the 1989 Constitution of Nigeria.* Ibadan, Nigeria: Spectrum Books, 1993.
Anjum, Ovamir. *Politics, Law, and Community in Islamic Thought: The Taymiyyan Moment.* Cambridge: Cambridge University Press, 2012.

Annual Report of the Education Department of Northern Nigeria, 1952–1953. Kaduna: Government Printer, 1954.
Asad, Talal. *Formations of the Secular: Christianity, Islam, Modernity*. Stanford: Stanford University Press, 2003.
Ayandele, Emmanuel Ayankanmi. *The Missionary Impact on Modern Nigeria, 1842–1914: A Political and Social Analysis*. London: Longmans, 1966.
Ayandele, E. O. "The Missionary Factor in Northern Nigeria 1870–1918." In *The History of Christianity in West Africa*, edited by Ogbu Kalu, 133–158. London: Longman, 1982.
Ayoub, Samy. *Law, Empire, and the Sultan: Ottoman Imperial Authority and Late Hanafi Jurisprudence*. Oxford: Oxford University Press, 2019.
Ayuba, Jonathan Mamu. "The Bible and Political Revolution: Religion and Minority Politics in Northern Nigeria, 1945–1957." *Journal of the Historical Society of Nigeria* 17, (2007): 138–150.
Backwell, Henry Flemming. *The Occupation of Hausaland, 1900–1904, Being a Translation of Arabic Letters Found in the House of the Wazir of Sokoto Bohari in 1903*. London: Frank Cass, 1969.
Balogun, Ismail A. B. *The Life and Works of Uthman Dan Fodio: The Muslim Reformer of West Africa*. Lagos: Islamic Publications Bureau, 1975.
Bamali, Nuhu. "Islamic Courts Must Remain." *Nigerian Citizen*. October 27, 1955.
Banerjee, Prathama. "Re-Presenting Pasts: Santals in Nineteenth-Century Bengal." In *History and the Present*, edited by Partha Chatterjee and Anjan Ghosh. Delhi: Permanent Black, 2002.
Barnes, Andrew E. "Christianity and the Colonial State in Northern Nigeria: 1900–1960." In *Nigeria in the Twentieth Century*, edited by Toyin Falola, 281–292. Durham, NC: Carolina Academic Press, 2002.
——— "'Evangelization Where It Is Not Wanted': Colonial Administrators and Missionaries in Northern Nigeria during the First Third of the Twentieth Century." *Journal of Religion in Africa* (1995): 412–441.
——— *Making Headway: The Introduction of Western Civilization in Colonial Northern Nigeria*. Rochester: University of Rochester Press, 2009.
——— "The Colonial Legacy to Contemporary Culture in Northern Nigeria 1900–1960." In *Power and Nationalism in Modern Africa: Papers in Honor of Don Ohadike*, edited by Toyin Falola and Salah M. Hassan, 257–262. Durham, NC: Carolina Academic Press, 2008.
——— "The 'Great Prohibition': The Expansion of Christianity in Northern Nigeria," *History Compass* 8, no. 6 (2010): 440–454.
Bates, Miner Searle. *Religious Liberty: An Inquiry*. New York and Landon: Harper Bros, 1945.
Belich, James. *The Victorian Interpretation of Racial Conflict: The Maori, the British, and the New Zealand Wars*. McGill: Queen's University Press, 1989.

Bell, George K. *The Kingship of Christ: The Story of the World Council of Churches*. Middlesex: Penguin Books, 1954.
Bello, Ahmadu. "Reply to Mr. Justin Price's Attacks on the Legal Reforms in Northern Nigeria." *Lagos Magazine*, October 28, 1961.
Work and Worship: Selected Speeches of Sir Ahmadu Bello, Sardauna of Sokoto. Zaria: Gaskiya Corporation, 1986.
Berman, Nathaniel. "'But the Alternative Is Despair': European Nationalism and the Modernist Renewal of International Law." *Harvard Law Review* 106, no. 8 (1993): 1792–1903.
Bhargava, Rajeev. *Secularism and Its Critics*. New York: Oxford University Press, 1999.
Bingham, Rowland Victor. "Britain's Crisis in Missionary Policy: A Missionary Secretary's Appeal for Prayer, and a Protest against an Un-British Autocracy in a Great British Colony." *The Evangelical Christian* (1919): 165.
Boer, Jan Harm. *Missionary Messengers of Liberation in a Colonial Context: A Case Study of the Sudan United Mission*. Amsterdam: Rodopi, 1979.
Bouwman, Bastiaan. "From Religious Freedom to Social Justice: The Human Rights Engagement of the Ecumenical Movement from the 1940s to the 1970s." *Journal of Global History* 13, no. 2 (2018): 252–273.
Brooke, Neville J. *Report of the Native Courts (Northern Provinces) Commission of Inquiry Laid on the Table of the House of Representatives as Sessional Paper No. 1 of 1952*. Lagos, Nigeria: Federal Government Printer, 1952.
Brown, Callum. *The Death of Christian Britain: Understanding Secularisation, 1800–2000*. London: Routledge, 2009.
Brown, Wendy. "Civilizational Delusions: Secularism, Tolerance, Equality." *Theory & Event* 15, no. 2 (2012).
Brunner, Emil. "Secularism as a Problem for the Church." *International Review of Mission* 19, no. 76 (1930): 498.
Buell, Raymond Leslie. *The Native Problem in Africa*, Vol. 1. New York: Macmillan, 1928.
Bukhari, Muhammad bin Ismail. *Sahih Bukhari*. Translated by Dr. Muhammad Muhsin Khan. India: Darussalam, 1997.
Bunza, Mukhtar Umar. *Christian Missions among Muslims: Sokoto Province, Nigeria 1935–1990*. Trenton, NJ: Africa World Press, 2007.
Burak, Guy. *The Second Formation of Islamic Law*. New York: Cambridge University Press, 2015.
Burguière, André, and Raymond Grew, eds. *The Construction of Minorities: Cases for Comparison across Time and around the World*. Ann Arbor: University of Michigan Press, 2001.
Buxton, Thomas Fowell. *The African Slave Trade and Its Remedy*. London: Murray, 1840.
Cady, Linell and Elizabeth Hurd. *Comparative Secularism in a Global Age*. New York: Palgrave MacMillan, 2010.

Cameron, Donald. "Native Administration in Tanganyika and Nigeria." *Journal of the Royal African Society* 36, no. 145 (1937): 3–29.
 The Principles of Native Administration and Their Application. Lagos, Nigeria: The Government Printer, 1934.
Casanova, José. *Public Religions in the Modern World*. Chicago: University of Chicago Press, 2011.
 "The Secular and Secularisms." *Social Research: An International Quarterly* 76, no. 4 (2009): 1049–1066.
Chanock, Martin. *Law, Custom, and Social Order: The Colonial Experience in Malawi and Zambia*. Cambridge: Cambridge University Press, 1985.
Chatterjee, Nandini. *The Making of Indian Secularism: Empire, Law and Christianity, 1830–1960*. New York: Palgrave Macmillan, 2011.
Chatterjee, Partha. "Secularism and Toleration." *Economic and Political Weekly* 29, no. 28 (1994): 1768–1777.
Chaudhry, Ayesha. *Domestic Violence and the Islamic Tradition*. Oxford: Oxford University Press, 2013.
Christelow, Allan. "Islamic Law and Judicial Practice in Nigeria: An Historical Perspective." *Journal of Muslim Minority Affairs* 22, no. 1 (2002): 185–204.
 "Persistence and Transformation in the Politics of Shariʿa, Nigeria, 1947–2003: In Search of an Explanatory Framework." In *Muslim Family Law in Sub-Saharan Africa: Colonial Legacies and Post-colonial Challenges*, edited by Shamil Jeppie, Ebrahim Moosa, and Richard Roberts, 247–272. Amsterdam: Amsterdam University Press, 2010.
 "Three Islamic Voices in Contemporary Nigeria." In *Islam and the Political Economy of Meaning*, edited by William Roff, 234–235. Oakland: University of California Press, 1987.
 ed. *Thus Ruled Emir Abbas: Selected Cases from the Records of the Emir of Kano's Judicial Council*. East Lansing: Michigan State University Press, 1994.
Clapperton, Hugh. *Journal of a Second Expedition into the Interior of Africa from the Bight of Benin to Soccatoo*. Philadelphia: Carey, Lea and Carey, 1829.
Clarke, Morgan. *Islam and Law in Lebanon: Shariʿa within and without the State*. Cambridge: Cambridge University Press, 2018.
Colonial Reports-Annual, no. 346, Northern Nigeria, 1900–01. His Majesty's Stationery Office: 1902.
Colonial Reports-Annual, no. 409, Northern Nigeria, 1902. His Majesty's Stationery Office: 1903.
Colonial Reports-Annual, no. 437, Northern Nigeria, 1903. His Majesty's Stationery Office: 1905.
Colonial Reports-Annual, no. 551, Northern Nigeria, 1906. His Majesty's Stationery Office: 1907.
Colonial Reports-Annual, no. 704, Northern Nigeria, 1910–11. His Majesty's Stationery Office: 1913.

Colonial Reports-Annual, no. 738, Northern Nigeria, 1911. His Majesty's Stationery Office, 1912.

Comaroff, Jean, and John L. Comaroff. *Of Revelation and Revolution: Christianity, Colonialism, and Consciousness in South Africa*, Vol. 1. Chicago: University of Chicago Press, 2008.

Theory from the South: Or, How Euro-America Is Evolving toward Africa. New York: Routledge, 2015.

Comaroff, John. "Colonialism, Culture, and the Law: A foreword." *Law & Social Inquiry* 26, no. 2 (2001): 305–314.

Comaroff, John. "Reflections on the Rise of Legal Theology: Law and Religion in the Twenty-First Century." *Social Analysis* 53, no. 1 (2009): 193–216.

The Politics of Custom: Chiefship, Capital, and the State in Contemporary Africa. Chicago: University of Chicago Press, 2018.

Committee Representing Principal Cultures of the World. "The Statement of Essential Human Rights." *The American Law Institute*, December 10, 2018, www.ali.org/news/articles/statement-essential-human-rights/.

Cooper, Frederick, and Ann Laura Stoler, eds. *Tensions of Empire: Colonial Cultures in a Bourgeois World*. Berkeley: University of California Press, 1997.

Copland, Ian. "Christianity as an Arm of Empire: The Ambiguous Case of India Under the Company, c. 1813–1858." *Historical Journal* 49, no. 4 (2006): 1025–1054.

Cossman, Brenda, and Ratna Kapur. *Secularism's Last Sigh?: Hindutva and the (Mis) Rule of Law*. Oxford: Oxford University Press, 2001.

"Secularism's Last Sigh: The Hindu Right, the Courts, and India's Struggle for Democracy." *Harvard International Law Journal* 38, no. 1 (1997): 113.

Coulson, Noel James. *A History of Islamic Law*. New Brunswick, NJ: Aldine Transaction, 2011.

Crampton, Edmund Patrick Thurman. *Christianity in Northern Nigeria*. London: Burns and Oates, 1979.

Crocker, Walter Russell. *Nigeria: A Critique of British Colonial Administration*. London: Allen and Unwin, 1936.

Dajani, Adel A. *From Jerusalem to a Kingdom by the Sea*. London: Zuleika Books, 2021.

Daly, Samuel Fury Childs. *A History of the Republic of Biafra: Law, Crime, and the Nigerian Civil War*. Cambridge: Cambridge University Press, 2020.

Danchin, Peter G. "Islam in the Secular Nomos of the European Court of Human Rights." *Michigan Journal of International Law* 32, no. 4 (2010): 663–748.

Dudley, Billy. *Parties and Politics in Northern Nigeria*. London: Routledge, 2013.

Dudley, Billy J. "Federalism and the Balance of Political Power in Nigeria." *Journal of Commonwealth & Comparative Politics* 4, no. 1 (1966): 16–29.

Dulles, John F. *A Just and Durable Peace: Discussion of Political Propositions (Six Pillars of Peace)*. New York: Commission to Study the Bases of a Just and Durable Peace, 1943.
Elias, Taslim O. *The Nigerian Legal System*. London: Routledge, 1963.
Eliot, Thomas Stearns. *Essays Ancient and Modern*. New York: Harcourt Brace, 1936.
——— *The Idea of a Christian Society*. New York: Harcourt Brace and Company, 1940.
Eltantawi, Sarah. *Shari'ah on Trial: Northern Nigeria's Islamic Revolution*. Oakland: University of California Press, 2017.
Emon, Anver M. *Religious Pluralism and Islamic Law: Dhimmis and Others in the Empire of Law*. Oxford: Oxford University Press, 2012.
Enwerem, Iheanyi M. *A Dangerous Awakening: The Politicization of Religion in Nigeria*. Ibadan, Nigeria: IFRA-Nigeria, 1995.
Evans, Malcom D. *Religious Liberty and International Law in Europe*. Cambridge: Cambridge University Press, 2008.
Ezera, Kalu. *Constitutional Development in Nigeria*. Cambridge: Cambridge University Press, 1960.
Falola, Toyin, ed. *Nigeria in the Twentieth Century*. Durham, NC: Carolina Academic Press, 2002.
Falola, Toyin. *Violence in Nigeria: The Crisis of Religious Politics and Secular Ideologies*. Rochester: University of Rochester Press, 2001.
Falola, Toyin, and Salah M. Hassan, eds. *Power and Nationalism in Modern Africa: Papers in Honor of Don Ohadike*. Durham, NC: Carolina Academic Press, 2008.
Feinstein, Alan. *African Revolutionary: The Life and Times of Nigeria's Aminu Kano*. New York: Quadrangle, 1973.
Feldman, Noah. "Religion and the Earthly City." *Social Research: An International Quarterly* 76, no. 4 (2009): 989–1000.
Fika, Adamu Mohammed. *The Kano Civil War and British Over-rule: 1882–1940*. New York: Oxford University Press, 1978.
Fuerst, Ilyse R. Morgenstein. *Indian Muslim Minorities and the 1857 Rebellion: Religion, Rebels and Jihad*. London: Bloomsbury Publishing, 2017.
Gailey, Harry A. *Sir Donald Cameron: Colonial Governor*. Stanford, CA: Hoover Institution Press, 1974.
Galanter, Marc. "Secularism, East and West." *Comparative Studies in Society and History* 7, no. 2 (1965): 133–159.
Gana, Idris. "Not Necessarily." *Nigerian Citizen*, November 10, 1955.
Gest, John Marshall. "The Influence of Biblical Texts upon English Law." *University of Pennsylvania Law Review and American Law Register* 59, no. 1 (1910): 15–38.
Glendon, Mary Ann. *A World Made New: Eleanor Roosevelt and the Universal Declaration of Human Rights*. New York: Random House Trade Paperbacks, 2001.

Gloster, Patricia C. "The Evolution of Maliki Law in Northern Nigeria 1930–1960." PhD diss. Columbia University, 1987.
Gluckman, Max. "The Village Headman in British Central Africa: Introduction." *Africa: Journal of the International African Institute* 19, no. 2 (April 1949): 89–94.
Goldstick, Isidore. "Where Jews Can't Pray." *Contemporary Jewish Record* 6, no. 6 (1943): 587.
Graham, Sonia. "A History of Education in Relation to the Development of the Protectorate of Northern Nigeria 1900–1919, with Special Reference to the Work of Hans Vischer." PhD diss. University of London, 1955.
    Government and Mission Education in Northern Nigeria 1900–1919: With Special Reference to the Work of Hanns Vischer. Ibadan, Nigeria: Ibadan University Press, 1966.
Green, Arnold H., ed. In *Quest of an Islamic Humanism: Arabic and Islamic Studies in Memory of Mohamed al-Nowaihi.* Cairo: American University in Cairo Press, 1986.
Greenberg, Udi. "Catholics, Protestants and the Tortured Path to Religious Liberty." *Journal of the History of Ideas* 79, no. 3 (2018): 461–479.
    "Protestants, Decolonization, and European integration, 1885–1961." *The Journal of Modern History* 89, no. 2 (2017): 314–354.
Grubb, Kenneth, "London Conference Faces Problems." *The Church of England Newspaper*, May 31, 1957.
Grubb, Kenneth George. *Crypts of Power: An Autobiography.* London: Hodder and Stoughton, 1971.
Gründer, Horst. "Christian Missionary Activities in Africa in the Age of Imperialism and the Berlin Conference of 1884–1885." In *Bismarck, Europe, and Africa: The Berlin Africa Conference 1884–1885 and the Onset of Partition*, edited by Stig Förster, Wolfgang J. Mommsen, and Ronald Robinson. New York: Oxford University Press, 1988.
Gumi, Abubakar. *Where I Stand.* Ibadan, Nigeria: Spectrum Books, 1992.
Hailey, William Malcolm. *Native Administration and Political Development in British Tropical Africa.* Nenldeln, Liechtenstein: Kraus Reprint, 1979.
    Native Administration in the British African Territories: West Africa: Nigeria, Gold Coast, Sierra Leone, Gambia, Vol. 3. London: HM Stationery Office, 1951.
Hallaq, Wael. *Shari'a: Theory, Practice, Transformations.* New York: Cambridge University Press, 2009.
Hargreaves, John D. *Decolonization in Africa.* London: Routledge, 2014.
Harnischfeger, Johannes. *Democratization and Islamic Law: The Sharia Conflict in Nigeria.* Frankfurt: Campus Verlag, 2008.
Hashmi, Sohail H., ed. *Just Wars, Holy Wars, and Jihads: Christian, Jewish, and Muslim Encounters and Exchanges.* Oxford: Oxford University Press, 2012.
Hassan, Ahmad. "The Principle of Istiḥsān in Islamic Jurisprudence." *Islamic Studies* 16, no. 4 (1977): 347–362.

Hatch, John Charles. *Africa: The Rebirth of Self-Rule*. Oxford: Oxford University Press, 1967.

Hill, Enid. "Al-Sanhuri and Islamic Law: The Place and Significance of Islamic Law in the Life and Work of 'Abd al-Razzaq Ahmad Al-Sanhuri, Egyptian Jurist and Scholar, 1895–1971." *Arab Law Quarterly* 3, no. 1 (1988): 33–64.

Hirschl, Ran. *Constitutional Theocracy*. Cambridge, MA: Harvard University Press, 2010.

Hirschl, Ran and Ayelet Shachar. "Competing Orders? The Challenge of Religion to Modern Constitutionalism." *The University of Chicago Law Review* 85, no. 2 (2018): 425–455.

Hiskett, Mervyn. *The Course of Islam in Africa*. Edinburgh: Edinburgh University Press, 1994.

"Kitāb Al-Farq: A Work on the Habe Kingdoms Attributed to 'Uthmān Dan Fodio." *SOAS Bulletin* 23, no. 3 (1960): 558–579.

The Sword of Truth: The Life and Times of the Shehu Usuman dan Fodio. Oxford: Oxford University Press, 1973.

Hoffmann, Stefan-Ludwig, ed. *Human Rights in the Twentieth Century*. Cambridge: Cambridge University Press, 2011.

Hohfeld, Wesley Newcomb. "Some Fundamental Legal Conceptions as Applied in Judicial Reasoning." *The Yale Law Journal* 23, no. 1 (1913): 16–59.

Holt, Thomas. *The Problem of Freedom: Race, Labor, and Politics in Jamaica and Britain, 1832–1938*. Baltimore, MD: JHU Press, 1992.

Hooft, W. A. Visser't. *Memoirs of W. A. Visser't Hooft*. Philadelphia: Westminster Press, 1973.

Huntington, Samuel P. *The Clash of Civilizations and the Remaking of the Modern World*. New York: Simon and Schuster, 1996.

Hussin, Iza R. *The Politics of Islamic Law: Local Elites, Colonial Authority, and the Making of the Muslim State*. Chicago: University of Chicago Press, 2016.

Ibn Fuduye, Uthman. *Ihya' as-Sunnah wa Ikhmad a-Bid'ah*. Translated by Abu Alfa Umar Muhammad Shareef Bin Farid. Sennar, Sudan: Sankore, 1998.

Ibn Ishak, Khalil. *Précis de jurisprudence musulmane ou principes de législation musulmane civile et religieuse selon le rite malékite*. Translated by M. Perron. Paris: Imprimerie Nationale, 1848–52.

Ibn Taymiyya, Taqī al-Dīn Ahmad. *al-Siyāsa al-Shar 'iyya fī Islah al-Rā'ī wa-al-Ra 'iyya*. Beirut: Dār -al Kutub al 'ilmiyyah, 1988.

Ibrahim, Ahmed Fekry. *Pragmatism in Islamic Law: A Social and Intellectual History*. Syracuse, NY: Syracuse University Press, 2015.

Ikime, Obaro. "The Establishment of Indirect Rule in Northern Nigeria." *Tarikh* 3, no. 3 (1971): 1–15.

Ikime, Obaro. "Reconsidering Indirect Rule: The Nigerian Example." *Journal of the Historical Society of Nigeria* 4, no. 3 (1968): 421–438.

Iwobi, Andrew Ubaka. "Tiptoeing through a Constitutional Minefield: The Great Sharia Controversy in Nigeria." *Journal of African Law* 48, no. 2 (2004): 111–164.

Iwuchukwu, Maurinius. *Muslim-Christian Dialogue in Post-Colonial Northern Nigeria: The Challenges of Inclusive Cultural and Religious Pluralism*. Berlin: Springer, 2013.

Jega, Attahiru, Haruna Wakili, Mustapha Ahmad, and Mahmoud Lawal, eds. *Mallam Aminu Kano: Selected Speeches and Writings 1950–1982*. Kano, Nigeria: Mambaya House, Bayero University, 2002.

Jellinek, Georg. *The Declaration of the Rights of Man and of Citizens: A Contribution to Modern Constitutional History*, translated by Max Farrand. New York: H. Holt, 1901.

Jeppie, Shamil, Ebrahim Moosa, and Richard L. Roberts, eds. *Muslim Family Law in Sub-Saharan Africa: Colonial Legacies and Post-colonial Challenges*. Amsterdam: Amsterdam University Press, 2010.

Jonathan T. Reynolds, *The Time of Politics (Zamanin Siyasa): Islam and the Politics of Legitimacy in Northern Nigeria, 1950–1966*. San Francisco: International Scholar Publications, 1998.

Jones, Thomas Jesse. *Education in Africa: A Study of West, South, and Equatorial Africa by the African Education Commission, Under the Auspices of the Phelps-Stokes Fund and Foreign Mission Societies of North America and Europe*. New York: Phelps-Stokes Fund, 1922.

Juma, Dan. "The British Tradition of Federal Ideas: Kenya and Rhodesia in the Interwar and Postwar Years circa 1925–1960." PhD diss. Harvard Law School, 2017.

Kalu, Ogbu, ed. *The History of Christianity in West Africa*. London: Longman, 1982.

Kamali, Mohammad Hashim. *Crime and Punishment in Islamic Law: A Fresh Interpretation*. Oxford: Oxford University Press, 2019.

Principles of Islamic Jurisprudence, 3rd ed. Cambridge: Islamic Texts Society, 2005.

Kane, Ousmane. *Muslim Modernity Postcolonial: Nigeria: A Study of the Society for the Removal of Innovation and Reinstatement of Tradition*. Leiden: Brill, 2003.

Kano, Aminu. "NEPU Would Not Do Away with Islamic Courts-But Sleepy Alkalis, Squatters and 'go-betweens' must all look out." *Nigerian Citizen*, November 10, 1955.

Kastfelt, Niels. *Religion and Politics in Nigeria. A Study in Middle Belt Christianity*. New York: Tauris, 1994.

Kelsay, John. "Saudi Arabia, Pakistan and the Universal Declaration of Human Rights." In *Human Rights and the Conflict of Cultures: Western and Islamic Perspectives on Religious Liberty*, edited by David Little, John

Kelsay, and Abdulaziz A. Sachedina. Columbia: University of South Carolina Press, 1988.

Kendhammer, Brandon. *Muslims Talking Politics: Framing Islam, Democracy, and Law in Northern Nigeria.* Chicago: University of Chicago Press, 2016.

Kennedy, Dane. *Britain and Empire, 1880–1945.* London: Routledge, 2014.

Kennedy, David. "International Human Rights Movement: Part of the Problem?" *Harvard Human Rights Journal* 15 (2002): 101.

Kennedy, Duncan. "Three Globalizations of Law and Legal Thought: 1850–2000." In *The New Law and Economic Development: A Critical Appraisal*, edited by Trubek, David M., and Alvaro Santos. Cambridge: Cambridge University Press, 2006.

Khan, Naveeda. *Muslim Becoming: Aspiration and Skepticism in Pakistan.* Durham, NC: Duke, 2012.

Khan, Zafrullah. *Islam and Human Rights.* Islamabad: Islam International Publications Ltd., 1988.

Kirk-Greene, Anthony H. M. *Crisis and Conflict in Nigeria: A Documentary Sourcebook, 1966–1969*, Vol. 1. New York: Oxford University Press, 1971.

Principles of Native Administration in Nigeria. London: Oxford University Press, 1965.

Kocamaner, Hikmet. "Regulating the Family through Religion: Secularism, Islam, and the Politics of the Family in Turkey." *American Ethnologist* 46, no. 4 (2019): 495–508.

Kolff, Dirk H. A. "The Indian and the British Law Machines: Some Remarks on Law and Society in British India." In *European Expansion and Law: The Encounter of European and Indigenous Law in Nineteenth and Twentieth Century Africa and Asia*, edited by W. J. Mommsen and J. A. de Moor, 201–235. Oxford: Berg, 1992.

Koshenniemi, Martti, Monica Garcia-Salmones Rovira, and Paolo Amorosa, eds. *International Law and Religion: Historical and Contemporary Perspectives.* Oxford: Oxford University Press, 2017.

Kukah, Matthew Hassan. *Religion, Politics and Power in Northern Nigeria.* Ibadan: Spectrum Books, 1993.

Kukah, Matthew Hassan, and Toyin Falola. *Religious Militancy and Self-Assertion: Islam and Politics in Nigeria.* Aldershot, UK: Avebury, 1996.

Kumo, Suleimanu, and Abubakar Aliyu, eds. *Issues in the Nigerian Draft Constitution: Report Conference Held at the Institute of Administration, Ahmadu Bello University, 21st–24th March, 1977.* Zaria, Nigeria: Ahmadu Bello University, 1977.

Laitin, David, "The Sharia Debate and the Origins of Nigeria's Second Republic." *Journal of Modern African Studies* 20, no. 3 (1982): 411–430.

Lange, Christian. "Crime and Punishment in Islamic History (Early to Middle Period): A Framework for Analysis." *Religion Compass* 4, no. 11 (2010): 698.

Last, Murray. *The Sokoto Caliphate.* London: Open Humanities Press, 1967.
Lazarus-Black, Mindie, and Susan F. Hirsch. *Contested States: Law, Hegemony and Resistance.* New York: Routledge, 2012.
Lewis, Bernard. "Siyasa." In *Quest of an Islamic Humanism: Arabic and Islamic Studies in Memory of Mohamed al-Nowaihi*, edited by Arnold H. Green. Cairo: American University in Cairo Press, 1986.
Lindkvist, Linde. "The Politics of Article 18: Religious Liberty in the Universal Declaration of Human Rights." *Humanity: An International Journal of Human Rights, Humanitarianism, and Development* 4, no. 3 (2013): 429–447.
——— *Shrines and Souls: The Reinvention of Religious Liberty and the Genesis of the Universal Declaration of Human Rights.* Lund, Sweden: Bokbox förlag, 2014.
Little, David, John Kelsay, and Abdulaziz A. Sachedina, eds. *Human Rights and the Conflict of Cultures: Western and Islamic Perspectives on Religious Liberty.* Columbia: University of South Carolina Press, 1988.
Loimeier, Roman. *Islamic Reform and Political Change in Northern Nigeria.* Evanston: Northwestern University Press, 2011.
Louis, William Roger. *The Transfer of Power in Africa: Decolonization, 1940–1960.* New Haven, CT: Yale University Press, 1982.
Lucy, Henry William, ed. *Speeches of the Marquis of Salisbury: With a Sketch of His Life.* London: Routledge, 1885.
Lugard, Fredrick John Dealtry. *Political Memoranda, Revision of Instructions to Political Officers on Subjects Chiefly Political and Administrative 1913–1918.* London: Frank Cass, 1970.
——— *Report by Sir F. D. Lugard on the Amalgamation of Northern and Southern Nigeria, and Administration, 1912–1919.* London: H.M. Stationery Office, 1920.
——— *The Dual Mandate in British Tropical Africa.* Edinburgh: W. Blackwood, 1922.
Lydon, Ghislaine. "Inventions and Reinventions of Sharia in African History and the Recent Experiences of Nigeria, Somalia and Mali." *Ufahamu: A Journal of African Studies* 40, no. 1 (2018): 100.
Lynn, Martin. "British Policy, Trade, and Informal Empire in the Mid-Nineteenth Century." In *The Oxford History of the British Empire: Volume III: The Nineteenth Century*, edited by Andrew Porter, 101–121. Oxon: Oxford University Press, 1999.
Macmillan, Harold. "The Wind of Change Speech, Address by Harold Macmillan to Members of Both Houses of the Parliament of the Union of South Africa, Cape Town, 3 February 1960." Accessed December 17, 2021. https://web-archives.univ-pau.fr/english/TD2doc1.pdf.
Magaji, Danbatta. "Religious Freedom Move Can Be Disastrous." *Nigerian Citizen*, June 20, 1956.
Mahmood, Saba. *Religious Difference in a Secular Age: A Minority Report.* Princeton, NJ: Princeton University Press, 2015.

Mahmood, Saba, and Peter G. Danchin. "Immunity or Regulation? Antinomies of Religious Freedom." *South Atlantic Quarterly* 113, no. 1 (2014): 129.

Mahmud, Abdulmalik Bappa. *A Brief History of Shari'ah in the Defunct Northern Nigeria*. Jos, Nigeria: University of Jos Press, 1988.

Malik, Charles Habib. "The Universal Declaration of Human Rights." In Frederick Nolde, *Free and Equal: Human Rights in Ecumenical Perspective with Reflections on the Origin of the Universal Declaration of Human Rights*. Geneva: World Council of Churches, 1968

Mamdani, Mahmood. *Citizen and Subject: Contemporary Africa and the Legacy of Late Colonialism*. Princeton, NJ: Princeton University Press, 1996.

——. *Define and Rule: Native as Political Identity*. Cambridge: Harvard University Press, 2012.

——. *Good Muslim, Bad Muslim: America, the Cold War, and the Roots of Terror*. New York: Pantheon Books, 2004.

——. "Historicizing Power and Responses to Power: Indirect Rule and Its Reform." *Social Research* 66, no. 3 (1999): 859–886.

——. *Neither Settler Nor Native: The Making and Unmaking of Permanent Minorities*. Cambridge, MA: Harvard University Press, 2020.

Mantena, Karuna. *Alibis of Empire: Henry Maine and the Ends of Liberal Imperialism*. Princeton, NJ: Princeton University Press, 2010.

March, Andrew. *Islam and Liberal Citizenship: The Search for an Overlapping Consensus*. Oxford: Oxford University Press, 2009.

Markus, Robert Austin. *Saeculum: History and Society in the Theology of St Augustine*. Cambridge: Cambridge University Press, 1988.

Martin, B. G. "A Muslim Political Tract from Northern Nigeria: Muhammad Bello's Usul al-Siyasa." In *Aspects of West African Islam*, edited by Daniel F. McCall and Norman R. Bennett, 63–86. Boston: African Studies Center, Boston University, 1971.

Massoud, Mark Fathi. "Islamic Law, Colonialism, and Mecca's Shadow in the Horn of Africa." *Journal of Africana Religions* 7, no. 1 (2019): 121–130.

——. *Law's Fragile State: Colonial, Authoritarian, and Humanitarian Legacies in Sudan*. Cambridge: Cambridge University Press, 2013.

——. *Shari'a, Inshallah: Finding God in Somali Legal Politics*. New York: Cambridge University Press, 2021.

Masud, Muhammad, and Armando Salvatore, eds. *Islam and Modernity: Key Issues and Debates*. Edinburgh: Edinburgh University Press, 2009.

Masuzawa, Tomoko. *The Invention of World Religions: Or, How European Universalism Was Preserved in the Language of Pluralism*. Chicago: University of Chicago Press, 2005.

Mawani, Renisa, and Iza Hussin. "The Travels of Law: Indian Ocean Itineraries." *Law and History Review* 32, no. 4 (2014): 733–747.

Maxwell, J. Lowry. *Half a Century of Grace: A Jubilee History of the Sudan United Mission*. Westcliff-on-Sea, UK: Sudan United Mission, 1953.

Mazower, Mark. "Minorities and the League of Nations in Interwar Europe." *Daedalus* 126, no. 2 (1997): 47–63.
  No Enchanted Palace: The End of Empire and the Ideological Origins of the United Nations. Princeton, NJ: Princeton University Press, 2009.
  "The Strange Triumph of Human Rights, 1933–1950." *Historical Journal* 47, no. 2 (2004): 379–398.
McCall, Daniel F., and Norman R. Bennett, eds. *Aspects of West African Islam*. Boston: Boston University, African Studies Center, 1971.
McConnell, Michael, W. "Why Protect Religious Freedom?" *The Yale Law Journal* 123, no. 3 (2013): 770–810.
Merivale, Herman. *Lectures on Colonization and Colonies Delivered before the University of Oxford in 1839, 1840 and 1841*. London: Longman, Orme, Brown, Green, and Longmans, 1861.
Messick, Brinkley M. *The Calligraphic State: Textual Domination and History in a Muslim Society*. Berkeley: University of California Press, 1993.
Metcalf, Thomas R. *Aftermath of Revolt: India 1857–1970*. Princeton, NJ: Princeton University Press, 2015.
  Imperial Connections: India in the Indian Ocean Arena, 1860–1920. Berkely: University of California Press, 2008.
Milner, Alan. *African Penal Systems*. London: Routledge, 1969.
Mitoma, Glenn. "Charles H. Malik and Human Rights: Notes on a Biography." *Biography* 33, no. 1 (2010): 222–224.
Moosa, Ebrahim. "Colonialism and Islamic Law." In *Islam and Modernity: Key Issues and Debates*, edited by Muhammad Khalid Masud, 158–184. Edinburgh: Edinburgh University Press, 2009.
Morel, Edmund Dene. *Affairs of West Africa*. New York: Routledge, 2013.
  Nigeria: Its People and Problems. Oxfordshire: Taylor and Francis, 1968.
Morsink, Johannes. *The Universal Declaration of Human Rights: Origins, Drafting, and Intent*. Philadelphia: University of Pennsylvania Press, 1999.
Moustafa, Tamir. *Constituting Religion: Islam, Liberal Rights, and the Malaysian State*. Cambridge: Cambridge University Press, 2018.
  "Judging in God's Name: State Power, Secularism, and the Politics of Islamic Law in Malaysia." *Oxford Journal of Law and Religion* 3, no. 1 (2013): 156.
  "The Judicialization of Religion." *Law & Society Review* 52, no. 3 (2018): 685–708.
Moyn, Samuel. *Christian Human Rights*. Philadelphia: University of Pennsylvania Press, 2015.
Moyn, Samuel. "The First Historian of Human Rights." *The American Historical Review* 116, no. 1 (2011): 58.
Moyn, Samuel. "Hannah Arendt on the Secular." *New German Critique* 35, no. 3 (105) (2008): 71–96.
  The Last Utopia: Human Rights in History. Cambridge: Harvard University Press, 2012.

"Personalism, Community, and the Origins of Human Rights." In *Human Rights in the Twentieth Century*, edited by Stefan-Ludwig Hoffmann. Cambridge: Cambridge University Press, 2011.

Mutua, Makau. *Human Rights: A Political and Cultural Critique*. Philadelphia: University of Pennsylvania Press, 2013.

Myers, Frank. "Harold Macmillan's 'Winds of Change' Speech: A Case Study in the Rhetoric of Policy Change." *Rhetoric and Public Affairs* 3, no. 4 (2000): 555–575.

Native Courts and Native Customary Law in Africa: Judicial Advisers Conference 1953. A Special Supplement to the Journal of African Administration. London: Her Majesty's Stationery Office, 1953.

Nchi, Suleiman Ismaila, and Samaiʻla Abdullahi Mohammed, eds. *Alhaji Sir Ahmadu Bello, Sardauna of Sokoto: His Thoughts and Vision in His Own Words: Selected Speeches and Letters of the Great Leader*. Makurdi, Nigeria: Oracle, 1999.

Nigeria Constituent Assembly. *Proceedings of the Constituent Assembly*. Lagos: Federal Ministry of Information, Printing Division, 1977.

Nigeria Constituent Assembly. *Proceedings of the Nigeria Constituent Assembly: Official Report 1977*, Vols. 1 and 2. Lagos: Federal Ministry of Information, 1977.

Nigeria. *Federal Census Office. Population Census of Nigeria, 1952–3*. Lagos: The Census Superintendent, 1953.

Nigeria. *Federal Census Office. Population Census of Nigeria, 1963*, Lagos: The Census Superintendent, 1964.

Nigeria. *Proceedings of the Constituent Assembly, Nigeria, 1978*, Vols. 1 and 2. Lagos: Federal Government Press, 1978.

Nigerian Citizen. "Christmas Day Message: Forget Religious Differences Says North Premier." December 28, 1957.

Nigerian Supreme Council for Islamic Affairs. "What We Stand For." New Nigerian, January 23, 1987.

"About." NSCIA. Accessed January 7, 2023. www.nscia.com.ng/about.

Nigerian Tribune. "Fundamental Rights May Be Started in 1959." August 11, 1958.

Nmehielle, Vincent O. "Sharia Law in the Northern States of Nigeria: To Implement or Not to Implement, the Constitutionality Is the Question." *Human Rights Quarterly* 26, no. 3 (2004): 730–759.

Nolde, O. Frederick. *Free and Equal: Human Rights in Ecumenical Perspective with Reflections on the Origin of the Universal Declaration of Human Rights*. Geneva: World Council of Churches, 1968.

———, ed. *Freedom's Charter: The Universal Declaration of Human Rights*. New York: Foreign Policy Association, 1949.

———. "Review: Religious Liberty: An Inquiry, by M. Searle Bates." *The Annals of the American Academy of Political and Social Science* 243, no. 1 (1946): 150–151.

Nurser, John. *For All Peoples and All Nations: The Ecumenical Church and Human Rights.* Washington, DC: Georgetown University Press, 2005.

Nzeogwu, Chukwuma Kaduna. "Radio Broadcast by Major Chukwuma Kaduna Nzeogwu – Announcing Nigeria's First Military Coup on Radio Nigeria, Kaduna on January 15, 1966." *Vanguard,* September 30, 2010, www.vanguardngr.com/2010/09/radio-broadcast-by-major-chukwuma-kaduna-nzeogwu---announcing-nigeria's-first-military-coup-on-radio-nigeria-kaduna-on-january-15-1966/.

Oba, Abdulmumini. "Islamic Law as Customary Law: The Changing Perspective in Nigeria." *International and Comparative Law Quarterly* 51, no. 4 (2002): 817–850.

Obadare, Ebenezer. *Pentecostal Republic: Religion and the Struggle for State Power in Nigeria.* London: Zed Books, 2018.

Ochonu, Moses. *Colonialism by Proxy: Hausa Imperial Agents and Middle Belt Consciousness in Nigeria.* Bloomington, IN: Indiana University Press, 2014.

Odumosu, Olu. "The Northern Nigerian Codes." *The Modern Law Review* 24, no. 5 (September 1961): 612–615.

Oduntan, Oluwatoyin B. "Decolonization and the Minority Question in Nigeria: The Willink Commission Revisited." In *Minority Rights and the National Question in Nigeria,* edited by Uyilawa Usuanlele and Bonny Ibhawoh, 17–39. Cham, Switzerland: Palgrave Macmillan, 2017.

Ofonagoro, Walter Abiola Ojo, and Adele Jinadu, eds. *The Great Debate: Nigerian Viewpoints on the Draft Constitution.* Apapa-Lagos, Nigeria: Daily Times Publication, 1989.

Oldham, Joseph Houldsworth. "'The Educational Work of Missionary Societies." *Africa: Journal of the International African Institute* 7, no. 1 (1934): 47–59.

———. *The Oxford Conference: (Official Report).* Chicago and New York: Willett, Clark, 1937.

Oliver, Roland. "Prologue: The Two Miss Perhams." In *Margery Perham and British Rule in Africa,* edited by Alison Smith and Mary Bull, 2. London: Routledge, 1991.

Orsi, Robert A., ed. *The Cambridge Companion to Religious Studies.* Cambridge: Cambridge University Press, 2011.

Ostien, Philip, "An Opportunity Missed by Nigeria's Christians: The 1976–78 Sharia Debate Revisited." In *Muslim-Christian Encounters in Africa,* edited by Benjamin F. Soares, 221–255. Leiden: Brill, 2006.

———, ed. *Sharia Implementation in Northern Nigeria 1999–2006: A Sourcebook,* Vols. 1, 2, and 3. Ibadan, Nigeria: Spectrum Books, 2007.

Paden, John N. *Ahmadu Bello, Sardauna of Sokoto: Values and Leadership in Nigeria.* Zaria, Nigeria: HudaHuda, 1986.

Padmore, George. "The Kano Riot: The Background." *West African Pilot,* May 29, 1953.

Parkinson, Charles. *Bills of Rights and Decolonization: The Emergence of Domestic Human Rights Instruments in Britain's Overseas Territories.* Oxford: Oxford University Press, 2007.

Peiponen, Matti. *Ecumenical Action in World Politics: The Creation of the Commission of the Churches on International Affairs 1945–1949.* Helsinki: Luther-Agricola-Society, 2012.

Perham, Margery Freda. *Lugard: The Years of Authority, 1898–1945.* London: Collins, 1968.

——— *Native Administration in Nigeria.* New York: Oxford University Press, 1937.

Peters, Rudolph. *Crime and Punishment in Islamic Law: Theory and Practice from the Sixteenth to the Twenty-First Century.* Cambridge: Cambridge University Press, 2006.

Porter, Andrew N., ed. *The Oxford History of the British Empire: Volume III: The Nineteenth Century.* Oxford: Oxford University Press, 1999.

——— "Religion and Empire: British Expansion in the Long Nineteenth Century, 1780–1914." *The Journal of Imperial and Commonwealth History* 20, no. 3 (1992): 370–390.

——— "Margery Perham, Christian Missions and Indirect Rule." *Journal of Imperial and Commonwealth History* 19, no. 3 (October 1991): 83–99.

——— "War, Colonialism and the British Experience: The Redefinition of Christian Missionary Policy, 1938–1952." *Kirchliche Zeitgeschichte* 5, no. 2 (1992): 273–274.

Potter, David C. *India's Political Administrators: From ICS to IAS.* Oxford: Oxford University Press, 1996.

Prasch, Thomas. "Which God for Africa: The Islamic-Christian Missionary Debate in Late-Victorian England." *Victorian Studies* 33, no. 1 (1989): 51–73.

Price, Justin. "Criminal Law Reform in Northern Nigeria: Retrograde Legislation in Northern Nigeria?" *The Modern Law Review* 24, no. 5 (1961): 604–611.

Quraishi-Landes, Asifa. "Islamic Constitutionalism: Not Secular, Not Theocratic, Not Impossible." *Rutgers Journal of Law and Religion* 16, no. 3 (2014): 553–579.

——— "Who Says Shari'a Demands the Stoning of Women? A Description of Islamic Law and Constitutionalism." *Berkeley Journal of Middle Eastern and Islamic Law* 1, no. 1 (2008): 163–178.

Rashid, Syed Khalid, ed. *Islamic Law in Nigeria: Application and Teaching.* Lagos: Islamic Publications Bureau, 1988.

Rawls, John. *A Theory of Justice.* Cambridge: Harvard University Press, 1971.

——— *Political Liberalism.* New York: Columbia University Press, 2005.

Razaq, Abdul G. F. "A Barrister Says North Is Not Ready to Do Away with Them." *Nigerian Citizen*, November 10, 1955.

Reinhart, Kevin, and Robert Gleave. *Islamic Law in Theory: Studies on Jurisprudence in Honor of Bernard Weiss.* Leiden: Brill, 2014.

Renaud, Terence. "Human Rights as Radical Anthropology: Protestant Theology and Ecumenism in the Transwar Era." *The Historical Journal* 60, no. 2 (2017): 493–518.

Reynolds, Jonathan. "Good and Bad Muslims: Islam and Indirect Rule in Northern Nigeria." *International Journal of African Historical Studies* 34, no. 3 (2001): 601–618.

———. *The Time of Politics (Zamanin Siyasa): Islam and the Politics of Legitimacy in Northern Nigeria, 1950–1966.* San Francisco: International Scholars Publications, 1998.

Reynolds, Justin. "Against the World: International Protestantism and the Ecumenical Movement between Secularization and Politics, 1900–1952." PhD diss. Columbia University, 2016.

Richardson, Sam Scruton. *No Weariness: The Memoir of a Generalist in Public Services in Four Continents.* Wiltshire, UK: Malt House Publishing, 2001.

Robbins, Keith. *England, Ireland, Scotland, Wales: The Christian Church 1900–2000.* Oxford: Oxford University Press, 2008.

Robinson, Kenneth E. "Margery Perham and the Colonial Office." *Journal of Imperial and Commonwealth History* 19, no. 3 (October 1991): 185–196.

Roff, William, ed. *Islam and the Political Economy of Meaning.* Oakland: University of California Press, 1987.

Roosevelt, Eleanor. "Introduction." In *Freedom's Charter: The Universal Declaration of Human Rights,* edited by Frederick O. Nolde, 3–4. New York: Foreign Policy Association, 1949.

Russell, Ruth B., and Jeanette E. Muther. *A History of the United Nations Charter: The Role of the United States 1940–1945.* Washington, DC: Brookings Institution, 1958.

Ruxton, Fitz Herbert. *Mâliki Law: Being a Summary from French Translations of the Mukhtasar of Sîdî Khalîl: With Notes and Bibliography.* Wesport: Hyperion Press, 1916.

Saeed, Asmau G. "British Fears over Mahdism in Northern Nigeria: A Look at Bormi 1903, Satiru 1906 and Dumbulwa 1923." *Frankfurter Afrikanistische Blätter* 4 (1992): 34–46.

Salomon, Noah. *For Love of the Prophet: An Ethnography of Sudan's Islamic State.* Princeton, NJ: Princeton University Press, 2016.

Sandel, Michael J. "Religious Liberty: Freedom of Choice and Freedom of Conscience." In *Secularism and Its Critics,* edited by Rajeev Bhargava. New York: Oxford University Press, 1999.

Sanneh, Lamin. *The Crown and the Turban: Muslims and West African Pluralism.* New York: Routledge, 2018.

Schacht, Joseph. "Islam in Northern Nigeria." *Studia Islamica,* no. 8 (1957): 123–146.

Scott, Joan Wallach. *The Politics of the Veil.* Princeton, NJ: Princeton University Press, 2009.

Scott, Peter H. G. *A Survey of Islamic Law in Northern Nigeria in 1952*. Nigeria: Government Printer, 1953.
Seignette, Napoléon. *Code Musalman par Khalil*. Paris: Challamel aîné, 1878.
Singh, Pritam. "Hindu Bias in India's 'Secular' Constitution: Probing Flaws in the Instruments of Governance." *Third World Quarterly* 26, no. 6 (2005): 909–926.
Shankar, Shobana. *Who Shall Enter Paradise? Christian Origins in Muslim Northern Nigeria, ca. 1890–1975*. Athens, OH: Ohio University Press, 2014.
Shapiro, Martin. "Islam and Appeal." *California Law Review* 68, no. 2 (1980): 350–381.
Sharkey, Heather, J. "Jihads and Crusades in Sudan from 1881 to the Present." In *Just Wars, Holy Wars, and Jihads: Christian, Jewish, and Muslim Encounters and Exchanges*, edited by Sohail H. Hashmi, 263–282. Oxford: Oxford University Press, 2012.
Sharp, H., ed. *Selections of Educational Records, Part 1, 1781–1839*. Calcutta: Superintendent, Government Printing, 1920.
Sharwood-Smith, Bryan. *But Always as Friends: Northern Nigeria and the Cameroons, 1921–1957*. London: Allen and Unwin, 1969.
Sklar, Richard L. *Nigerian Political Parties: Power in an Emergent African Nation*. Princeton, NJ: Princeton University Press, 2015.
Skuy, David. "Macaulay and the Indian Penal Code of 1862: The Myth of the Inherent Superiority and Modernity of the English Legal System Compared to India's Legal System in the Nineteenth Century." *Modern Asian Studies* 32, no. 3 (1998): 513–557.
Slotte, Pamela. "Whose Justice? What Political Theology? On Christian and Theological Approaches to Human Rights in the Twentieth and Twenty-first Centuries." In *International Law and Religion: Historical and Contemporary Perspectives*, edited by Martti Koskenniemi, Mónica García-Salmones Rovira, and Paolo Amorosa, 196–218. Oxford: Oxford University Press, 2017.
Smith, Alison, and Mary Bull, eds. *Margery Perham and British Rule in Africa*. London: Routledge, 1991.
Smith, Donald Eugene. *India as a Secular State*. Princeton, NJ: Princeton University Press, 2015.
Smith, Wilfred Cantwell. *The Meaning and End of Religion*. Minneapolis: Fortress Press, 1959.
Soares, Benjamin F., ed. *Muslim-Christian Encounters in Africa*. Leiden: Brill, 2006.
Spivak, Gayatri Chakravorty. *A Critique of Postcolonial Reason*. Cambridge, MA: Harvard University Press, 1999.
Stanley, Brian. *The Bible and the Flag: Protestant Missions and the British Empire in the Nineteenth and Twentieth Centuries*. Townbridge: Apollos, 1990.

The World Missionary Conference, 1910. Grand Rapids: Eerdmans Publishing, 2009.

Stepan, Alfred. *Arguing Comparative Politics*. Oxford: Oxford University, 2001.

——. "Religion, Democracy and the 'Twin Tolerations.'" *Journal of Democracy* 11, no. 4 (2000): 37–57.

Stephens, Julia. *Governing Islam: Law, Empire, and Secularism in Modern South Asia*. Cambridge: Cambridge University Press, 2018.

Stilt, Kristen. *Islamic Law in Action: Authority, Discretion, and Everyday Experiences in Mamluk Egypt*. Oxford: Oxford University Press, 2011.

Stoler, Ann Laura. "Colonial Archives and the Arts of Governance." *Archival Science* 2, no. 1–2 (2002): 87–109.

Su, Anna. *Exporting Freedom: Religious Liberty and American Power*. Cambridge: Harvard University Press, 2016.

Suberu, Rotimi T. "Religion and Institutions: Federalism and the Management of Conflicts over Sharia in Nigeria." *Journal of International Development* 21, no. 4 (2009): 547–560.

Sulaiman, Ibraheem. "Conflict of Values in Nigeria: A Background to the Encounter between Islam and Western Civilization." Paper presented at the Conference on the National Question, Abuja, 1986.

Sulaiman, Ibraheem. *The Islamic State and the Challenge of History: Ideals, Policies and Operation of the Sokoto Caliphate*. London: Mansell, 1987.

Sullivan, Winnifred Fallers. *The Impossibility of Religious Freedom*. 2nd ed. Princeton, NJ: Princeton University Press, 2018.

Sullivan, Winnifred Fallers, Elizabeth Shakman Hurd, Saba Mahmood, and Peter G. Danchin, eds. *Politics of Religious Freedom*. Chicago: University of Chicago Press, 2015.

Taylor, Charles. *A Secular Age*. Cambridge: Harvard University Press, 2007.

——. "Modes of Secularism." In *Secularism and Its Critics*, edited by Rajeev Bhargava. New York: Oxford University Press, 1999.

Temple, Charles L. *Native Races and Their Rulers*. Cape Town: Argus, 1918.

Temple, William. *Papers for War Time: Christianity and War*. Oxford: Oxford University Press, 1914.

Tertsakian, Carina. "Political Shari'a: Human Rights and Islamic Law in Northern Nigeria." *Human Rights Watch* 16, no. 9a (2004), www.hrw.org/report/2004/09/21/political-sharia/human-rights-and-islamic-law-northern-nigeria.

Thompson, Cliff F. "The Failure of Continental Codes in the Democratic Republic of the Sudan – An Analysis," *Verfassung Und Recht in Übersee/Law and Politics in Africa, Asia and Latin America* 8, no. 3/4 (1975): 407–421.

Thompson, Edward Palmer. *Whigs and Hunters: The Origin of the Black Act*. New York: Pantheon Books, 1975.

Thompson, Michael G. *For God and Glove: Christian Internationalism in the United States between the Great War and the Cold War*. New York: Cornell University Press, 2015.

Thompson, Todd. *Norman Anderson and the Christian Mission to Modernize Islam*. Oxford: Oxford University Press, 2018.

Tibenderana, Peter K. "The Emirs and the Spread of Western Education in Northern Nigeria, 1910–1946." *Journal of African History* 24, no. 4 (1983): 517–534.

"The Irony of Indirect Rule in Sokoto Emirate, Nigeria, 1903–1944." *African Studies Review* 31, no. 1 (1988): 67–92.

Turaki, Yusufu. *The British Colonial Legacy in Northern Nigeria: A Social Ethical Analysis of the Colonial and Post-colonial Society and Politics in Nigeria*. Jos, Nigeria: Challenge Press, 1993.

Ubah, Chinedu Nwafor. "Problems of Christian Missionaries in Muslim Emirates, 900–1928." *Journal of African Studies* 3, no. 3 (1976), 351–371.

Umar, Muhammad Sani. *Islam and Colonialism: Intellectual Responses of Muslims of Northern Nigeria to British Colonial Rule*. Leiden: Brill, 2006.

"Hausa Traditional Political Culture, Islam, and Democracy: Historical Perspectives on Three Political Traditions." In *Democracy and Prebendalism in Nigeria: Critical Interpretations*, edited by Wale Adebanwi and Ebenezer Obadare, 177–200. New York: Palgrave Macmillan, 2013.

United Middle Belt Congress. *The Constitution of the United Middle Belt Congress*. Kaduna, Nigeria: Ola Moduro Press, 1955.

Usman, Yusuf Bala. *Beyond Fairy Tales: Selected Historical Writing of Yusuf Bala Usman*. Zaria, Nigeria: Abdullahi Smith Centre for Historical Research, 2006.

The Manipulation of Religion in Nigeria 1977–1987. Kaduna, Nigeria: Vanguard Press, 1987.

Usuanlel, Uyilawa, and Bonny Ibhawoh, eds. *Minority Rights and the National Question in Nigeria*. Cham, Switzerland: Palgrave Macmillan, 2017.

Utuk, Efiong Isaac. *Britain's Colonial Administrations and Developments, 1861–1960: An Analysis of Britain's Colonial Administrations and Developments in Nigeria*. Portland: Portland State University, 1975.

van der Veer, Peter. *Imperial Encounters: Religion and Modernity in India and Britain*. Princeton, NJ: Princeton University Press, 2001.

Vaughan, Olufemi. *Religion and the Making of Nigeria*. Durham, NC: Duke University Press, 2016.

Viswanathan, Gauri. *Outside the Fold: Conversion, Modernity, and Belief*. Princeton, NJ: Princeton University Press, 1998.

Vogel, Frank. "Tracing Nuance in Māwardī's al-Aḥkām al-Sulṭāniyyah: Implicit Framing of Constitutional Authority." In *Islamic Law in Theory: Studies on Jurisprudence in Honor of Bernard Weiss*, edited by Reinhart and Gleave, 331–359 (Leiden: Brill, 2014).

von Albertini, Rudolf. *Decolonization: The Administration and Future of the Colonies, 1919–1960*. Garden City, NY: Doubleday, 1971.
Wael, B. Hallaq. *Shari'a: Theory, Practice, Transformations*. New York: Cambridge University Press, 2009.
   The Impossible State: Islam, Politics, and Modernity's Moral Predicament. New York: Columbia University Press, 2014.
Walzer, Michael, *Exodus and Revolution*. Michigan: Basic Books, 1985.
Watts, Michael J. *Silent Violence: Food, Famine, and Peasantry in Northern Nigeria*, Vol. 15. Athens, GA: University of Georgia Press, 2013.
Wight, Martin. "The Church, Russia, and the West." *The Ecumenical Review* 1, no. 1 (1949): 30.
   The Development of the Legislative Council, 1606–1945. London: Faber and Faber, 1946.
Willink, Henry, ed. *Nigeria: Report of the Commission Appointed to Enquire into the Fears of Minorities and the Means of Allaying Them*. London: Her Majesty's Stationery Office, 1958.
Witte, John. *Religion and the American Constitutional Experiment*. Boulder, CO: Westview Press, 2005.
World Missionary Conference. *Report of Commission VII. Missions and Governments: With Supplement: Presentation and Discussion of the Report in the Conference on 20th June 1910*. Edinburgh: Oliphant, Anderson and Ferrier, 1910.
World Missionary Conference. *Record of the Proceedings of World Missionary Conference, 1910*. Edinburgh: Oliphant, Anderson and Ferrier, 1910.
World Missionary Conference. *Report of the World Missionary Conference Commission I: Carrying of the Gospel to All the Non-Christian World*. Edinburgh: World Missionary Conference, 1910.
Wright, Quincy. "Human Rights and the World Order." *International Conciliation*, no. 389 (1943): 238–262.
Wyndham, Hugh Archibald. "The Native Problem in Africa by Raymond Leslie Buell." *Journal of the Royal Institute of International Affairs* 7, no. 5 (1928): 335–337.
Yadudu, Auwalu H. "Colonialism and the Transformation of the Substance and Form of Islamic Law in the Northern States of Nigeria." *Journal of Law and Religion* 9, no. 1 (1991): 17–47.
Youé, Chris. "Mamdani's History." *Canadian Journal of African Studies* 34, no. 2 (2000): 397–408.
Yusuf, Ahmed Beita. *Nigerian Legal System: Pluralism and Conflict of Laws in the Northern States*. New Delhi: National Publishing House, 1982.
Zubovich, Gene. "The Global Gospel: Protestant Internationalism and American Liberalism, 1940–1960." PhD diss. University of California, Berkeley, 2014.

PUBLISHED CASES

(1985) 1 Sharia Law Reports of Nigeria 94 (FCA/K) (no. CA/3/16S/84).
A.G. Kano v. A.G. Federal Republic of Nigeria (2007) 3 SC.
Ado and Rabi v. Dijjah, Ado v. Dije (1983) 2 Federation of Nigeria Law Reports 213 (FCA/K).
Lagos State Government and others v. Asiyat Abdulkareem and others (Suit SC 910 2016, delivered on June 17, 2022).
Dahlab v. Switzerland (Application no. 42393/98, ECHR 2001-V).
Effiong Ekpo v. Kano N.A (1957) N.R.N.L.R 129.
Fagoji v. Kano NA (1957) NRNLR. 57 (S.C.).
J.S. Olawoyin & Six Others. v. Commissioner of Police (1961) (Supreme Court of Nigeria) 1 All N.L.R. (Part 2) 203.
Katsina NA v. Yakudi of Hababa and Dankoko of Renage (unreported).
Lautsi and ors v. Italy (App no 30814/06 IHRL 3688 ECHR, 2011).
Maizabo v. NA (1957) NRNLR. 133 (S.C).
Manohar Joshi vs. Nitin Bhaurao Patil All India Reports, 1996 SC 796.
Sahin v. Turkey, Application no. 44774/98, Council of Europe.
Tsofo Gubba v. Gwandu Native Authority (1947) WACA vol. 12.
Walz v. Tax Comm'n, 397 U.S. 664, 668–69 (1969).

LEGISLATION

Borno State Repeals and Savings Provisions Law (2000).
Cantonment Courts Proclamation (1902) (N.Ng.).
Ceylon Constitution Order in Council, 1946.
Constitution of the Federal Republic of Nigeria, 1960.
Constitution of the Federal Republic of Nigeria, 1979.
Constitution of the Federal Republic of Nigeria, 1989.
Constitution of the Federal Republic of Nigeria, 1999.
Convention for the Protection of Human Rightsand Fundamental Freedoms, 1950
Criminal Code, 1916 (Ng.).
Education Ordinance, 1916 (N. Ng.).
General Act of the Berlin Conference on West Africa, 1885.
Giwa Local Government (Kaduna State) by-law on liquor, gambling and prostitution (1999).
Kano State Prostitution and Other Immoral Acts (Prohibition) Law (2000).
Kano State's State Censorship Film Board Law (2001).
Lord Chancellor (Tenure of Office and Discharge of Ecclesiastical Functions) Act 1974.
Moslem Court of Appeal Law, no. 10, 1956.
Native Courts (Amendment) Proclamation (no. 10, 1908) (N.Nig.), 1911.

Native Courts Ordinance (no. 5, 1918) (Ng.).
Native Courts Proclamation (no. 2/1900) (N.Ng.).
Native Courts Ordinance (no. 44, 1933) (N.Ng.).
Native Courts Ordinance (no. 45, 1933) (N.Ng.).
Native Courts Ordinance (no. 46, 1933) (N.Ng.).
Native Courts Ordinance (no. 36, 1948) (N.Ng.).
Native Courts (Amendment) Ordinance (no. 2, 1951) (N.Ng.).
Northern Nigerian Penal Code, 1960.
Protectorate Courts Proclamation (1900) (N.Ng.)
Roman Catholic Relief Act, 1829.
Niger State Liquor Law (as amended 2001).
Nigeria (Legislative Council) Order in Council, 1922.
Nigeria (Legislative Council) Order in Council, 1946.
Nigeria (Legislative Council) Order in Council, 1954.
Slavery Proclamation, 1900 (N.Ng.).
Slavery Proclamation, 1907 (N.Ng.).
West African Court of Appeal Ordinance (no. 47 of 1933) (Ng.).
Zamfara State Anti-Corruption Commission Law (2003).

NEWSPAPERS AND PERIODICALS

Lagos Weekly Record. January 29, 1898.
Times Weekly Edition. June 22, 1900.
Church Missionary Gleaner. August 1, 1900.
Church Missionary Intelligencer. 1897.
Sudan Leaflet, no. 1. January 1890.
Gazette. July 1917.
West Africa Magazine. June 24, 1933.
Daily Comet. November 11, 1950.
Daily Comet. June 22, 1960.
Daily Comet. June 14, 1954.
Daily Comet. April 27, 1960.
New Nigerian. April 1978.
New Nigerian. June 1, 1987.
Monthly Life. December 1987.
Journal of African Society. July 1911.

INDEX

Abu Rannat, Sayyed Mohammed, 163, 167, 170–171, 176
Abul Gasim, Mohammed, 172
abuses, 162, 174
Achimugu, Peter, 144, 165, 168
Action Group (AG), 124, 125, 127, 180, 212, 220
activism (judicial), 100
Adamawa (province), 46, 114, 120–121, 123
Adamu (student), 180
Adamu, Mahdi, 241
Adcock, C.S., 9
Aden Protectorate, 9, 76, 152
Ado and Rabi v. Dijah, 256–258
adultery, 176, 264
Africa, 32–33, 53, 92, 192–193, 209,
  see also Muslim states
African Colonization Expedition, 41
Africans. *see also* natives; non-Muslims; religious minorities
  Cameron on, 18, 63, 69, 92
  devotion of, 59
  Lugard on, 52, 58, 69
  native aliens and, 44
  racialized identity of, 44
AG (Action Group), 124, 125, 127, 180, 212, 220
A.G. Kano v. A.G Federal Republic of Nigeria, 270
Agrama, Hussein Ali, 36, 48, 263
Ahl al-Kitāb (People of the Book), 10, 204
Ahmed, Gambo, 140
Ajetunmobi, Musa Ali, 240
Akilu, Ali, 156
El-Alem, Mohamed Abulasad, 145, 164
Algernon Brown, Thomas, 184
alkalai (judge-jurists)
  abolition of courts, 234, 235
  Dan Fodio on, 80, 81
  Emirs and. *see* Emirs and *siyasa*
  Gubba decision, 99
  non-Muslims, jurisdiction over, 95, 154
  Penal Code and, 146, 176–178
All Nigerian Judges Conference, 244
almsgiving (zakat), 37, 261
Alvarez, T.E., 58

Amalgamation Report (Lugard), 84, 91
Amana ("entrusted" people), 131
American Law Institute (ALI), 207
Ames, Justice, 96–97
Amina Lawal v. State, 264
Aminu Kano, 116, 117, 157, 188, 242
Amir al-Mu'minin, 73
Anderson, John Norman Dalrymple
  Abu Rannat and, 167
  on *diya*, 171
  on guarantee of non-interference, 153
  on indirect rule, 100–103
  on Islamic law, 8, 100–103
  on Penal Code, 146, 154, 158–163, 170, 178–180, 184
  on *siyasa*, 77–78, 147, 159, 173
Aniagolu, Anthony Nnaemezie, 259
anti-colonialism, 75
anti-secularism, 22, 23
apostasy (*ridda*), 44, 193, 203, 210
appellate courts
  Cameron on, 91, 92
  homicide and, 178
  Lugardian reforms of, 86–88
  Muslim Court of Appeal, 158, 177
  Native Courts Ordinance and, 95
  Penal Code and, 177
  personal law and, 177, 230, 241, 245
  West African Court of Appeal, 96, 97
Arabs, 45
aristocracy, 55, 111, 213
Arnett, E., 88
Article 18. *see* Universal Declaration of Human Rights Article 18
Asad, Talal, 14, 71, 103, 268
Asia, 193
assassinations, 233
atheism, 239
Attahiru I, Sultan of Sokoto, 72
authoritarianism, 203, 204
authorities, 71, 159, 186
authority
  Gumi and, 239
  of Islamic law, 147, 148, 150, 155, 261, 265
  missionary enterprise and, 47, 48, 53, 55, 62
  of residents, 65

301

INDEX

Ayandele, Emmanuel A., 36
Ayoub, Samy, 150
Al-Azhar University, 145

Babangida, Ibrahim Badamosi, 259
Bachama, 120, 134
bail, 139
Balewa, Abubakar Tafawa, 115, 130, 219
Bamali, Nuhu, 155
Barnes, Andrew, 35
Baroody, Jamil, 209
Basa case, 93
Bates, Miner Searle, 203–206
Bauchi (province), 45
beheading, 91
Bell, Gawain Westray, 166–168, 171, 178
Bell, Hesketh, 58, 61
Bello, Abdullah, 80
Bello, Ahmadu
　in general, 115
　assassination of, 233
　on guarantee of non-interference, 221
　on indirect rule, 137
　Islamic law and, 160
　on missionary enterprise, 136
　Penal Code and, 179, 183
　on religious difference, 218
　on religious minorities, 134
　on *siyasa*, 174
Bello, Muhammed, 80
Benghazi, 165
Benue (province), 46
Benue (river), 42
Berlin General Act of 1885, 7
Berlin Treaty, 42
Berom Group, 134
Berom Progress Union (BPU), 113, 133
Bhabha, Homi, 15
Bible
　Caesar-God analogy, 198
　Luke (gospel), 130
　Mark (gospel), 120
　Matthew (gospel), 120
　political identity and, 120
　testimonies and, 90
Bida (town), 57
Bilad al Sudan ("land of the Blacks"), 32, 191
bills of rights, 201, 205, 206, 211, 220
Binji, Haliru, 144, 174
blasphemy, 205
blood money, 171
Borno (province), 45, 165
Boxer rebellion, 31
boycotts, 20
BPU (Berom Progress Union), 113, 133

Brice-Smith, Hugh Middleton, 61
Britain
　Attahiru I on, 72
　Christian identity of, 39
　constitutions and, 212
　indirect rule by. *see* indirect rule
　missionaries and, 31, 33, 38, 41–45, 193
　religious liberty, 34, 207
　tolerance, 204
British Council of Churches, 211, 214
British Protectorate of Northern Nigeria
　missionary enterprise and, 5, 32, 53, 58, 68, 193
　Sokoto Caliphate, fall of, 41, 42
Brooke Commission, 52, 100
Bukuru (city), 113
Burdon, John, 75
bureaucracy, 213
Buxton, Thomas Fowell, 41

Caesar, 117, 194, 198, 237
Cameron administration
　on Africans, 18, 63, 69, 92
　on appeals, 91, 92
　on Eluaka case, 94
　indirect rule, 17, 51, 63, 92
　Islamic institutions, 18, 20–22, 269
　judicial reforms. *see* courts, Cameron reforms of
　Lugardians and, 64–66, 91
　missionaries and, 64
　on missionary activity, 66–68, 114
　on natives, 63
　on neutrality, 17, 51, 68
　siyasa, 82, 185
Canada, 207
Cantonments Proclamation, 59
capital punishment, 85, 88, 89, 97, 99, 171, 176, 264
Carrow, John H., 85
Catholic Church, 23, 38, 135, 203, 204, 206, 236
CCN (Christian Council of Nigeria), 119, 121, 129, 134, 142, 211, 213, 236
Certificates of Occupancy, 65
Chamba, 123, 133
Chamberlain, Joseph, 42, 55
Chief Justices, 87
chiefs, 8, 46, 51, 61, 84, 134
China, 31, 207
Christian Association of Nigeria (CAN), 22, 26, 236, 240, 243, 260, 262
Christian Council of Nigeria (CCN), 119, 121, 129, 134, 142, 211, 213, 236
"Christian Human Rights" (Moyn), 191
Christian society, 199

302

INDEX

Christianity
  Catholic Church. *see* Catholic Church
  colonial ideals and, 151
  conversion to. *see* conversion and converts
  in Europe, 197
  missionary enterprise. *see* missionary enterprise
  morality, 50, 53
  personalism, 200, 201, 207, 211
  Protestantism. *see* Protestantism
  in United States, 205
Christianizing and Unchristianizing of the World, The (Oldham), 196
Christians
  as minority group, 214, 233
  devotion, lack of, 59
  education of, 112
  Middle Belt state and, 119–122, 132
  Muslims and, 218
  in NML, 114
Church of England, 31, 33, 38, 205
Church Missionary Intelligencer (magazine), 54
Church Missionary Society (CMS)
  in general, 2, 33
  British government and, 42
  on dissociation of culture from religion, 62
  Eluaka case, 94
  Kano mission station, 65
  lepers settlement, 67
  Lugard and, 53, 56
  on Masu Sarauta, 49
  on religious liberty, 48–51
churches, 23, 62
Churchill, Winston, 57
Church-State report, 198
citizenship, 37
civil law, 148, 230, 241, 258, 260, *see also* personal law
civil obligations, 49
civil war, 235, 237
civilization
  Cameron on, 63, 92
  colonialism as civilizing enterprise, 2, 36, 39–40, 92
  Lugard on, 52
  missionary enterprise and, 36, 39–40, 53
  religious toleration and, 19
classification
  in general, 109
  by Willink Commission, 126, 129, 131, 138, 141
  Muslim vs. non-Muslim binary, 10, 37, 45, 109–111, 123–124, 126, 134, 138, 142
  territorial, 126, 129, 131, 138, 141
Clifford, Hugh, 60, 62, 63
CMS (Church Missionary Society). *see* Church Missionary Society (CMS)

coalitions, 122, 124
codification. *see* Penal Code
colonial law, 9, 78
colonial office, 22, 27, 100, 102, 114, 128, 142, 158
colonialism, 2, 7, 12, 24, 36, 39–40, 92, 185, 262
Colonialism by Proxy (Ochonu), 8
Commission of the Churches on International Affairs (CCIA), 200, 207, 211
Committee of Advisors on Human Rights, 207
common law, 23, 175
commoners (*talakawa*), 112, 118
communion, 38
communism, 196, 203, 223
compensation, 85, 93, 133
"compensation" (*diya*), 88, 89, 171–174
compliance, 74, 86
conscience of the state, 194
conscience, freedom of, 7, 19, 48, 61, 89, 218, 222
Constituent Assembly, 23, 245, 254–256, 259
Constituting Religion (Moustafa), 9
Constitution Drafting Committee (CDC), 244, 245, 248, 254
Constitutional Conferences
  of 1953, 117, 211
  of 1957/1958, 115, 124, 169, 178, 215, 217–220
  of 1977, 22, 23, 224, 229–233, 242, 245, 254–256
  of 1988, 259
constitutional politics
  Article 18. *see* Universal Declaration of Human Rights Article 18
  in Britain, 205, 212
  in Egypt, 204
  human rights, constitutionalization of, 27, 108, 189, 212
  in India, 15
  missionaries and, 62
  secularism and, 199
  in US, 205
  Willink Commission and, 126
constitutions
  of 1946, 111, 124, 130
  of 1960, 221–222
  of 1999, 271
consuls, 42
conversion and converts. *see also* missionary enterprise
  Bible and, 120
  in Egypt, 155
  freedom to convert, 49, 189, 207
  Hausa (ethnic group), 19, 54

303

INDEX

conversion and converts (cont.)
  in India, 203
  intolerance, leading to, 53
  jurisdiction over converts, 154
  missionary education and, 112
  of Muslims, 233
co-option. *see* indirect rule
Cornes, John, 84
corruption, 155, 261
council of *ulama* (jurists), 261
coups d'état, 233–235
court cases
  A.G Kano v. A.G Federal Republic of Nigeria, 270
  Ado and Rabi v. Dijah, 256–258
  Amina Lawal, 264
  Basa, 93
  Eluaka case, 94, 113
  Fagoji v. Kano NA, 99
  Hassana of Fura, 87
  Katsina NA v. Yakudi of Hababa and Dankoko of Renage, 85
  Lagos State Government and others v. Asiyat Abdulkareem, 271
  Magudama v. Bornu NA, 96
  Maizabo v. NA, 99
  Nyali Bridge case, 184
  Reg v. Ilorin, 89
  Tsofo Gubba v. Gwandu N.A., 97–100, 107, 129, 151
  Umary Fannami v. Bukar Sarkiu, 258
courts
  appellate. *see* appellate courts
  Bello and, 175
  classification and, 46
  deference, 96–97, 107
  Federal Court of Appeal, 257, 258
  Federal Sharia Court of Appeal. *see* Federal Sharia Court of Appeal (FSCA)
  High Court, 141, 154, 181, 244
  Islamic. *see* courts, Islamic
  Muslim Court of Appeal, 158, 177
  Protectorate, 87–88
  Shari'a Court of Appeal. *see* Shari'a Court of Appeal;Sharia Court of Appeal
  Supreme Court. *see* Supreme Court
  West African Court of Appeal, 96, 97
courts, Cameron reforms of
  Emirs, 92
  mixed courts, 95
  native courts and appellate channels, 82, 91, 92, 96–103, 177
courts, Islamic
  Anderson on, 101
  capital punishment, 88
  classification, 46
  Metteden on, 155

  non-Muslims tried before, 89–90, 94–95, 136, 252
  protectorate and, relationship between, 88
  superior courts and, 95
courts, Lugardian reforms of
  in general, 161
  appeals, 86–88
  Maliki law, 90–91
  siyasa, 82, 84–86, 151, 187
Crewe, Robert Offley Ashburton Crewe-Milnes, Marquis of, 65
Criminal Code, 88, 96, 97, 99
criminal law, 9, 77
Criminal Procedure Code, 175
Crown and the Turban, The (Sanneh), 268
culture, dissociating from religion, 62
Cunliffe-Lister, Phillip, 94
customary law, 46, 62, 89, 166

Dajjani, Auni, 144, 164
damages, 94
Dan Fodio, Uthman, 32, 80, 81, 115, 116, 187, 258
"dan kirki," 161
Danchin, Peter, 190
death penalty, 85, 88, 89, 97, 99, 171, 176, 264
declaration of tolerance, 136
deference, 96–97, 107
Define and Rule (Mamdani), 109
delegations, 164–167, 169, 174, 247
democracy, 127, 221, 234, 260
denationalization, 59
Denning, Alfred Thompson, 167, 184
Department of Education, 60
deportations, 76, 114
Dhimmah ("protected" people), 131
Diplock, Kenneth, 184
direct rule, 17, 54, *see also* indirect rule
disempowerment, 128, 132, 240, 244, 250
disestablishment of religion, 4, 198, 200
disputes, 80, 90, 261
dissidents, 73, 139–141
district commissioners, 51, 83, 134
district officers, 64, 86, 158
disturbances, political, 114
diversity, religious. *see* religious difference
divorce, 186
diya ("compensation"), 88, 89, 171–174
Doktori (Protestant), 115
drowning, 91
Dual Mandate (Lugard), 57
Dulles, John Foster, 201, 207, 208
Dutch Missionary Conference, 196

Eastern Nigeria, 235
Eastern Nigerian Catholic Church, 236

304

ECHR (European Convention on Human Rights), 162, 211, 220, 221, *see also* Universal Declaration of Human Rights Article 18
eclecticism, 248, 265
economy, 133, 242
ecumenical movement. *see also* conversion and converts; missionary enterprise; missionary restrictions; Protestantism
  Article 18, 162, 189, 191–195, 208, 211, 214–215, 223, 224, 230
  Catholic Church and, 23, 236
  Christian Council of Nigeria and, 236
  Middle Belt State and, 120, 123
  on morality, Christian, 50
  Protestant ecumenism, 119, 124
  on religious liberty, 200, 202, 204
  religious minorities and, 124, 135
  secularism and, 21, 189, 194–199, 204, 223
  Universal Christian Council for Life and Work, 197–201
  World Missionary Conference, 5, 33, 50, 189, 198
education
  in general, 60
  in constitution, 222
  of Federal Court of Appeal judges, 255
  in Lokoja, 133
  madrasah, 239
  missionary. *see* missionary education
  of politicians in Muslim coalition, 239
  public, 38, 60
Education Ordinance, 60, 67
Egypt
  Article 18, 209
  Bates on, 203, 204
  Biblical metaphors from, 120
  Civil Code, 148, 154–157
  missionary activity in, 192, 194
  Penal Code, 146
  religious difference in, 15, 48
Elgin, Victor Alexander Bruce, Earl of, 57
Elias, Taslim, 91
Eliot, T.S., 199
El-Rayah, Bashir, 20
Eltantawi, Sarah, 10, 263
Eluaka, Victor, 94, 113
emancipation, 110, 120, 128, 142, 223, 265
Emir of Fika, 93
Emir of Kano, 42, 55, 94, 171, 182
Emir of Zaria, 171
Emirs
  in general, 6, 45
  Article 18, 212
  Cameron administration, 20–22, 63, 92–94
  Christianising of, 66
  guarantee of non-interference and, 7, 72, 100
  indirect rule, 54
  missionary activity, 64, 65
  missionary restrictions and, 36, 54, 56, 67
  non-Muslims and, 131
  Penal Code, 182–185
  source of law of, 185
  Willink Commission on, 136
Emirs and *siyasa*
  Anderson on, 173
  Cameron reforms, 92–94
  judicial restrictions, 80
  Lugardian reforms, 17, 82, 84–88, 187
  Native Courts Ordinance, 99
  relation with *alkalai*, 11, 20, 82, 84–86, 183
Emon, Anver, 186
enfranchisement, 38
English Common Law, 87, 147, 184, 241, 248, 253
English Criminal Code, 87
"entrusted" people (*Amana*), 131
equality, 48, 247, 266, 270
Europe, 39, 197
European Convention on Human Rights (ECHR), 162, 211, 220, 221, *see also* Universal Declaration of Human Rights Article 18
Evangelicalism. *see* missionary enterprise
evidence (legal), 85, 89, 95, 97, 252
exceptionalism, 22
executions, 75
exodus metaphor, 120
exotic other, 52, 83
exploitation, 119

Fagoji v. Kano NA, 99
Fani-Kayode, Remi, 130–131
Farrant, H.G., 52, 67
fatwa, 20
Federal Council of Churches (FCC), 201, 207
Federal Court of Appeal, 255, 257, 258
Federal Military Government, 260
Federal Sharia Court of Appeal (FSCA)
  in general, 229
  CDC on, 244, 255–256
  jurisdiction, 244
  non-Muslims, jurisdiction over, 252
  opposition to, 246, 259
  secularism and, 22
federalism
  Middle Belt state and, 123, 127
  NEPU on, 141
  NPC on, 129
  religious liberty and, 250, 254
  in US, 205
  Willink Commission on, 126

INDEX

fiqh (Islamic jurisprudence)
  Egyptian Civil Code and, 149
  human fallibility and, 246
  siyasa and, 10–12, 17, 20, 79, 153, 186
First Amendment (US Constitution), 205
flogging, 93
Foreign Missions Conference, 202
forgiveness, 85
Formations of the Secular (Asad), 14, 71, 103, 268
Forster, Canon, 214
France, 15, 33, 39, 148, 207
free exercise, 217
Freed Slaves Home, 56
freedom of conscience, 7, 19, 48, 61, 89, 218, 222
FSCA (Federal Sharia Court of Appeal). *see* Federal Sharia Court of Appeal (FSCA)
Fulani ethnic group, 18, 54, 116, 134
Fulani War, 19, 32, 54, 80
fundamental rights, 216
Future of Law in Africa Conference, 167, 184

Galanter, Marc, 16
Garam town, 61
Germany, 33, 67, 196, 207
Girouard, Percy, 57–60
Gluckman, Max, 174
God, 59, 72, 198, 239
Godfrey, William, 214
Good Muslim, Bad Muslim (Mamdani), 73
good order exception, 46, 91, *see also* order
governance. *see* direct rule; indirect rule; guarantee of non-interference; secularism
Governance of India Act of 1858, 7, 40, 43
Greece, 210
Gresswell, R.E., 94
Grey, Ralph, 158
grievous bodily harm, 90
Grubb, Kenneth, 128, 213–215
guarantee of non-interference
  in general, 7, 43, 68
  Anderson on, 153
  Article 18 and, 217, 221
  Bello on, 221
  Brooke Commission on, 100
  Emirs and, 7, 72, 100
  Gubba decision and, 97–100
  imperial secularism and, 8, 17, 27
  Islamic institutions and, 17, 21, 43, 72–73
  lack of neutrality of, 7
  Lugardian, 72–73
  Masu Sarauta and, 19, 27, 73
  missionary restrictions, 34, 43, 55, 63, 216
  religious liberty and, 55, 62
  Shari'a and, 98
  Sharwood-Smith on, 161

Gubba decision, 97–100, 107, 129, 151
Gumi, Abubakar, 174, 177, 234, 238, 239
Gwari (tribe), 135

hadd penalties, 90
Hadejia, Mohammad Danjani, 182
hadith, 157, 246
Hafsatu (wife of Ahmadu Bello), 233
Hallaq, Wael B., 11, 79
Hanafism, 150, 186
Hassana of Fura case, 87
Hastings, Warren, 3, 160
Hausa (ethnic group), 18, 54, 60, 180
Hausseleiter, G., 194–195
Headman of Tuwam, 61
headscarves, 15
heathen rites, 61
High Commissioner of Northern Nigeria. *see* Lugard, Frederick
High Court, 98, 99, 141, 181, 244
Hindu-Christianity conversions, 203
Hindutva (ideology), 15
hisbah (morality police), 261, 264, 270
homicide
  appeals and, 178
  diya, 173
  Gubba case, 97, 98
  Islamic courts, 88, 100
  Lugardian reforms, 85, 86
  Native Courts Ordinance, 99–100
  Protectorate Courts, 88
House of Assembly, 111–113
House of Chiefs, 179
Huber, Max, 198, 207
human rights
  Article 18. *see* Universal Declaration of Human Rights Article 18
  constitutionalization of, 27, 108, 189, 212
  Nolde on, 207
human self-sufficiency, 196

Ibn Taymiyya, 149
Idea of a Christian Society, The (Eliot), 199
identity
  Christian, 39, 120, 234, 257
  dissident, 73
  ethnic, 109, 122, 134
  European, 39
  Islamic, 54
  Muslim, 114, 234
  native, 109
  NPC on, 134–136
  political, 109, 118, 120, 121
  Protestant, 109, 122
  racial, 44
  religious difference and, 118, 126, 130

306

religious minorities, 108–111, 121, 123, 130, 134–136, 138, 140, 142, 230
Tijanniyyah, 75
tribal, 109
Willink Commission on, 126, 128, 130, 138
Ige, Bola, 255
Ihya' as-Sunnah wa Ikhmad a-Bid'ah (Uthman Dan Fodio), 81
Ilorin (province), 46
Imams, 172, 258
impartiality, 4, 7, 46, 48, 134
imperial secularism. *see also* religious liberty and secularism; secularism
  guarantee of non-interference and, 8, 17, 27
  indirect rule and, 34, 68–69
  Middle Belt state and, 133
  order and, 48
  Penal Code and, 187
  postcolonial debate, 267–273
  religious liberty and, 26, 266
  religious minorities and, 110, 143
  Shari'a and, 82, 103, 231, 264
  Willink Commission and, 126
imprisonment, 61, 87, 139, 140, 176
independence
  Article 18 and, 211
  Catholics on, 135
  Constitutional Conferences. *see* Constitutional Conferences
  decolonization, 107
  district officers, 158
  inequality and, 27
  Islamic law and, 152–155, 166, 230, 249
  Libya as model of, 144
  Masu Sarauta, 155–158, 224, 241
  missionary activity and, 136
  non-Muslims and, 230
  NPC and, 115
  Penal Code and, 178
  postcolonial hierarchies after, 260
  religious liberty and, 108, 189, 230, 269
  religious minorities and, 27, 107–111, 229
  secularism and, 25, 240
  UMBC on, 124–125
  Willink Commission and, 128
India
  Article 18, 213
  church-state separation in, 2, 38
  common law, 184
  conversions, 203
  Hindutva (ideology), 15
  indigenous religion in, 194
  Lugard in, 53
  modernizing law of, 168
  mutiny, 2, 5, 39, 43, 110
  Penal Code, 175
  siyasa, 160

indirect rule
  in general, 5–6, 9, 68, 76, 104
  Aminu Kano on, 117
  Anderson on, 100–103
  Bates on, 204
  Bello on, 137
  Cameron administration, 17, 51, 63, 92
  classification and, 10–13, 109
  imperial secularism and, 34, 68–69
  Islamic law and, 71, 78
  Lugard administration, 44, 51–57, 83
  Masu Sarauta, 54, 70, 121
  missionaries and, 17, 18, 36, 41–43, 54
  NEPU on, 118
  NPC on, 137
  order and, 48
  racial distinctions, 45
  religious difference, 101
  religious liberty, 68
  religious minorities, 121, 133, 134
  secularism and, 1–3, 9, 41–44, 267
Indonesia, 213
inequality, 101, 111, 223
Institute of Administration, 239, 249, 254
instructions, 82–85
International Bill of Rights, 206
International Charter of Liberties, 206
international law, 162
International Missionary Council, 193, 196, 200
intolerance, 203
Iraq, 203
Islam
  Bates on, 206
  Lugard on, 52
  nationality and, 59
  state-defined, 10, 13, 139, 187
Islamic courts. *see* courts, Islamic
Islamic institutions
  in general, 223
  Cameron administration and, 18, 20–22, 269
  guarantee of non-interference and, 17, 21, 43, 72–73
  Lugard administration and, 17–20, 27, 43, 54, 269
  missionary enterprise and, 49, 58, 59, 77
  secularism and, 11, 25, 27, 230, 62–66
Islamic jurisprudence
  fiqh. *see fiqh* (Islamic jurisprudence)
  FSCA and, 245, 248
  Maliki, 81, 90–91, 96, 264
  paganism and, 10
  Penal Code and, 147
  precolonial, 11, 17, 77
  schools of, 81
  siyasa. *see siyasa* ("discretionary powers of political rulers")

INDEX

Islamic law
  abolition, 108, 153, 230
  adultery, 176
  Anderson on, 8, 77–78, 100–103, 152–153
  appeals, 245–247
  Dijah case, 257
  diya, 172
  Federal Court of Appeal, 255
  Gubba decision, 97–100, 107, 129, 151
  independence and, 152–155, 166, 230, 249
  indigenous law, preferred over, 97
  indirect rule, 78
  Judicial Adviser's Conference on, 152
  jurisdiction, 6, 260
  jurisprudence, 108
  modernity and, 146–150, 155, 158, 160, 182, 263
  NEPU on, 154–158
  Penal Code and, 20, 21, 102, 146, 147, 170, 176, 230, 259
  personal law and, 77, 145, 164, 176
  provocation, 97
  religious liberty, 210
  renewal, 249, 255, 261
  Schacht on, 77
  secularism and, 8, 70, 164, 240, 263
  siyasa and, 71
  territorial classification, 46
  transformation, 10–13, 17, 20
Islamization
  Bello, 233
  Christianity and, 249
  and secularism, 237
  Sharia Court of Appeal and, 254
istihsan (preferential reasoning), 157
Italy, 207
Izala movement, 238

Jama'atu Nasril Islamiyyah (JNI), 238
Jama'atu Izalatil Bid'ah Wa Iqamatus Sunnah, 238
Jesus, 32
Jinnah, Muhammad Ali, 165
Jizyah (tax), 37
JNI (Jama'atu Nasril Islamiyyah), 238
Joint Committee on Religious Liberty (JCRL), 202, 204, 207, 211
Jones, Arthur Creech, 107
Judaism, 120
judges
  Cameron years, 92, 96
  education, 239
  English, 92, 98, 182
  Hallaq on, 79
  High Court, 257
  on Sharia Court of Appeal, 244

Sharia Court of Appeal, 253
superior courts, 97
Judicial Advisers' Conference, 152, 158
judiciary. *see* courts
Junaidu, Muhammadu, 165
jurisprudence. *see* Islamic jurisprudence; *fiqh* (Islamic jurisprudence)
jurists, 20, 81, 146, 177, 186
Al-Juwaynī, 186

Kabba (province), 46
Kabwir district, 61
Kachia, Toro, 252
kafiri (pagan). *see* paganism
Kamuku (tribe), 135
Kanem–Bornu Empire, 33, 258
Kano (province)
  as Type I area, 45
  missionary activity in, 65
  non-Muslims, use of evidence in courts, 90
  protest in, 140
  riots and protest in, 125, 129
Kano, Aminu, 116, 117, 157, 188, 242
Katsina (province), 45
Katsina NA v. Yakudi of Hababa and Dankoko of Renage, 85
Kendhammer, Brandon, 24
Khan, Zafrullah, 210
killing, 171, 235, *see also* manslaughter; murder
Kobo, Muhamadu, 144, 164
Kukah, Matthew Hassan, 234
Kumo, Sule, 248

labor, 61
Labour Party, 107
Lagos, 125
Lagos State Government and others v. Asiyat Abdulkareem, 271
Lake Chad Basin, 33
Lamido, 123
language, 60, 86
Latin America, 207
law
  civil, 148, 230, 241, 258, 260
  colonial, 9, 78
  common, 23, 175
  criminal, 9, 77
  customary, 46, 62, 89, 166
  English, 83, 177, 239, 240, 244, 249
  English Common Law, 87, 147, 184, 241, 248, 253
  High Court Law, 257
  imperial, 146
  international, 162
  Islamic. *see* Islamic law
  Maliki. *see* Maliki law

INDEX

personal. *see* personal law
public, 77, 164
Roman, 157
sacred, 239
social, 62, 89
statutory, 248
Western, 156
Law, Empire and the Sultan (Ayoub), 150
Lawal, Amina, 264
lawyers, 96, 98, 156, 178, 220, 244
Lebanon, 203
legal representation, 177
legal theory, 16
Legislative Council, 102
Lennox-Boyd, C.A., 124, 129
Lepers Settlements, 66
Lethem, G.J., 76
liberalism, 9, 41, 168, 191
Libya, 144, 163, 164, 169, 174, 175, 179, 203
Limits of Tolerance, The (Adcock), 9
Lokoja Improvement Union, 133
Lot, David, 113
Lugard, Frederick John Dealtry
  Amalgamation Report, 84, 91
  on Christianity, 53–55
  CMS and, 53
  Dual Mandate, 57
  in India, 53
  orientalism, 52, 83
  Political Memoranda, 57, 90
Lugardian administration
  on Africans, 58, 69
  anti-Lugardian views and, 212
  Cameron administration and, 64–66, 91
  CMS and, 56
  guarantee of non-interference. *see* guarantee of non-interference
  indirect rule, 44, 51–57, 83
  Islamic institutions, 17–20, 27, 43, 54, 269
  judicial reforms. *see* courts, Lugardian reforms of
  Masu Sarauta and, 17, 19, 54, 55, 57, 129, 151
  Middle Belt state and, 128
  missionary education, 53, 56–57
  missionary restrictions, 46, 55, 57–62
  NPC and, 129, 137
  religious liberty and, 17, 51, 58
  secularism and, 17, 43
Luke (gospel), 130
Lyndon, Ghislaine, 264
Lyttleton, Oliver, 211–213

Macaulay, Thomas Babington, 168
madrasah education, 239
Magaji, Dambatta, 217
Magistrates, 87

Maguzawa (tribe), 10, 33, 37, 68, 234
Magudama v. Bornu NA case, 96
Mahdism, 12, 75
Mahdist War, 47
Mahmood, Saba, 10, 15, 110, 190, 222, 265
Mahmud, Abdulmalik Bappa, 241, 257, 258
Maine, Henry, 100
Maizabo v. NA, 99
Majalla Code, 148, 150
Majiyagbe, J.B., 257
majus (Zoroastrians), 10
Makurdi (city), 249
Malaysia, 15
Malik, Charles, 208–209
Maliki law
  adultery and, 264
  jurisprudence, 81, 90–91, 96, 264
  Penal Code, 181
  reforms, 90, 169
  Supreme Court and, 99
Mamdani, Mahmood, 17, 73, 109
manslaughter, 88, 97, 99, *see also* murder
marginalization
  enfranchisement and, 38
  Middle Belt state and, 128, 132–134, 141
  Sharia Court of Appeal and, 177
  Willink Commission and, 111, 138
Mark (gospel), 120
Marshall, Hedley, 161
martyrdom, 234
Masu Sarauta ("possessors of governance"). *see also* Northern People's Congress (NPC)
  in general, 6
  on abolition of alkalai courts, 157–158
  Aminu Kano on, 117
  Article 18, 211, 215, 217
  CMS on, 49
  Colonial Office, 158
  Constitution of 1946 and, 111
  education, 112
  guarantee of non-interference and, 19, 27, 73
  independence and, 155–158, 224, 241
  indirect rule and, 54, 70, 121
  Lugardian administration and, 17, 19, 54, 55, 57, 129, 151
  Middle Belt state and, 115, 120, 128–130
  missionary activity and, 55, 64, 65, 68
  NEPU and, 116–118, 141, 158
  Panel report, 179
  Penal Code and, 146, 183, 187
  religious difference and, 12, 17, 23, 46, 70, 72–76, 138, 236
  religious liberty, 65, 68
  secularism and, 13–18, 26, 48
  siyasa, 93

309

INDEX

Mataszu (town), 67
materialism, 199
Matthew (gospel), 120
Maxwell, J.L., 119
McPetrie, James, 215
merchants, 74
mercy, prerogative of, 173
messiah, 12, 75
Metteden, Mallam A.K., 155–156
Middle Belt state
  in general, 127–129
  imperial secularism and, 133
  Lugardians and, 128
  Masu Sarauta and, 115, 120, 128–130
  natives on, 136
  NEPU on, 124, 129, 141
  non-Muslims, 132
  religious minorities and, 108, 120–125, 134–137
Middle Zone League (MZL), 121, 128
Miller, Walter Richard Samuel, 52, 53, 65
Minorities Commission. *see* Willink Commission
missionaries. *see* Church Missionary Society (CMS)
missionary education
  in Constitution, 222
  Education Ordinance, 60, 67
  freedom of, 200
  leading to positions in government, 111, 133
  Lugard on, 53, 56–57
missionary enterprise
  in Africa, 32–33, 192–193
  Bello on, 136
  Cameron administration and, 18, 66–68, 94, 269
  classification and, 37
  Hausa (ethnic group), 19, 54
  indirect rule, 18
  Islamic institutions and, 49, 58, 59
  Islamic law and, 153, 154
  Masu Sarauta and, 64, 68
  Middle Belt state and, 128
  Penal Code and, 180
  political autonomy of, 121
  religious liberty, 20
  secularism and, 2, 19, 25, 26, 237
  "special protection," 42
missionary restrictions
  in general, 2, 5, 9, 33, 36
  in Africa, 192
  anti-mission bill of 1949, 112–113
  Britain, relationship with, 31, 33, 38, 41–45, 193
  bureaucracy, 212
  Cameron administration and, 64, 114
  distestablishment and, 4
  Emirs, 36, 54, 56, 67
  good order exception, 46–48
  guarantee of non-interference, 34, 43, 55, 63, 216
  house-to-house visitation, 66
  independence and, 22, 108
  indirect rule and, 17, 36, 41–43, 54
  Islamic law and, 203
  Lugard administration, 46
  Lugardian administration, 19, 55, 57–62, 114
  Masu Sarauta and, 55, 65
  Middle Belt state and, 132
  Muslims and, 203
  opposition to, 236
  political interference, 118
  preaching, 65, 66
  religious liberty and, 48
  by Residents, 64
  Salisbury on, 31, 33, 38, 55
  territorial classification, 6, 46, 56, 234
  Willink Commission on, 136
modernity
  Islamic law and, 146, 147–150, 155, 158, 160, 182, 263
  Muslim states, 102, 153, 162, 163, 175, 179
  Penal Code and, 146
  secularism and, 103
Moosa, Ebrahim, 79
morality, 50, 53
morality police (*hisbah*), 261, 264, 270
Morel, Edmund Dene, 58
mosques, 139
Moustafa, Tamir, 9
Moyn, Samuel, 191
Muffet, David, 160
Muftis, 118, 172
Muhammad (prophet), 116, 117
mujtahid (Muslim jurist), 81, 186
Mukthasar Khali (Maliki text), 147
murder, 87, 97, 171, 173, *see also* manslaughter
Muslim Court of Appeal, 158, 177
Muslim states
  Article 18, 210
  Bates on, 203
  modernity, 102, 153, 162, 163, 175, 179
  religious liberty, 219
Muslim sub-imperialism, 7, 25, 70, 109, 110, 113
Muslims
  binary, non-Muslims vs., 10, 37, 45, 109–111, 123–124, 126, 134, 138, 142
  Christians and, 218
  conversion of, 233
  ideal, 73–76, 138, 165

identity, 114, 234
Islamic institutions and, 19
jurisdiction over, 230
jurists, 20, 81, 146, 168, 177, 186
Lugard on, 69
marginalization of, 140, 256
Masu Sarauta and, 12
missionary restrictions and, 203
political participation, 235, 239
Mussolini, Benito, 203, 204
mutilation, 90
mutiny, 2, 5, 39, 43, 110, *see also* protests; rebellion; revolts; riots
mutum ya kasha maliki. see Richardson, Sam Scruton
MZL (Middle Zone League), 121, 128

Nasir, Mamman, 165
Nasser, Gamal, 155
National Council of Nigeria and the Cameroons (NCNC), 212
nationalism, 112, 203, 204
nationalization, 236, 238
Native Administration in Nigeria (Perham), 151
native aliens, 44
Native Authority Police, 93, 95, 134, 140
Native Courts Appellate Division, 181
Native Courts Ordinances, 95, 97, 99
Native Courts Proclamation, 91
natives
  in general, 6
  Cameron administration and, 63, 82, 91, 92, 96–103, 177
  chiefs, native, 84
  converts, 6
  customary law, 46, 62, 89, 166
  in India, 194
  indirect rule, governing through. *see* indirect rule
  institutions. *see* Islamic institutions
  on Middle Belt state, 136
  missionary education and, 57
  non-native vs., 88
  pagan as colonial ideal of non-Muslim, 5, 10, 12, 37
  as political identity, 109
  racialized construction of, 44–45
  religions, 33, 34, 40
  territorial classification of, 6, 46, 153
Nazism, 196, 223
NCNC (National Council of Nigeria and the Cameroons), 212
NEPU. *see* Northern Elements Progressive Union (NEPU)
Newton, C.C., 42
Ngileruma, Muhammad Isa, 165
Niger (province), 46

Niger (river), 42
Nigeria. *see* British Protectorate of Northern Nigeria; Eastern Nigeria; Northern Nigeria; Southern Nigeria
Nigeria (Legislative Council) Order in Council, 107
Nigeria Working Group, 215–216, 220
Nigerian Criminal Code, 175
Nigerian Supreme Council for Islamic Affairs (NSCIA), 238, 243, 249, 262
Niven, Rex, 112
Nolde, Otto Frederick, 202, 207
Non-Muslim League (NML), 113–114, 119, 121, 128
non-Muslims. *see also* paganism
  binary, Muslims vs., 10, 37, 45, 109–111, 123–124, 126, 134, 138, 142
  diya, 171
  identity, 134
  independence and, 230
  jurisdiction over, 89–90, 94–95, 132, 136, 154, 252
  Middle Belt state and, 121, 122, 123, 132, 141
  territorial classification of, 46
  Willink Commission and, 131, 136
Noon, Firoz Khan, 164
Northern Elements Progressive Union (NEPU)
  Article 18, 212, 217
  indirect rule, 118
  Islamic law, 154–158
  Masu Sarauta and, 116–18, 141, 158
  on Middle Belt state, 124, 129, 141
  NPC and, 116–119
  on Penal Code, 181–182, 187
  siyasa utilized against, 93, 140, 141
  Tijaniyyahs and, 13, 139–141
  Women's Wing, 140
Northern Nigeria
  in general, 1
  independence. *see* independence
  indirect rule. *see* indirect rule
  missionaries and, 32, 35, 42
  natives. *see* natives
  orthodoxy and secularism, 21
  population, 5, 53, 84, 124
  religion in, 68
  territorial classification, 126, 129, 131, 138, 141
Northern People's Congress (NPC)
  in general, 114–119
  Article 18, 217, 221
  Bello. *see* Bello, Ahmadu
  egalitarianism, 115
  independence and, 115
  on indirect rule, 137

311

INDEX

Northern People's Congress (NPC) (cont.)
  Islamic law and, 154
  Lugardians and, 129, 137
  on Middle Belt state, 124–125, 128–130, 132, 134–136
  on missionary enterprise, 219
  MZL and, 121
  NEPU and, 116–119
  "One North, One People," 114, 130, 134
  Penal Code, 181
  repression by, 139
NSCIA (Nigerian Supreme Council for Islamic Affairs), 238, 243, 249, 262
Nupe Group, 134
Nyali Bridge case, 184
Nzeogwu, Chukwuma Kaduna, 233

oaths, 72, 88, 89, 95, 252
observance, religious, 209, 217, 222
Ochonu, Moses, 8
Odumosu, Olu, 183
Offa (region), 180
Okogie, Olubunmi, 237
Olawoyin, J.S., 180
Oldham, Joseph Houldsworth, 64, 192, 196, 199, 237
"One North, One People," 114, 130, 134
oppression, 140, 231
order, 46–48, 65–66, 79, 81, 91
orientalism, 52, 83
orthodoxy
  Anderson on, 77
  Article 18 and, 209
  Bates on, 203, 204, 206
  ecumenical movement and, 21, 189, 191, 199, 223
  JNI and, 238
  Maliki law, 90
  secularism and, 15
Othman, Musa, 168
Ottoman Empire, 148, 150

paganism
  as colonial ideal of non-native Muslim, 5, 10, 12, 37
  ecumenists on, 196, 197
  Eliot on, 199
  evidence in court and, 90
  legal representation and, 178
  Lugard on Islam and, 52
  maguzawa and, 10
  religious diversity amongst, 131
  Type III areas and, 46
Pakistan, 146, 162, 164–166, 175, 210, 213, 220
Palestine, 203
pamphlets, 43, 66
Parson (CMS official), 180

Penal Code. *see also* Islamic law
  in general, 185–188
  alkalai and, 176–178
  Anderson on, 146, 179, 184
  Bello and, 179, 183
  imperial secularism and, 187
  Islamic law and, 20, 21, 102, 146, 147, 176, 230, 259
  Masu Sarauta and, 146, 183, 187
  missionaries on, 180
  Muslim states, 102, 153, 162, 163, 175, 179
  NEPU on, 181–182, 187
  opposition to, 180, 182–185, 187
  Panel of Jurists on, 166–169, 173, 175–180
  postcolonial, 261, 264
  religious minorities and, 162, 181
  secularism and, 176
  Tanzimat reforms and, 147–149
penalties. *see* punishment
People of the Book (*Ahl al-Kitāb*), 10, 204
Perham, Margery, 57, 150
persecution, 140
personal law
  appellate courts and, 22, 177, 230, 241, 245
  Islamic law and, 77, 145, 164, 176
personalism, 200, 201, 207, 211
Perth, John David Drummond, Earl of, 214–215, 217
Plateau (province), 46, 113, 133
Poland, 207
police
  hisbah, 261, 264, 270
  Native Authority Police, 93, 95, 134, 140
Political Liberalism (Rawls), 13
Political Memoranda (Lugard), 57, 90
polygamy, 53, 59, 166
Prasch, Thomas, 32
preaching, 47, 65, 66, 119, 189, 193, 200, 207
Price, Justin, 182–184
Principles of Native Administration and Their Application (Cameron), 92
prison. *see* imprisonment
private law. *see* personal law
private sphere, 13, 39, 48, 252
proselytize, right to, 214, 219, 220
"protected" people (*Dhimmah*), 131
Protestantism. *see also* conversion and converts; missionary enterprise; missionary restrictions
  Article 18 and, 214
  Bates on, 206
  Bible and, 120
  identity, 108–111, 122
  as minority group, 214
  personalism, 200, 201, 207, 211

public education and, 38
religious freedom, 222, 224, 269
rights recommendation, 142
UMBC and, 123
in US, 207
protests, 99, 125, 140, 258, *see also* mutiny; rebellion; revolts; riots
provocation, defence of, 97
public education, 38, 60
public law, 77, 164
public sphere, 39, 48, 241
punishment
  of adultery, 176
  of apostasy, 210
  of Basa, 93
  Cameron administration reforms of, 94, 99
  capital punishment, 85, 88, 89, 97, 99, 171, 176, 264
  executive power and, 81
  flogging, 93
  Lugardian reforms of, 85, 90
  siyasa powers, 173

Qadiriyyah Sufism, 12, 74, 139
Quraishi-Landes, Asifa, 246
Quran
  abolition from Islamic law and, 145
  alkalai on, 86
  on apostasy, 210
  diya, 172
  legal authority of, 86, 155
  Muftis, 172
  NEPU on, 157
  Shari'a, 98
  Sunnah, 172
  testimonies and, 89

race, 3, 44–45, 59, 200
Rashid, Syed Khalid, 240
Rawls, John, 13
Razaq, Abdul G.F., 156
rebellion, 62, *see also* mutiny; protests; revolts; riots
reforms
  in Adamawa, 82, 123
  Cameron administration. *see* courts, Cameron reforms of
  Lugardian. *see* courts, Lugardian reforms of
  Penal Code. *see* Penal Code
  Tanzimat, 148
Reg v. Ilorin, 89
religion
  disestablishment of, 4, 198, 200
  indigenous, 4, 5, 33, 34, 40, 49, 122, 123
  state-defined, 10, 13, 126, 139, 187, 272
  symbols, religious, 15

religious difference. *see also* religious minorities
  Article 18 and, 222
  civil war and, 235
  colonial governance and, 2, 3, 5, 9, 10, 27, 45, 110
  enfranchisement and, 38
  "grid of intelligibility," 5
  identity and, 118
  indirect rule and. *see* indirect rule
  intra-Muslim dichotomy, 76
  liberal imperialism and, 3, 10
  Masu Sarauta and, 12, 17, 23, 46, 70, 72–76, 138, 236
  Middle Belt state and, 130
  Penal Code and, 187
  secularism and, 13, 252
  territorial classification, 126, 129, 131, 138, 141
  Willink Commission on, 125–126, 137–142
religious exemption, 72
"Religious Freedom Move Can be Disastrous," 217
religious instructions, 67
religious intolerance, 129
religious liberty
  Article 18. *see* Universal Declaration of Human Rights Article 18
  Bates on, 203
  discrimination and, 190
  Dulles on, 201
  ecumenists on, 200, 202, 204
  federalism and, 250, 254
  good order, 48
  guarantee of non-interference and, 34, 55, 62
  human right, 20, 21
  imperial secularism and, 26, 266
  independence and, 108, 189, 230, 269
  indirect rule, 68
  Islamic law and, 210
  Lagos State Government and others v. Asiyat Abdulkareem, 271
  Lugardian administration, 17, 51, 58
  Lyttleton on, 212
  Masu Sarauta and, 65, 68
  missionary restrictions and, 49
  of Muslims states, 219
  postcolonial debate on, 232
  religious minorities and, 190
  ridda (apostasy), 203
  rights recommendation, 142
  secularism and. *see* religious liberty and secularism
  in US, 205
  Willink Commission on, 136

313

INDEX

Religious Liberty (Bates), 202–209
religious liberty and secularism
  in general, 4, 8, 16
  Article 18 and, 190, 222–225
  Bates on, 204
  enfranchisement and, 38
  missionaries on, 19, 232
  postcolonial debate, 265
  Shari'a, separation from, 22–24, 252
  state-religion separation and, 15–17, 21–22, 35, 40, 44, 46, 62, 172, 214–215, 245
religious minorities. *see also* religious difference
  Bello on, 134
  Christians as, 214, 233
  ecumenical movement and, 124, 135
  identity, 108–111, 121, 123, 130, 134–136, 138, 140, 142, 230
  imperial secularism and, 110, 143
  independence and, 27, 107–111, 107–109, 229
  indirect rule, 121, 133, 134
  Middle Belt state and, 108, 120–125, 127, 130–137
  non-Muslim bloc, 22, 229
  Penal Code and, 162, 181
  political alliance of, 121
  religious liberty and, 190
  secularism and, 15
  Willink Commission on, 125, 132, 134–136, 140
"religious toleration," 7, 19
representatives, 111, 112
repression, 75, 76, 93, 138, 141, 252
reservations (*Sabon Guruwa*), 45, 59
Residents
  homicide and, 86
  instructing Emirs, 83–85
  jurisdiction of, 87
  missionary activity and, 56, 64, 114
  Provincial Courts and, 87
  reforms, entrusted with, 83
  segregation system institutionalized by, 59
restitution, 91
restrictions to missionary activity. *see* missionary restrictions
retaliation, 171
revolt, 31, 161, 235, *see also* mutiny; protests; rebellion; riots
Richardson, Sam Scruton, 144–146, 164, 168, 170, 171, 178, 258
ridda (apostasy), 44, 193, 203, 210
rights recommendation, 142
riots, 129, *see also* mutiny; protests; rebellion; revolts
rituals, 62, 89
Robertson, James, 128, 163, 167, 214

Roberts-Wray, Kenneth, 152, 159, 162
Roman Catholic Church. *see* Catholic Church
Roman Catholic Relief Act of 1829, 38
Roman law, 157
Roosevelt, Eleanor, 208
Roosevelt, Franklin D., 201
Rotimi Williams, Frederick, 244, 245, 251, 254
Royal African Society, 58
Royal Nigeria Company, 54
Russia, 67, 196, 203, 207
Ruxton, F. H., 90

Sabon Guruwa (reservations), 45, 59
Sacramental Test Act of 1828, 38
Salisbury, Robert Cecil, Marquess of, 31, 33, 38, 55
"Salt of the Earth" metaphor, 120
sanctions, 114
Sanhuri, Abdur-Razaq, 148
Sani, Muhammad, 144
Sanneh, Lamin O., 267
Sardauna ("Head of the Sultan's Guards"), 115, 160, 174, 181
Satiru colonial expedition, 75
Saudi Arabia, 177, 209
Schacht, Joseph, 8, 77, 84, 91, 100
school. *see* education
Scott, P.H.G., 97
secession, 235
secularism
  in general, 1, 25, 267–273
  Article 18 and, 191
  Bates on, 203
  CDC on, 255
  defining religion, 10
  dual imperative of, 15–16, 34
  ecumenical movement, 21, 189, 194–199, 204, 223
  Eliot on, 199
  enfranchisement and, 38
  entanglement, 13–18, 23–25, 36, 263
  imperial. *see* imperial secularism
  independence and, 240
  in India, 39
  indirect rule and, 1–3, 9, 41–44, 267
  Islamic institutions and, 11, 25, 27, 62–66, 230
  Islamic law and, 8, 164, 240
  Islamization, 237
  Lagos State Government and others v. Asiyat Abdulkareem, 271
  Lugardian administration, 17, 43
  Masu Sarauta and, 13–18, 26, 48
  missionaries and, 2, 19, 25, 26, 237
  Penal Code and, 176
  postcolonial debate, 262

privileging the majority, 15, 48, 62–66, 230, 239, 253
Protestantism and, 224
religious difference, 13
religious liberty and. *see* religious liberty and secularism
scholarship on, 71
Shari'a and, 237–240, 263
Shari'a Court of Appeal and, 22, 230, 244
state-religion separation and, 5–77, 22, 35, 40, 44, 46, 62, 172,175–6, 209, 214–215, 218, 241
in US, 205
sedition, 117
segregation, 45, 59
self-determination, 108–111, 121, 123, 124, 128, 143, 154
self-government. *see* independence
self-sufficiency, human, 196
separation, church state; state-religion, 15–77, 22, 35, 40, 44, 46, 62, 172,175–6, 209, 214–215, 218, 241.
religious liberty and. *see* state-religion separation and religious liberty.
secularism and. *see* state-religion separation and secularism
sexual intercourse outside of wedlock (*zina*), 264
Shafism, 186
Shari'a
Anderson on, 159
diya and, 173
freedom of religion, 250
guarantee of non-interference and, 98
imperial secularism and, 82, 103, 231, 264
independence and, 249
Al-Juwaynī on, 186
Masu Sarauta on, 20
modernity and, 146, 147–150, 164, 175
postcolonial debate, 23–25, 258–266
secularism and, 22–23, 263
siyasa, 11, 17, 76–82, 86, 92, 147, 149, 186
Shari'a Court of Appeal
abolition of, 235
CDC on, 254
independence and, 230
jurisdiction, 244
opposition to, 231, 237, 250
Panel of Jurists on, 177
secularism and, 22, 230, 244
Shari'a Criminal Procedure Codes, 261
"Shari'a statism," 27, 82, 264, 265, 269, *see also siyasa* ("discretionary powers of political rulers"):statist
Shari'ah on Trial (Eltantawi), 10
Sharif, Mohammed, 168, 171, 176
Sharwood-Smith, Bryan, 129, 161–164

Shettima, Kashim, 165, 168
SIM (Sudan Interior Mission), 113
Six Pillars of Peace (Dulles), 201
siyasa ("discretionary powers of political rulers")
Anderson on, 77–78, 101, 147, 159, 173
Bello on, 174
Cameron administration. *see* courts, Cameron reforms of
Emirs. *see* Emirs and *siyasa*
fiqh and, 10–12, 17, 20, 79, 153, 186
Islamic law and, 71
Lugardian reform of, 82, 84–86, 151, 187
Masu Sarauta and, 93
Penal Code, 183
Schacht on, 100
Shari'a and, 11, 17, 76–82, 86, 92, 147–150, 186
Sokoto Caliphate, 80
statist, 84, 88
slander, 93
slavery, 56, 59
Smith, Gordon, 215
Smith, Maurice, 162
socialism, 116
Society for the Propagation of the Gospel in Foreign Parts, 31
Society of Removal of Innovation and Re-establishment of the Sunnah, 239
Sokoto Caliphate
in general, 32
fall of, 41, 42, 47, 54
Hausa-Fulani identity in, 54
Masu Sarauta and, 19
religious diversity in, 37
siyasa, 79–80
as Type I area, 45
Somaliland, 203
Southern Nigeria, 62, 98
Soviet Union, 67, 196, 203, 207
Spain, 203, 206
Spivak, Gayatri, 24
State Judicature Committee, 259
states, 194
States (Creation and Transitional Provisions) Decree, 235
Stokes report, 60
subordination, 27, 132, 136, 214, 243
Sudan
Article 18 and, 209, 213
Bates on, 203
ecumenists on, 194
Mahdist War, 47
missionary activity, 192
Penal Code, 165, 167, 170, 175, 179
Sudan Interior Mission (SIM), 113
Sudan United Mission, 52, 67, 113, 114

INDEX

Sufism
  Qadiriyyah, 12, 74, 139
  Tijaniyyah, 13, 74, 93, 118, 138–140
Suleiman, Ibraheem, 240
Sultan of Sokoto, 43, 55, 115, 140, 238
Sultans, 12, 80
Sunnah, 172
Supreme Court, 98, 99, 244, 245, 255, 271
Swar El Dahab, Mohammed, 20
Sweden, 210
Syria, 207

ta'azir (offences against public order), 81
Tabbat Hakika (Uthman Dan Fodio), 187
Tabsirat al-Hukam (Maliki text), 94
takhayyur (selecting opinions), 81, 148
talakawa (commoners), 112, 118
talfiq (amalgamating opinions), 81, 148
Tanbih al-raqid (Bello), 80
Tanzimat (reforms), 147–150
Tarka, Joseph, 132
taxation, 37, 53, 60, 74, 94, 139
Temple, Charles, 57, 58, 59
Temple, William, 197
territorial classification, 126, 129, 131, 138, 141
testimonies, 252
theocracy, 8, 244, 262
theology, 64, 73–76, 117, 119, 139, 200
Thomson, Graeme, 64, 65
Tijaniyyah (Sufi order), 13, 74, 93, 118, 138–140, see also Northern Elements Progressive Union (NEPU)
tin mining companies, 133
Tingary, Annur, 20
Tiv Group, 134
tolerance, 4, 46, 62, 64, 204, 205
Tong chief, 61
torture, 90, 139
Tsofo Gubba v. Gwandu N.A., 97–100, 107, 129, 151
Turkey, 204
Tuwam (village), 61
Type I areas, 6, 60, 261
Type II areas, 6, 49, 60, 111, 121, 133
Type III areas, 6, 57, 60, 111, 121, 133, 135

Ubah, C.N., 36
UDHR (Universal Declaration of Human Rights), 208, see also Universal Declaration of Human Rights Article 18
Umary Fannami v. Bukar Sarkiu, 258
unchristian separation. see secularism
uniformity, 168, 204, 246

United Middle Belt Congress (UMBC), 122–125, 127, 132, 134, 141
United Nations (UN), 166, 170, see also Universal Declaration of Human Rights Article 18
United States, 201, 205, 207
Universal Christian Council for Life and Work, 197–201, 206, 237
Universal Church in the World of Nations, The (report), 197, 201
Universal Declaration of Human Rights (UDHR), 208
Universal Declaration of Human Rights Article 18. see also European Convention on Human Rights (ECHR); religious liberty
  in general, 21, 189–192
  Ceylon provision, 213
  domestication of, 22, 189, 211–216, 222, 230
  ecumenical movement's influence on, 162, 189, 191–195, 208, 211, 214–215, 223, 224, 230
  guarantee of non-interference and, 217, 221
  Masu Sarauta on, 211, 215, 217
  NEPU on, 212, 217
  NPC on, 217, 221
  opposition to, 209–211, 215–220
  secularism and, 191
Usman, Yusufu Bala, 44, 242
Uthman Dan Fodio, 32, 80, 81, 115, 116, 187, 258

Veer, Peter van der, 4, 39, 41
Verity, Chief Justice, 97
Victoria, Queen of England, 7, 40, 43
violence, 47, 50, 56, 75, 125, 139, 218, 235, 260

Wali of Borno, 165
Wallahi Wallahi (Uthman Dan Fodio), 187
war, 42, 72
WCC (World Council of Churches), 21, 200
Weatherhead, A.T., 171
West Africa (magazine), 58
West Africa Group, 215
West African Court of Appeal, 96, 97
West African Frontier Force, 42
Western State Joint Muslim Organization (WESTJOMO), 238
whipping, 94
Williams, Robert, 50
Williamson, Tom, 215
Willink Commission
  on economy, 132–133
  imperial secularism and, 126
  on jurisprudence, 154

316

Middle Belt state, 127, 136
Muffet and, 161
NEPU and, 139
religious difference, 111, 125–126, 137–143
on religious liberty, 136
religious minorities, 125, 132, 134–136, 140
rights recommendation, 142
territorial classification, 126, 129, 131, 138, 141
Willink, Henry, 129
Women Wing's (NEPU), 140
World Council of Churches (WCC), 21, 200
World Missionary Conference, 5, 33, 50, 189, 198
worship, 145, 200, 207, 209, 239

Yobe (province), 93
"Young Turks," 160

zakat (almsgiving), 37, 261
Zamfara (state), 261
Zaria (city), 46, 57, 60, 67, 140, 171
zina (sexual intercourse outside of wedlock), 264
Zoroastrianism, 10

CAMBRIDGE STUDIES IN LAW AND SOCIETY

Books in the Series

Diseases of the Will: Alcohol and the Dilemmas of Freedom
Mariana Valverde

The Politics of Truth and Reconciliation in South Africa: Legitimizing the Post-Apartheid State
Richard A. Wilson

Modernism and the Grounds of Law
Peter Fitzpatrick

Unemployment and Government: Genealogies of the Social
William Walters

Autonomy and Ethnicity: Negotiating Competing Claims in Multi-Ethnic States
Yash Ghai

Constituting Democracy: Law, Globalism and South Africa's Political Reconstruction
Heinz Klug

The Ritual of Rights in Japan: Law, Society, and Health Policy
Eric A. Feldman

Governing Morals: A Social History of Moral Regulation
Alan Hunt

The Colonies of Law: Colonialism, Zionism and Law in Early Mandate Palestine
Ronen Shamir

Law and Nature
David Delaney

Social Citizenship and Workfare in the United States and Western Europe: The Paradox of Inclusion
Joel F. Handler

Law, Anthropology, and the Constitution of the Social: Making Persons and Things
Edited by Alain Pottage and Martha Mundy

Judicial Review and Bureaucratic Impact: International and Interdisciplinary Perspectives
Edited by Marc Hertogh and Simon Halliday

Immigrants at the Margins: Law, Race, and Exclusion in Southern Europe
Kitty Calavita

Lawyers and Regulation: The Politics of the Administrative Process
Patrick Schmidt

Law and Globalization from Below: Towards a Cosmopolitan Legality
Edited by Boaventura de Sousa Santos and César A. Rodríguez-Garavito

Public Accountability: Designs, Dilemmas and Experiences
Edited by Michael W. Dowdle

Law, Violence and Sovereignty among West Bank Palestinians
Tobias Kelly

Legal Reform and Administrative Detention Powers in China
Sarah Biddulph

The Practice of Human Rights: Tracking Law between the Global and the Local
Edited by Mark Goodale and Sally Engle Merry

Judges beyond Politics in Democracy and Dictatorship: Lessons from Chile
Lisa Hilbink

Paths to International Justice: Social and Legal Perspectives
Edited by Marie-Bénédicte Dembour and Tobias Kelly

Law and Society in Vietnam: The Transition from Socialism in Comparative Perspective
Mark Sidel

Constitutionalizing Economic Globalization: Investment Rules and Democracy's Promise
David Schneiderman

The New World Trade Organization Knowledge Agreements: Second Edition
Christopher Arup

Justice and Reconciliation in Post-Apartheid South Africa
Edited by François du Bois and Antje du Bois-Pedain

Militarization and Violence against Women in Conflict Zones in the Middle East: A Palestinian Case-Study
Nadera Shalhoub-Kevorkian

Child Pornography and Sexual Grooming: Legal and Societal Responses
Suzanne Ost

Darfur and the Crime of Genocide
John Hagan and Wenona Rymond-Richmond

Fictions of Justice: The International Criminal Court and the Challenge of Legal Pluralism in Sub-Saharan Africa
Kamari Maxine Clarke

Conducting Law and Society Research: Reflections on Methods and Practices
Simon Halliday and Patrick Schmidt

Planted Flags: Trees, Land, and Law in Israel/Palestine
Irus Braverman

Culture under Cross-Examination: International Justice and the Special Court for Sierra Leone
Tim Kelsall

Cultures of Legality: Judicialization and Political Activism in Latin America
Javier Couso, Alexandra Huneeus, and Rachel Sieder

Courting Democracy in Bosnia and Herzegovina: The Hague Tribunal's Impact in a Postwar State
Lara J. Nettelfield

The Gacaca Courts, Post-Genocide Justice and Reconciliation in Rwanda: Justice without Lawyers
Phil Clark

Law, Society, and History: Themes in the Legal Sociology and Legal History of Lawrence M. Friedman
Edited by Robert W. Gordon and Morton J. Horwitz

After Abu Ghraib: Exploring Human Rights in America and the Middle East
Shadi Mokhtari

Adjudication in Religious Family Laws: Cultural Accommodation, Legal Pluralism, and Gender Equality in India
Gopika Solanki

Water on Tap: Rights and Regulation in the Transnational Governance of Urban Water Services
Bronwen Morgan

Elements of Moral Cognition: Rawls' Linguistic Analogy and the Cognitive Science of Moral and Legal Judgment
John Mikhail

Mitigation and Aggravation at Sentencing
Edited by Julian V. Roberts

Institutional Inequality and the Mobilization of the Family and Medical Leave Act: Rights on Leave
Catherine R. Albiston

Authoritarian Rule of Law: Legislation, Discourse and Legitimacy in Singapore
Jothie Rajah

Law and Development and the Global Discourses of Legal Transfers
Edited by John Gillespie and Pip Nicholson

Law against the State: Ethnographic Forays into Law's Transformations
Edited by Julia Eckert, Brian Donahoe, Christian Strümpell and Zerrin Özlem Biner

Transnational Legal Ordering and State Change
Edited by Gregory C. Shaffer

Legal Mobilization under Authoritarianism: The Case of Post-Colonial Hong Kong
Waikeung Tam

Complementarity in the Line of Fire: The Catalysing Effect of the International Criminal Court in Uganda and Sudan
Sarah M. H. Nouwen

Political and Legal Transformations of an Indonesian Polity: The Nagari from Colonisation to Decentralisation
Franz von Benda-Beckmann and Keebet von Benda-Beckmann

Pakistan's Experience with Formal Law: An Alien Justice
Osama Siddique

Human Rights under State-Enforced Religious Family Laws in Israel, Egypt, and India
Yüksel Sezgin

Why Prison?
Edited by David Scott

Law's Fragile State: Colonial, Authoritarian, and Humanitarian Legacies in Sudan
Mark Fathi Massoud

Rights for Others: The Slow Home-Coming of Human Rights in the Netherlands
Barbara Oomen

European States and Their Muslim Citizens: The Impact of Institutions on Perceptions and Boundaries
Edited by John R. Bowen, Christophe Bertossi, Jan Willem Duyvendak, and Mona Lena Krook

Environmental Litigation in China: A Study in Political Ambivalence
Rachel E. Stern

Indigeneity and Legal Pluralism in India: Claims, Histories, Meanings
Pooja Parmar

Paper Tiger: Law, Bureaucracy and the Developmental State in Himalayan India
Nayanika Mathur

Religion, Law and Society
Russell Sandberg

The Experiences of Face Veil Wearers in Europe and the Law
Edited by Eva Brems

The Contentious History of the International Bill of Human Rights
Christopher N. J. Roberts

Transnational Legal Orders
Edited by Terence C. Halliday and Gregory Shaffer

Lost in China? Law, Culture and Society in Post-1997 Hong Kong
Carol A. G. Jones

Security Theology, Surveillance and the Politics of Fear
Nadera Shalhoub-Kevorkian

Opposing the Rule of Law: How Myanmar's Courts Make Law and Order
Nick Cheesman

Ironies of Colonial Governance: Law, Custom and Justice in Colonial India
James Jaffe

The Clinic and the Court: Law, Medicine and Anthropology
Edited by Ian Harper, Tobias Kelly, and Akshay Khanna

The World of Indicators: The Making of Government Knowledge through Quantification
Edited by Richard Rottenburg, Sally E. Merry, Sung-Joon Park, and Johanna Mugler

Contesting Immigration Policy in Court: Legal Activism and Its Radiating Effects in the United States and France
Leila Kawar

The Quiet Power of Indicators: Measuring Governance, Corruption, and Rule of Law
Edited by Sally Engle Merry, Kevin E. Davis, and Benedict Kingsbury

Investing in Authoritarian Rule: Punishment and Patronage in Rwanda's Gacaca Courts for Genocide Crimes
Anuradha Chakravarty

Contractual Knowledge: One Hundred Years of Legal Experimentation in Global Markets
Edited by Grégoire Mallard and Jérôme Sgard

Iraq and the Crimes of Aggressive War: The Legal Cynicism of Criminal Militarism
John Hagan, Joshua Kaiser, and Anna Hanson

Culture in the Domains of Law
Edited by René Provost

China and Islam: The Prophet, the Party, and Law
Matthew S. Erie

Diversity in Practice: Race, Gender, and Class in Legal and Professional Careers
Edited by Spencer Headworth, Robert L. Nelson, Ronit Dinovitzer, and David B. Wilkins

A Sociology of Constitutions: Constitutions and State Legitimacy in Historical-Sociological Perspective
Chris Thornhill

A Sociology of Transnational Constitutions: Social Foundations of the Post-National Legal Structure
Chris Thornhill

Genocide Never Sleeps: Living Law at the International Criminal Tribunal for Rwanda
Nigel Eltringham

Shifting Legal Visions: Judicial Change and Human Rights Trials in Latin America
Ezequiel A. González-Ocantos

The Demographic Transformations of Citizenship
Heli Askola

Criminal Defense in China: The Politics of Lawyers at Work
Sida Liu and Terence C. Halliday

Contesting Economic and Social Rights in Ireland: Constitution, State and Society, 1848–2016
Thomas Murray

Buried in the Heart: Women, Complex Victimhood and the War in Northern Uganda
Erin Baines

Palaces of Hope: The Anthropology of Global Organizations
Edited by Ronald Niezen and Maria Sapignoli

The Politics of Bureaucratic Corruption in Post-Transitional Eastern Europe
Marina Zaloznaya

Revisiting the Law and Governance of Trafficking, Forced Labor and Modern Slavery
Edited by Prabha Kotiswaran

Incitement on Trial: Prosecuting International Speech Crimes
Richard Ashby Wilson

Criminalizing Children: Welfare and the State in Australia
David McCallum

Global Lawmakers: International Organizations in the Crafting of World Markets
Susan Block-Lieb and Terence C. Halliday

Duties to Care: Dementia, Relationality and Law
Rosie Harding

Insiders, Outsiders, Injuries, and Law: Revisiting "The Oven Bird's Song"
Edited by Mary Nell Trautner

Hunting Justice: Displacement, Law, and Activism in the Kalahari
Maria Sapignoli

Injury and Injustice: The Cultural Politics of Harm and Redress
Edited by Anne Bloom, David M. Engel, and Michael McCann

Ruling Before the Law: The Politics of Legal Regimes in China and Indonesia
William Hurst

The Powers of Law: A Comparative Analysis of Sociopolitical Legal Studies
Mauricio García-Villegas

A Sociology of Justice in Russia
Edited by Marina Kurkchiyan and Agnieszka Kubal

Constituting Religion: Islam, Liberal Rights, and the Malaysian State
Tamir Moustafa

The Invention of the Passport: Surveillance, Citizenship and the State, Second Edition
John C. Torpey

Law's Trials: The Performance of Legal Institutions in the US "War on Terror"
Richard L. Abel

Law's Wars: The Fate of the Rule of Law in the US "War on Terror"
Richard L. Abel

Transforming Gender Citizenship: The Irresistible Rise of Gender Quotas in Europe
Edited by Eléonore Lépinard and Ruth Rubio-Marín

Muslim Women's Quest for Justice: Gender, Law and Activism in India
Mengia Hong Tschalaer

Children as 'Risk': Sexual Exploitation and Abuse by Children and Young People
Anne-Marie McAlinden

The Legal Process and the Promise of Justice: Studies Inspired by the Work of Malcolm Feeley
Jonathan Simon, Rosann Greenspan, Hadar Aviram

Gift Exchanges: The Transnational History of a Political Idea
Grégoire Mallard

Measuring Justice: Quantitative Accountability and the National Prosecuting Authority in South Africa
Johanna Mugler

Negotiating the Power of NGOs: Women's Legal Rights in South Africa
Reem Wael

Indigenous Water Rights in Law and Regulation: Lessons from Comparative Experience
Elizabeth Jane Macpherson

The Edge of Law: Legal Geographies of a War Crimes Court
Alex Jeffrey

Everyday Justice: Law, Ethnography, and Injustice
Sandra Brunnegger

The Uncounted: Politics of Data in Global Health
Sara L. M. Davis

Transnational Legal Ordering of Criminal Justice
Gregory Shaffer and Ely Aaronson

Five Republics and One Tradition
Pablo Ruiz-Tagle

The Law Multiple: Judgment and Knowledge in Practice
Irene van Oorschot

Health as a Human Right: The Politics and Judicialisation of Health in Brazil
Octávio Luiz Motta Ferraz

Shari'a, Inshallah: Finding God in Somali Legal Politics
Mark Fathi Massoud

Policing for Peace: Institutions, Expectations, and Security in Divided Societies
Matthew Nanes

Rule of Law Intermediaries: Brokering Influence in Myanmar
Kristina Simion

Lactation at Work: Expressed Milk, Expressing Beliefs, and the Expressive Value of Law
Elizabeth A. Hoffmann

The Archival Politics of International Courts
Henry Redwood

Global Pro Bono: Causes, Context, and Contestation
Edited by Scott L. Cummings, Fabio de Sa e Silva and Louise G. Trubek

The Practice and Problems of Transnational Counter-Terrorism
Fiona de Londras

Decoupling: Gender Injustice in China's Divorce Courts
Ethan Michelson

Anti-Constitutional Populism
Martin Krygier, Adam Czarnota and Wojciech Sadurski

The Ghostwriters: Lawyers and the Politics behind the Judicial Construction of Europe
Tommaso Pavone

The Sentimental Court: The Affective Life of International Criminal Justice
Jonas Bens

Practices of Reparations in International Criminal Justice
Christoph Sperfeldt

Seeking Supremacy: The Pursuit of Judicial Power in Pakistan
Yasser Kureshi

The Power of the Jury: Transforming Citizens into Jurors
Nancy S. Marder

Undue Process: Persecution and Punishment in Autocratic Courts Fiona Feiang Shen-Bayh

Discounting Life: Necropolitical Law, Culture, and the Long War on Terror
Jothie Rajah

Clean Air at What Cost? The Rise of Blunt Force Regulation in China
Denise Sienli van der Kamp

Law and Precarity: Legal Consciousness and Daily Survival in Vietnam
Tu Phuong Nguyen

Prosecutors, Voters and The Criminalization of Corruption in Latin America: The Case of Lava Jato
Ezequiel A. Gonzalez-Ocantos and Paula Muñoz Chirinos

For EU product safety concerns, contact us at Calle de José Abascal, 56–1°,
28003 Madrid, Spain or eugpsr@cambridge.org.

www.ingramcontent.com/pod-product-compliance
Lightning Source LLC
LaVergne TN
LVHW020340260326
834688LV00045B/1465